AN AUDIT APPROACH TO COMPUTERS

AN AUDIT APPROACH TO COMPUTERS

BRIAN JENKINS MA FCA
PETER COOKE BSc(Econ) FCA
PETER QUEST MA FCA
Coopers & Lybrand

The Institute of Chartered Accountants
in England and Wales,
Chartered Accountants' Hall,
Moorgate Place,
London, EC2P 2BJ.
1992

ISBN 1 85355 229 1

First published 1966
Second edition 1978
Third edition 1986
Fourth edition 1992
Reprinted 1995

Photoset by Rowland Phototypesetting Limited
Bury St Edmunds, Suffolk
Printed and bound in Great Britain by
Creative Print and Design Wales, Ebbw Vale, Gwent

Acknowledgements

The authors wish to thank the many people who have assisted them in writing this book. In this connection they are grateful to the computer audit specialist partners and senior staff of Coopers & Lybrand. Within the UK particular thanks go to:

Mollie Bickerstaff	(London)	Iain McCusker	(London)
Pat Cavanagh	(London)	Daryl Ogden	(Edinburgh)
James Fanshawe	(Northampton)	Erik Samuelson	(London)
John Holt	(Leeds)	Geoff Smart	(London)
Henry Kenyon	(Bristol)	Graham Williams	(London)
Richard Lambert	(Birmingham)	Richard Williamson	(Reading)

Thanks are also due to the following of our computer audit specialist partners overseas whose co-operation and constructive comment has been invaluable:

Patrick Gaudron	(France)	European Computer Audit Committee
Frits Hoek	(The Netherlands)	European Computer Audit Committee
Hans Jacobsson	(Sweden)	European Computer Audit Committee
Rainer Kemnitzer	(Germany)	European Computer Audit Committee
Lukas Marbacher	(Switzerland)	European Computer Audit Committee
Al Decker	(USA)	
Michael Stoneham	(Canada)	
Jan Muysken	(Australia)	

Preface

Scope and relevance of the book

The principal purpose of this book which is intended to take the place of a book with the same title published in 1986, is to describe a practical approach to the expression of an audit opinion on the financial statements of companies where the processing and storage of accounting data is by computer. This approach is summarised in Chapter 1 and dealt with in greater detail, together with the related audit techniques and documentation, in Chapters 2 to 13. The book will thus be of particular relevance to the **practising accountant** involved in audits of this nature.

The approach suggested in this book also forms a suitable practical basis of work for an **internal audit department**. Indeed, in a number of instances, for example when dealing with many of the computer assisted audit techniques, the techniques have been described in detail since they may be of relevance to the internal auditor, even though the external auditor is unlikely to find it efficient to use them frequently. The methods and documentation outlined in this book can be amended to suit the particular objectives of an internal audit department which often include efficiency reviews. Accordingly, in the discussions of computer systems and controls in Chapters 2, 3, 5, 6, 7 and 8, the desirable features for increasing the efficiency of computer processing have been mentioned, where appropriate.

Recent years have seen significant growth in the use of electronic data interchange (EDI) and electronic funds transfer (EFT) to improve business efficiency and effectiveness by linking computer systems with those of trading partners and banks. The use of these technologies and their effects on controls are described in Chapter 14.

Computer fraud, computer misuse and computer security have become issues of increasing importance for both external and internal auditors as a result of increasing dependence of companies on their computer systems and the rapid growth of on-line systems which allow extensive user access to computer resources and information through terminals. Independent reviews of security procedures are becoming commonplace. Chapter 15 deals with computer fraud and computer misuse, including the provisions of the Computer Misuse Act 1990 which provides legal penalties against computer hacking and the promulgation of computer viruses. Chapter 16 deals with computer security and with the requirements of the Data Protection Act which provides protection in respect of data relating to living individuals and processed by automatic means.

Chapter 17 includes some practical suggestions on the organisation and training of the staff of a practising accountant to carry out computer audit work. These suggestions may also prove helpful to internal audit departments.

It is hoped that this book will also be of interest to **management**. Management has the responsibility of establishing satisfactory controls for computer systems. This is not always easy and it is hoped that the information regarding computer systems and controls outlined in Chapters 2, 3, 5, 6, 7 and 8, which are based on wide practical experience, will be of assistance.

Finally, it is hoped that the contents of this book will be of assistance both to **tutors** concerned with the teaching of either computer or audit personnel and to **students**. There will be an increasing demand for those competent in the methods and techniques mentioned in this book.

Terminology used

Definitions

Where it is considered helpful, definitions of the words and phrases used have been given. The definition is normally provided on the first occasion when the word or phrase is used and reference can be made thereto from the index.

Computer user

The computer user is referred to throughout as either the **company** or the **client**. The reader is asked to substitute an alternative term if more appropriate.

The auditor

Throughout the discussion of the audit approach in Chapters 2 to 13 the general term **auditor** is used and no attempt is made to indicate what type (general auditor or computer audit specialist) or level (senior, manager or partner) of auditor is involved at each stage. However, practical suggestions regarding the type and level of staff that would be suitable for the various aspects of the work are made in Chapter 17. The pronoun 'he' which has been used for convenience to refer to the auditor is intended to encompass both the male and female gender.

Brian Jenkins
Peter Cooke
Peter Quest

The authors

Brian G Jenkins

Brian Jenkins is a senior partner in the United Kingdom firm which is part of Coopers & Lybrand (International), a Past President of the Institute of Chartered Accountants in England & Wales, and Lord Mayor of London in 1991–1992. He was for many years the national partner in charge of computer auditing and was closely involved in the establishment of the Institute's Information Technology Group. He has spoken widely on computer matters at courses and conferences arranged by the Institute, the London and other district societies and many other bodies in the United Kingdom and other countries.

Peter J Cooke

Peter Cooke is a computer assurance services partner in the United Kingdom firm which is part of Coopers & Lybrand (International). He is a member of the firm's European Computer Audit Committee and of the committee of the IT Faculty of the Institute of Chartered Accountants in England and Wales. He is chairman of the IT Faculty's technical committee and has chaired Institute working parties on computer fraud and computer misuse. He has spoken on computer audit and related subjects for the Institute and other bodies.

Peter J Quest

Peter Quest is a computer assurance services partner in the United Kingdom firm which is part of Coopers & Lybrand (International). He is the national practice area leader for computer assurance within the UK firm and chairman of its Computer Assurance Services Committee. He is a member of the firm's international IT Audit Committee and was a member of the Institute of Chartered Accountants in England and Wales working party on the impact of IT on the audit. He has spoken on computer audit and related subjects for the Institute and other bodies.

Contents

Chapter 3. Understanding and Recording the System

Chapter 3, Appendix A. Examples of Computer Systems

Chapter 4. Evaluation of Internal Control: The Audit Approach

Chapter 6. Evaluation of Controls: Information Technology (IT) Controls (1)

Chapter 7. Evaluation of Controls: Information Technology (IT) Controls (2)

Chapter 8. Evaluation of Controls: Information Technology (IT) Controls (3)

Chapter 9. Testing Controls and the Response to Weaknesses

Chapter 9, Appendix C. Examples of the Use of Audit Test Data

Chapter 9, Appendix D. The Use of Program Code Analysis

Chapter 10. Substantive Tests

Chapter 10, Appendix A. Example of a Programme of Substantive Tests

Chapter 10, Appendix B. Examples of the Use of Computer Audit Programs

Chapter 11. The Use of File Interrogation Software

Chapter 17. Organisation and Training

List of Figures

1

An Audit Approach to Computers

Introduction

1.01 This book is based on the principles and documentation of an audit approach which has been designed for computerised accounting systems, although capable of being applied whatever the method adopted for the processing of data. In this chapter this audit approach is summarised and the main features of its application to computer systems are outlined.

The Audit Approach

1.02 The audit approach is designed to enable the auditor to achieve in the most efficient manner the principal objective of the audit, which is to ascertain whether, in his opinion, the financial statements on which he is reporting show a true and fair view of the state of affairs at a given date and of the results for the period ended on that date.

Principal features

1.03 Before outlining the steps in the overall audit approach it may be helpful to mention certain of its principal features. First, the audit procedures and documentation are designed to enable the auditor to perform his audit in the most efficient manner by concentrating his efforts on those items and activities which are likely to affect the overall truth and fairness of the financial statements. To achieve this efficiency, the audit approach is risk based in that the auditor assesses the risks of material misstatements in the financial statements in determining his audit procedures. He pays less attention to items where risk is lower or which are immaterial, and need not concern himself with items which are not relevant to the truth and fairness of the financial statements. Items would not be relevant if they related solely to efficiency of processing and would be immaterial if an error of such size as to distort the truth and fairness of the financial statements could not arise.

1.04 The second principal feature is that the auditor has considerable flexibility in the manner in which the elements of the audit approach are combined to meet the differing circumstances of each client. All stages in the audit are related to one another and, as part of the audit planning process, the auditor will select the procedures which he believes to be most appropriate for each aspect of the financial statements. The most obvious choice is the option of placing reliance for audit purposes on the system of internal control and carrying out an extended assessment thereof, or deciding it is more efficient to place no reliance on controls and to proceed instead to substantive audit work on the financial statements themselves.

1.05 The third major feature is that the approach is designed so that managers and partners are involved at each important stage of the audit. While it has always been the practice for managers and partners to review the work done, they have sometimes been insufficiently involved at the planning stage. As a result, required work may not have been carried out and time may have been spent on unnecessary procedures. Using the approach suggested in this book, managers and partners are required to decide on, for example, the audit approach to be adopted, the levels of test to be carried out and the audit response where weaknesses are found. The role of the manager and partner is further considered in Chapter 17.

1.06 The fourth important feature is that the approach and documentation were developed internationally. As a result, a few of the phrases and definitions may seem strange to the UK reader. No attempt has been made to adapt these phrases and definitions as it is not thought that they will lead to difficulty. Indeed, it is considered noteworthy that the approach and documentation outlined in this book are in daily use on a world-wide basis. However, in so far as they depend on statutory requirements, the detailed practices described in this book are based on UK law and may need amendments to suit the requirements of countries where the statutory obligations of the auditor are different.

1.07 Finally, the approach included in this book is in compliance with UK Auditing Standards and Guidelines.

1.08 The principal steps in carrying out the audit approach are as follows:

- Determination of the audit strategy.
- Understanding and recording the system.
- Evaluation of internal control.

- Testing controls and the response to weaknesses.
- Substantive tests.

In the following paragraphs each step is briefly described, together with the main features of its application to the audit of computer systems. The audit approach is summarised in chart form in Figure 1.

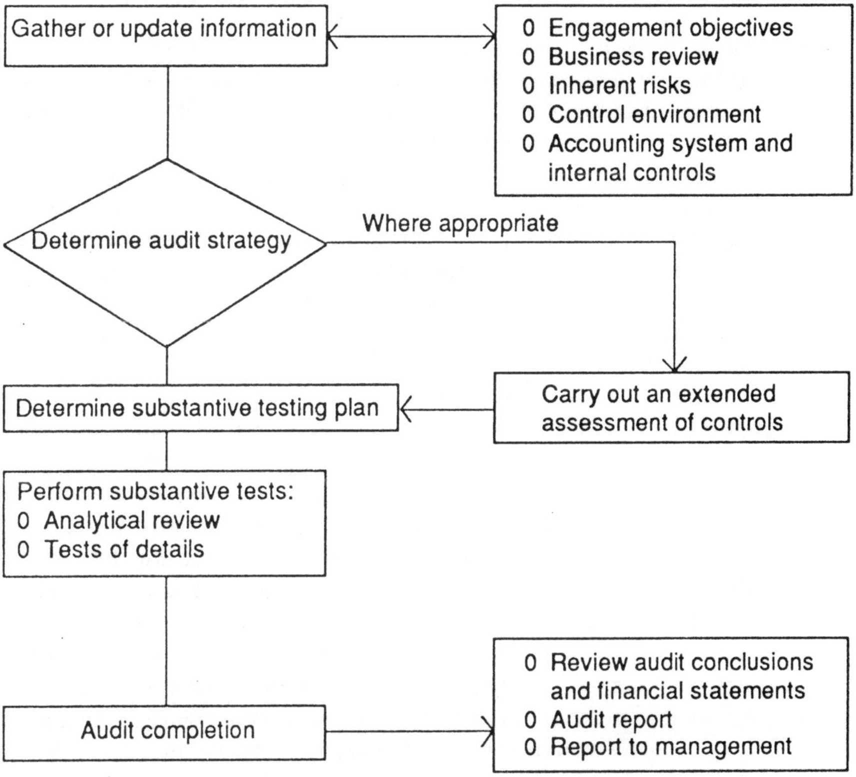

FIG. 1. Steps in the audit approach (para. 1.08)

Determination of the audit strategy

General approach

1.09 The first stage in the audit approach is for the auditor to determine the most efficient and effective audit strategy for each aspect of the financial statements. In order to determine the audit strategy the auditor will need to consider the objectives of the particular audit engagement and to gain an understanding of the business being audited and of the risks of material misstatements being contained in the financial statements. In the light of these risks, the auditor will carry out a "top down" overview of, firstly, the overall control environment within the business, then the accounting systems and finally the related internal controls. The audit strategy for each item in the financial statements will be determined in relation to specific **audit objectives** such as completeness, accuracy, cut-off and valuation as described in Chapter 2.

1.10 Based on his preliminary understanding the auditor will decide on the extent to which he considers it efficient to make an extended assessment of internal control so as to be able to rely on the controls that reduce the risk of misstatements in the financial statements. In the light of this decision he will also determine the broad nature, extent and timing of his substantive tests. The auditor should document the audit strategy, perhaps in the form of a memorandum, and will need to monitor, and perhaps amend it, as the audit progresses.

Computer systems

1.11 The particular factors relating to the determination of the audit strategy in computer systems are dealt with in Chapter 2. Although the principles of determining audit strategy are the same as for non-computerised systems, in practice the process is more complicated. This is because, in addition to the manual controls carried out on the data being processed, referred to herein as user controls, the auditor will be concerned with the other types of procedures and controls which are unique to computer systems, termed **programmed procedures** and **information technology (IT) controls**. Programmed procedures include steps in the computer programs that may assist in the control of the data being processed, while IT controls are the controls, mainly in the computer department, over, *inter alia*, the implementation, security and use of programs and security of data. The user controls and programmed procedures, which together directly control the data in a computer application, are collectively known as **application controls**.

1.12 The auditor will need to satisfy himself that significant programmed procedures on which he wishes to rely continue to operate properly and he may do this by tests of IT controls or possibly by tests of user controls or direct tests of the programmed procedures themselves.

1.13 The auditor will need to gain a preliminary understanding of application and IT controls and suitable documentation to achieve this is included in Chapters 3 and 4.

Understanding and recording the system

General approach

1.14 Where the auditor decides in determining his audit strategy to place reliance on internal controls, he will need to gain and record an understanding of the procedures and controls comprising a company's accounting system. The auditor normally obtains his understanding by reading systems descriptions and by discussions with company staff. He usually records his understanding of the system by use of overview or detailed flowcharts or, in those cases where it is considered to be more efficient, by narrative notes.

1.15 Where the audit strategy for an item in the financial statements is to rely principally on substantive tests, the auditor will require a sufficient understanding of the accounting system to enable him to devise and perform these tests. An adequate level of understanding for this purpose may have been obtained at the time of determining the audit strategy, perhaps in the form of an overview flowchart. If not, a sufficiently detailed understanding should be obtained and recorded to enable the substantive tests to be designed and carried out.

Computer systems

1.16 There are particular features in understanding computer systems because of the distinctive nature of computer processing. These features are discussed in the first part of Chapter 3 and examples of typical computer systems are described in the appendix to that chapter. Particular points in recording computer systems are dealt with in the second part of Chapter 3.

Evaluation of internal control

General approach

1.17 The auditor is concerned with a company's system of internal control because he may wish, where possible, to place reliance thereon in order to limit, and phase the timing of, his subsequent audit work on the financial statements. A further important purpose is to report to management weaknesses that come to his notice, so as to assist management in carrying out its obligations to establish and maintain controls that will ensure, as far as possible, the reliability of the company's accounting records and the safeguarding of its assets.

1.18 Internal accounting controls consist of application controls and IT controls. Application controls are all those controls designed to ensure that data on files from which the financial statements are derived is properly maintained between transaction updates **(file controls)**, and that valid transactions, and only valid transactions, are processed and recorded completely and accurately in the accounting records **(transaction controls)**. They include user controls and programmed procedures. IT controls are designed to ensure that the programmed procedures within a computer application are appropriately designed, implemented, maintained and operated and that only authorised changes are made to computer programs and data.

1.19 If application and IT controls are to be effective in practice, there should be adequate supervision of control procedures by responsible officials and a suitable division of duties in the performance of procedures and related internal accounting controls.

Computer systems

1.20 The nature and the method of evaluating internal controls in computer systems are considered in Chapters 2 and 4. A suitable document for evaluating and testing controls the **control assessment and record of tests (CART)** is described. Extracts of those parts of the CART which are needed to evaluate computer systems are contained in the appendix to Chapter 4 for illustration purposes.

1.21 A more detailed consideration of the control requirements and techniques in computer systems, and how they can be evaluated using the CART, is contained in Chapter 5, as regards application controls, and in Chapters 6, 7 and 8, as regards IT controls.

Testing controls and the response to weaknesses

General approach

1.22 Where the auditor decides to carry out an extended assessment of controls as part of his audit strategy, he will need to carry out tests to satisfy himself that the controls have operated effectively and continuously throughout the period under audit. In general, the auditor will seek to perform the minimum amount of testing necessary to provide the degree of assurance that he requires on the operation of the controls.

1.23 The auditor obtains direct and indirect evidence of the effective operation of controls from many aspects of his audit work and, in deciding the extent of testing which is necessary, he will take into account all other relevant work he has performed. Where an audit has been carried out in earlier years the auditor will have knowledge of the previous operation of the business, of overview and possibly extended assessments of controls and of substantive testing performed. Where the results of this work were satisfactory the auditor should take this into account in deciding the extent of testing necessary in the current year.

1.24 The auditor will have gained further information from the work performed to determine the audit strategy, and in particular his review of the overall control environment, and to evaluate controls in the current year. Where the control environment is favourable, it will provide the auditor with a significant degree of assurance that application controls subject to the environment are effective. Where the auditor wishes to satisfy himself as to the effective operation of programmed procedures, he will normally evaluate and test the IT controls. The extent of testing of the application controls will be a matter for judgement in each case taking into account all the above factors but, provided the results of the work on the control environment and IT controls are satisfactory, the auditor should be able to be selective in deciding which systems and controls to test and should not need to test every control on which he wishes to rely. This is because assurance on the consistency of operation of user controls and programmed procedures in the applications will be provided by the work performed on the control environment and IT controls.

1.25 Testing will for the most part comprise what are termed in this book "observation and enquiry", "examination of evidence" and "reperformance". **Observation and enquiry** comprises the viewing of the actions of employees in their work environment and the making of specific enquiries of management and staff, for example, observing the physical inspection of goods received. **Examination of evidence** consists of the inspection of records, documents, reconciliations and reports for evidence that a control has been properly carried out. An example is the inspection of signatures or initials on a supplier's invoice evidencing that the invoice has been matched with a goods received note. **Reperformance** consists of the repetition, either in whole or in part, of the same work processes as those performed by the company's employees or a computer program, for example, the actual matching by the auditor of a supplier's invoice with the corresponding goods received note, in order to obtain assurance that the evidence seen on the supplier's invoice really does mean that the matching process has been carried out.

1.26 Where testing reveals weaknesses in or the absence of controls, the auditor will need to consider whether these are significant to his overall assessment of the effectiveness of the controls. If the weaknesses lead the auditor to conclude that the overall control environment is not favourable, then he will not be able to rely on his assessment of it to provide a degree of assurance on the reliable operation of the underlying application controls. He may need to perform significantly more work on the application controls to prove their reliability in such circumstances and may need to reconsider whether an extended assessment of controls is an efficient audit strategy.

1.27 Where there are weaknesses in the application or IT controls, the auditor will need to consider whether these are so significant as to prevent overall reliance on the controls. If so he will need to reconsider his audit strategy, but he should avoid giving undue weight to individual or less serious weaknesses in making this assessment. With the exception of insignificant matters, weaknesses should normally be reported to the client.

Computer systems

1.28 The techniques for testing in computer systems are considered in Chapter 9 and specimen tests for use when testing the more common controls and procedures are contained in Appendix A to that chapter.

1.29 A feature in computer systems may be the inability to carry out conventional audit tests because visible evidence is not available as a routine. Alternative techniques, which may be employed where it is deemed necessary to carry out detailed testing, include the use of software, audit test data and program code analysis. These techniques, which are unique to computer systems, are described in Chapter 9 and Appendices B and C (audit test data) and Appendix D (program code analysis).

1.30 Examples of common weaknesses and breakdowns in computer systems are also considered in Chapter 9.

Substantive tests

General approach

1.31 Substantive tests represent the final stage of the audit and in conjunction with any tests of internal controls and other audit work must be adequate to support the audit opinion expressed on the financial statements. They have as their main objective the substantiation of account balances and other information contained in the financial statements. In addition, substantive tests complement tests of controls since they provide further evidence as to whether the internal controls have continued to operate.

1.32 Substantive tests consist of analytical review and tests of details. **Analytical review** involves comparison of recorded amounts with expectations of what such amounts should be. **Tests of details** may include direct tests of account balances or transactions, or more general procedures, such as a review of minutes of the board of directors.

1.33 Normally the most important factors governing the nature and extent of substantive tests are the auditor's assessment of inherent risks relating to the financial statements and the effectiveness of controls, the materiality of the item, the assurance concerning the item which the auditor obtains from substantive tests of related items and the auditor's judgement of the most efficient and effective combination of substantive testing procedures. It is often desirable to perform substantive tests at a date prior to the year end, particularly if the client wishes the audit to be completed shortly after the year end. This may be done in appropriate circumstances without impairing the effectiveness of the audit, particularly if the client has an effective system of controls or institutes special control procedures for the period between the date of early testing and the year end.

1.34 Where substantive testing reveals exceptions the auditor will need to consider the potential for material misstatement in the financial statements. Further investigation may be necessary to justify the account balance, and this may well be performed by the client. If, after such investigation, the auditor is unable to conclude that the account balance is not materially misstated he will need to consider a qualification in the audit report.

Computer systems

1.35 Where records supporting balance sheet and income and expenditure accounts are maintained by computer, the objectives of the substantive tests and the relationship between the system of internal control and the substantive tests remain the same. However, because of, first, the opportunity to make use of the computer to assist in substantive testing, and, second, the distinctive control features in computer systems, there are often changes in the substantive tests. In Chapter 10 general matters relating to the nature, timing and extent of substantive tests are discussed, together with the impact that computers may have on them.

1.36 The audit use of file interrogation software to examine data held on computer files represents the most common use of the computer to assist in substantive testing. The two most significant features in using computer programs are that, first, all relevant items are normally examined, whereas when manual tests are used only a sample is normally examined, and, second, additional information of assistance to the auditor can often be produced. The combination of these two factors may enable the auditor to carry out more effective or more efficient substantive tests than are practicable by manual means.

1.37 Examples of the wide uses of interrogation software for substantive test purposes and the procedures for incorporating them into the other substantive tests are outlined in Chapter 10. Two illustrations of the use of interrogation software to assist in the substantive testing of accounts receivable and inventories are included in Appendix B to that chapter.

1.38 Extensive use has been made by auditors of general purpose computer programs which can carry out similar tasks on a variety of files and installations. Programs of this type are termed **file interrogation packages** in this book. It is not intended to review and analyse the various file interrogation packages. However, in Chapter 11 the more important facilities, based on practical experience, that should be available in a file interrogation package are indicated.

1.39 It is advisable to establish formal procedures to control the use of computer software. This will help ensure that software is only used in cases where the cost can be justified, that the contemplated objectives are appropriate, and that the costs are controlled. Examples of suitable procedures are outlined in Chapter 11.

Microcomputers in the audit practice

1.40 Auditors are making increasing use of microcomputers within the audit process. In some cases the uses are administrative in nature, common examples being the preparation of audit budgets or the maintenance of a database of client information. Microcomputers are also used in performing audit work, for example, in the preparation of audit working papers, in analytical review, and for file interrogation software. The uses of microcomputers for such purposes and guidance on their acquisition and use within an audit practice are included in Chapter 12.

Small computer systems

1.41 In recent years there has been a dramatic increase in the use of small computer systems for accounting purposes. The audit approach outlined above can be applied equally to small or large computer systems. However, the extensive use of bought-in packaged software in small computer systems and the limited number of people involved in operating such a system mean that there are particular considerations regarding application and IT controls in small computer systems. These are dealt with in Chapter 13.

Summary

1.42 The audit approach in a computer system is similar to that in a non-computer system. The auditor should plan and control his approach to the audit so as to ensure that it is performed in the most efficient manner. He will need to gain a preliminary understanding of the nature of the client's business, of particular areas of risk and of the control environment, accounting system and internal controls in order to determine his audit strategy. Where his strategy is to place reliance on internal controls he will need to gain and record an understanding of the accounting system, evaluate the system of internal control and carry out tests to satisfy himself that the controls are working in practice. In a computer system the auditor will have to consider programmed procedures and IT controls, and in performing tests of controls he may need to use computer assisted audit techniques such as audit software or test data.

1.43 The auditor's object in placing reliance on the system of internal control is to limit and phase the timing of his subsequent audit work on the financial statements. Where his audit strategy is to rely on controls he must therefore assess the effect of control weaknesses on the nature, timing and extent of his procedures. The auditor will carry out substantive tests comprising analytical review and tests of details. In performing substantive tests in computer systems the auditor may be able to make efficient use of file interrogation software.

2

Determination of the Audit Strategy

General Approach

2.01 The first stage in the audit approach is for the auditor to plan his audit procedures so as to ensure that the audit is carried out in the most efficient manner. This will require determination of the most efficient and effective audit strategy for each aspect of the financial statements. In order to determine the audit strategy the auditor will need to consider the objectives of the engagement and to gain an understanding of the nature of the business being audited, of the risk of material misstatements being contained in the financial statements, of the overall control environment within the business and of the accounting systems and related internal controls.

2.02 Based on his preliminary understanding the auditor will decide on the extent to which he considers it efficient to make an extended assessment of internal control so as to be able to rely on the controls that reduce the risk of misstatements in the financial statements. In the light of this decision he will also determine the broad nature, extent and timing of his substantive tests. Before considering these matters in detail, it is helpful to discuss the concepts of materiality, audit objectives and audit risk which underlie the determination of the strategy.

Materiality, Audit Objectives and Audit Risk

Materiality

2.03 In relation to financial statements, a matter should be judged material if knowledge of the matter would be likely to influence a user of the financial statements. Materiality is not absolute but can only be considered in relation to context. For example, an error of £100,000 may be immaterial in the context of debtors but material as regards the profit and loss account.

2.04 Materiality is important to the auditor because the materiality of an item in the financial statements will determine its importance and therefore the amount of audit effort to be devoted to it, and because in relation to misstatements it defines the threshold at which adjustment would need to be made to the financial statements. In determining his audit strategy and deciding on the extent of his further detailed work, the auditor will have materiality in mind since he will wish to detect material misstatements in the financial statements. His initial judgements on materiality will need to be reassessed as the audit progresses to take account of any significant changes in his understanding of the facts and circumstances surrounding the engagement.

Audit objectives

2.05 Management is responsible for the preparation of the financial statements and, in compiling them, makes certain assertions regarding the information which they contain, for example, that inventories as stated in the balance sheet actually exist, are owned by the entity and are stated at a proper value. Most of the auditor's work in forming an opinion on the financial statements consists of obtaining and evaluating evidence to corroborate management's assertions that are embodied in the financial statements. In obtaining and evaluating that evidence it is helpful for the auditor to direct attention to specific audit objectives that correspond to management's assertions.

2.06 The audit objectives that the auditor will wish to see achieved are as follows:

- **Completeness** – all account balances and transactions that should be included in the financial statements are included.
- **Accuracy** – recorded transactions and account balances are mathematically accurate, are based on correct amounts, have been allocated to the proper accounts and have been accurately summarised and posted to the general ledger.
- **Existence** – recorded assets and liabilities exist at the balance sheet date; recorded transactions have occurred and are not fictitious.
- **Cut-off** – transactions are recorded in the correct period.
- **Valuation** – appropriate accounting measurement and recognition principles are properly selected and applied.
- **Rights and obligations** – recorded assets are rights of the entity and recorded liabilities are obligations of the entity at the balance sheet date.

- **Presentation and disclosure** – account balances and classes of transactions are properly classified and described; appropriate disclosures are made.

2.07 Although the audit objectives remain the same from engagement to engagement, they are not equally relevant to all account balances and transactions. For example, valuation is commonly a very important objective when related to inventories but is not a significant issue when related to cash balances.

2.08 The accounting system and related internal controls generally address the objectives of completeness and accuracy. The auditor's work on internal controls will, if satisfactory, serve as a basis for restricting substantive tests directed to one or both of these objectives.

2.09 The existence objective may be addressed by the system of internal controls to the extent that controls are present to ensure that fictitious transactions are not processed and to ensure the continued existence of the related assets and liabilities. Internal controls may also address the cut-off objective, although substantive tests are often performed to address this objective.

2.10 The objectives of valuation, rights and obligations and presentation and disclosure are related to management's subjective judgements and estimates, and often are not addressed by the system of internal control. The risks of misstatement associated with these objectives are often higher than the risks related to other audit objectives where less judgement is required.

Audit risk

2.11 The term **audit risk** is used to describe the risk that the auditor will issue an incorrect opinion on the financial statements. For example, there is a risk that the auditor will issue an unqualified opinion when the financial statements taken as a whole are materially misstated. The auditor should design and perform audit procedures that will permit the expression of an opinion on the financial statements with a low overall risk that the opinion will be inappropriate. Because of the limitations inherent in both the preparation and the audit of financial statements, it is not possible to eliminate completely the risk that the audit opinion will be inappropriate.

2.12 Audit risk should be assessed in relation to the account balance or class of transactions, and has two major components, as follows:

- **The risk of material misstatement.** This is a combination of the inherent risk that items in the financial statements will be materially misstated, either individually or in aggregate, and the risk that the controls will not be effective in preventing or detecting those misstatements.

- **Detection risk.** This is the risk that misstatements contained within the financial statements will not be detected by the audit.

Inherent risk

2.13 Inherent risk is the susceptibility of an account balance or class of transactions to material misstatement before taking into account the effectiveness of controls. The misstatement may arise as a result of error, through unintentional misstatements in, or omissions from, the accounting records or financial statements, or from fraud. The misstatement may result from conditions that exist at the macroeconomic, industry, or company level (**inherent risk conditions**) or from characteristics of the account balance or class of transactions (**inherent risk characteristics**).

2.14 At the macroeconomic level inherent risk conditions may include the state of the economy, the political climate and exchange rate and interest rate volatility. For example, the recoverability of receivables may be adversely affected in a recession. At the industry level examples would include legislative changes related to the industry, overcapacity within the industry and technological change which could render inventory obsolete. At the company level an example might be a new product about which there is uncertainty as to the level of demand. Some inherent risk conditions may be pervasive in that they affect more than one account balance. For example, a risk relating to whether the entity remains a going concern will affect many account balances.

2.15 Inherent risk conditions may change from year to year and the auditor should reassess them at the beginning of every audit. They are not normally addressed by the system of internal accounting control, although the entity may perform special procedures in relation to them. Examples of such procedures include special reviews of inventory obsolescence or of doubtful accounts receivable.

2.16 Inherent risk characteristics are attributable to specific account balances or classes of transactions and may affect all audit objectives. Examples of account balances that display inherent risk characteristics include:

(a) account balances involving complex judgements, for example, the recognition of revenue on long-term construction contracts;

(b) account balances representing assets that are susceptible to theft in the absence of strong controls, for example, precious metals;

(c) account balances derived from unusual or complex transactions where there may be limited procedures or experience to deal with such transactions.

2.17 Inherent risk characteristics usually change only as a result of changes in the business. They are often addressed by internal accounting controls. The auditor should assess at an early stage in the audit whether changes in the business have had an effect on inherent risk characteristics and whether the internal control structure has been revised to respond to such changes.

Control risk

2.18 Control risk is the risk that the internal controls will not prevent or detect material misstatements on a timely basis. When assessing controls the auditor is seeking to determine how effective they are in preventing or detecting such misstatements.

Detection risk

2.19 Detection risk is the risk that the auditor's substantive tests will not detect material misstatements in the financial statements. It differs from inherent and control risk in that it can be controlled by the auditor. The assessment of inherent risk and of the effectiveness of controls gives the auditor a better understanding of the risk of material misstatement in the financial statements, but it does not reduce or otherwise change that risk. Detection risk can be controlled by varying the nature, extent and timing of substantive tests.

2.20 The assessment of inherent risk and of the effectiveness of controls determines the acceptable level of detection risk and, thereby, affects the nature, extent and timing of substantive tests. As the risk of material misstatement decreases due to lower inherent risk or more effective controls, so the amount of assurance required from substantive tests decreases. The auditor seeks to keep detection risk to an acceptably low level by designing an effective programme of substantive tests and carrying them out thoroughly.

2.21 There is always a risk that the auditor will reach an inappropriate conclusion in performing and evaluating the results of his audit procedures. This risk has two components, namely **sampling risk**, which is present only when tests involving sampling are performed, and

non-sampling risk, which is present when any auditing procedures, including tests involving sampling, are performed.

2.22 Sampling risk is the risk that the results of a test involving a sample will lead to a conclusion that would have been different had the entire population been examined. It is reduced by designing the sample effectively. Non-sampling risk is the risk that any factor other than the sample selected will cause the auditor to draw an incorrect conclusion about an account balance or the effectiveness of control. Examples include the omission of essential audit procedures, such as a review of board minutes, or the improper performance of procedures, for example, failure to follow up queries arising from a circularisation of receivable balances.

Factors Affecting the Audit Strategy

2.23 The audit strategy describes, in broad terms, the principal features of the proposed approach to the audit and it provides a basis for planning and controlling the subsequent audit work. In determining the audit strategy, the auditor will undertake the following activities:

(a) determine the objectives of the engagement;

(b) carry out a review of the business being audited to gain an understanding of it;

(c) evaluate inherent risks; and

(d) make an initial assessment of internal control, including the overall control environment of the business, the principal features of the accounting system and the related internal accounting controls.

The objectives of the engagement

2.24 The auditor will normally be appointed in accordance with the Companies Act 1985 and the audit will be carried out in accordance with approved Auditing Standards. Consequently, the auditor is normally primarily concerned with the truth and fairness of the financial statements being audited. However, it is also necessary to consider whether additional responsibilities arise from requests of management or because the business is required to conform to special regulatory or other requirements that are not normally applicable. For example, the auditors of building societies in the United Kingdom are required by the Building Societies Act 1986 to form an opinion as to whether the society has maintained a satisfactory system of control over the conduct of the society's business and over the accounting and other records and this obliges them to evaluate controls including those relating to computer systems. A further example occurs in local authority and other public sector audits where the auditor may be asked to carry out value for money auditing as part of his engagement.

2.25 The auditor may decide to go beyond his statutory obligations in order to enhance the service provided to his client. For example, he may decide, or be asked by management, to evaluate controls in order to bring any weaknesses to the attention of management even though there are no regulatory or other requirements to do so. Because management recognise the dependency of the business on its computer systems, they will often request a review of controls within the computer department even though the auditor does not need to review them for the purpose of his audit.

2.26 The responsibilities of the internal auditor are somewhat different in that often his primary function is to report to management on the effectiveness of controls. As a result the internal auditor will usually choose to evaluate and test controls in the system in preference to substantive testing. However, he too may need to carry out substantive tests to ascertain the effect on the financial statements of a lack of control or as part of a special investigation for management.

Reviewing the business

2.27 In determining his audit strategy the auditor should obtain a knowledge of the business being audited and the industry in which it operates. This will assist in planning his subsequent audit procedures by giving him an understanding of the types and levels of business activities in which the entity is involved, the industry and economic conditions affecting the business and the inherent risks to which the business is subject. For a continuing audit, much of this information will already be known to the auditor, although it should be updated each year.

2.28 External factors which the auditor will consider include macroeconomic factors such as government policies and industry factors including information about the market, the main competitors in the industry, industry practices with audit implications and specialised reporting, accounting and regulatory matters. Internal factors to be reviewed include the location and size of the operations, the nature of the products and production methods, major capital and research projects, management's concerns and plans, and finance, marketing and personnel policies. The auditor will gather his information from discussions with management, visits to principal locations and external and internal reports and publications.

2.29 As part of the review of the business, the auditor may well perform some preliminary analytical review of high level aggregations of data, often using management accounts. This will assist in establishing familiarity with cash flows, operating results and the financial position and in identifying unusual or unexpected relationships or balances. The auditor will also gain an understanding of the significant accounting policies used by the business and consider whether they are appropriate in the light of legislation, accounting standards, industry norms and good practice. In the light of his review of the business, the auditor will make preliminary judgements concerning materiality, although these judgements may be affected by matters that arise subsequently.

Evaluating inherent risks

2.30 The auditor's objective in evaluating inherent risk is to assess the risk of material misstatement for all significant audit objectives for each individual account balance and class of transactions. This assessment will be used as the basis for planning subsequent audit procedures to gain assurance that the financial statements are not materially misstated. The auditor will search for inherent risks by considering the results of his review of the business, the characteristics of account balances or classes of transactions and whether there is any history of fraud or error affecting particular account balances.

2.31 Having identified inherent risks, the auditor will evaluate their significance. In so doing he will take the following into account:

(a) The operating environment of the business and the external factors that affect it. For example, in the case of a software development company the auditor might conclude, based on his understanding of industry trends, that there was a higher than normal inherent risk of inventory obsolescence.

(b) Whether there is any particular motivation for management to distort the financial statements. For example, management may have greater motivation to distort the financial statements if results were falling short of a publicly announced profit forecast than if the forecast were for internal purposes only.

(c) Whether the risk is of fraud or error. For example, with an electronic funds transfer system used to pay suppliers, the auditor might conclude that a risk of error is mitigated by the likelihood that, if such an error occurred, recompense could be obtained from the supplier, whereas a risk of material fraud would not be similarly mitigated.

(d) The number of risks affecting the audit objective. For example, the inherent risk normally associated with calculating an inventory obsolescence estimate would be greater if the product were new and management had little experience in developing such estimates. It would increase further if management had a history of error in developing other estimates.

2.32 In assessing the significance of inherent risks, the auditor will consider the likelihood of the risk crystallising into a fraud or error and the likely materiality of any consequent misstatement. The auditor will also relate the risks identified to audit objectives for each account balance and class of transaction. For example, the risk of inventory obsolescence in a software development company referred to in paragraph 2.31(a) would relate principally to the valuation audit objective for inventories. In general, risks associated with estimates will relate to the audit objectives of valuation, rights and obligations, cut-off and presentation and disclosure. The risk of fraud relates principally to the audit objective of existence because where assets are susceptible to theft this is the objective which could be affected and because employee frauds are often concealed by overstating expenses and assets.

Initial assessment of internal control

2.33 In order to determine the audit strategy the auditor will need to make an initial assessment of the quality of internal control within the business. In practice, there will be a hierarchy of procedures and controls which the auditor will consider, comprising the following elements:

- The control environment.
- The accounting systems.
- Internal accounting controls.

The control environment

2.34 The control environment encompasses the overall attitudes, abilities, awareness and actions of the personnel within the business, and particularly those of its management, concerning the importance of control and the emphasis given to it. The leadership and support of senior management are essential if a favourable control environment is to be established and maintained. The key elements of the control environment are as follows:

(a) the effectiveness of the organisational structure;
(b) the role of the board of directors and key management;
(c) the existence and role of the audit committee and internal audit;
(d) the reasonableness of management plans and budgets;
(e) the relevance and reliability of management information;
(f) the reliability of management estimates;
(g) the existence of adequate policies and procedures for controlling the business;
(h) the risk that management might override internal controls or intentionally misstate the financial statements; and
(i) the effectiveness of management control over computer operations and in other areas.

2.35 Favourable or unfavourable control environment features have a significant effect on the quality of internal accounting controls, on the degree of control exercised by management over the business operations and, ultimately, on the fair presentation of its financial statements. The auditor will make his assessment of the control environment through enquiry, observation, review of evidence of management's controls and discussions with management. On continuing audits the auditor will also draw on the knowledge obtained in prior years, updated to take account of developments in the current year.

2.36 The assessment of the control environment will normally identify positive and negative features. A favourable overall assessment of the control environment will provide the auditor with considerable assurance concerning the effective operation of internal accounting controls carried out by users. Where the control environment is unfavourable it will generally not be efficient for the auditor to make an extended assessment of internal control.

Accounting systems

2.37 An accounting system consists of a series of procedures for recording and processing transactions and for recording resources and their use. Such procedures may be performed manually, for example, the recording of goods received, or by computer, for example, the automatic generation of cheques to pay suppliers. Computerised accounting procedures are referred to as programmed accounting procedures. A computerised system normally comprises a series of both manual and computer procedures which record transactions from their inception to their entry in the general ledger.

2.38 The accounting system should be designed in the light of factors such as the nature of the business, its size and organisational structure, the types and volumes of transactions and whether it is subject to the requirements of any regulatory bodies. It should take into account any relevant inherent risk characteristics of the account balances and classes of transactions. The auditor will need to gain an initial understanding of the accounting systems in order to determine the audit strategy. Overview flowcharts, described in Chapter 3, may well be used for this purpose. The auditor should also gain and record an initial understanding of the computer environment within which the accounting applications are processed including details of the computer hardware and software in use.

Initial assessment of internal accounting controls

2.39 In determining the audit strategy the auditor will need to make an initial assessment of the effectiveness of the internal accounting controls designed to ensure the consistent and proper operation of the accounting systems. The auditor's objective at this stage is to make preliminary judgements as to whether the internal accounting controls are likely to be strong enough to enable him to place reliance on them and to assess the relative cost-effectiveness of performing an extended assessment of internal control as compared to relying on substantive tests.

2.40 The auditor will obtain a preliminary understanding of the internal controls from discussions with the client's management and from limited reviews of documents. For continuing audits the information will already be available and will merely need to be updated for changes to the controls. The assessment of controls at this stage will be limited to obtaining prima facie evidence of the existence or otherwise of the principal controls, and will not normally include any testing of those controls. Nevertheless, the auditor will need to assess their likely effectiveness and to relate them to other controls so as to be able to judge the likely overall strength of controls. For this reason the preliminary assessment of controls is a task requiring considerable skill and expertise in reviewing and testing controls.

2.41 In order to determine the most efficient strategy it is necessary that the auditor should understand clearly the nature and different types of internal control and the way in which they relate to one another. In the remainder of this chapter the main elements of controls, the way in which they relate to each other, and the options which the auditor has in determining the audit strategy are described under the following headings:

- Internal Controls.
- Determining the Audit Strategy.

Internal Controls

2.42 In some countries, the phrase "internal control" is often taken to cover the methods, procedures and organisational arrangements adopted not only for the safeguarding of assets and ensuring the reliability of the accounting records, but also for the promotion of operational efficiency and adherence to management policies. Those internal controls which are relevant to the expression of an audit opinion on financial statements are classified as **internal accounting controls** and the others are classified as **operational controls**. In practice, some internal accounting controls will also have operational aspects. For the purpose of this book, the phrase internal controls is used for internal accounting controls.

2.43 The approach and documentation outlined in this book are directed primarily to the evaluation of internal controls. This is because the operational controls are not relevant to the expression of an audit opinion on financial statements. However, the evaluation of operational controls, particularly by the internal auditor, is often an important aid to management. The approach outlined in this book can also be applied to the evaluation of operational controls; additional material would then need to be included in the documentation for this purpose.

The nature of controls

2.44 Internal accounting controls consist of:

- Application controls.
- Information technology (IT) controls.

Application controls are defined as all those controls and procedures designed to ensure that data on files from which the financial statements are derived is properly maintained between transaction updates (**file controls**) and that valid transactions, and only valid transactions, are processed and recorded completely and accurately in the accounting records (**transaction controls**). They may be manual procedures carried out by users (**user controls**) but will often rely on procedures performed by computer programs (**programmed procedures**). IT controls are designed to ensure that the programmed procedures within a computer system are appropriately designed, implemented, maintained and operated and that only authorised changes are made to computer programs and data.

2.45 The structure of controls is more complex in a computer system than in a manual system because of the existence in a computer system of programmed procedures and the need for IT controls. Furthermore, in a manual system the controls may develop over a period as a result of experience. In a computer system the controls must be built in when it is implemented, since computer systems are difficult and expensive to change later. Consequently, the controls in a computer system need to be specified more formally than in a manual system.

2.46 Frequently, the auditor will find that the type of control in force varies according to the type of organisation. In large organisations, with high volumes of transactions, a formalised system of controls with supervision of their performance and division of duties between staff is necessary in order to run the business effectively. By contrast, in small organisations the opportunity and the need for formal control and supervision and division of duties are less, and such organisations tend to rely on a basic level of controls coupled with a greater degree of management involvement in the day-to-day transactions of the company. The auditor should beware of concluding that such a system is uncontrolled since the controls in force may be adequate for the type of organisation.

Application controls

File controls

2.47 The account balances within the financial statements are normally held on computer files. Not all files are of equal significance and the auditor is principally concerned with files that support material items in the financial statements. Within these files certain data elements will be of greater importance to the auditor, for example, the inventory balance, while others will be of less significance, for example, information held for operational reasons such as year to date sales by individual employees. In a database system there are not normally discrete data files supporting account balances, and the auditor therefore identifies the key data elements in the database in which he is interested. The objectives of file controls are:

(a) **file continuity**, to ensure that, once data is updated to a file, the data remains correct and current on the file; and

(b) **asset protection**, to ensure that the assets represented by the balances on the file are suitably protected by physical security procedures, proper approval and recording of movements and security procedures over stored data to prevent unauthorised access to data files.

Transaction controls

2.48 Transaction controls have the following objectives:

(a) **completeness**, to ensure that all transactions are recorded, input to the computer and processed through the accounting system;

(b) **accuracy**, to ensure that transactions are accurately recorded, input to the computer and processed through the accounting system; and

(c) **authorisation**, to ensure that only valid transactions are processed.

File and transaction controls will normally comprise a mixture of manual controls carried out by users and programmed procedures carried out within computer programs. The nature of such user controls and programmed procedures is explained in paragraphs 2.49 to 2.53.

User controls

2.49 User controls are defined as manual controls carried out on the data being processed. Users, for this purpose, may include all those who are not involved in computer operations. They thus include user departments and, in some cases, control sections within computer departments.

2.50 Some user controls will be unrelated to computer processing. These would include such controls as checking the quality and condition of goods received or ensuring that all transactions are initially recorded. Other user controls will rely for their effectiveness on the continued and proper operation of a related programmed procedure. For example, the investigation of items reported by the computer as missing or exceptional will only be effective if the missing or exceptional items are properly reported. In a few cases, there will be other user controls which have as their purpose the checking of programmed procedures, for example, the detailed checking to source data of a print-out of standing data amendments.

2.51 The three types of user control are illustrated in Figure 2 which shows part of a simplified sales accounting system. The checking of quantities shipped is unrelated to computer processing. The investigation of missing items is related to computer processing and will only be effective if the related programmed procedure, in this case the checking of the sequence of despatched documents, operates properly. The review of invoices has as its purpose the checking of a programmed procedure – the calculation of invoices.

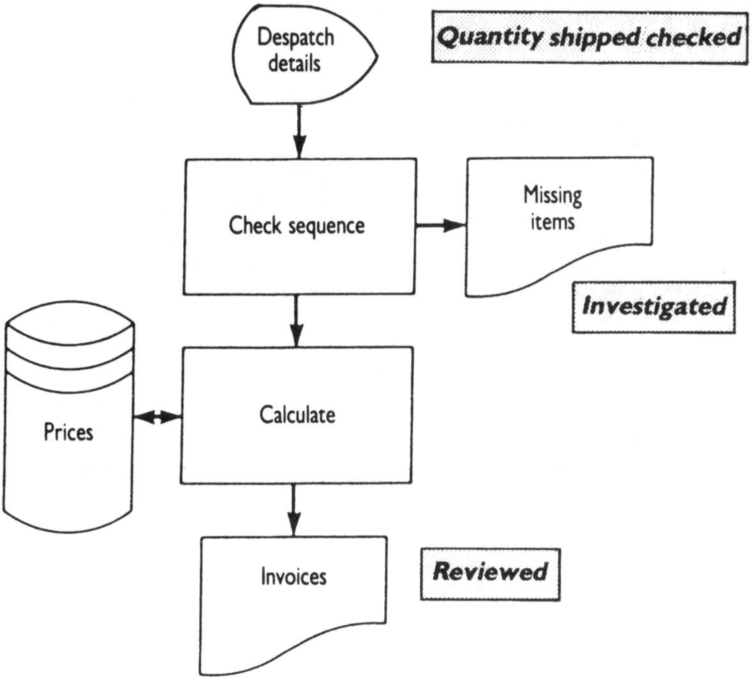

Fig. 2. Types of user controls (para. 2.51)

Programmed procedures

2.52 Programmed procedures can be divided into two types:

- Programmed control procedures form part of *control functions previously carried out manually*. They may test the completeness, accuracy and validity of the data being processed. They include edit tests, the accumulation of the data being processed and agreement with control totals, the accumulation of items on master files and reconciliation with file totals and the identification and reporting of incorrect, exceptional and missing data. In many cases, for control to be effective the programmed procedure will need to be combined with suitable manual control procedures, for example, the follow up of items failing edit tests or reported as incorrect, exceptional or missing.

- Programmed accounting procedures replace *manual operations of an accounting rather than control nature*, for example, the calculation and production of sales invoices and payrolls, the updating of master files and the generation of data within the computer.

2.53 The extract of a sales accounting system previously used to illustrate user controls is shown again in Figure 3 to illustrate examples of the two types of programmed procedures, the checking of the sequence of despatch numbers, which replaces a manual control, and the calculation of invoices, which replaces a manual accounting function.

IT controls

2.54 IT controls are those controls, normally carried out in the data processing department, that are concerned with the computer programs and data files. It is convenient for audit purposes to divide the IT controls according to their objective, using the terms by which they will be referred to in this book, as follows:

- **Implementation controls**, designed to ensure that appropriate programmed procedures are effectively included in the program, both when the system originally becomes operational and when changes are subsequently made. They include the controls over the design, testing and taking into operational use of new systems and program changes and the related documentation.

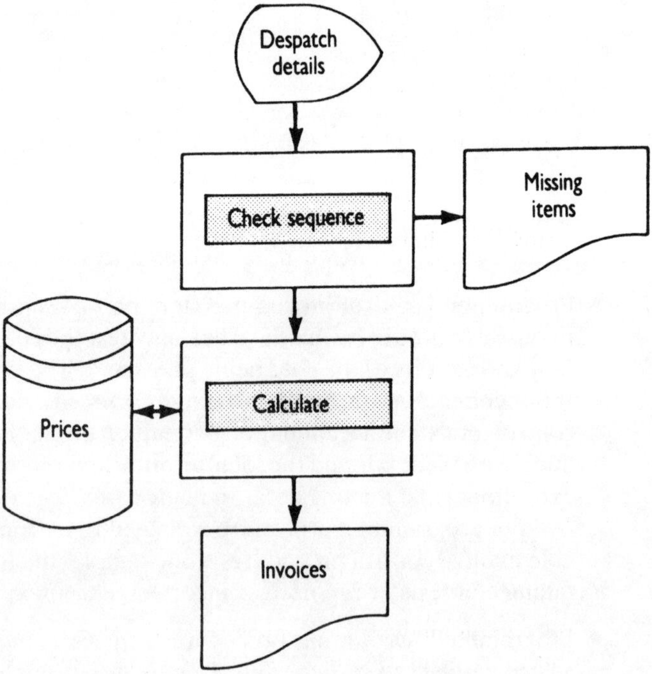

FIG. 3. Types of programmed procedures (para. 2.53)

- **Security controls**, designed to ensure that unauthorised changes cannot be made to programmed procedures and data. They include the controls over the security of programs and data, both from unauthorised access through terminals and when they are stored in a separate physical library.
- **Computer operations controls**, designed to ensure that programmed procedures are consistently applied. They include the controls that programs and data are properly set up on the system and that they are used in accordance with authorised instructions.

2.55 The IT controls will be a combination of manual controls and procedures included in what is termed in this book the system software. **System software** may be defined as those programs, such as the operating system, on whose functioning the auditor may wish to place reliance, although they do not process accounting data. The extent of reliance on system software will vary. For example, when programs are not being used for processing, they may be held under manual control in a physical library or under software control on the computer.

2.56 Commonly, the same IT controls are applied to all systems being developed or processed at a computer installation. Because of this the IT controls will assist in ensuring the effectiveness of programmed procedures and security in all systems within the environment. However, in some cases the controls will differ from one system to another, and the auditor may thus need to evaluate several sets of controls. This can be the case, for example, in large organisations where teams of programmers and analysts are permanently assigned to each system and adopt implementation controls appropriate to the complexity and importance of their individual systems.

2.57 The extract of a sales accounting system previously used to illustrate user controls and programmed procedures is shown again in Figure 4 to illustrate the scope of IT controls. The implementation, security and computer operations controls relate to the programmed procedures (sequence check and calculation of invoices) and the security controls also protect the data stored on the prices file.

Supervision and division of duties

2.58 If application and IT controls are to be effective in practice, there should be adequate supervision of control procedures by responsible officials and a suitable division of duties in the performance of procedures and related internal accounting controls.

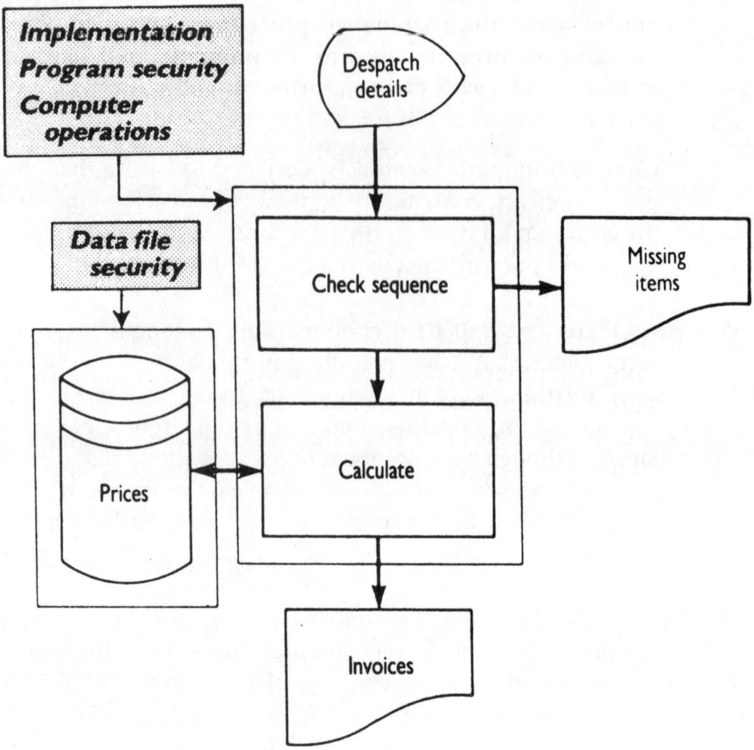

FIG. 4. The scope of IT controls (para. 2.57)

Supervision

2.59 Supervision comprises a regular check or review by a responsible official that a control continues to operate effectively. For example, in a user department, there would need to be a regular check by a responsible official that the investigation of data rejected by the computer is being carried out regularly. Likewise, in the data processing department, the adequacy of testing procedures for program changes would require to be reviewed and approved by a suitable data processing department manager.

Division of duties

2.60 Division of duties involves the work of one person providing a check over the operation of another. It includes both separation of the responsibility for the custody of assets from the records which account for them, and the separation of functions related to control in the accounting or data processing areas. An example of the separation of responsibility for the custody of assets from the related records is that the user controls relating to a computer inventory file should be performed or checked by persons other than those involved in maintaining physical custody of the inventory. In relation to user controls an obvious example is that the persons carrying out controls on data should be independent of computer operations. In relation to IT controls it is important, for example, that those responsible for testing and implementing new systems should not also be responsible for operating those systems.

2.61 The extract of a sales accounting system previously used to illustrate user controls, programmed procedures and IT controls is shown again in Figure 5 to illustrate examples of supervision and division of duties relating to user controls. Those persons checking quantities shipped should not also have custody of inventories, the work of investigating

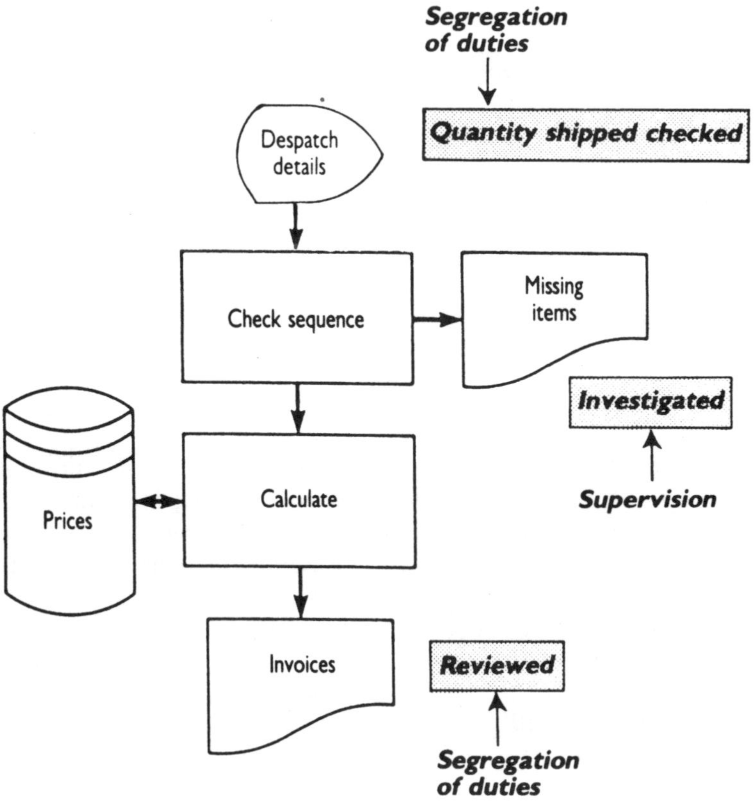

FIG. 5. Examples of supervision and division of duties relating to user controls (para. 2.61)

missing items should be supervised and those persons responsible for reviewing sales invoices should be independent of computer operations. In practice, further controls would be required both as regards the user controls illustrated and the IT controls.

Determination of the Audit Strategy

2.62 The auditor will determine the audit strategy based on the results of the initial work performed to determine engagement objectives, review the business being audited, evaluate inherent risks and assess the control environment, accounting systems and internal controls. In particular, the auditor will decide:

(a) the degree to which he will carry out an extended assessment of controls in order to reduce substantive testing; and

(b) the broad nature, extent and timing of substantive tests to be performed.

Extended assessment of controls

2.63 In some circumstances deciding whether to carry out an extended assessment of controls will be straightforward. For example, for a small client with unsophisticated systems it may require very little investigation to establish that the assurance needed to support the audit opinion would most efficiently be obtained from substantive tests. Similarly, in the following circumstances, substantive testing would be likely to be the most efficient approach:

(a) if the control environment were unfavourable;

(b) if the previous year's audit or subsequent information indicated that the application controls or IT controls were not effective; or

(c) if the volume of transactions was low, or if the nature of the assets, liabilities or operations or the composition of the account balance made substantive testing relatively cost-effective.

2.64 However, before deciding to obtain all required assurance from substantive tests, the auditor should consider whether, by so doing, he will be meeting the engagement objectives. For example, a reporting deadline might make it impracticable to obtain the required assurance solely from substantive tests because there was insufficient time to perform the tests before the deadline. In this case an extended assessment of controls might be performed. Alternatively, management might request the auditor to report in detail on controls, even where it would be more efficient for audit purposes to rely on substantive testing.

2.65 As set out in paragraphs 2.08 to 2.10 the accounting system and related internal controls principally address the completeness and accuracy audit objectives and to some degree the existence and cut-off objectives. Where the auditor decides to carry out an extended assessment of internal controls in respect of some or all of these objectives he will, if the results are satisfactory, restrict his substantive tests relating to them. The auditor will normally design substantive tests to address the valuation, rights and obligations and presentation and disclosure objectives.

2.66 Where the circumstances in paragraph 2.63 do not apply the auditor will consider whether it is efficient to perform an extended assessment of controls. This will be the case if the savings resulting from reductions in the assurance required from substantive tests exceed the costs of making the extended assessment of controls. To a significant degree the decision will depend upon the quality of the control environment and the IT controls. Where the control environment is favourable this will provide the auditor with a significant degree of assurance that user controls subject to the environment are effective. Where the IT controls are effective this will provide significant assurance over the effective operation of programmed procedures and the security of programs and data. The auditor will also need to carry out an extended assessment of controls in systems subject to the control environment and IT controls. However, he should be able to be selective in deciding which systems or controls to test and should not need to test every control on which he wishes to place reliance on the basis that, if the results of his tests are satisfactory, other controls subject to the same control environment and IT controls will also operate satisfactorily. The extent of testing necessary will be a matter for judgement in each case.

2.67 As noted in paragraph 2.63, where the control environment is unfavourable it is unlikely to be efficient to perform an extended assessment of controls. Where the IT controls are generally unsatisfactory the auditor will not be able to rely on them to ensure the effective operation of programmed procedures. The user controls may ensure the continued and proper operation of the programmed procedures if they reperform or check the procedures. In these circumstances, reliance on IT controls will not be necessary. However, as computer systems and their programmed procedures become more sophisticated and users gain confidence in them it is unlikely that user controls will seek to check the operation of the programmed procedures in detail. Frequently, computer systems now produce summarised information or report only exceptional or unusual items as the basis for user controls, since this is generally more helpful to the user. It is neither practical nor cost effective for the user to check manually the operation of the programmed procedure in these cases.

2.68 If the auditor is to rely on programmed procedures when the IT controls and user controls do not ensure their continued and proper operation, then he will need to test them directly. Most computer systems are likely to include a significant number of programmed procedures and, in general, it is unlikely to be efficient for the auditor to test a large number of procedures directly as part of an extended assessment of controls. He may, however, decide to test selected programmed procedures directly as part of his audit strategy. For example, the auditor may decide to test the programmed procedure which calculates interest charges in a bank because of its importance, even though he has performed an extended assessment of IT controls. As a further example, where the computer systems are relatively simple, the auditor may combine tests of user controls with direct tests of the significant programmed procedures rather than examining IT controls in detail. The internal auditor may also wish to test programmed procedures directly where his objective is to examine the operation and control of a system in detail. A variety of techniques are available for testing programmed procedures including manual reperformance, use of test data, analysing program logic and reperforming the procedure with computer programs written by the auditor.

Reliance on IT controls

2.69 The cost and effectiveness of testing IT controls will depend on the number and complexity of the programmed procedures and on the type and strength of the IT controls in force. In large computer installations, where many of the systems are developed internally, there will often be well developed and highly formalised IT controls, backed up by extensive supervision and by sophisticated computer programs which control access to, and use of, the computer. Frequently, the auditor will be able to place a high degree of reliance on them. In addition, there are likely to be a large number of significant programmed procedures and considerable dependence by the business on computer processing. In these circumstances it is likely that the auditor will wish to evaluate and test the IT controls.

2.70 In small computer installations where packaged software supplied by external vendors is used, the degree of formalisation and complexity of IT controls required will be reduced. This will particularly be the case where the package in use is well established and the source code is not supplied to users or where users, in practice, make no changes to it. Operations procedures are often relatively straightforward in such cases, being built into the operation of the software itself. In these circumstances it may well be efficient for the auditor to rely on IT controls over implementation, maintenance and computer operations to ensure the continued and proper operation of programmed procedures. Controls over the security of programs and data are often relatively weak in small installations and the auditor will need to perform other procedures, such as substantive tests, to determine whether there are any material misstatements arising as a result of the weaknesses.

2.71 Where the auditor's preliminary assessment reveals weaknesses in some aspects of the IT controls, he may still be able to rely on other elements of them as part of his audit strategy. For example, where weaknesses in controls over the implementation of new systems have arisen during the year under audit, the auditor may still be able to rely on IT controls if no significant new systems have been implemented during the year. If a significant system was implemented during the year the auditor may still be able to rely on an extended assessment of application and IT controls where his tests of application controls cover the new system. Weaknesses in certain aspects of security controls may give rise principally to a risk of fraudulent amendment to programs or data, enabling the auditor to continue to rely on IT controls to protect against errors in the operation of the programmed procedures.

Substantive testing plan

2.72 The auditor is not expected to design the detailed programme of substantive tests when determining his audit strategy but he will establish their broad nature, extent and timing. As part of this he will consider any particular substantive testing response to inherent risks identified, and the efficiency of performing some substantive testing prior to the period end.

Documenting the Audit Strategy

2.73 The auditor will need to document his audit strategy both to help him clarify his thoughts and as evidence of the purpose and nature of his audit work. It is normally suitable to do this in the form of a memorandum summarising the factors affecting the audit strategy, the audit approach adopted for each significant aspect of the financial statements and the reasons for the decisions taken. The audit strategy memorandum may also deal with administrative matters, such as timetables, budgets and staffing of the work. In addition, the auditor will normally wish to record his preliminary assessment of the accounting systems and related controls, and for this purpose it may be suitable to use the overview documentation described in Chapters 3 and 4. The audit strategy will be monitored as the audit progresses and may be amended in the light of information which changes the auditor's preliminary judgements.

Summary

2.74 In order to ensure that the audit is carried out effectively and efficiently the auditor will need to plan his audit procedures in relation to each significant balance or group of balances in the financial statements. A major choice facing the auditor is whether to make an extended assessment of internal control in order to restrict his substantive testing. In determining his audit strategy the auditor will also decide on the broad nature, extent and timing of his substantive tests.

2.75 The audit strategy will be influenced by the objectives of the audit, the nature of the business and the risks affecting it, by the nature of the balances and by the strength of the controls over the accounting systems which generate them. For each significant balance or group of balances, the strategy will be determined in relation to the audit objectives of completeness, accuracy, existence, cut-off, valuation, rights and obligations and presentation and disclosure. The auditor will want to choose the strategy which achieves his objectives in the most efficient way.

2.76 In considering controls the auditor will first review the overall control environment which encompasses the attitudes, abilities, awareness and actions of the personnel within the business concerning the importance of control and the emphasis given to it. Controls within the computer systems consist of application controls and IT controls. Application controls are controls carried out within a specific computer system, such as accounts receivable. They may be performed by users but will often rely on programmed procedures. IT controls are controls over the design, security and operation of computer systems, and the auditor may wish to place reliance on them to ensure the continued and proper operation of significant programmed procedures. The need for the auditor to assess programmed procedures and IT controls is one of the principal differences between auditing computer and manual systems.

2.77 Where the control environment is favourable, and his initial review shows application and IT controls to be effective, the auditor may decide to carry out an extended assessment of controls. The extent of testing performed will be a matter of judgement in each case, but, where the control environment and tests of IT controls are satisfactory, this will provide some assurance over the consistency of operation of controls and programmed procedures, so that the auditor should not need to test every application control on which he wishes to rely. Where IT controls are not fully effective the auditor may be able to rely on them selectively or to rely on user controls or direct tests of the programmed procedures in performing his extended assessment of controls.

3

Understanding and Recording the System

General Approach

3.01 Where the auditor decides, in determining his audit strategy, to place reliance on internal controls, he will need to gain and record an understanding of the procedures and controls comprising a company's accounting system. The auditor normally obtains his understanding by reading systems' descriptions and by discussions with company staff. He usually records his understanding of the system by use of **flowcharts** or, in those cases where their preparation may be more efficient, by narrative notes.

3.02 The auditor's understanding of the accounting system is ultimately confirmed during the audit by the performance of audit tests. However, in order to reduce the risk that time may be wasted in devising and attempting to perform audit procedures on the basis of an incorrect understanding of the accounting system, the auditor may wish to confirm his understanding before performing audit tests. He can do this, for example, by inspecting or reviewing transactions, records, documents or reports.

3.03 There are particular features in understanding computer systems because of the distinctive nature of computer processing. These features are discussed in the first part of this chapter and examples of typical computer systems are described in the appendix to this chapter. Particular points in recording computer systems are dealt with in the second part of the chapter.

Understanding Computer Systems

Technical computer knowledge required

3.04 In order to understand and record computer systems effectively, the auditor must have a basic understanding of the principles of computers and computer processing and it is assumed that the reader of this book will have such an understanding. This would include a knowledge of the basic units of a computer configuration, their inter-relationship, the nature of computer processing from input to output, the concepts of programming and the functions of the operating system. If the reader does not have this basic knowledge, it is readily available from existing literature and courses. Any further detailed knowledge required will vary from system to system and depend primarily on the complexity of computer processing in any particular system and the resulting impact on the controls.

Computer processing in business

3.05 The individual business is faced with a wide choice of equipment and methods when considering how to make the best use of computer technology. The choice no longer rests upon which machine to buy but rather how to organise the transfer of information within the business. This change has been reflected in the terminology used to describe computer processing in business.

Data processing

3.06 The term "data processing" has been used for many years to describe the use of computers to process data. In the early computer systems this referred to the receipt of data, usually in batch form and most commonly relating to accounting systems, by a centralised computer operations department, its subsequent manipulation and storage and the provision of printed output to the various users reflecting the processing carried out.

3.07 Subsequent to this period, the ways in which computer systems were organised and data was processed began to change. On-line and real-time systems emerged, databases began to be used and distributed systems became feasible as the technology of communications improved. These terms are explained later in this chapter.

Office automation

3.08 As these changes took place, so the computer industry began to widen the scope of data processing to incorporate many of the clerical functions carried out in the office. This was referred to as "office automation".

3.09 Office automation includes the use of computerised telephone exchanges offering facilities for recording and analysing calls made, for abbreviated dialling functions by storing numbers in memory, for conference calls by joining additional parties to a conversation, and for automatic routing of calls when there is no reply. In addition to simple improvement to telephone facilities, word processing using computers has replaced the typewriter. Only when the text can be seen to be correct is it printed out in final form often using a letter quality printer to give a good finished document.

3.10 Office automation also includes electronic filing and electronic mail. Electronic filing means that copies of documents are no longer kept in hard copy but are held on the memory of the computer. Any workstation – a desk top terminal or computer connected to the main computer, usually by cabling known as a local area network (LAN) – can, if permitted, access that "copy" document. Recently "image processing" systems have been developed to capture, store, manipulate and present information in visual form. Such systems can capture large volumes of documentation and allow rapid access to it. They commonly involve the use of optical scanners, large capacity storage devices such as optical disks, high resolution screens, database and graphics software.

3.11 Electronic mail enables messages to be sent from workstation to workstation by keying in a message and putting an "address" on it, which is recognised by the computer. At the receiving workstation, the individual enquires from time to time if there are any messages. If so, the message is displayed. Electronic mail is now available on an international basis to anyone who wishes to subscribe to one of a number of different systems. Its effectiveness is clearly dependent upon all the persons whom the individual might wish to contact also being subscribers to the system.

Information technology

3.12 Clearly, these different systems and developments cannot all reside in isolation in one part of an organisation. It is desirable to integrate them in the organisation's general use of computing. In addition, two other features have gained widespread acceptance. The first is the use of individual microcomputers as a powerful tool to carry out a variety of tasks at an individual or departmental level. Such tasks include, for example, maintaining customer lists and information, modelling and cash flow projections. The term "personal computing" has come into being. In some organisations, the personal computing facilities provided by the microcomputer are centralised and provided by linking individual users to the organisation's central computer.

3.13 The second feature is an extension of the use of computing into functional systems connected with the operation of the business rather than with processing accounting data. These systems include, for example, reservation systems, production planning systems, dealing systems for the financial markets, computer-aided design facilities and, perhaps of more direct significance to the auditor, automated payment systems and systems for electronic funds transfer (EFT).

3.14 As a result, today the term "information technology" is being used increasingly. Information technology covers all uses of computers, peripheral devices and communications to receive, process, store and transfer information, whether that information be textual or numerical, and regardless of whether the information is in electronic, hard copy, image or voice form.

Executive information systems

3.15 In order to enable management to make effective use of the information available in the growing range of information systems within a business, recent years have seen the development of "executive information systems". These systems are designed to provide information to executives in a form which is easy to access and use covering a range of functional areas within the business, such as finance, marketing, manufacturing and human resources. The systems typically provide information in a summary form but then allow the user to access more detailed information to investigate a particular item. Frequently, graphics are used in presenting information on screen. Information must be gathered from a variety of systems within the business, which may be incompatible with one another, and recorded in a common format for presentation. To be successful the system should establish appropriate relationships between the information gathered and present it in a meaningful way rather than simply summarising it. Careful analysis of the requirements of the users is needed to achieve this.

Electronic data interchange

3.16 In order to take advantage of the improvements in communications and reduce the need for exchange of paper documents, businesses are increasingly using electronic data interchange (EDI) to exchange business documents by computer. For example, purchase orders may be sent to a supplier electronically rather than on paper. As well as cutting out paperwork, the speed of the whole process can be increased. The sending and receiving organisations must be able to communicate and will use EDI software to process electronic transactions and pass them to existing application systems. Transmissions may be made directly between trading partners, but very commonly they use a valued added network (VAN) to provide a store and forward service which is an electronic mailbox. A number of document standards have been developed to enable documents to be exchanged in a common format.

3.17 EDI is being used increasingly in a variety of industries including insurance, manufacturing, retail and distribution, international trade and transport and financial services. As well as reducing costs and improving speed of processing, it can assist in reducing errors, improving inventory and cash management and in enhancing relations with customers and suppliers. EDI and EFT are considered further in Chapter 14, "Electronic Data Interchange (EDI) and Electronic Funds Transfer (EFT)".

Open systems

3.18 Traditionally computer vendors have supplied their own proprietary hardware and software which did not communicate easily with the products of other vendors. In recent years there have been significant moves towards "open systems" to enable effective interaction of a variety of vendors' products. This is being achieved by the development of standards in such areas as communications.

Expert systems

3.19 The growth in computer power and storage has offered opportunities to extend not only the range of computer systems but also their nature. This has led to discussion and research work on the nature of "intelligence" and the ways by which artificial intelligence, that is to say a thinking machine, might be created. Expert systems are one application of artificial intelligence.

3.20 An expert system is a system where knowledge on a subject is held within the system and applied to particular circumstances by the use of rules which are coded into the system. The most commonly quoted example is that of a medical diagnostic system in which the patient's symptoms are input. The system matches the symptoms to its knowledge base of symptoms and diseases, uses the rules to determine the likely disease and issues the diagnosis. It can be seen, therefore, that there are two main elements to an expert system, the knowledge – often referred to as the "knowledge base", and the codified rules – often referred to as the "inference engine".

Computer processing features of audit relevance

3.21 The auditor has to understand the computer processing features that are of audit relevance. He must, therefore, identify those systems that process the transactions which make up the financial statements. Having identified the systems, the auditor can examine the features of the system that are of primary concern in processing significant accounting data. It is not a purpose of this book to describe in detail the methods of computer processing. However, in this chapter, the main features are outlined and defined. For convenience, the features are considered under the headings below, which can be applied to any computer system regardless of its nature:

- **Input** – the initiation of a transaction and subsequent activity until it is written to a magnetic file in the computer system.
- **Processing** – all the work carried on within the computer system including calculations, analysis and the transmission of data between different computers or locations.
- **Output** – the provision of information by the computer normally to a file or in the form of a screen display or print-out.

3.22 It is also convenient to subdivide the types of computer system according to the ways in which data is input, processed and output because of the different types of control to be found. The principal types of system referred to in this and subsequent chapters are:

- **Real-time systems** – where data is input through a computer terminal as it arises, and immediately checked by the computer, processed and written to the relevant computer files.

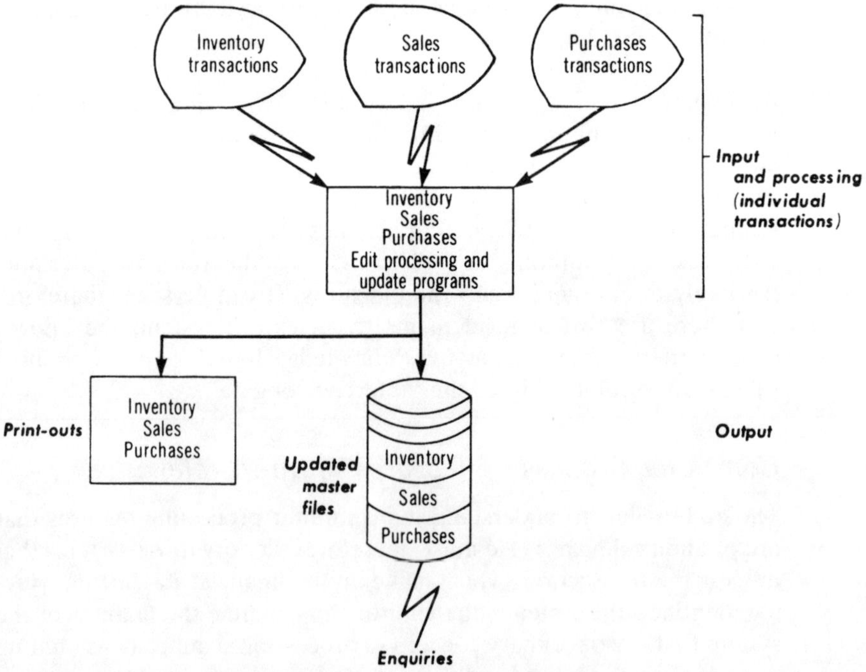

FIG. 6. Real-time system (para. 3.23)

- **On-line systems** – where data is input through a computer terminal as it arises and some checking is carried out immediately, but the data is then stored temporarily for processing and updating at some later time.
- **Batch systems** – where the data is collected into batches of similar items which are input and processed together periodically, frequently passing through a number of distinct stages of processing.

3.23 In real-time systems, where users may invoke any program at any time from their terminals, all programs and data files must be continuously available ("on-line"). In on-line systems, the programs and data files used for input, including those required for any programmed checking of input, must be available at all times. By contrast, in batch systems, programs are run by a separate computer operations department in a pre-planned sequence, and only those programs and data files currently in use are required to be loaded into the computer. Outlines of real-time and on-line systems are shown in Figures 6 and 7 respectively.

3.24 The principal features of input, processing and output are described in the following paragraphs in relation to real-time and on-line systems. Next the particular features of batch systems are described. A description of the particular features of systems where data is organised as a database is then given. Finally, the distinguishing features of distributed processing systems, in which various elements of input, processing and output are carried out in different locations, are considered.

Real-time and on-line systems

Input

3.25 The work of input can be divided into two distinct functions: initiating a transaction; and entering it into the computer system. These do not necessarily take place in this order, as on occasions the computer may be programmed to initiate data itself. This happens, for example, where the computer is programmed to produce purchase orders when the balance of stock on hand falls below a minimum level. This type of activity is more conveniently considered under processing. Manual procedures which take place before the data is entered into the computer are, in principle, the same as in non-computer systems and are not considered here.

3.26 The major differences between real-time and on-line systems concern the methods of processing of data. Therefore, in considering input, the two types of systems are considered together and any differences discussed where they arise.

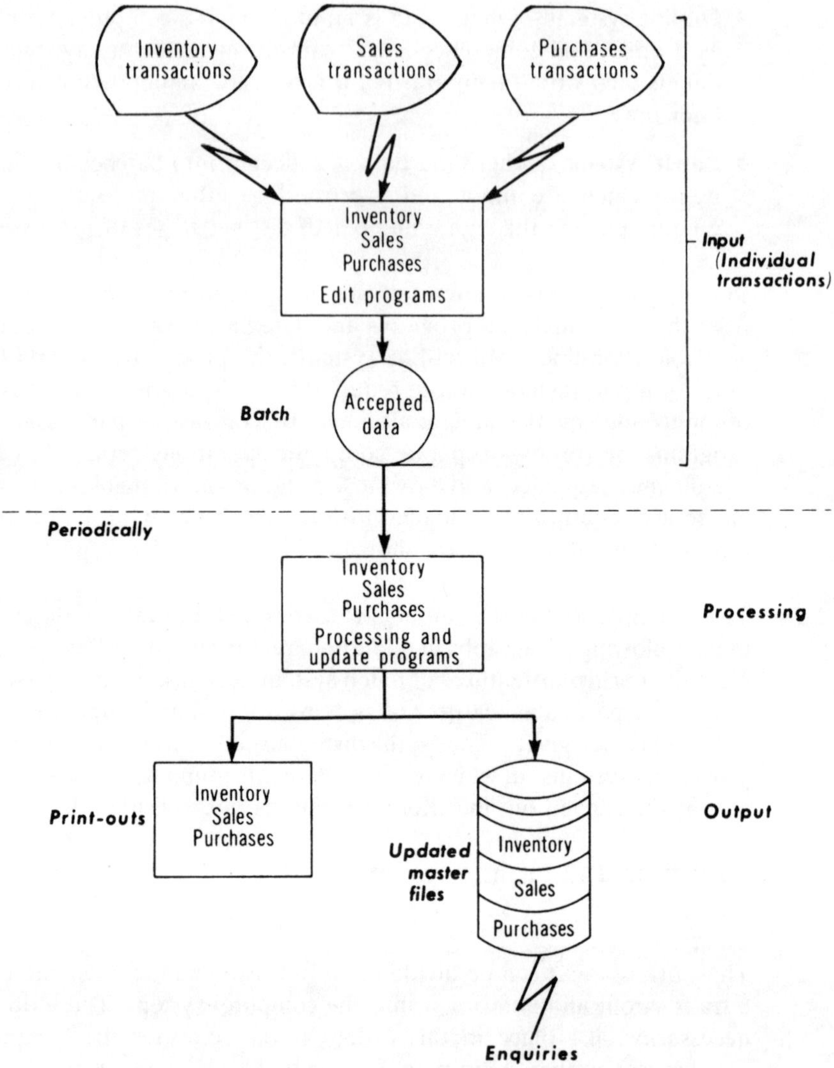

FIG. 7. On-line system (para. 3.23)

3.27 In real-time and on-line systems, data is usually entered into the computer by the use of a terminal which is continuously connected to the computer ("on-line"). Typically, transactions are input at the time when they occur. The advantage of this is that the computer can be programmed to check the data comprehensively at the outset, with the result that errors are detected and queries identified at an early stage. For example, sales orders may be received by telephone and keyed into the computer while the customer is still on the line. The computer can then check that sufficient stock is available to meet the order and that the customer's credit rating is satisfactory, and the customer can be told immediately whether his order can be accepted. The computer files will generally be more up to date in a real-time system than in an on-line system, so the programmed checking can be more rigorous.

3.28 The user of a real-time or on-line system will normally wish to be able at any time to use the system in any one of many different ways. These may include the input of different types of transaction, the display on the terminal of different types of data from computer files, or the production of documents and reports. Such a system must include programs to decide what type of input, processing or output the user has requested and react accordingly. In many older systems this is achieved by means of a command input by the user which the system recognises, but this has the disadvantage that the user must remember or look up the necessary commands.

3.29 In most modern systems a *menu* or list of the available options is displayed on the terminal by the system and the user has only to press the appropriate key to select the option he requires. Where there are more options than can conveniently be displayed at once he may have to select from a master-menu and then select again from sub-menus. Figure 8 illustrates the use of menus in an accounting system where the user wishes to input a purchase invoice.

3.30 Variations on the use of menus include:

- The use of touch-sensitive screens where the user can select an option by touching it on the screen with his finger.
- The use of a device, commonly called a *mouse*, whose movements are sensed by the computer and reproduced by an indicator on the screen. The user can move the mouse around his desk, and thus move the indicator to point to an option on the screen. The option is then selected by pressing a button on the mouse.
- The use of pictorial symbols, known as *icons*, on the screen instead of writing to describe the available options in a menu.

3.31 There are other methods that can be used to input data into real-time and on-line systems:

- Light pens are sensory devices which are used to read and transmit information. They may be used to read information on coded labels, such as that commonly encoded in the form of vertical bars of

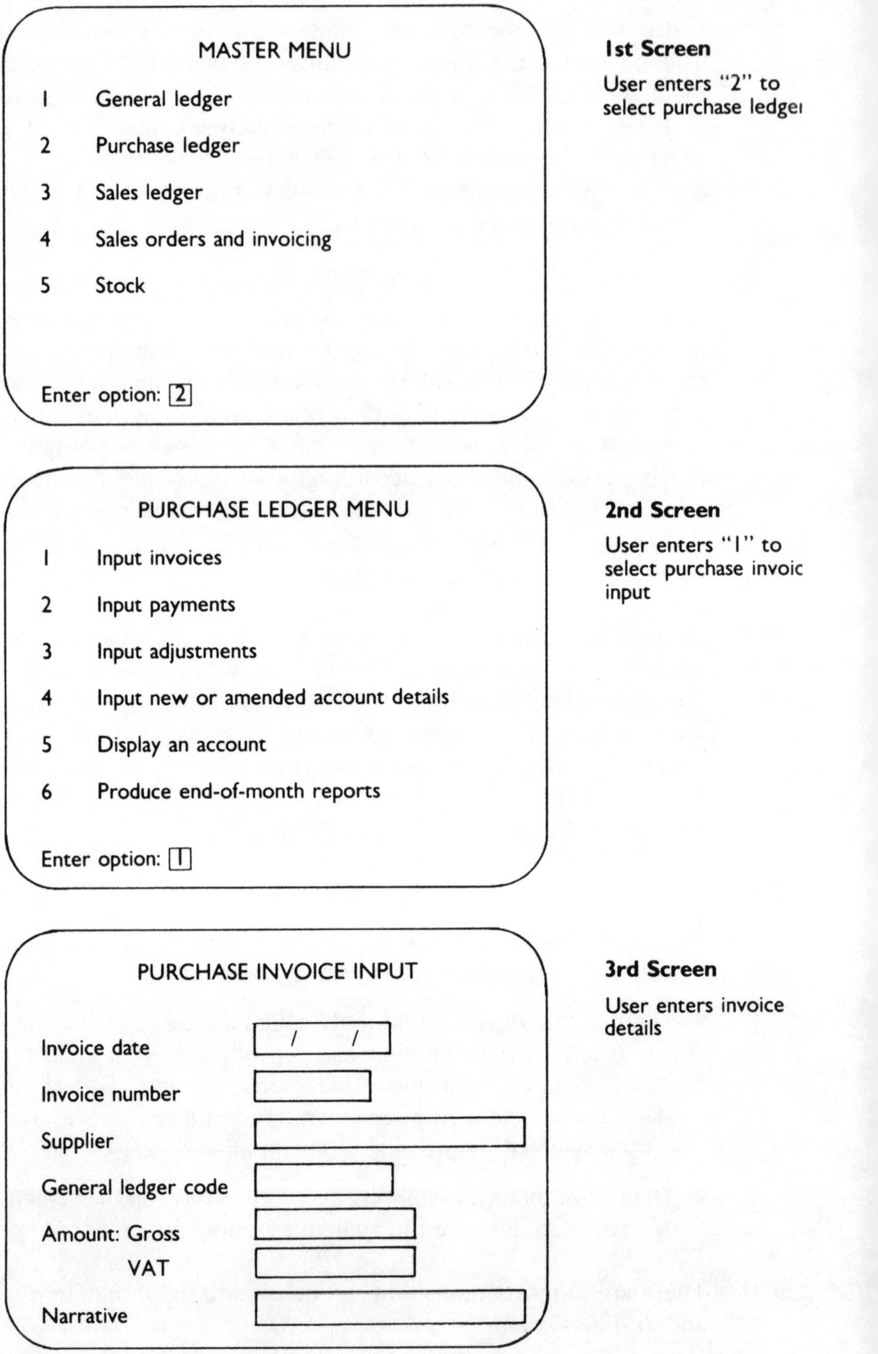

MASTER MENU
1 General ledger
2 Purchase ledger
3 Sales ledger
4 Sales orders and invoicing
5 Stock
Enter option: 2
1st Screen
User enters "2" to select purchase ledgei
PURCHASE LEDGER MENU
1 Input invoices
2 Input payments
3 Input adjustments
4 Input new or amended account details
5 Display an account
6 Produce end-of-month reports
Enter option: 1
2nd Screen
User enters "1" to select purchase invoic input
PURCHASE INVOICE INPUT
Invoice date / /
Invoice number
Supplier
General ledger code
Amount: Gross
VAT
Narrative
3rd Screen
User enters invoice details

FIG. 8. Use of menus in a real-time or on-line system (para. 3.29)

varying widths on the products in a shop or on library books. They are sometimes used in conjunction with point of sale terminals in retail organisations in order to input accounting data at the time that a transaction is concluded. Light pens may also be used to point to items displayed on a terminal, for example, to select screen options from a menu.

- Magnetic ink character recognition (MICR) and optical character recognition (OCR) systems allow the computer to read information written in letters similar to the conventional alphabet. The information will have been encoded, usually mechanically, using a special type fount which emphasises the distinctive features of different letters, and for MICR systems using a special magnetic ink. A common example of this method of input is the characters printed on cheques identifying the bank account on which they are drawn.

- Optical mark recognition (OMR) is a simpler form of optical character recognition, where a sensor simply registers the presence or absence of a hand-written mark in a particular position on a document.

- The recognition of hand-written or ordinary typed characters is not yet in widespread use in accounting systems because of the technical difficulties involved. However, devices that can read most standard type faces are in use for input of text in many text retrieval systems.

- Considerable investment is being made in the area of voice recognition, and primitive devices with limited vocabularies are now available although they are not in widespread use in commercial systems.

3.32 It is a feature of real-time and on-line systems that a large number of people outside the traditional data processing department use on-line computer terminals continually in the normal course of their work to input data and to display information from computer files. Complex software is needed to organise the input and enquiry activity of all users so that the system responds to all users without undue delay, even when many people are using it simultaneously. Furthermore, such systems must include strong controls, which normally include controls within the software, to ensure that:

(a) data is protected from the errors which can arise from two or more users trying to update the same item of data simultaneously; and

(b) users cannot amend, display or print data or computer programs unless they are authorised to do so.

Processing

3.33 Processing may be defined as all the work carried on in the computer. Although by no means exhaustive, the following is a useful summary of the processing work that will normally be of significance to the auditor:

- Editing.
- Calculating, summarising and categorising.
- Initiating transactions.
- Updating master or pipeline files.

These functions are described in the following paragraphs.

Editing

3.34 **Editing** is the programmed checking normally carried out when data is first input into the computer. It typically consists of a mixture of:

(a) Checking the validity of an item which has to be in a particular format, for example, a date.

(b) Checking that data is reasonable in relation to fixed limits or other data previously input.

(c) Matching the data to information already held on computer files.

3.35 In real-time and on-line systems, comprehensive editing can be carried out during input because of the availability of data files against which the input data can be checked. Further editing may also take place during subsequent processing, particularly in on-line systems.

Calculating, summarising and categorising

3.36 **Calculating** is defined as using two sets of data and generating a third set, for example, multiplying hours by rate to produce pay, or multiplying quantity shipped by a sales price to produce the sales value. The process typically consists of matching standing data, for example, the price, which is held permanently on a master file, with transaction data, for example, quantity, which is input and processed once only. **Summarising** means the accumulating of all transactions, often after calculating as explained above, and the generating of a total, for example, total value of sales for the day. **Categorising** consists of analysing a summarised total, for example, sales analysed by area. Categorising is normally carried out by reference to a code included in the data input for each transaction.

Initiating transactions

3.37 The computer can be programmed to **initiate** transactions in two ways:

(a) The processing of a transaction may create the condition. For example, the processing of a stock issue reduces stock below minimum level and a purchase order is produced. In these cases the condition is normally recognised by a comparison with standing data, for example the minimum stock level. This form of generation of data is likely to be particularly common where the files are organised as a database.

(b) A signal to initiate transactions may be input. For example, the input of a date will lead to the production of cheques for all suppliers' invoices dated prior to a certain date; the input of a stage of production reached will generate the appropriate charges to work in progress; the input of a requisition code will generate a listing of the components to be issued.

Updating master or pipeline files

3.38 **Master files** are similar to ledgers in a non-computer system and may be defined as those files holding financial and reference data of importance to more than one processing run, for example, accounts receivable and inventory ledgers, and price files. **Pipeline files** are temporary files similar to suspense accounts in a non-computer system and normally only hold transaction data, for example, outstanding orders or records of goods received. **Updating** may be defined as the process of writing transactions to or from master or pipeline files, for example, in the case of accounts receivable, writing invoices and cash receipts to the file or deleting dormant customer accounts from the file.

3.39 The method of updating depends on the file organisation in use. Files held on disc can be accessed directly by reading and, where necessary, updating each data item on the file individually. It is also possible to process disc files sequentially by processing each item in turn, and this may be more efficient if a large number of the records on the file are to be updated. By contrast, files held on tape can only be processed sequentially. Updating such a file is a matter of reading sequentially all the records on the old master file together with all those on the file of items to be updated to it and writing a complete new master file.

3.40 In real-time systems processing is carried out on individual transactions as and when they occur and data files are normally accessed for individual records only. Consequently, files will be held on disc rather than tape so that direct access can be used. In on-line systems files are also normally held on disc since direct access to individual items is required for enquiry purposes. Where in on-line systems input is stored on pipeline files for subsequent processing, these files may be accessed and updated sequentially during subsequent processing.

Output

3.41 **Output** is defined to include both the updated master files and any related reports in the form of listings, analyses and exception reports whether produced in printed form or as a screen display. It also includes accounting documents, for example, invoices. Information for third parties is sometimes transferred directly on magnetic file, for example, credit transfer details from the bank to its customer and sales statistics from branches to head office for consolidation. Output may also be converted to microfiche or film.

Batch systems

3.42 Batch systems differ from real-time and on-line systems in that data items are collected into batches containing a number of similar items which are input and processed together. Typically, in batch systems data is recorded manually on documents, checked manually and sent to a separate data entry or data control department for conversion into computer readable form. The complete batch of input, or frequently a number of batches, is input to the computer together. Processing proceeds in a number of discrete "runs", each comprising one or more programs. These are carried out in a pre-planned sequence and are usually controlled by a separate computer operations department. Typically, there might be an edit run which identifies and reports any errors in the data which might otherwise cause the system to fail, followed by an update run which updates the data to the relevant computer files. Batch processing is illustrated in Figure 9.

3.43 In batch systems there are a number of methods of converting data into computer readable form. The most common are devices for recording data directly onto magnetic discs or tapes. These are often arranged as a number of operator key stations linked to a small computer which can be programmed to carry out limited checking on the data before it is submitted to the main computer. Other methods include the traditional punched cards (becoming rare), and the automatic character and mark sensing devices discussed earlier under real-time and on-line systems.

3.44 The advantage of batch processing systems is that they are easier to design and more efficient in their use of the computer. However, the disadvantage is that it takes longer for the data to be processed in

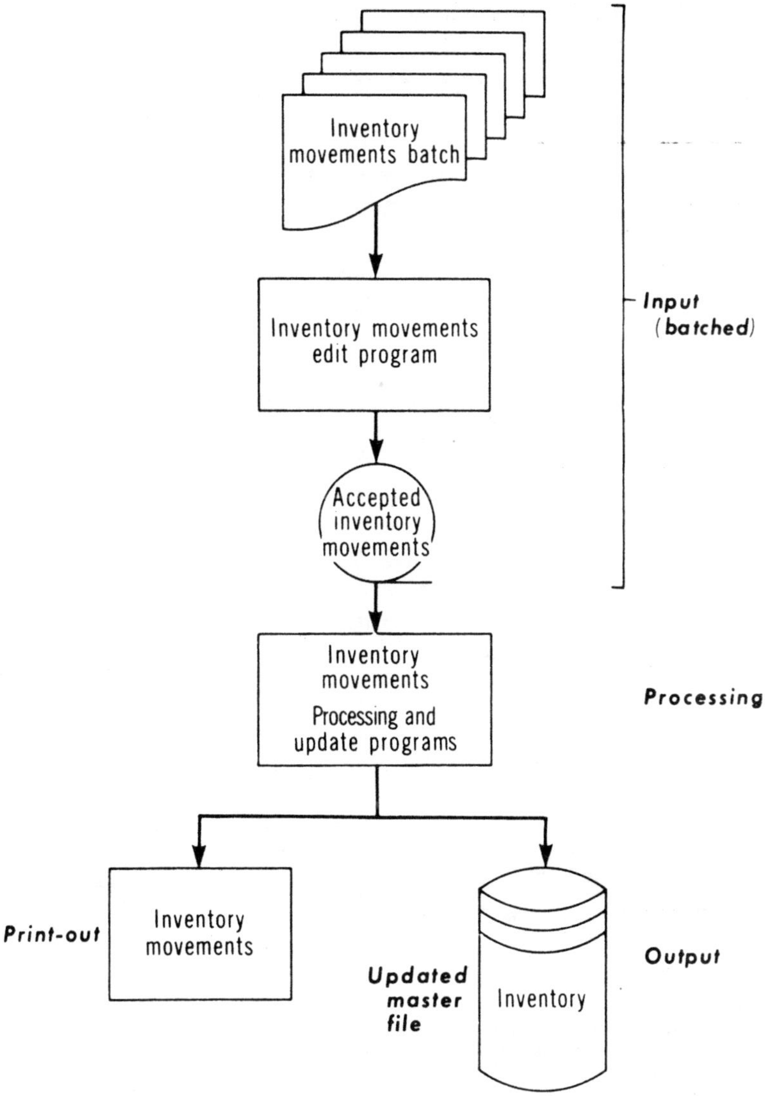

FIG. 9. Batch system (para. 3.42)

batch systems. Typically it might take one or two days for a batch to be input and the edit report to be returned to the users, and a week for the files to be updated. Consequently, as greater computer power becomes more readily available, new systems are being designed as real-time or on-line systems.

Database organisation

3.45 The term **database** is commonly used to describe a collection of data organised and maintained through a **database management system** (DBMS). It is a form of data organisation which stores data in a manner suitable for use for more than one application. In conventional systems data is usually organised by means of a predetermined access key, either in a physical sequence or by means of a random direct access method. For example, data may be stored physically in ascending order of stock code number or the physical location of the data may be generated from the stock code number. Such systems suffer from the deficiency that they are organised to answer readily only enquiries based on the access key field.

3.46 A DBMS physically organises data according to an extensive set of logical relationships defined by pointers, indices or tables. This set is known as a **schema**. Application programs are permitted access to sub-sets of the logical database known as **sub-schemas** or views and all interaction with the data itself is handled by the DBMS. The terms schema and sub-schema were established by the Conference on Data Systems Languages (CODASYL). Application programs communicate with the DBMS by special instructions in a very high level language commonly called a **data manipulation language** (DML). This process is illustrated in Figure 10.

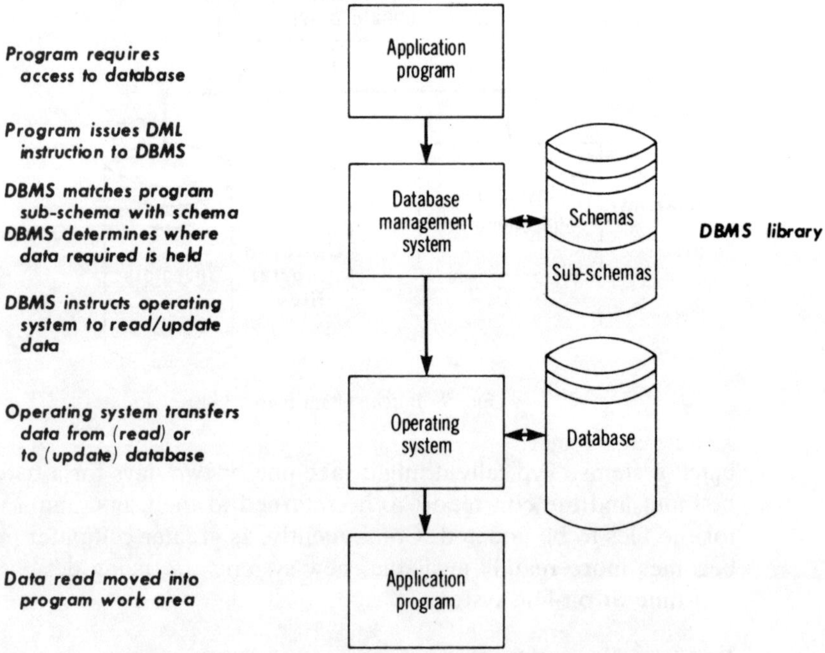
Program requires access to database
Program issues DML instruction to DBMS
DBMS matches program sub-schema with schema
DBMS determines where data required is held
DBMS instructs operating system to read/update data
Operating system transfers data from (read) or to (update) database
Data read moved into program work area
Application program
Database management system
Schemas
Sub-schemas
DBMS library
Operating system
Database
Application program

FIG. 10. Database – reading and updating (para. 3.46)

3.47 A database permits rapid access to any individual items provided the access depends on one of the many logical relationships defined in the schema. The nature of the relationships which are possible and the extent to which new relationships can readily be defined in an existing database depends on the type of DBMS. The principal categories are commonly known as **hierarchical**, **network** and **relational** databases, the first two names being derived from the possible relationships between data items when expressed in diagrammatic form and "relational" from the methodology which holds relationships and reference to data in tables rather than as part of a more rigidly defined structure. The advantages and disadvantages of each type will depend on the needs of the user but, in general, hierarchical databases are the most difficult to restructure and relational databases the easiest.

3.48 In addition to the ability to organise data more effectively and to control access to it, databases have other advantages, principally:

(a) Data in the database can be used by more than one application, for example, data from the personnel records might be used in the preparation of the payroll. Hence, it is not necessary to repeat the same data in separate files for each application using it. This elimination of redundancy reduces both the work required to maintain each version and the risk of inconsistency between different versions of the data.

(b) A DBMS usually incorporates options for sophisticated checks over processing and for recovery from processing failures. Where these options are implemented they are powerful tools for ensuring the reliability of the processing of data.

(c) Much of the code in an application program relates to the definition of the elements of data on a file and identification of the appropriate records. This has to be repeated for all programs accessing the file. With a DBMS most of these functions are removed to the definitions associated with DBMS itself (for example, via a data dictionary, see below) and to the DML and application programming is made easier.

(d) Data which in conventional systems would have been spread over several physical files is contained on a single file, which facilitates housekeeping.

3.49 The advantages of a database are achieved through the use of a DBMS to manage data by means of a logical organisation, which may be related to the physical data in a variety of ways (pointers, indices, tables). This implies that a considerable amount of processing takes place for each access of the database.

3.50 This is likely to be efficient for on-line, transaction-driven systems, where successive transactions access entirely different parts of the database. The processing overhead for each transaction may be negligible compared to the amount of searching which would be required with conventional organisation of data. However, in sequential processing of a database when an entire section of a database has to be read the overhead is much greater than in conventional systems. This is of particular relevance in accounting systems where large amounts of sequential processing are often required at the end of accounting periods, for example, when all ledgers are added up and many exception reports are generated. Most databases can be tuned but the tuning methods tend to optimise processing performance for either batch or on-line work at the cost of degrading performance for the other option.

3.51 The balance between efficiency of on-line processing and inefficiency of batch sequential processing is in favour of databases for small to medium sized collections of data and adverse for very large ones (the size criteria clearly being relative to the computing capacity available). This is one of the reasons why most businesses use databases for selected groups of related applications, but few have implemented "corporate databases" spanning all aspects of their activity.

3.52 Since a database relies on the relation of the logical schema to the physical data, it is essential that this relationship remains intact, i.e. that the *integrity* of the database is preserved. Databases can become corrupted for a variety of reasons including the incorrect use of system software utilities, recovery mechanism failures or poor application programming/design. DBMS therefore incorporate integrity check utilities which can be run periodically to ensure that any corruption is detected and corrected.

Data dictionaries

3.53 It has already been stated that a major characteristic of database systems is the sharing of data by more than one application. Even in non-database environments, systems are commonly encountered where data is used by more than one program although this is likely to be confined to sharing within specific applications. This gave rise to the establishment of **data dictionary directory** systems, either manual or programmed, the purpose of which was to establish a record of all data items in the system, their characteristics and how they were used by the application programs.

3.54 With the advent of databases, and the possibility of sharing data between applications on a wider and more complex scale than before, the establishment of a data dictionary directory became an important aid to the efficient design and maintenance of a database. Dictionaries for database systems are programmed rather than manual and are usually integrated with the DBMS.

3.55 The information about each data item typically maintained by the data dictionary system includes:

(a) Descriptions (names used for data item; description of content).

(b) Relationships with other data items.

(c) Departments and source documents using the data item.

(d) Programs and transactions accessing the data item and for what reason (insert; amend; delete; read only).

(e) Output containing the data item.

(f) Edit tests applied to the data item (format; reasonability; compatibility).

(g) Picture statement (numeric; alphanumeric).

(h) How held on database (compacted; encrypted).

(i) Logical address and physical location.

Distributed processing

3.56 As the name implies, **distributed processing** refers to the processing of different components of a system on different computers. Processing on each individual computer falls into one of the categories already described and information is passed between the processors as required. The traditional distributed processing model comprises a central computer performing head office functions supported by a hierarchy of smaller machines performing local operations. Summaries of local transactions such as sales would be passed to the centre and relevant central detailed information such as current price lists would be passed outwards.

3.57 The principal advantages of distributed processing are:

(a) Distributed processing gives local management responsibility for its own local computing, in accordance with many current management philosophies.

(b) A distributed system has much greater resilience in that if there are operating problems with one processor, only a part of the system is not functioning. With a single computer the whole system would be out of action.

(c) The workload at a central site is reduced by spreading it over several computers providing much greater flexibility in computer resource planning.

3.58 Two trends have promoted the viability of distributed processing. First, the introduction of good quality, high capacity transmission lines at a reasonable cost makes telecommunication links between processors more reliable and more cost-effective. Secondly, the rapid developments in microprocessor technology have made similar improvements in the effectiveness of local computing resources such that point-of-sale and other intelligent terminals, both of which are programmable processors, are now commonplace. Because of the range of equipment available the potential for variety in distributed systems is large and, coupled with the advantages described above, it is clear that distributed processing will become increasingly common.

3.59 The individual computers making up the distributed system may be connected together in a number of different ways, including:

- A hierarchical network where connection goes down from the main computer in an organised defined way diagrammatically such as a family tree.
- A ring network where the computers are connected in a ring each to its two neighbours.
- A star network where all computers are connected to a central computer and where they can only communicate with one another through the central computer.
- A fully interconnected network where all computers are connected to all other computers in the network.

The network organisation is a crucial element of the distributed system and the organisation selected should reflect the structure of the company's places of business and its organisational and processing requirements.

3.60 Since a distributed system comprises several components with interfaces between them it is analogous to several conventional, integrated systems. Individual components are often separately programmed and the form and content of the information transferred between the processors must be clearly understood if the whole is to function as intended. Furthermore, the timing of various elements of interrelated processing may be important, for example, a company operating a number of department stores may have local point-of-sale terminals for invoicing and day-to-day stock management but may need direct local access to the latest customer account balances for credit control purposes.

Examples of computer systems

3.61 Having described in general terms those features of computer processing that may be of significance to the auditor, their application to specific accounting systems can be reviewed. This is done by describing typical computer systems using, where applicable, the definitions already given in this chapter. Although the details of computer systems differ, depending on the systems' requirements and the precise method of design, their main outlines are often similar. The typical systems are described in the appendix to this chapter and comprise:

- Sales accounting.
- Purchase accounting.
- Inventory control.
- Payroll.
- Fixed assets.

It is likely that most computer systems processing these activities will be similar to those described.

Recording the System

The advantages of flowcharting

3.62 Where the auditor decides, in determining his audit strategy, to place reliance on internal controls, he will need to record his understanding of the system as a basis for evaluating the controls. In more complex systems flowcharting is usually preferable to narrative because greater discipline can be applied to the preparation and contents of flowcharts and they are easier to understand and review. Flowcharting enables the recording to be standardised so that new staff can work with flowcharts prepared by other staff in earlier years. This is particularly important in recording computer systems which are normally more complex than non-computer systems. As a result, it is normally preferable to record computer systems principally in flowchart form.

3.63 It is not a purpose of this book to elaborate in detail on any particular method of flowcharting. There are several well-proven methods in use and software packages are available which computerise the proofs. Most general flowcharting techniques are easily applied to recording computer systems. However, there are certain points of particular relevance in flowcharting such systems. In the following paragraphs a particular flowcharting technique is outlined, so as to provide a framework within which to describe and illustrate these particular points.

A flowcharting technique

3.64 This particular flowcharting technique has been specifically designed to record a company's system in a convenient manner to enable the auditor to determine the controls that are significant for his purposes. Separate flowcharts are prepared for each transaction processing system or major part thereof. The principal features of the system are that only those operations or documents that are of audit significance are shown, with the flowlines depicting the flow of information and the sequence of operations. This enables the relevant parts of the system to be represented clearly and avoids confusing the flowchart with unnecessary detail. The flowchart records the processing of transactions from their inception to their recording in the accounting records.

3.65 Within this framework the following important conventions are applied:

(a) Standard symbols are used which are, so far as possible, self-explanatory.

(b) Flowlines run as far as possible from left to right and top to bottom of the page.

(c) Significant copies of documents are explained and accounted for.

(d) Departments or organisational units are represented by vertical bands across the flowchart, and operations are depicted within the department in which they occur.

(e) Narrative is kept to a minimum. Where detailed descriptions are needed, they are attached as appendices.

The flowchart for part of the sales processing in a non-computer system is shown in Figure 11.

Flowcharting computer systems

3.66 An important aim when flowcharting computer systems is to integrate into a single flowchart the computer and non-computer parts of the system. This is achieved easily with the flowcharting method described above. The flowline moves on the flowchart into and out of the com-

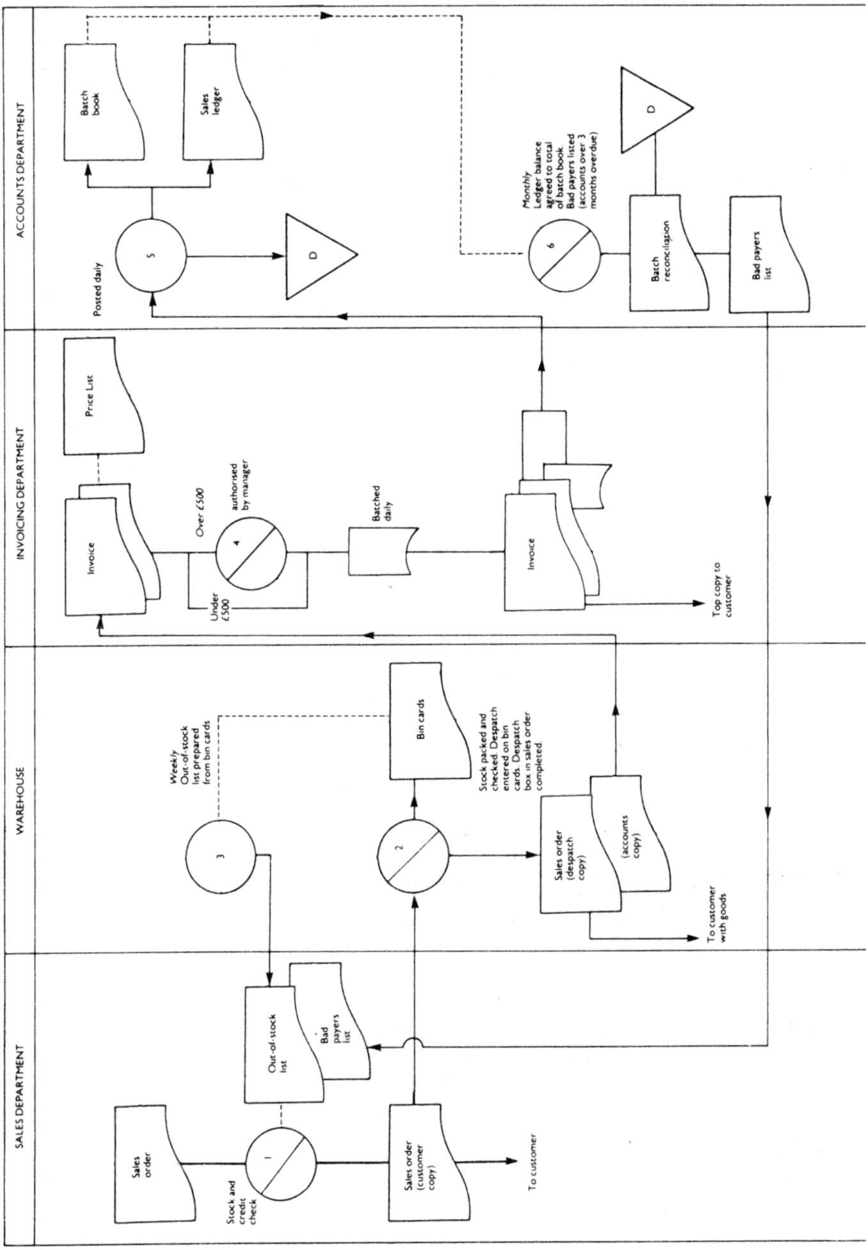

FIG. 11. Sales orders, despatching and invoicing – manual system (para. 3.65)

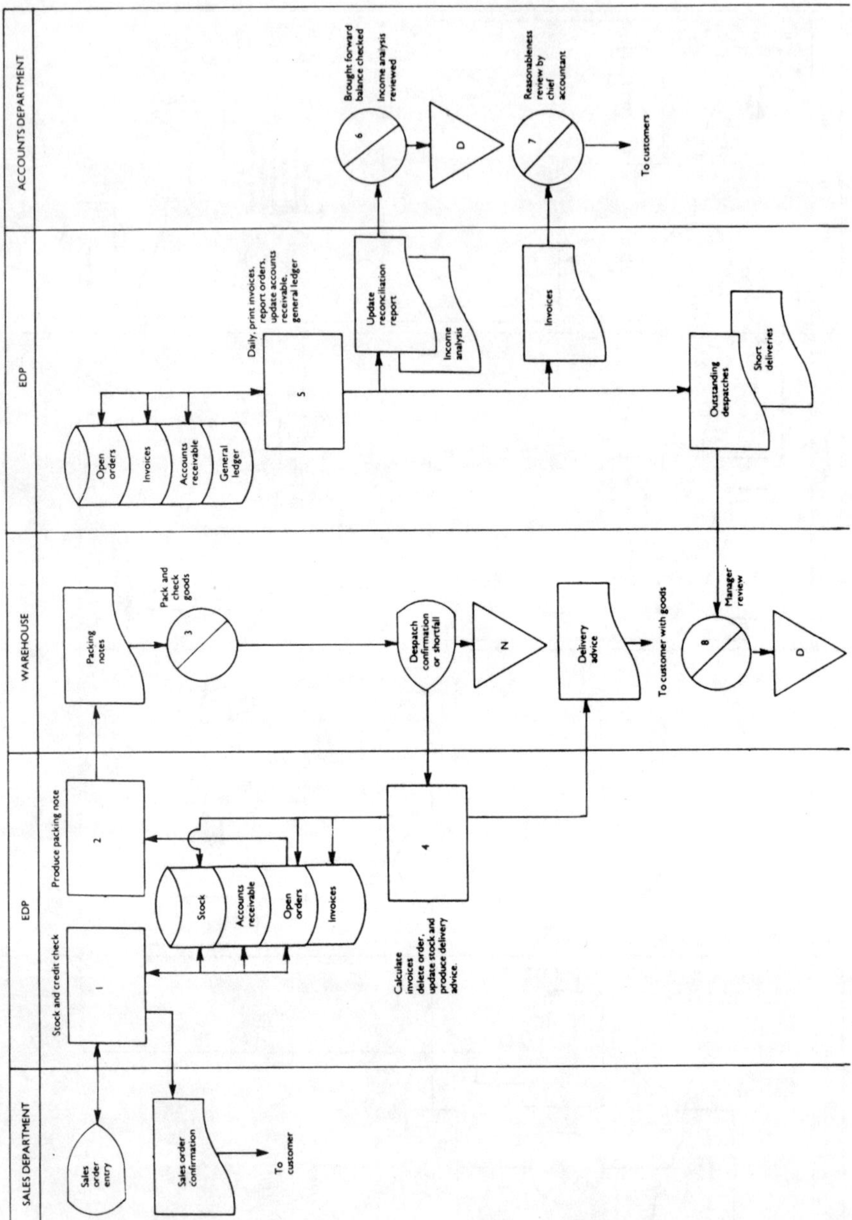

FIG. 12. Sales orders, despatching and invoicing – computer system (para. 3.66)

puter department at the appropriate stages and, where necessary, computer operations can be shown taking place in a user department. An example of this might be the input of sales information to a real-time airline booking system. As far as possible, the same flowcharting conventions and symbols (as for non-computer systems) are used to illustrate the processing in that department. Additional symbols are, of course, required for devices unique to computer systems, such as terminals and disc files, but these are readily understandable. Flowcharts for part of the sales processing in a computer system are shown in Figure 12. A comparison of these flowcharts with those in Figure 11 illustrates the similarity of the flowcharts prepared for computer and non-computer systems.

3.67 Another important aim when recording the computer parts of a system is to keep the flowcharts and narrative as simple as possible. This facilitates understanding by non-technical audit staff and highlights the operations of importance to the auditor. Various aids to simplification are discussed in the following paragraphs.

Overview flowcharts

3.68 It is desirable at the audit strategy stage to prepare an overview flowchart summarising the main features of the system as a basis for determining the audit strategy. An example of an overview flowchart is shown in Figure 13 and further illustrations are given with the examples of computer systems in the appendix to this chapter.

3.69 The overview flowcharts shown summarise diagrammatically the main input, data files and output. In complex systems it is desirable also to show the flow of data between separate sub-systems. From this information it is possible to deduce the principal controls required (from the transactions and files) and the controls that are likely to exist (from the listings and exception reports). Thus the auditor can form an immediate impression of the system, its relationship to other systems, and the likely controls. He may find that the overview flowchart provides an adequate understanding of the system and that he does not need to prepare more detailed flowcharts.

Programmed operations

3.70 When preparing the flowcharts, the recording of programmed operations can usually be limited to those of significance to the auditor. These operations would include all programmed procedures, as defined in paragraph 4.17, and the other operations that are necessary to understand the overall flow of processing.

3.71 Programmed operations are recorded as a rectangular symbol whilst manual operations are shown with a circular symbol. There will need

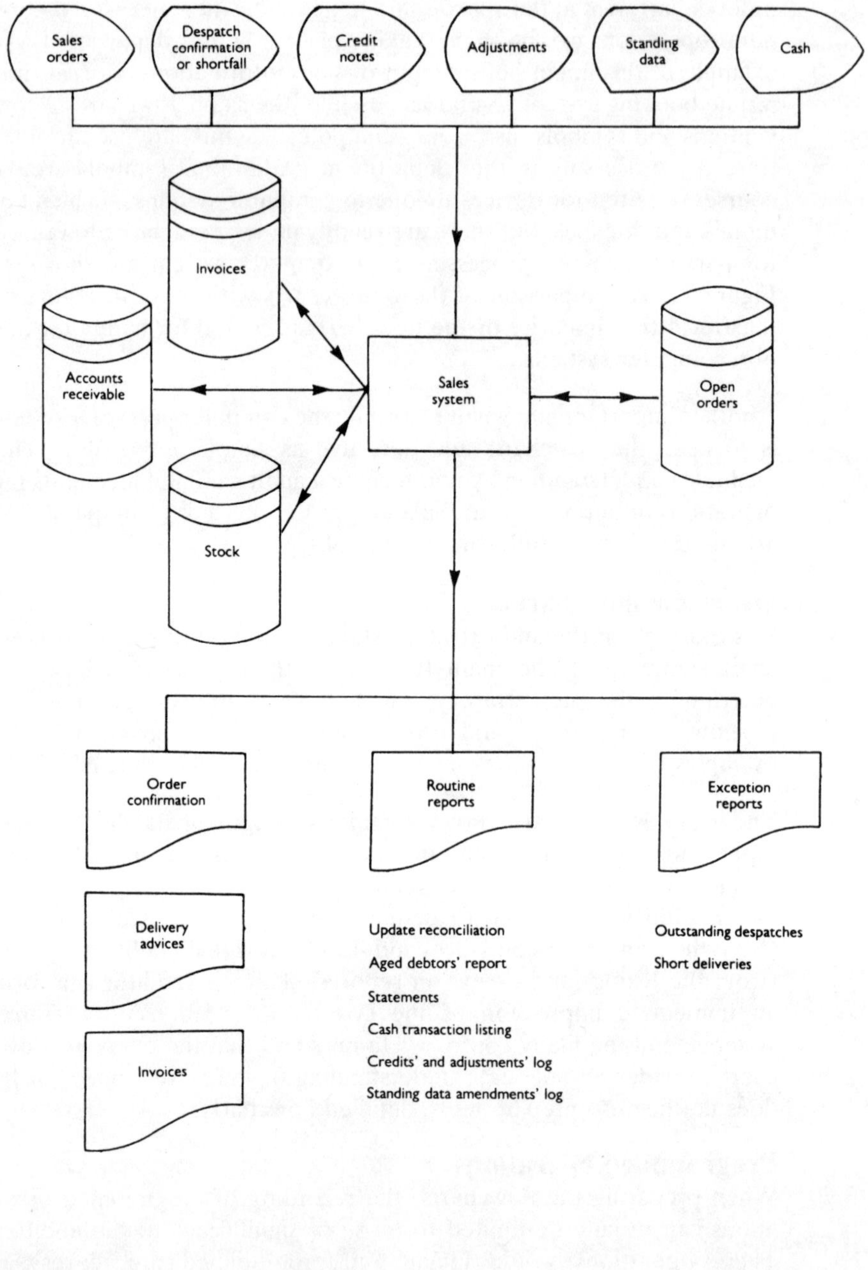

FIG. 13. Overview flowchart for a computer-based sales system (para. 3.68)

to be a description of the functions carried out by the program. Where lengthy explanations are required, a cross reference can be inserted on the flowchart to the client's detailed program documentation or to a narrative description following the flowchart.

Standing data amendments

3.72 The procedures relating to the amendments of standing data are usually difficult to incorporate in the flowcharts dealing with the processing of the master files concerned. It is preferable to prepare separate flowcharts or narrative records for these procedures.

Standard procedures

3.73 Many companies have standard procedures for carrying out certain types of operation, which apply to many different systems. Examples of these might be the procedures for logging on to a computer terminal, the procedures for investigating and resubmitting rejections, or the periodic procedures for reconciling the movements on a master file to totals of transactions accumulated during input. Such procedures may often be more conveniently recorded in a separate flowchart or by a supplementary narrative, and cross references made to this on other flowcharts whenever the procedures arise.

IT controls

3.74 IT controls, while relevant to the consistency of processing, generally operate separately from the flow of data through the accounting system. Accordingly, it is not practicable to incorporate them in the main flowcharts of the accounting applications. As the procedures will usually be relevant to all accounting applications processed, they should be separately flowcharted or, more commonly, recorded in narrative form.

Company documentation

3.75 Company documentation is usually of considerable use to the auditor in understanding and recording computer systems. This is because it often needs to be more detailed and precise than that prepared for non-computer systems. Two distinct groups of documentation will be of importance to the auditor – the documentation prepared for particular accounting systems and the documentation prepared for the general work of design, implementation and operation of systems as a whole. These may be termed **systems documentation** and **standards documentation** respectively and are discussed in the following paragraphs.

Systems documentation

3.76 Systems documentation consists of a general description of the system and more detailed descriptions and related documentation of the manual and programmed procedures. The general description is normally called an outline systems description and provides a helpful overall description in terms that are easily understandable. It will usually outline the complete system, comprising both manual and programmed procedures, and will show the interrelationship of the various parts.

3.77 For the clerical procedures, manuals are normally prepared for staff in user departments detailing the procedures to be followed in respect of data collection and input, and the action to be taken on rejections and output. These manuals are a useful source of information for understanding and recording manual procedures.

3.78 For the programmed procedures, there will be various levels of detailed documentation, including systems descriptions, containing details of the individual programs within each application, and a description of the contents of each program. Both of these descriptions provide the auditor, particularly in more complex systems, with a convenient source of information regarding the programmed procedures. At a more detailed level, there will be block diagrams and listings of the instructions in the programs.

Standards documentation

3.79 It is common for the procedures that are followed in the design, implementation and operation of computer systems to be standardised and explained in manuals. The design and implementation manuals will also often include details as to the procedures to be followed when systems and programs are amended. There will usually be operations manuals setting out the duties of operating staff and librarians. The operating instructions for particular systems will also normally be based on the standard procedures included in the manuals. These manuals are a useful source of information for understanding and recording those aspects of the IT controls with which the auditor is concerned.

Use of company documentation

3.80 When recording computer systems, there may be scope for making use of flowcharts prepared by the company, either as a substitute for the separate preparation of flowcharts or as a more detailed record of programmed procedures to which the auditor's flowcharts can be referenced. The auditor's flowcharts can also often be referenced to clerical procedure manuals. Likewise the narrative records of IT controls may be kept to a minimum by referencing to the company's standards documentation.

Confirmation of the Understanding of the System

3.81 Having completed his flowcharts or narrative record of the system, the auditor may wish to confirm his understanding before performing any further work. Although the understanding will ultimately be confirmed during the audit by the performance of audit tests, specific procedures to confirm the understanding will reduce the risk of wasting time by devising and attempting to perform audit procedures on the basis of an incorrect understanding. Confirmation may also assist new staff in gaining familiarity with the system in subsequent years.

3.82 The confirmation may involve inspection or review of transactions, records, documents or reports. In some cases one or more transactions may be selected and traced through each part of the accounting system to confirm the understanding. Where the confirmation or subsequent audit tests reveal that the auditor's initial understanding was not correct, then the procedures actually in force should be ascertained and the documentation of the system revised accordingly.

Summary

3.83 In order to understand and record computer systems effectively the auditor must have a basic understanding of the principles of computers and computer processing. The processing features of significance to the auditor can be divided between input, processing and output. Processing may include editing, calculating, summarising and categorising, initiating transactions and updating master or pipeline files. The manner in which transactions are processed and therefore controlled differs between real-time, on-line and batch systems. The way in which data is stored and controlled depends on the nature of the file organisation; particular considerations apply to databases.

3.84 There are advantages in recording computer systems by means of flowcharts. The computer and non-computer parts of the system should be integrated in a single flowchart. Thus, the same conventions and symbols, as are used in non-computer systems, should be used as far as possible in flowcharting computer systems. It is desirable to keep the flowcharts as simple as possible and various aids to clarification can be employed. These include suggested methods of recording programmed operations, standing data amendments and standard procedures. Overview flowcharts provide an efficient way of documenting a system. Use can often be made of company documentation.

3.85 The auditor may wish to confirm his understanding and recording of the system by inspection or review of transactions, records, documents or reports.

3: Appendix A

Examples of Computer Systems

Introduction

1 In this appendix typical examples of the following computer systems are described:

- Sales accounting.
- Purchase accounting.
- Inventory control.
- Payroll.
- Fixed assets.

As stated in paragraph 3.61, it is likely that most computer systems processing these activities will be similar to those described.

2 In practice, particularly as regards sales accounting, purchase accounting and inventory control, systems of differing complexity will be encountered depending upon the extent to which computer processing is used. In order to distinguish between systems of varying complexity it is convenient to break these systems down into their component parts and describe the features of computer processing in each component. After describing the components in this way, it can be seen how the components, whether computer or non-computer, are linked together to provide the total system. In practice, computer systems are often designed and implemented in just this manner, beginning with a simple system having only one computer-based component, and then gradually adding further computer-based components until finally a complex computer system exists.

3 In the descriptions and diagrams within this appendix the major master files within each system are illustrated and typical layouts of such files are shown. It should be remembered that although these files are illustrated as discrete files related to the particular application, they could equally be "logical" files of data held within a database system.

In this latter case they would represent the sub-schemas, i.e. the data on the database available to the particular program being executed.

Sales Accounting

The components

4 Most sales accounting systems comprise three components, **order processing**, the processing of orders resulting in the despatch of goods, **invoicing**, the processing of despatch details to produce invoices, and **accounts receivable processing**, the recording of transactions in the accounts receivable ledger. The computer is likely to be involved in each of these activities, as described in the following paragraphs.

Order processing

5 Order processing is illustrated in Figure 14. The initial input in this component will be *sales orders*. Two important checks may be carried out during *editing*. First, and most likely, the *finished goods' inventory file* may be referred to, in order to establish that there is sufficient stock to satisfy the order. Secondly, and less frequently, the *accounts receivable file* may be referred to, in order to assess the credit status of the customer. This latter test usually involves calculation. The order is evaluated, using prices held on a master file, shown in Figure 14 as the *finished goods' inventory file*, added to the customer's outstanding balance and the resulting notional balance is compared with the credit limit. The credit limit would be held as standing data in the customer's record on the accounts receivable file. Orders failing one of these tests are either *rejected* or, frequently, held in suspense on a *back orders file* until the stock is sufficient or the customer's balance outstanding reduced. Accepted orders are written to an *accepted orders' file*, usually both in quantity and value, and *despatch notes* are produced together with a *summary* for control purposes. Typically the orders would be input via an on-line terminal in the sales department, and the results of the tests would be displayed.

6 When the goods have been shipped, the *despatch notes* are re-input as illustrated in the second part of Figure 14, typically from an on-line computer terminal in the warehouse or despatching area. They are *matched* with the *accepted orders' file*. Matched items are deleted from the accepted orders file and written to a *matched despatches' file*. A *summary* is usually accumulated for control purposes. The file of matched despatches will be input for invoicing as described in paragraph 7. *Mismatched items* will be reported or rejected. The *accepted orders' file* at any time thus contains details of despatch notes produced

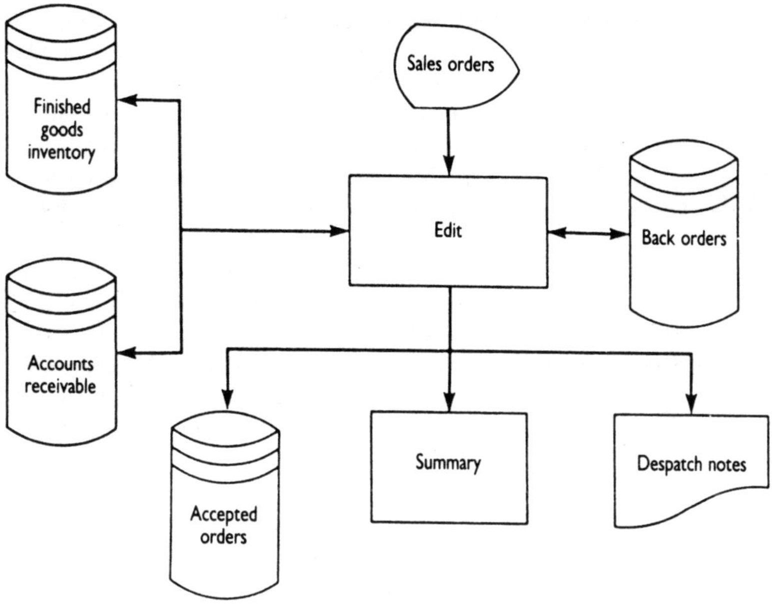

FIG. 14(1). Sales accounting – order processing (para. 5)

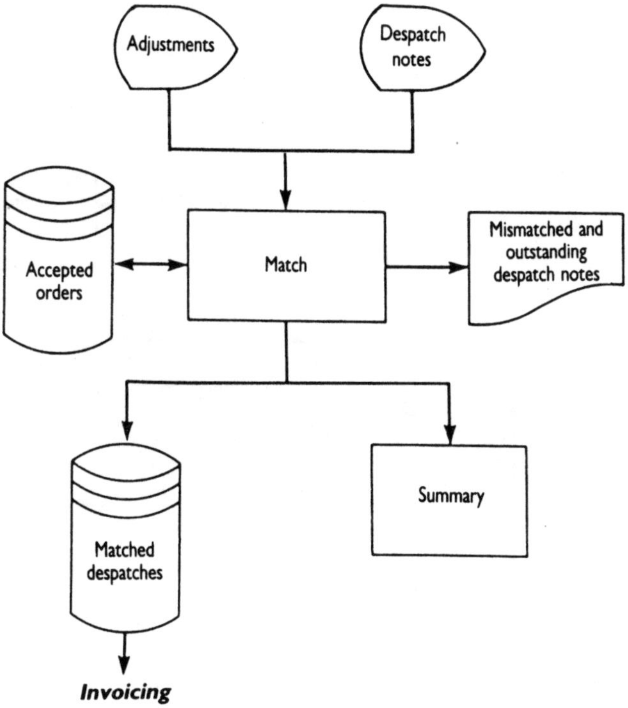

FIG. 14(2). Sales accounting – order processing (para. 6)

but not yet re-input. This file, which is a pipeline file, will be read periodically and rccords remaining unmatched for a given period printed out. The print-out thus provides details of *outstanding despatch notes*. A facility is usually necessary to process adjustments to the pipeline file so that entries on the file can be amended, for example, where the goods actually despatched differ from those ordered, or can be eliminated, for example, in respect of cancelled orders.

Invoicing

7 Invoicing is illustrated in Figure 15. The input to the invoicing component will be *despatch details*. These will either be *files of matched despatches*, if order processing is by computer, or *documents*, if order

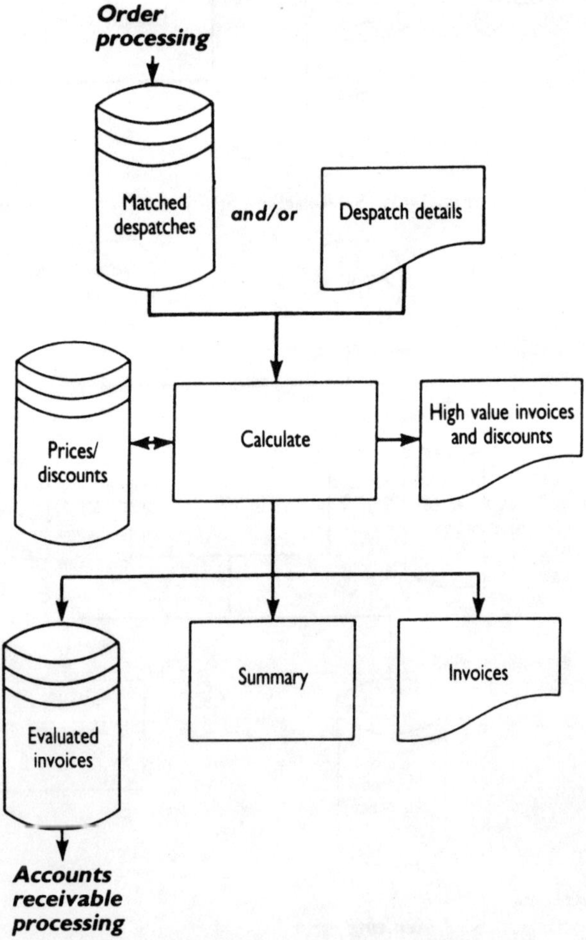

Fig. 15 Sales accounting – invoicing (para. 7)

processing is carried out manually. Often there will be both a file and documents, for example, a file for home sales and documents for export sales. The computer will *calculate* the value of each transaction, if this has not already been carried out during order processing, by matching quantities despatched with the relevant *price* held as standing data on a master file, usually the inventory file or a separate prices file. *Quantity discounts* can be calculated and applied in a similar manner. The computer will produce *invoices* and a *file of evaluated invoices* which will be input to accounts receivable processing, as described in paragraph 8. A *summary* is often produced for control purposes. *Exception reports* may be produced as a result of the calculation (for example, high value invoices or discount).

Accounts receivable processing

8 Accounts receivable processing is illustrated in Figure 16. The *accounts*

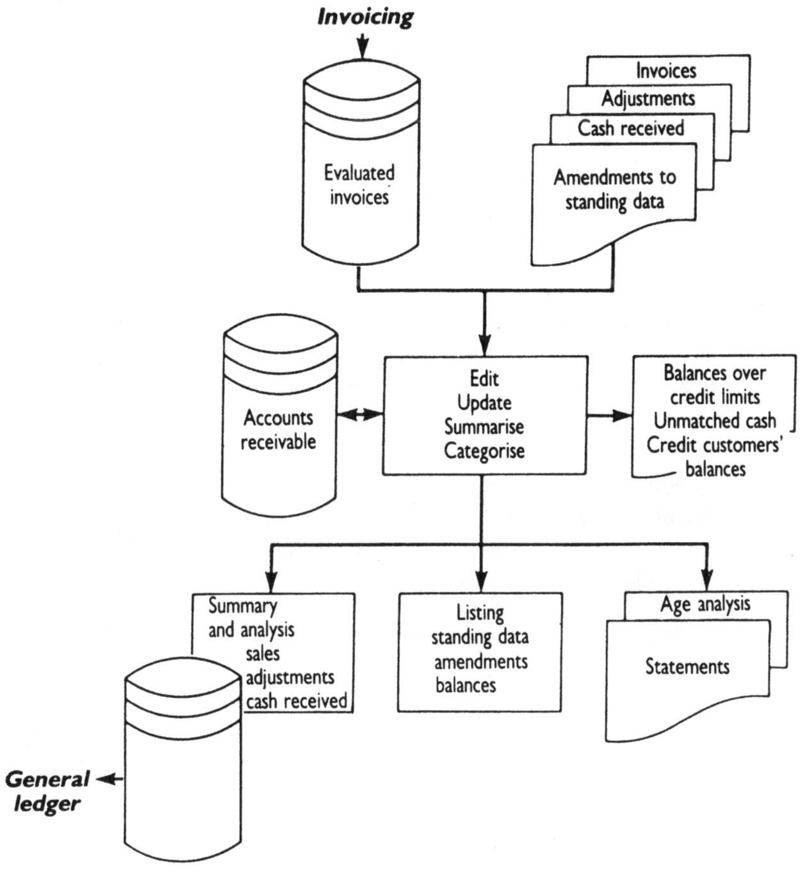

FIG. 16. Sales accounting – accounts receivable processing (para. 8)

receivable file will be updated by both transaction data and standing data. The main types of transaction data will be charges to customers, adjustments and cash received from customers. Charges to customers will be input in the form of a *file of evaluated invoices*, if invoicing is by computer, or in the form of *documents* if invoices are manually prepared.

9 The computer will *update* the customers' accounts on the accounts receivable file with the evaluated despatches or invoices and *summarise* the total of sales transactions for posting to the general ledger. This total may then be *categorised* by reference to an input code for financial reasons, for example, as a basis for the payment of commission, or for operational reasons, for example, geographically. The summaries of sales transactions may be printed out or written to a file for direct input into a *general ledger* computer application. Where the processing of the general ledger is integrated with accounts receivable processing, the updating may be simultaneous. An *exception report* may be produced of balances over credit limits as a result of updating charges to customers.

10 Procedures will always be necessary to input corrections in respect of mispostings arising from incorrect input coding or to write off a small balance where a customer has not paid an invoice in full and it is not intended to press for payment. The input documents required are referred to as *adjustments*.

11 Where a single document is used for a variety of purposes, the particular purpose will be indicated by an input code. In more advanced systems, certain of the adjustments, for which the input of documents is needed in simpler systems, may be initiated by the computer. For example, the computer may be programmed to write off small balances outstanding for longer than a specified time. In addition to updating the accounts receivable file, the computer may *summarise* and *categorise* the total of adjustments for posting to the general and cost ledgers in the same way as for invoices.

12 The method of updating details of *cash received* will depend on the manner in which transaction data is stored on the accounts receivable file. Where all transactions, including paid invoices and cash receipts, are held on the file, the details of cash receipts are written to and stored on the customers' records. In this simple case, only the account number need be matched. Where, however, only unpaid invoices, usually referred to as open items, are held on the file, cash receipts are processed by indicating, and subsequently deleting, the related invoices which are paid from the file. In these cases it is necessary to

match cash receipts against the related invoices. This can be done in one of four ways:

(a) Manual allocation prior to processing.

(b) Programming the computer to allocate the cash to the relevant items. This is normally practicable when only one periodic debit arises, as in the case of utilities or insurance companies, or where one specific sale is paid off over several instalments, as in the case of hire purchase companies.

(c) Programming the computer to allocate the cash against the earliest part of the balance. This method will not identify specific invoices remaining unpaid when later invoices are paid, for example, in respect of disputed items.

(d) Programming the computer to allocate the cash and make allowances for certain differences, for example, discount. Further small differences up to a certain amount may also be written off.

Cash received which cannot be matched (*unmatched cash*) will normally be reported for investigation.

13 *Amendments to standing data* will be processed to alter the standing data held on the accounts receivable file. They will be needed to open new customers' accounts and close old accounts. Their further use will depend largely on the extent of reference and financial standing data that is held on the file. A typical file layout is shown in Figure 17 illustrating the wide variety of data that may be stored and for which amendment routines may be necessary. In some systems the computer may calculate changes to standing data on the basis of input, for example rental based on the input of house characteristics. In advanced systems the computer may initiate amendments to standing data, for example, increments to discounts based on records of sales. A *listing of standing data amendments* made will normally be produced.

14 It would be normal for the accounts receivable file to be read periodically to:

(a) produce *statements*; and

(b) *categorise* open items or balances by age and *summarise* these categories to provide an *age analysis*.

During updating of the accounts receivable file, and these periodic readings of the file, the computer would normally *summarise* the items or balances and produce information for control purposes. *Lists of*

Accounts Receivable: Data elements

Description	**Number of Characters**
Customer details	
Closed account indicator	1
Account number	8
Previous account number if applicable	8
Depot number	4
Traveller number	4
Call day	4
Area number	4
Sales statistics code	4
Agent code	4
Agent commission	4
VAT code	1
Payment type indicator	1
Statement suppress indicator	1
Weekly statement indicator	1
Statement date	2
Date of last order	6
Overdue account indicator	1
Credit limit	8
Date last paid late	6
Bad debt indicator	1
Quantity discount rate code	3
Wholesale discount %	3
Wholesale discount indicator	1
Settlement date discount – 10 days %	3
Settlement date discount – 30 days %	3
Settlement date discount – 60 days %	3
Settlement date discount – 90 days %	3
Settlement date discount indicator	1
Special prices indicator – Group 1	1
Special prices indicator – Group 2	1
Special prices indicator – Group 3	1
Special prices indicator – Group 4	1
Special prices indicator – Group 5	1
Balance outstanding	8
Sales – this month	8
Sales – last 6 months	8
Sales – previous 6 months	8
Sales – budget for year	8
Sales for year – Group 1	8
Sales for year – Group 2	8
Sales for year – Group 3	8
Sales for year – Group 4	8
Sales for year – Group 5	8
Delivery name	34
Delivery address line 1	34
Delivery address line 2	34
Delivery address line 3	34
Delivery telephone number	12
Statement address indicator	1
Statement name	34

Fig. 17. Accounts receivable – data elements (para. 13)

Statement address line 1	34
Statement address line 2	34
Statement address line 3	34
Statement telephone number	12
	475
Transaction details	
Item type (invoice, credit note, cash, adjustment, discount)	1
Item reference number	6
Date	6
Net value	8
VAT value	8
Matched indicator	1
	30

FIG. 17 (continued). Accounts receivable – data elements (para. 13)

balances and *exception reports*, such as a list of credit balances, may be produced.

Utilities

15 Where a permanent or long-term service is provided rather than goods shipped, there may not be an input to start the billing cycle. In these cases, such as electricity and gas billing, the date on which a meter reading sheet should be initiated will be held as standing data. Current dates will be input as parameters and the computer will produce the relevant meter reading sheets, or renewal notices. Details of documents produced will be written to a pipeline file which will be processed as described in paragraph 6. Sometimes billing will combine transaction data, such as meter readings, and standing data, such as the rental.

The systems

16 The components described in paragraphs 4 to 14 may be combined to form any of the following sales accounting systems:

- Accounts receivable.
- Invoicing.
- Order processing.

The scope of each system is described in paragraphs 17 to 19. While systems do exist with only one or two components, increasingly new systems are comprehensive and will include all three components as set out in Figure 20.

Accounts receivable systems

17 The computer processes the accounts receivable ledger, and order processing and invoicing are non-computer operations. This type of system is illustrated in the overview flowchart in Figure 18.

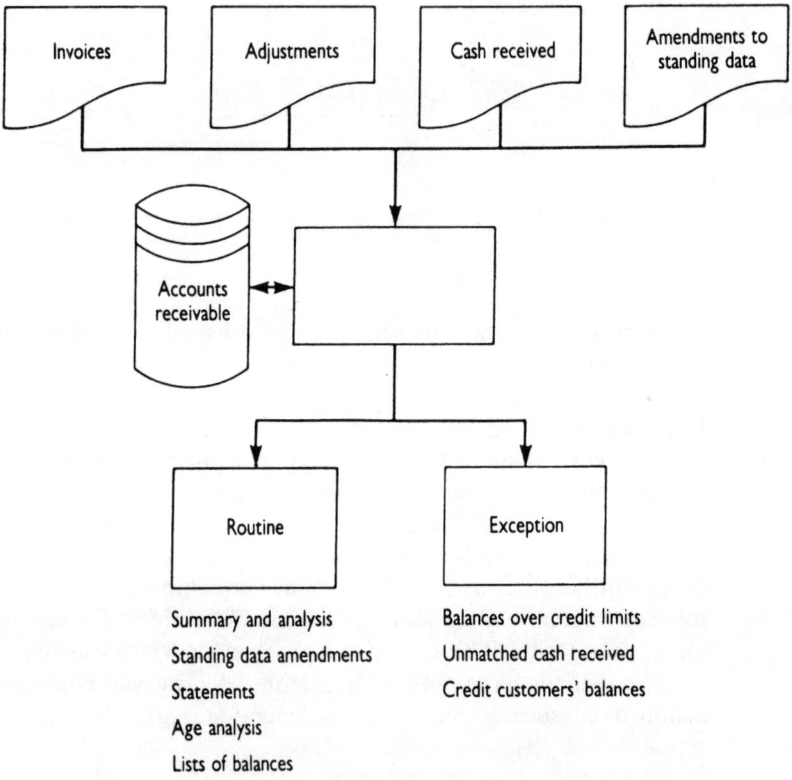

FIG. 18. Accounts receivable system – overview flowchart (para. 17)

Invoicing systems

18 The computer is involved in invoicing and processing the accounts receivable ledger, but order processing remains a manual operation. It is common for such systems to be integrated with the processing of inventory records for finished goods. The despatch details are used not

only to process sales but also to update the inventory file at the same time or subsequently. This type of system, including finished goods inventory, is illustrated in Figure 19.

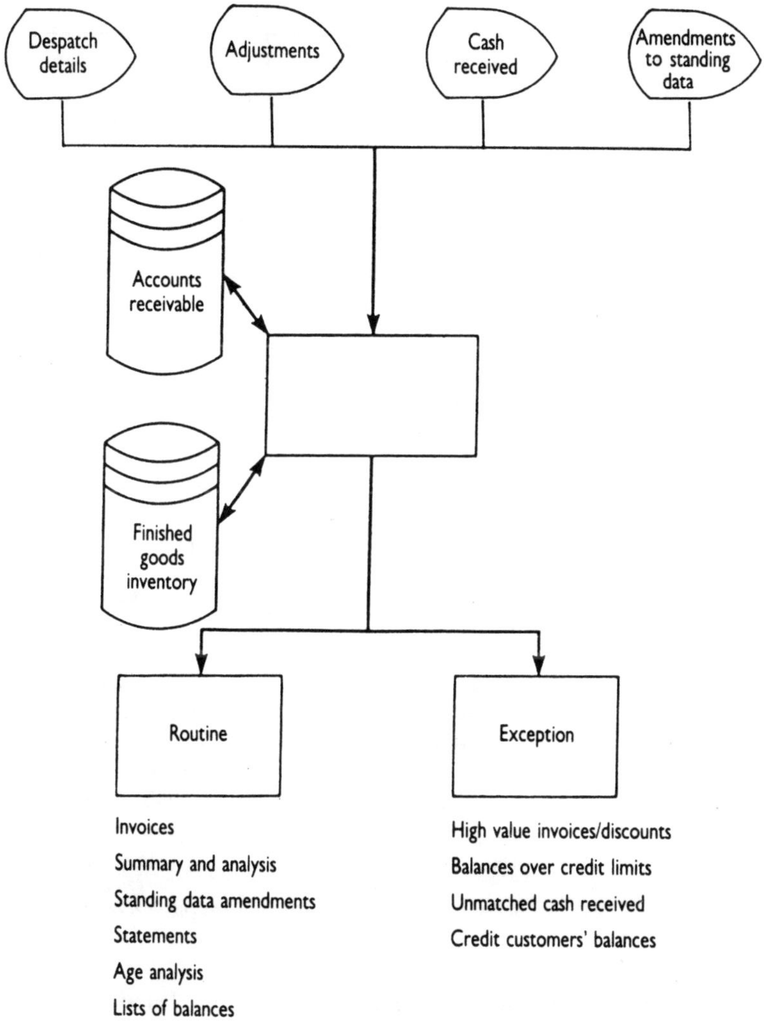

FIG. 19. Invoicing system – overview flowchart (para. 18)

Order processing systems

19 The computer is involved in the processing of all components of sales accounting. This type of system is illustrated in Figure 20. In some systems of this nature, sales orders are not only processed to produce despatch notes but also, at the same time, to produce invoices, update

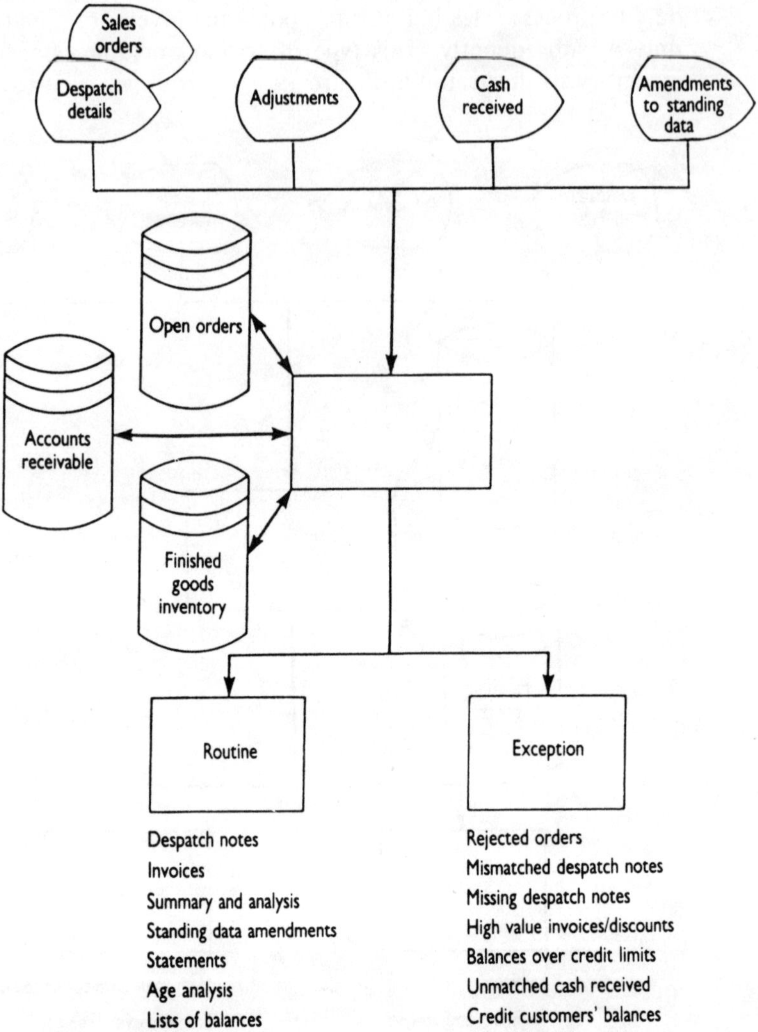

FIG. 20. Sales order processing system – overview flowchart (para. 19)

the accounts receivable ledger and provide sales totals. The subsequent despatch details are not re-input. These systems are often called "pre-debiting" systems. They can only be effective where it can be safely assumed that stocks are available for despatch, for example, in mail order companies, and are usually combined with computer inventory systems.

Purchase Accounting

The components

20 In a similar manner to sales, purchase accounting systems can be conveniently divided into three components, **order processing**, **goods received processing** and **accounts payable processing**. The computer may be involved in each of these activities, as described in the following paragraphs.

Order processing

21 Order processing is illustrated in Figure 21. Purchase orders are either *input* or *initiated* by the computer. A typical method for the computer to initiate orders is by comparing the stock balance with a minimum stock level held as standing data on the *inventory file*. Orders input, or initiated and printed by the computer, will be written to a pipeline record and a *summary* produced for control purposes. This may be on a separate file or on a master file, for example, the accounts payable file. (For consistency, the file is referred to throughout this description

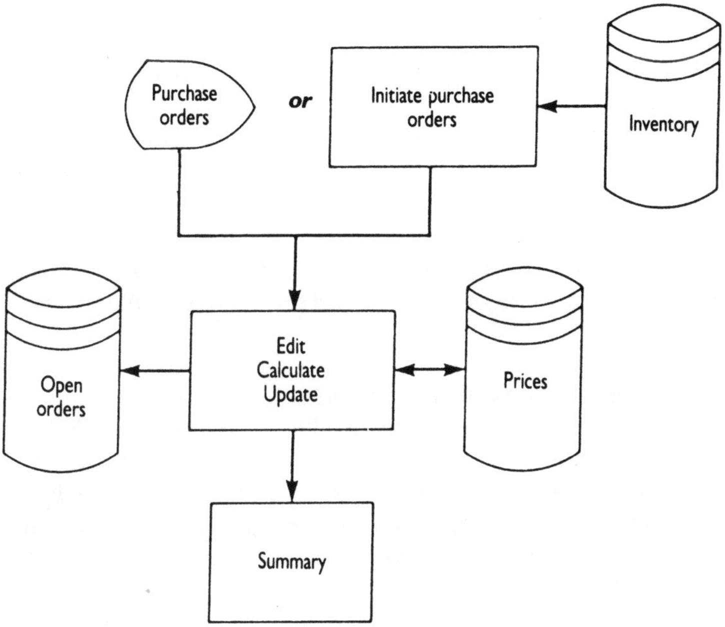

FIG. 21(1). Purchase accounting – order processing (para. 21)

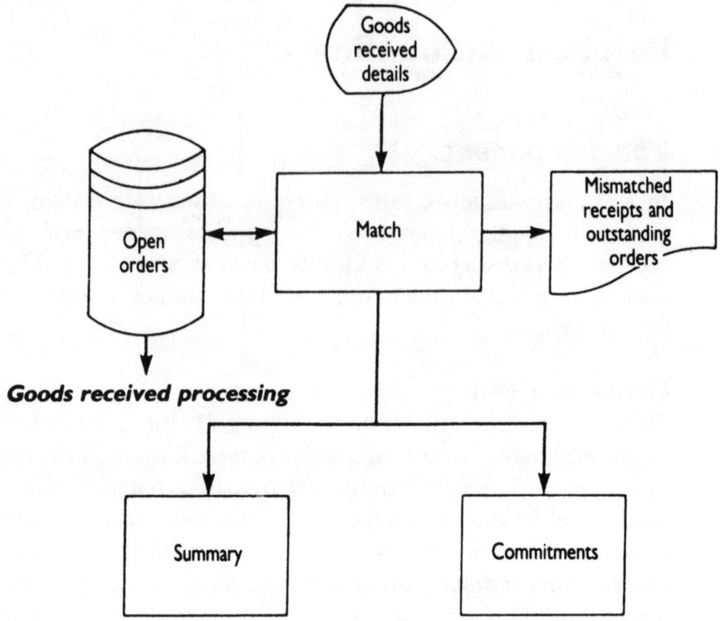

FIG. 21(2). Purchase accounting – order processing (para. 22)

as a *pipeline file*.) Sometimes the computer will *calculate* the value of orders input, or initiated, by reference to *prices* input or held as standing data on a master file.

22 *Open orders* will remain on the pipeline file until *matched* with the *details of goods received*. The pipeline file will be read periodically and orders for which goods have not been received for a given period will be printed out. Where the orders records are held in value, the value of *outstanding purchase commitments* can be summarised and printed out.

Goods received processing

23 Goods received processing is illustrated in Figure 22. *Goods received details* will be input and, if order processing is also by computer, *matched* with the order record on the *pipeline file*. When matched, it is usual for an indicator to be set on the record indicating that the goods have been received. Where order processing is not by computer, the goods received details will be written to the *pipeline file*, and a *summary* is normally produced for control purposes. It is common for the computer to calculate the value of goods received, if not already done in respect of orders. The computer will normally carry out this

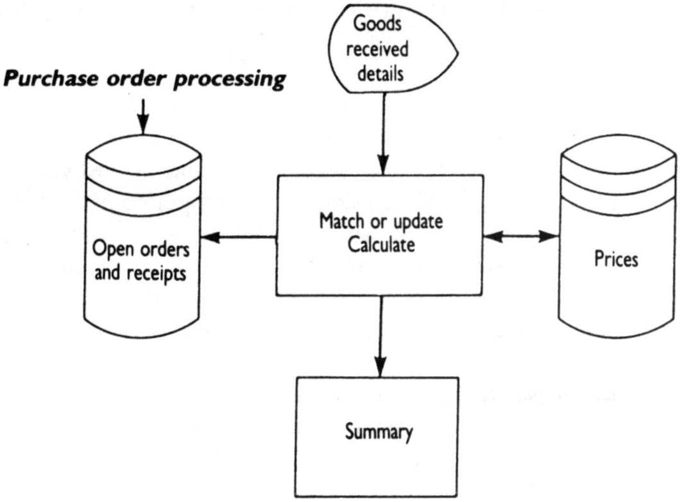

Fig. 22(1). Purchase accounting – goods received processing (para. 23)

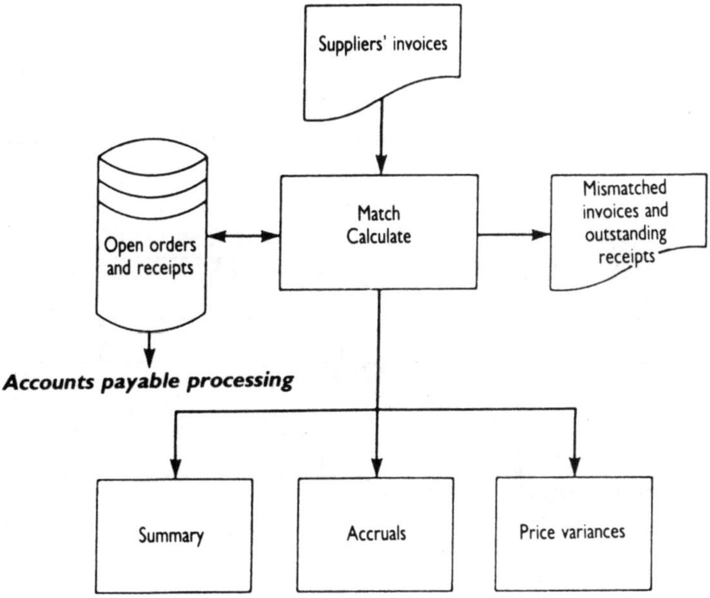

Fig. 22(2) Purchase accounting – goods received processing (para. 24)

calculation by reference to *standard prices* held as standing data on a master file.

24 Goods received details will remain on the pipeline file until *matched* with the *suppliers' invoice details*. At the time of matching, provided the goods received details are held at standard cost value, the computer may *calculate* the *price variance*. The pipeline file will be read periodically and goods received not matched with suppliers' invoices (*outstanding receipts*) for a given period will be printed out. Where the goods received records are held in value, the total *accrued liability* in respect of goods received can be summarised and printed out.

Accounts payable processing

25 Accounts payable processing is illustrated in Figure 23. The accounts payable file will be updated by both transaction data and standing data. The main types of transaction data will be suppliers' invoices,

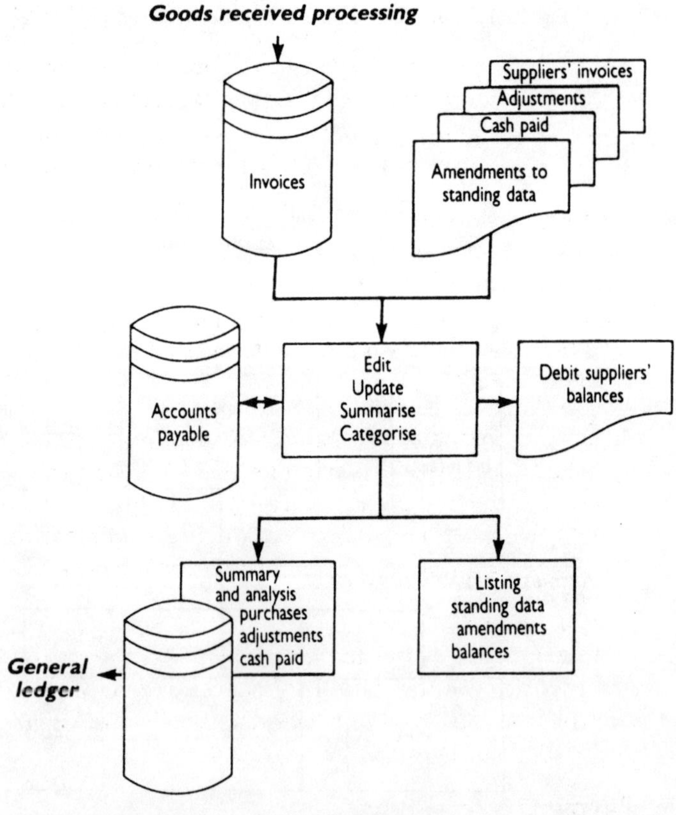

Fig. 23. Purchase accounting – accounts payable processing (para. 25)

adjustments and details of cash paid. Where goods received processing is by computer and *suppliers' invoices* are *matched* with goods received records, a facility must be incorporated in the system so that invoices relating to items other than inventory can be accepted. This is usually achieved by the input of dummy goods received details, or by including an indicator on the relevant invoices which the computer recognises as an instruction to by-pass the pipeline file for those items.

26 *Adjustments* will, as in sales systems, always be necessary to correct mispostings. They may also be needed for other purposes, for example, to facilitate quick payment of suppliers' invoices when the payer is entitled to a cash discount. An adjustment will then have to be made to the accounts payable file to record the discount taken.

27 The method by which *details of cash paid* are updated will depend on whether items are selected for payment manually or by the computer. Where items are selected manually, the details of items paid will require to be input and updated in the same manner as suppliers' invoices. The computer will match on either the account number alone or the account number, invoice number and value. Where the computer selects items for payment, the details will normally be updated at the time of selection. The methods of selection are dealt with later under the heading "Payment of creditors". Any manual changes to items selected will be input and updated as adjustments.

28 Suppliers' invoices and adjustments will be *summarised* and *categorised* for posting to the general and cost ledgers. These summaries may be printed out or written to a file for direct input into a *general ledger* computer application. Where the processing of the general and cost ledgers is integrated with accounts payable processing, updating may be simultaneous.

29 As in sales systems, *amendments to standing data* will be needed to open and close suppliers' accounts, and alter the various standing data fields. A file layout is shown in Figure 24 illustrating the wide variety of data that may be held and for which amendment routines may be necessary. A *listing of standing data amendments* made will normally be produced.

30 During updating of the accounts payable file the computer would normally *summarise* the items or balances and produce information for control purposes. *Lists of balances* and *exception reports*, for example, debit balances, may also be produced.

Payment of creditors

31 Any purchase accounting system may include computer involvement

Accounts Payable: Data Elements

Description	Number of Characters
Supplier details	
Supplier number	6
Supplier name	15
Date opened	6
Date last amended	6
Address line 1	20
Address line 2	20
Address line 3	20
Cheque limit	4
Terms	4
Value outstanding – credit	6
Value outstanding – debit	6
Payment due week 1	6
Payment due week 2	6
Payment due week 3	6
Payment due week 4	6
Cheque name	20
Rebate code	1
National giro number	8
Bank code	10
Total value invoices year to date	8
Total value invoices previous year	8
	192
Transaction details	
Transaction type	2
Date of transaction	6
Transaction number	6
Order number	6
Value (including VAT)	8
VAT	8
Discount on invoice	4
Nominal ledger code	6
Stock reference number	8
Payment date	6
Payment indicator	1
	61

Fig. 24. Accounts payable – data elements (para. 29)

in the payment of creditors. Within this definition of computer processing are included all cases where the computer selects items for payment. As a result of the selection the computer may produce:

(a) details from which cheques are manually or mechanically prepared;

(b) cheques for manual or mechanical signature;

(c) pre-signed cheques;

(d) tapes of payments for processing by a bank, for example, Bankers Automated Clearing Services (BACS) tapes. These tapes are physically delivered to BACS. Alternatively, data may be transmitted via a communications line;

(e) listings of items paid via electronic funds transfer systems.

32 The computer will also normally print out remittance advices and payment analyses showing the make-up of the payments. The normal selection criteria are date and, less frequently, discount indicator. The computer compares the dates on invoices with a date input as a constant and selects, for example, all items more than four weeks old. The computer may be programmed to recognise an indicator on invoices which means that discount is available if payment is prompt. The computer may also be programmed to calculate discount by reference to discount terms held as standing data. However, the processing of invoices by computer for early payment can be complex and invoices of this nature are sometimes diverted on receipt for separate manual payments. Manually produced cheques may also be required for other purposes. Details of such payments would be input as adjustments.

33 Payments via electronic funds transfer (EFT) systems are usually made by the treasury function, on the basis of selections of items identified by the computer. The benefits of EFT are that payments can be cleared more quickly and therefore transfers can be made at the last possible moment, optimising the cash management position of the business. The cost of making payments is also lower. Businesses are making increasing use of EFT systems for the payment of creditors and for transfer of loans, deposits and other money market activity both nationally and internationally. EFT systems are considered further in Chapter 14.

The systems

34 The components described in paragraphs 20 to 30 may be combined to form any of the following purchase accounting computer systems:

- Accounts payable.

- Goods received processing.
- Order processing.

The scope of each system is described in paragraphs 35 to 37. While systems do exist with only one or two components, increasingly new systems are comprehensive and include all of the components as set out in Figure 27. In addition, most systems will include facilities for payment selection and cheque production or automated payments.

Accounts payable systems

35 The computer processes the accounts payable ledger, and order processing and goods received processing are non-computer operations. This type of system is illustrated in Figure 25.

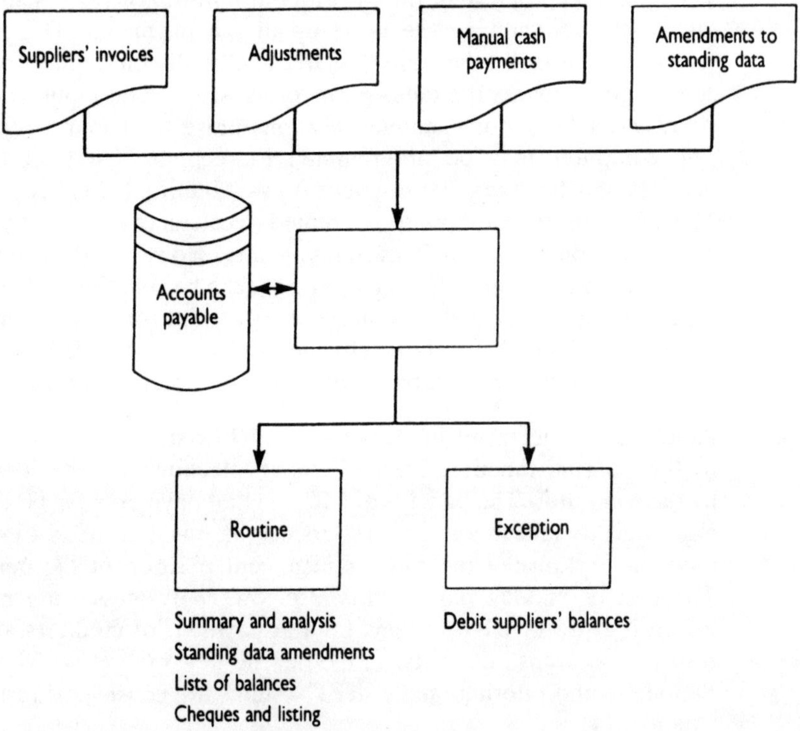

Fig. 25. Accounts payable system – overview flowchart (para. 35)

Goods received processing systems

36 The computer is involved in goods received processing and processing the accounts payable ledger, but order processing remains a manual operation. It is common for such systems to be integrated with the

processing of raw materials inventory records. The goods received details are used not only to process purchases, but also to update the inventory file for raw materials at the same time or subsequently. This type of system, including raw materials inventory, is illustrated in Figure 26.

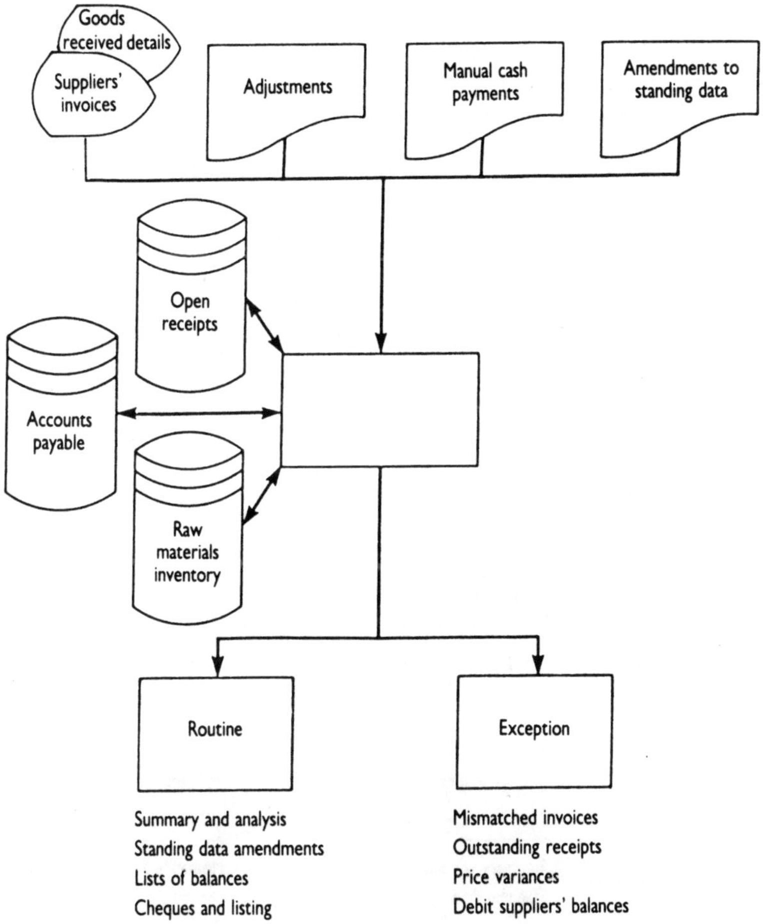

Fig. 26. Goods received processing system – overview flowchart (para. 36)

Order processing systems

37 The computer is involved in the processing of all components of purchase accounting. This type of system is illustrated in Figure 27.

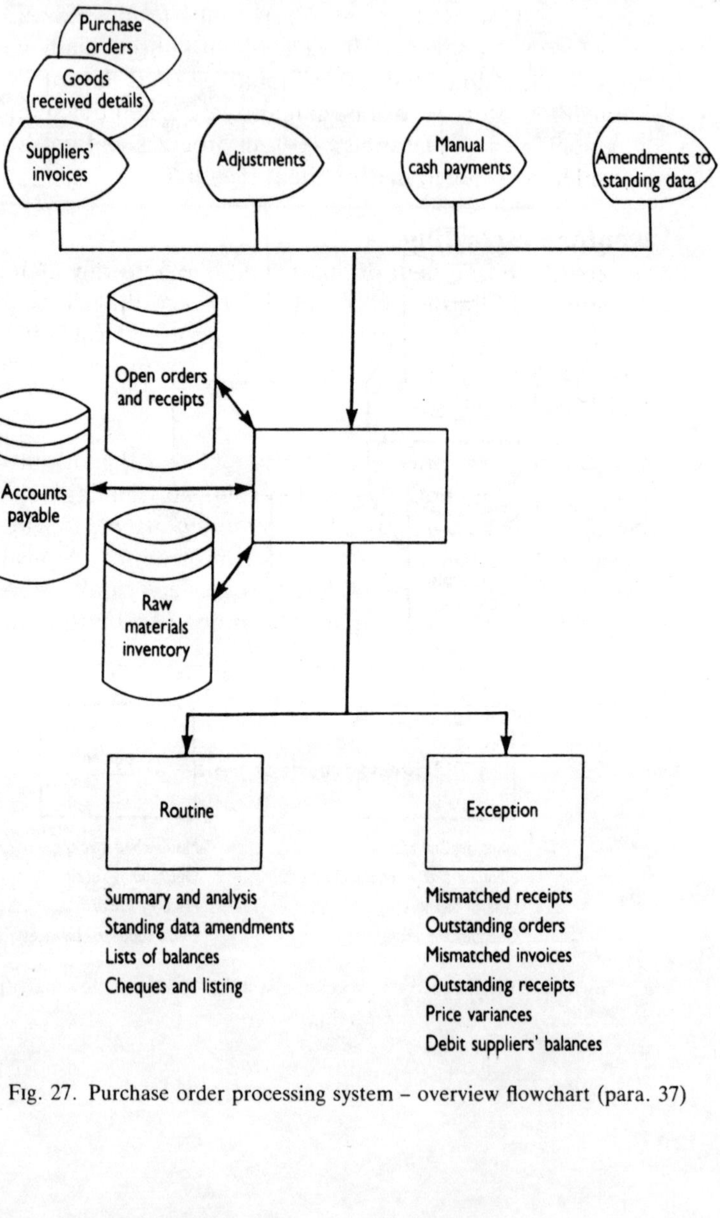

Fig. 27. Purchase order processing system – overview flowchart (para. 37)

Inventory Control

The components

38 Inventory control is a term commonly used for a wide variety of computer systems that process movements in inventories. Inventory control can be conveniently divided into three main components, **inventory recording**, **inventory valuation** and **inventory counting**. Although inventory recording can also be broken down into the three components of raw materials, work in progress and finished goods, it is considered easier to discuss them together.

Inventory recording

39 The records will be held on master files. Where raw materials, work in progress and finished goods inventory recording is integrated, it is normal for separate files to be maintained for each category. However, the maintenance of integrated inventory records is a typical use for database organisation.

40 The raw materials, work in progress and finished goods inventory files will be updated by both transaction data and standing data. The main types of transaction data will be *inventory movements*. There will also be a need for *adjustments* to correct mispostings. Adjustments may also be necessary to input differences between book and actual stock revealed by inventory counting. This is described further in paragraph

Inventory: Data elements

Description	**Number of Characters**
Part number details	
Part number	14
Product group	6
Stock description	30
Unit of measure code	1
Made in/Bought out indicator	2
Stores location	5
Latest purchase price	9
Reorder level	7
Reorder quantity	7
Safety stock	7
Maximum stock	7

Fig. 28. Inventory – data elements (para. 40)

Production reserve		7
Leadtime		3
Average weekly demand		7
Standard cost		9
Current selling price		11
Price effective date		6
New price increase percentage		5
New selling price		11
Bin stock		7
Allocated stock		7
Despatch stock		7
Outstanding sales orders		7
Outstanding purchase orders		7
Issues		7
Receipts	Current	7
Demand	Month	7
Despatches	Details	7
Adjustments		7
Issues		7
Receipts	Current	7
Demand	Year	7
Despatches	Details	7
Adjustments		7
Issues		7
Receipts	Monthly	7
Demand	Averages	7
Despatches		7
Adjustments		7
Last year's standard cost		9
Physical stock check count		3
Physical stock check frequency in weeks		2
Date of last physical count		6
Opening stock this year		7
Outstanding purchase requisition indicator		1
Outstanding purchase requisition quantity		7
Latest purchase quantity		7
Last issue date		6
Date of last purchase		6
Forecast total demand		7
Forecast spares demand		7
		362

Fig. 28 (continued). Inventory – data elements (para. 40)

47. *Summaries* and *analyses* of movements and adjustments will be produced. *Amendments to standing data* will be needed to open and close records of stock items and to alter the various standing data fields. A *listing of standing data amendments* made will normally be produced. An example of an inventory file layout is shown in Figure 28.

41 Particular features relating to raw materials, work in progress and finished goods inventory recording are outlined in the following paragraphs.

Raw materials

42 Raw materials recorded is illustrated in Figure 29. *Receipts of inventory* will be input from goods received records which, if the systems are integrated, will also be processed for *purchase accounting*. Issues to production may be made prior to computer processing, details being input from *production schedules* or requisitions. However, in more advanced systems the computer may be programmed to initiate the issues required on the basis of the input of a *production number*.

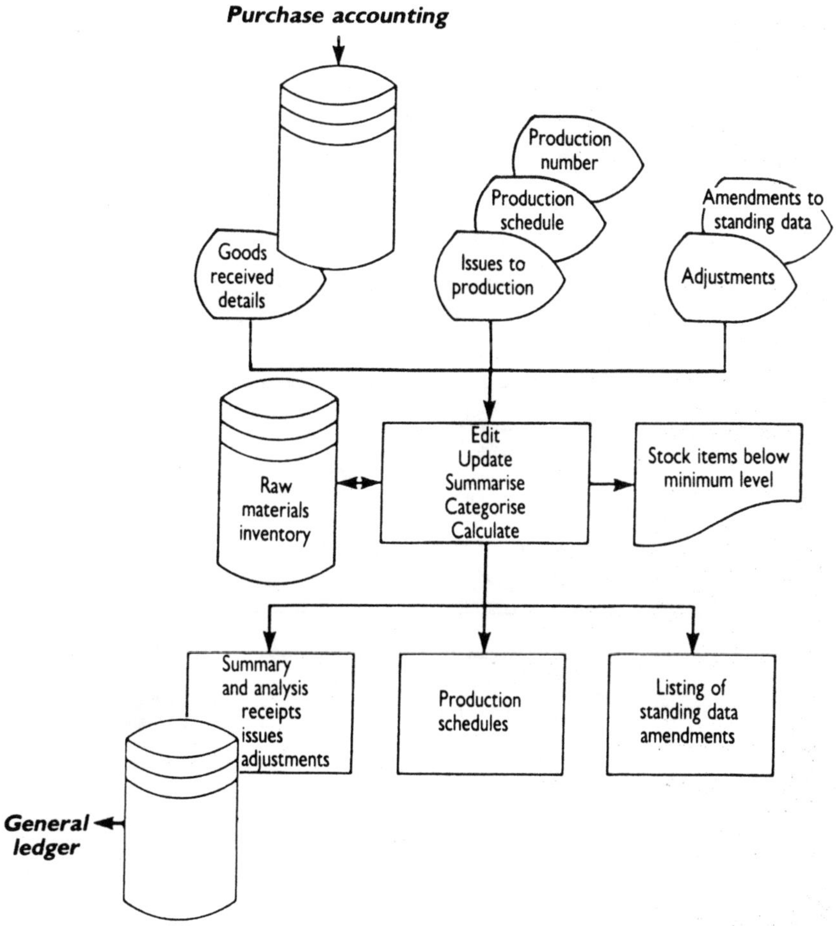

Fig. 29. Inventory control – raw materials recording (para. 42)

Information as to the materials necessary for the relevant job are held as standing data and the computer prints out the issue documentation, including *production schedules*, and updates the *raw materials file*. In these cases the file is updated in respect of issues prior to the actual issue from the stores. *Stock items below minimum levels* may be reported to assist in ordering.

Work in progress

43 Work in progress recording is illustrated in Figure 30. Details of *issues to production* will, as described above, be input from production schedules or requisitions or be initiated by the computer. The updating of the *work in progress file* is often carried out simultaneously with the updating of the raw materials file. *Labour charges* are usually input from manually prepared input documents or from a file produced dur-

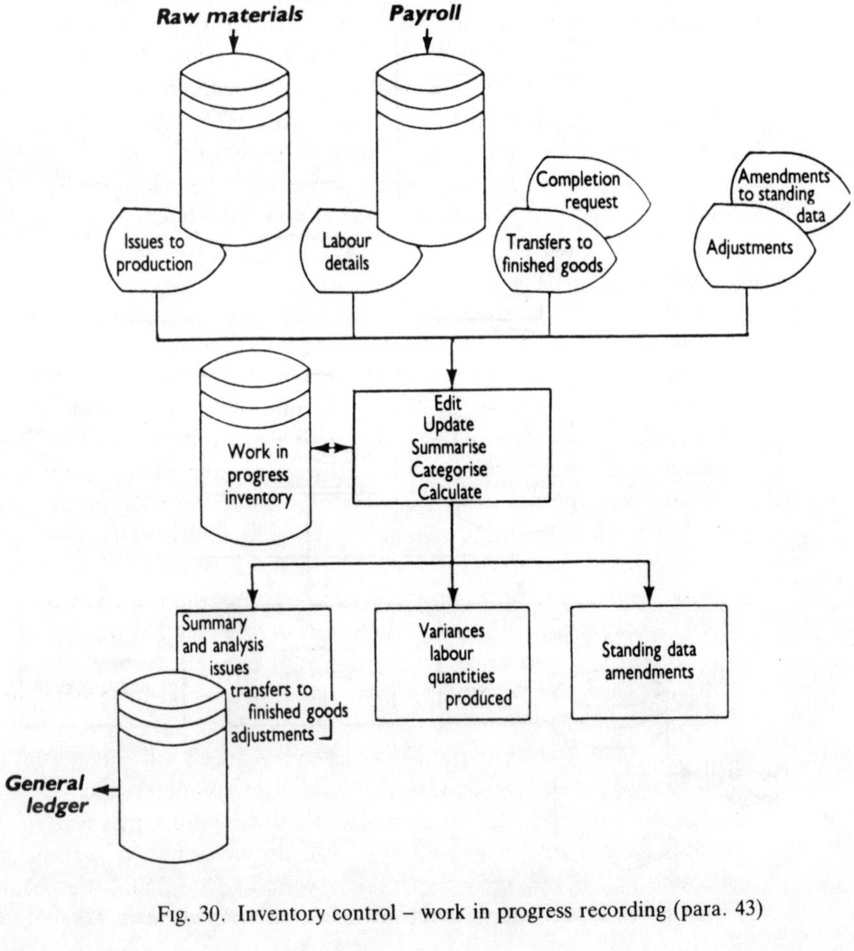

Fig. 30. Inventory control – work in progress recording (para. 43)

ing payroll production. Actual gross pay would be *categorised* by the computer by reference to an input code. In some cases standard labour charges are held as standing data and the computer may be programmed to calculate *variances*. Overhead rates are normally held as standing data on the work in progress inventory file and the computer calculates the appropriate amount. Details of *transfers to finished goods* will usually be input from manually prepared documentation. In advanced systems the computer may be programmed to initiate the details of the transfer on the basis of the input of a *completion request*. The transfer details are held on the work in progress inventory file as standing data. The computer may be programmed to calculate *variances* between actual and standard quantities produced.

Finished goods

44 Finished goods recording is illustrated in Figure 31. *Completed work* will, as described above, be input from manual documentation or initiated by the computer. The updating of the *finished goods file* is often carried out simultaneously with the updating of the work in progress file. When the finished goods are sold, *details of despatches* are input. Often the updating of the finished goods file will be integrated, as described earlier, with *sales accounting*. If the cost of finished goods is held on file, the cost of sales will be *summarised* by the computer. The unit cost of sales will normally be held as standing data.

Inventory valuation

45 Although it is normal for the inventory balances and movements to be held in quantities only, prices are also often held in the form of standing data. In this way the *value of inventory* can be regularly *calculated*. In the case of raw materials, the relevant cost may be the actual cost price, which will be updated every time a purchase is made, or an average cost price, which will be calculated after each purchase, or a standard cost price. If standard cost is used, the computer will be programmed to calculate *variances*. If average cost is used, the computer will often be programmed to calculate changes to average cost arising from each new purchase and report *changes over a certain norm*. These procedures are illustrated in the first part of Figure 32.

46 The computer may be programmed to *calculate* and report periodically information relevant to the value of inventory. Depending on the system this may include details as to excess stock, obsolete stock and slow-moving stock. *Excess stock* is usually calculated by comparing inventory on hand with past usage or future requirements. *Obsolete stock* is calculated by reference to past usage or by the setting of an indicator, for example, in respect of a component for a finished product which is no longer in production. *Slow-moving stock* is calculated by

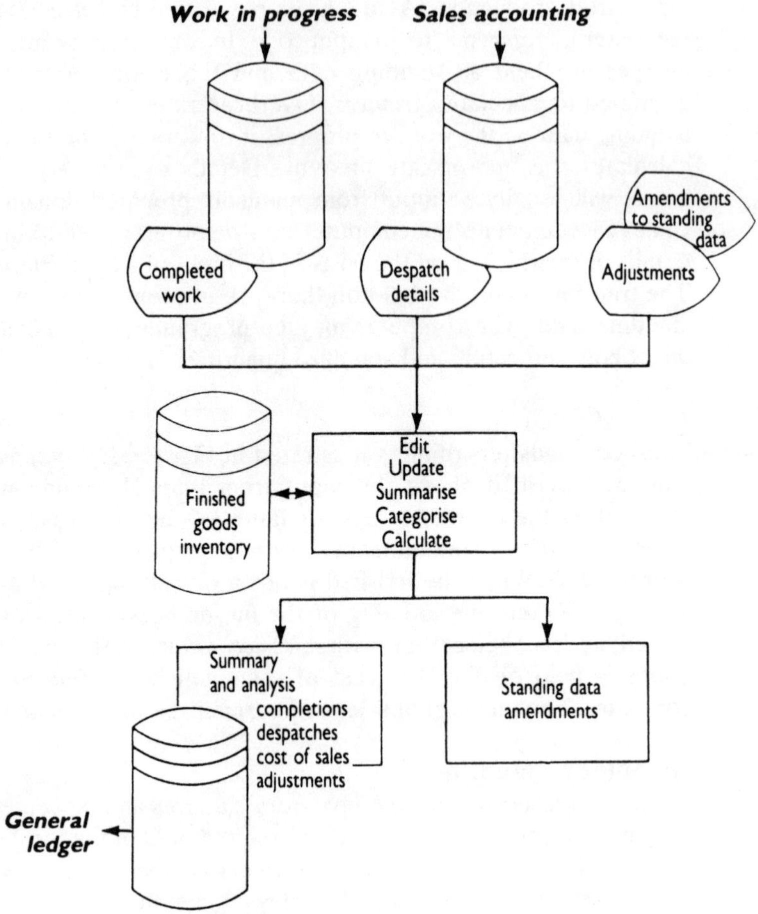

Fig. 31. Inventory control – finished goods recording (para. 44)

reference to the date of the last movement. The scope of reports of this nature is governed mainly by the range of information held on the file. These procedures are illustrated in the second part of Figure 32.

Inventory counting

47 The need for adjustments to input differences between book and actual stock has already been noted. These may result from a periodical count of all the stock. However, when inventory records are processed by computer, it is easier to ensure their reliability and thus continuous stocktaking becomes more likely. If continuous stocktaking is carried out, one of the following three methods will normally be followed:

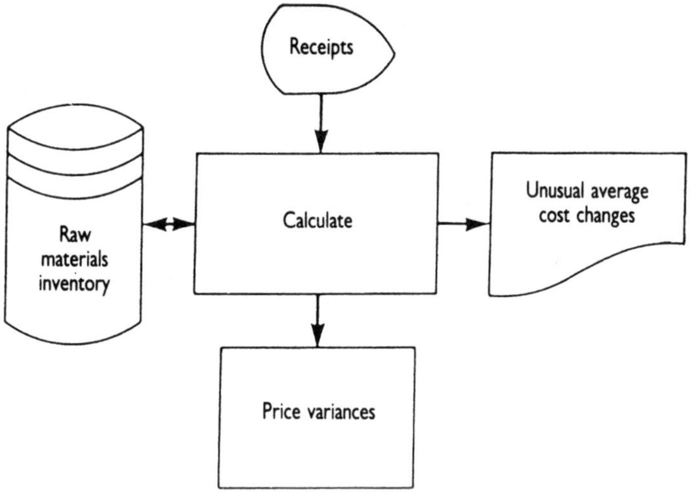

Fig. 32(1). Inventory control – inventory values (para. 45)

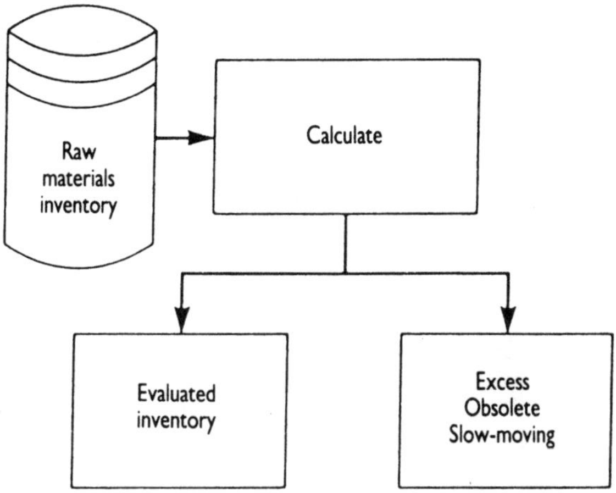

Fig. 32(2). Inventory control – inventory values (para. 46)

(a) The stock is counted and compared with the most recent balance on the file adjusted, where necessary, for outstanding issues and receipts. These adjustments can be made manually or by the computer. Differences are processed by the input of an *adjustment*. A manual record is kept of items to be counted.

(b) Stock is counted, compared and adjustments processed as in (a). At the same time as the adjustments are processed, the *date of the stock count* is input. The computer records the date and produces a regular report of *items which have not been counted* for a specified period.

(c) Stock is counted and the *details of the physical balances* are input. The computer calculates any differences between the physical and book inventory balance. The differences are often automatically processed and reported. In some cases, only *differences over a specified amount* are reported.

Provision will also often be made for *negative stock balances* to be reported. An example of inventory counting is illustrated in Figure 33.

The systems

48 The components described in paragraphs 38 to 47 can be combined to form a wide variety of computer systems that process inventory movements. They may vary from the simple recording of raw materials or finished goods to integrated recording, valuation and counting of materials, work in progress and finished goods and computer-controlled production planning. It has already been seen how inventory recording systems may be integrated with purchases and sales accounting and how replenishment of raw materials may be initiated by the computer. As a result it is not realistic to show a series of groupings of components. An example of an integrated inventory con-

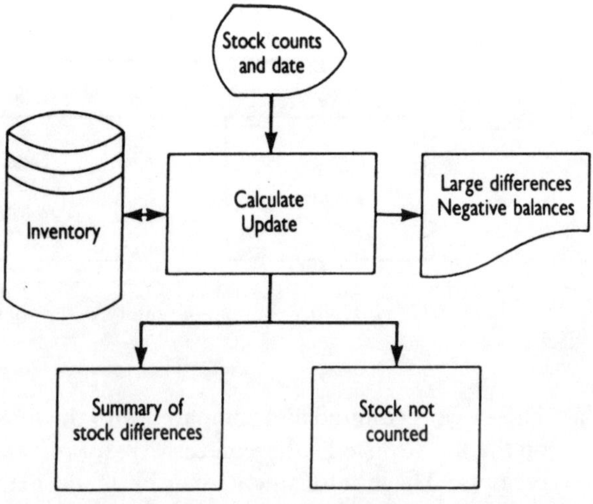

Fig. 33. Inventory control – inventory counting (para. 47)

trol system, combining most of the features discussed, is illustrated in Figure 34.

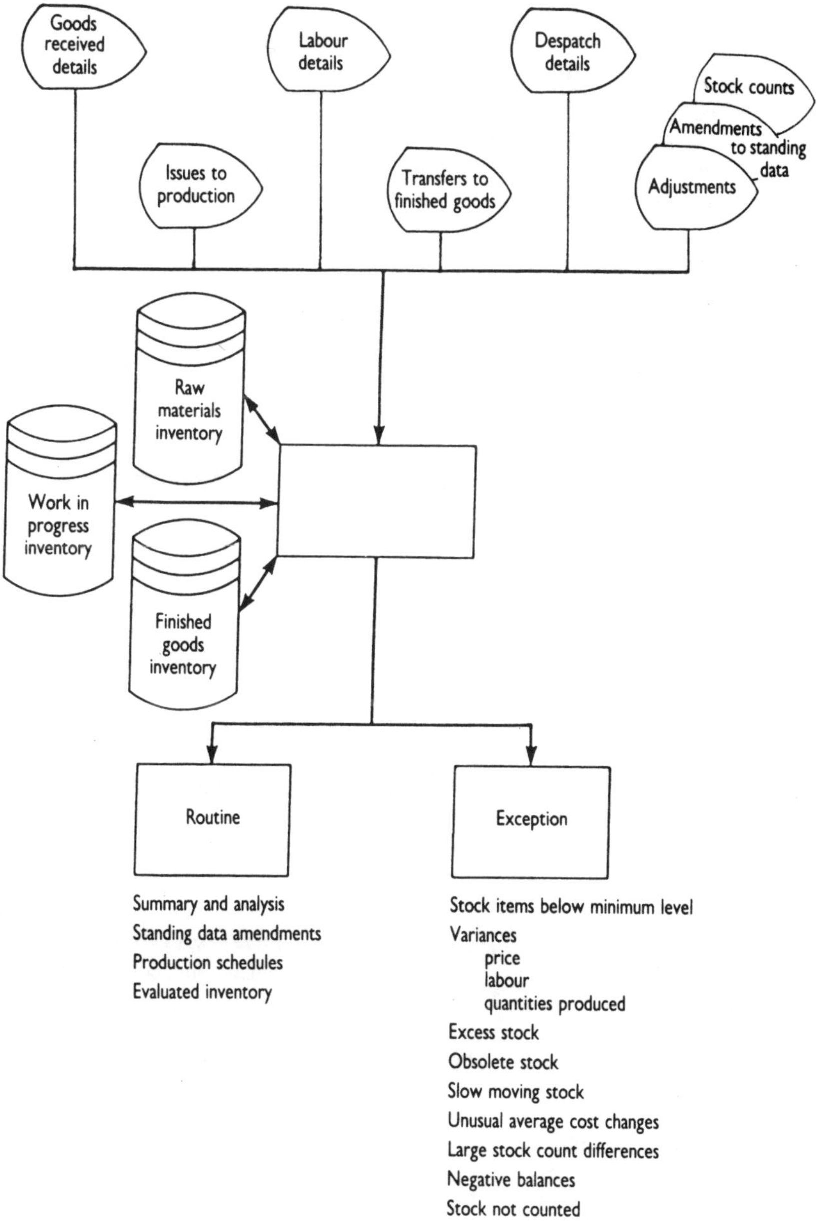

Fig. 34. Integrated inventory control system – overview flowchart (para. 48)

Payroll

49 In wages and salaries systems, which are illustrated in Figure 35, the most important output is usually the printed payroll with its various accounting totals of gross pay and deductions. Thus the principal concern is with the standing data held on the master files, for example, rates of pay, and the input and processing of the transaction data, for example hours worked or work done. When considering wages and salaries systems, it is convenient to deal with standing data before payroll production.

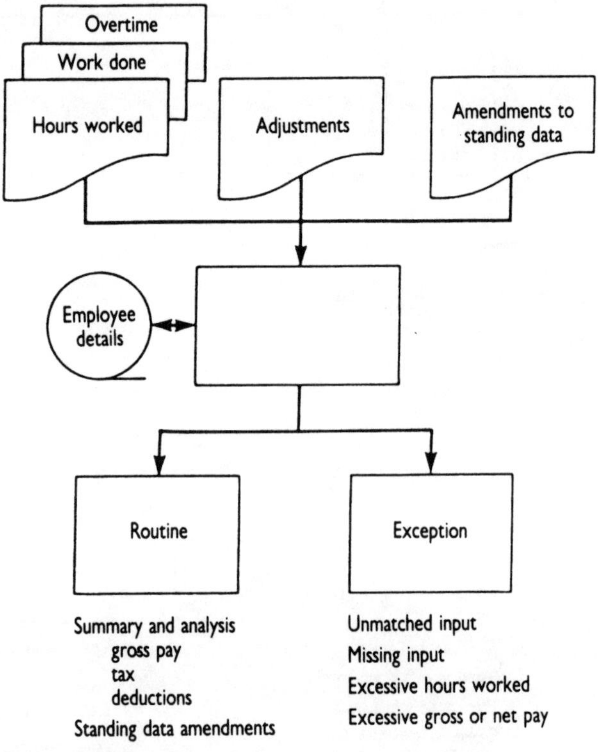

Fig. 35. Payroll – overview flowchart (para. 49)

Standing data

50 *Amendments to standing data* will be processed to record starters and leavers on the employee master file and to alter rates of pay, details of allowances and deductions. A typical employee details master file layout, illustrating the wide variety of data that may be held, and for which amendment routines may be necessary, is shown in Figure 36.

In some systems the computer may be programmed to calculate changes to standing data on the basis of input, for example, increments to rates of pay as a result of changes to personal details such as age or the passing of examinations. In advanced systems the computer may be programmed to initiate amendments to standing data, for example, increments to rates of pay on anniversary of starting date.

Payroll: Data elements

Description	**Number of Characters**
Employee details	
Employee's reference number	6
Sex	1
Starter/leaver indicator	1
Employee's title indicator	1
Employee's initials	5
Employee's surname	15
Employee's date of birth	6
National insurance number	9
Income tax code	5
Company number where employee works	4
Section number	2
Bank and branch sorting code	6
Bank account indicator	1
Date started	6
Date left	6
Staff coding	2
Basic annual salary	7
Previous salary prior to last increase/decrease	7
Date of last salary increase/decrease	6
Annual allowance – No 1	6
Annual allowance – No 2	6
Annual allowance – No 3	6
Total gross monthly standard salary	6
Pension fund indicator	1
Pension fund monthly contribution	5
Date of entry into pension fund	6
Pension fund accumulator for ½ year	6
Pension fund accumulator for 1 year	6
Pension fund accumulator for whole of service	7
National insurance code	3
Employer's national insurance contributions	4
Employee's national insurance contributions	4
Monthly loan repayments	5
Number of loan repayments outstanding	2
Number of monthly repayments at start	2
Accumulated gross pay to date	7
Accumulated gross pay to date from previous employment	7
Accumulated tax paid to date	6
Accumulated tax paid to date from previous employment	6
Tax free pay for one month	5
Tax month number	2
Tax district	15

FIG. 36. Payroll – data elements (para. 50) (continued overleaf)

Tax district reference number	11
Bank account number	8
Bank name	30
Bank address 1st line	30
Bank address 2nd line	30
Bank address 3rd line	30
	358

Fig. 36. Payroll – data elements (para. 50)

Payroll production

51 In wages systems it is usually necessary to input details of *hours worked* or *work done*. The input may be of all hours worked or variances from standard hours held as standing data. Variances would include *overtime*, *holidays* and *absences*. The computer is often programmed to report cases where *hours input exceed a defined norm*.

52 The transaction data will be *matched* with the relevant employee details on the master file. Unmatched input or employee details should be rejected, when there is duplicate input, or reported when there is no input. The computer will then *calculate* the pay details for each employee, *update* the transaction data on the master file and *summarise* the accounting totals for posting to the general ledger. The totals are often *categorised* as a basis for further processing, for example, posting to cost accounts. The summaries may be produced for non-computer processing or subsequent input to the *nominal* and *cost ledger* computer applications. This input may be by document or the file created during payroll production. The computer is often programmed to report cases where *gross* or *net pay* exceeds a defined norm.

53 In salaries systems it is normal for the monthly or annual salary to be held as standing data. The only input will be any *adjustments* or *overtime details*. The computer will be programmed to select or calculate the salary and take account of any input.

Fixed Assets

54 It is common to maintain records of fixed assets on computer. The cost of the fixed assets, depreciation rates and accumulated depreciation to date are normally held on the master file. The file layout for a typical fixed assets file is shown in Figure 37. *Purchases* will be input from

Fixed Assets: Data elements

Description	**Number of Characters**
Asset details	
Asset category	2
Asset reference number	10
Purchase date	6
Input document reference	6
Taxation code	3
Location code	3
Purchase method	1
Gross cost	8
Valuation method	1
Valuation	8
Valuation date	6
Standard life (months)	4
Depreciation method	1
All time cumulative depreciation	8
Residual life months	4
Rental method	1
All time cumulative rental	8
Rental suspension	1
Cumulative depreciation	8
Cumulative rental	8
Depreciation this month	8
Rental this month	8
Depreciation roundings	2
Rental roundings	2
Date of last physical inspection	6
Current cost	8
Current cost valuation method	3
	134

Fig. 37. Fixed assets – data elements (para. 54)

manually prepared documents or, as is often the case, from a categorised file from the purchase accounting application. Capitalised *wages* and *materials* will be dealt with in a similar manner. Input documents will be prepared for *disposals* and *adjustments*. It is normal for the fixed asset movements to be *summarised*, *categorised* and printed out for control purposes.

55 Depreciation rates will be held as standing data and may require to be amended from time to time. The computer will *calculate* and *summarise* depreciation for posting to the general ledger either by input documents or file. Information may be provided of *fully depreciated*

assets and *profits and losses* on disposals may be calculated. Details of *assets inspected* may be input and the computer can report *assets not inspected*.

56 A fixed assets system is illustrated in Figure 38.

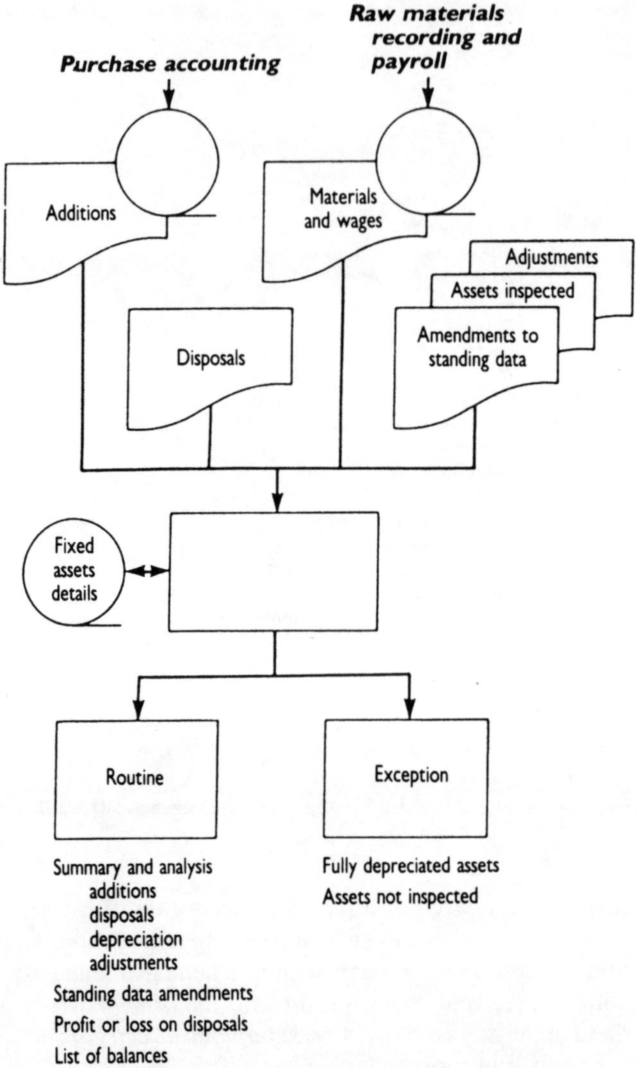

Fig. 38. Fixed assets – overview flowchart (para. 56)

4

Evaluation of Internal Control: The Audit Approach

General Approach

4.01 When, as part of his audit strategy, the auditor has decided to place reliance on his client's system of internal control, he will need to carry out an extended examination of the controls. He may also wish to evaluate controls in order to report to management weaknesses that come to his notice, so as to assist management in carrying out its obligations to establish and maintain controls that will ensure, as far as possible, the reliability of the company's accounting records and the safeguarding of its assets.

4.02 The approach suggested in this book is the use of an internal control questionnaire to evaluate and test the controls which should normally exist. This chapter describes the structure and use of such a questionnaire referred to as a Control Assessment and Record of Tests (CART).

4.03 In addition to a detailed CART, it is frequently helpful to summarise the principal controls over each system in a form that enables the auditor rapidly to gain an impression of the overall strength of control. This chapter describes one way in which this can be done using control matrices.

Additional services

4.04 The scope of the auditor's evaluation of control has already been outlined in paragraphs 2.42 and 2.43. In addition, in computer systems, there are three further services which the auditor is well suited to carry out on behalf of his client. Although these may enhance subsequent audit efficiency, it should be remembered that they are not of direct relevance to the forming of an audit opinion on financial statements.

4.05 First, it may be helpful for the auditor to provide advice on the general approach to controls in a computer system. The auditor is often well-qualified to provide this advice as he is likely to have wide experience of the controls applicable to computer systems.

4.06 Secondly, it can be very beneficial for the auditor to evaluate the controls in a computer system before it becomes operational whether or not he intends to examine those controls for audit purposes. This is more important than in a non-computer system because it is difficult to make changes to a computer system once it is operational. The auditor can make any suggestions or recommendations at the relevant stage of development so that they can be incorporated without problem. Indeed, clients often encourage or specifically require the auditor's evaluation and comments prior to implementation.

4.07 Thirdly, it may be helpful for the auditor to review and test the implementation controls, as applied to specific systems, during each important stage of development, although he does not himself propose to rely on the implementation controls. In this way he can bring any deficiencies that come to his notice to the client's attention in time for remedial action to be taken. Serious faults in operational systems, which, as indicated, can be difficult to correct, can be avoided by these means.

4.08 Where appropriate, the auditor may be able to arrange for additional features to be included in a new system that will assist his subsequent audit tests. For example, facilities may be arranged to obtain print-outs on request or for additional fields to be included on master files for subsequent examination by a computer audit program.

The Control Assessment and Record of Tests

Design of the CART

4.09 The CART described in this book has been designed to enhance audit efficiency by allowing one document to be used for recording the following:

- Details of control procedures additional to those recorded on flowcharts or narratives as discussed in Chapter 3.
- The evaluation of the effectiveness of the controls.
- Details of tests performed on the controls and conclusions drawn.

4.10 The CART includes separate sections for application controls and IT controls. The application controls CART illustrated in this book is designed for computerised accounting systems, although it includes questions on manual procedures which may form part of such a system, as appropriate. The application controls CART is divided into sections dealing with the purpose of controls, such as accuracy of input, and is not specific to particular applications such as sales or purchases.

Files and transactions

4.11 The application controls CART is separated into sections dealing with file controls and transaction controls. File controls are controls over the files from which amounts in the financial statements are derived. Transaction controls are controls over the transactions that update those files.

4.12 The file controls section of the CART is sub-divided into two sections as follows:

- **File continuity**, dealing with controls designed to ensure that the data which has been updated to a file remains correct and current.
- **Asset protection**, dealing with controls designed to ensure that the assets represented by the balances on the file are secure, by ensuring that movements are properly approved and recorded and that records are adequately protected from unauthorised or incorrect amendment.

4.13 The transaction controls section of the CART is sub-divided into five sections as follows:

- **Completeness of input**, dealing with controls designed to ensure that all necessary transactions are initiated, input and accepted for further processing.
- **Accuracy of input**, dealing with controls designed to ensure that data is accurately recorded, input and accepted for further processing.
- **Authorisation of transactions**, dealing with controls designed to ensure that only valid data is processed.
- **Generation of data/transactions**, dealing with controls designed to ensure that all data or transactions generated by computer processing are complete, accurate and valid.
- **Update of data onto files**, dealing with controls designed to ensure that all data input is completely and accurately processed through to update to the relevant key file.

4.14 Detailed questions for each of the above sections of the CART are included, for illustration purposes, in Appendix A to this chapter. Reference will be made to the questions in subsequent chapters.

Controls over standing data

4.15 If standing data is used in the processing of transactions, the auditor should identify the data file and data elements involved. For example, when invoices are generated, prices may be taken from a prices file held on the system. The auditor should consider whether control over the standing data elements and transactions affecting those data elements should be assessed. If so, sections of the CART should be completed with controls over the standing data file and the transactions which update it.

4.16 Sometimes it may not be appropriate for the auditor to assess controls over standing data. This would be the case if there is no risk of material misstatement as a result of an error in the standing data or if the completeness, accuracy and validity of the standing data used in processing are verified as part of the controls carried out by users on the results of processing.

Programmed procedures

4.17 When completing individual questions in the CART, the auditor is likely to identify controls which place reliance on the operation of programmed procedures. The CART includes a column to record whether the operation of each control is dependent upon the effective operation of programmed procedures. Where controls are dependent to a significant extent on the operation of programmed procedures, the auditor will need to gain assurance as to the continued and proper operation of the programmed procedures. This will usually be achieved by testing the IT controls.

IT controls

4.18 There is a separate section of the CART, the **IT CART** for use in assessing IT controls wherever the auditor decides as part of his audit strategy to place reliance on IT controls. The IT CART is divided into the following sections:

- **Implementation controls for new systems**, dealing with controls over the development and implementation of new computer programs.
- **System maintenance controls**, dealing with controls over changes to existing computer systems.

- **Computer operations controls**, dealing with controls over the set up and processing of computer programs and data files.
- **Program security controls**, dealing with controls designed to ensure that unauthorised changes cannot be made to computer programs.
- **Data file security controls**, dealing with controls designed to ensure that unauthorised changes cannot be made to data.
- **System software controls**, dealing with controls over programs which do not process accounting data but which form the operating environment in which all systems at the computer installation are processed.

4.19 Detailed questions for each of the above sections of the IT CART are included, for illustration purposes, in Appendix A to this chapter. Reference will be made to the questions in subsequent chapters.

The Control Matrices

4.20 It is frequently helpful to summarise the principal controls over a particular system in a form which shows clearly their overall structure and strength. Such a summary is of most use at the audit strategy stage, when it can be completed on the basis of discussions with management. It enables the auditor to make a preliminary assessment of the strength of controls and likely efficiency of evaluating and testing them. It also enables him to identify situations where several controls could be relied upon to achieve the same objectives, and therefore to choose the ones on which he will place reliance so as to maximise the efficiency of his audit. Documents suitable for summarising controls over a system, the file and transaction control matrices, are illustrated in Figures 39 and 40 (overleaf).

File control matrix

4.21 The file control matrix is used to record a concise statement of the principal controls over key files or data under the following headings:

- File continuity.
- Asset custody.
- Data file security.
- Division of duties.

File Control Matrix

Name of Client :

Financial statement account name and value	Key file(s) and/or data elements	File continuity					Asset custody	Data file security	Division of duties
		Total level	Detail level	C	A	E			
Accounts Receivable £12 million	Sales ledger masterfile: - customer name - customer no. - customer address - balance - transaction type - transaction date - transaction amount	Reconciliation of total to computer control log and general ledger.	Detailed review of accounts receivable aged analysis by credit controller.		√	√	N/A	See IT CART - controls over security of sales ledger masterfile	Despatches dealt with by warehouse. Invoices initiated by sales department. Customer remittances received in cash section. Computer operations performed centrally in data centre.
			Customer remittances matched to outstanding items on the file.	√	√	√			
Inventory £14 million	(details not recorded).								

C - Completeness
A - Accuracy
E - Existence

Fig. 39. File control matrix (para. 4.20)

Transaction Control Matrix

Name of client :

Significant transactions/Key fields	Input/Generation				Update		Division of duties
	Completeness	Accuracy	Standing data used	Authorisation	Key file(s) and/or data elements	Completeness and accuracy	
Despatch note copy of sales order (invoices). Data fields:- (a) customer no. (b) product no. (c) quantity (d) price	Sequence check	Data fields (a), (b), (d) - matching. Data field (c) - batching.	Customer name and address from sales ledger masterfile. Price and product no. checked to inventory masterfile.	**Validity** - only despatches accompanied by approved sales orders allowed past gatehouse. **Authorisation** - all sales orders over £500 approved by sales manager.	Sales ledger masterfile - transaction details - customer balance. Inventory masterfile - inventory balance.	As for input controls	See File Control Matrix
Customer and sales price change forms Data fields:- (a) customer no. name and address (b) product no. (c) price	Manual sequence check and 100 per cent comparison of input with output - all data fields.	As for completeness control	N/A	All forms approved by chief accountant.	Sales ledger masterfile - customer details Inventory masterfile - price and product details	As for input controls	Sales department responsible for standing data changes and invoices. Despatches and remittances dealt with by other departments as shown on File Control Matrix.
Customers' remittances Data fields:- (a) amount (b) customer no. (c) invoice no.	All cheques stamped "a/c payee only - not negotiable" on receipt and amounts banked per paying in slips agreed to cash edit report.	Data field (a) - as for completeness Data fields (b) and (c) - matching	Customer and invoice details matched to sales ledger masterfile.	N/A	Sales ledger masterfile - customer balance - invoice details	Data field (a) - cash receipts journal reconciled to edit report Data fields (b) and (c) - matching.	See File Control Matrix.

FIG. 40. Transaction control matrix (para. 4.20)

A separate file control matrix would normally be completed for each significant file for which the auditor wishes to make an overall assessment of controls.

4.22 Separate columns are provided for controls over file continuity at the total and detailed levels. This is because control techniques over the total on the file will normally differ from those which may provide assurance over the detailed balances and transactions held on the file. Controls over the protection of assets recorded on the file are documented in two columns dealing with direct custodial controls over the assets and indirect controls over security of the data. Ineffective data file security controls may facilitate manipulation of data and consequent loss of assets. A separate column is used to record whether division of duties in the operation of controls related to the file appears adequate.

Transaction control matrix

4.23 The transaction control matrix is used to summarise controls over the significant transactions that update the files under the following headings:

- Completeness of input.
- Accuracy of input.
- Authorisation of transactions.
- Completeness and accuracy of update of transactions to the files.
- Division of duties.

Programmed procedures

4.24 In completing the file and transaction control matrices the auditor may find it helpful to identify and record whether programmed procedures are relied upon in performing control techniques. This will assist the auditor in determining the significance of IT controls to the overall system of controls.

Completion of the CART

The extent of evaluation of controls

4.25 The extent of the auditor's detailed evaluation and testing of application controls and IT controls will be decided when determining the audit strategy in accordance with the principles set out in Chapter 2.

The auditor is unlikely to wish to rely on controls for systems where the transactions and related assets and liabilities are not material to the financial statements. In addition, the auditor may decide that it is more efficient to employ substantive tests on account activities and balances rather than to rely on the related control procedures.

4.26 Where the auditor does decide to perform a detailed evaluation and testing of controls, much of his other audit work will also provide some assurance about the effective operation of internal accounting controls. In particular, his work on assessing the control environment and documenting accounting systems in the light of the nature of the client's business and the risk of fraud or error in the financial statements will provide significant assurance on the operation of controls. Similarly, the results of substantive testing will indicate whether misstatements have occurred due to the ineffective operation of accounting controls. Finally, work performed by the auditor in previous years, both directly on controls and substantive testing, will provide evidence on whether an effective system of controls exists.

4.27 In most modern computerised accounting systems, significant reliance will be placed on the operation of programmed procedures in performing application controls. Where a detailed evaluation of controls is to be undertaken, assurance about the continued and proper operation of programmed procedures will normally be obtained by evaluation and testing of IT controls using the IT CART.

4.28 As regards the application controls performed by users, the auditor will not necessarily need to test every control on which he wishes to place reliance provided:

(a) Work on the control environment and IT controls shows them both to be effective.

(b) The results of detailed evaluation and testing which is carried out of application controls performed by users are satisfactory.

(c) Evidence from other audit procedures, including prior years' experience, shows controls to be satisfactory.

The precise extent of detailed evaluation and testing of application controls in each case will be a matter of judgement.

Selecting the questions

4.29 In using the application controls CART in practice, the auditor should first identify the file or files from which the account balance on which he is seeking assurance are derived. For example, the accounts receivable balance will normally come from the accounts receivable masterfile. In some cases there may be separate files for transaction data and customer standing data. The auditor will complete the file sections of the CART for those files on which he has decided to evaluate controls.

4.30 The significant transactions which update the files should then be identified and appropriate sections of the transaction CART should be completed for each significant transaction which the auditor has decided to evaluate. A straightforward accounts receivable system, such as that illustrated in paragraph 17 of Appendix A to Chapter 3, has four main transactions being invoices, adjustments, cash received and amendments to standing data. If the auditor has decided to evaluate this system, each section of the transaction CART would normally be completed for each transaction, with the exception of the generation of data/transactions section on the basis that no data or transactions are generated by the computer in this system.

Form of the CART

4.31 The application controls CART is divided into the following columns, as illustrated in the extract in Figure 41:

- Control question.
- "Yes/No" columns.
- Programmed procedure ("PP") column.
- Tests column.

4.32 The control question seeks to identify whether or not a control exists. Space is provided beneath each question for recording the following details for each control procedure:

(a) The name and job title of the person who usually carries out the procedure.

(b) A brief description of the procedure.

(c) The frequency with which the procedure is performed.

(d) A description of any programmed procedure involved.

Where appropriate this column may be cross referenced to flowcharts or supporting working papers on which details of controls are recorded.

4.33 Each question has been framed so that it may be answered "yes" if control is adequate or "no" if not, indicated by a tick in the appropriate

FILE CONTINUITY - TOTALS				
Questions	Yes	No	PP	Tests
FILE CONTINUITY - COMPUTER CHECKED 1 Is the total of items on file regularly reconciled by computer to an independently established total on a suitably timely basis (e.g. by computer agreement to a control record)? Sales ledger total reconciled monthly to computer control log and general ledger.	✓		✓	Reviewed control log reconciliation reports for September and January. Reports initialled by F. Green as checked to sales ledger and general ledger. Signature and date J.S.T. 6/4
2 Is the computer control total stored on an independent control file, so that any use of an incorrect file or loss of data from the file would be detected? Control log updated independently with totals of invoices and remittances prior to update of sales ledger.	✓		✓	Reviewed flowchart and discussed with F. Green on 5/4/9X. Confirmed that control log is updated independently from sales ledger. Signature and date J.S.T. 6/4

FIG. 41. CART – specimen layout (para. 4.31)

column. The programmed procedure column should be ticked if a programmed procedure is involved in the control and the procedure should be described in the control question column. This provides an indication of the degree of reliance by the client upon IT controls.

4.34 The tests column is provided to enable tests of the controls to be recorded. The following details would normally be recorded:

(a) The name and job title of the person with whom the procedure was discussed, or who was observed carrying out the procedure.

(b) The date of the discussion or observation.

(c) Details of the discussion, observation, evidence examined or other tests carried out.

(d) The level and spread of tests.

Where appropriate, reference should be made to working papers on which the details of tests are recorded. Tests of controls are discussed in detail in Chapter 9 "Testing Controls and the Response to Weaknesses".

4.35 The IT CART has a similar layout to the application controls CART except that it does not have a programmed procedure column since it is itself designed to assess controls which ensure the continued and proper operation of programmed procedures.

Assessment of answers

4.36 Where there are "no" answers to individual questions within the CART it is still possible that the overall objective of the relevant section is achieved if the weaknesses identified are not significant. The auditor should consider whether this is the case and should also make an overall assessment of the effectiveness of the client's control procedures in the light of all his audit evidence. Undue weight should not be given to individual or isolated weaknesses but where significant weaknesses are identified the effect on the audit strategy, and specifically whether reliance on controls is still appropriate, should be considered. Detailed discussion of weaknesses in controls is included in Chapter 9 "Testing Controls and the Response to Weaknesses".

Summary

4.37 The auditor may wish to carry out a detailed evaluation of controls either because he intends to place audit reliance on them or because he wishes to report any weaknesses to management.

4.38 As a means to evaluate controls, a questionnaire known as the Control Assessment and Record of Tests (CART) is suggested. It includes separate sections to evaluate application controls and IT controls. The application controls CART deals with controls over files and transactions, including controls over standing data. Questions are grouped by the purpose of the control and are not specific to any particular application such as sales or purchases. The IT CART is used to assess controls over the implementation, maintenance, operation and security of computer programs and the security of data files.

4.39 In addition to the detailed evaluation carried out using the CART, it is sometimes useful, particularly when carrying out a preliminary assessment of controls in order to determine the audit strategy, to summarise the control strengths and weaknesses of a system. File and transaction control matrices are suggested for this purpose.

4: Appendix A

Control Questions

1 This appendix includes the detailed questions for the application controls and IT controls CARTs. They are included for illustration purposes and tailoring or enhancement may be required in applying them in practice. The questions in the application controls CART are explained in Chapter 5, and those in the IT CART are explained in Chapters 6, 7 and 8. The design of the application controls CART and the IT CART is explained in Chapter 4.

Application Controls CART

File Continuity

File continuity at the total level

File continuity – computer checked

1 Is the total of items on file regularly reconciled by computer to an independently established total on a suitably timely basis (e.g. by computer agreement to a control record)?

2 Is the computer control total stored on an independent control file, so that any use of an incorrect file or loss of data from the file would be detected?

3 Are all the differences reported?

4 Are there adequate procedures to investigate and correct differences disclosed by the reconciliation?

5 Is the investigation and correction of differences performed or checked by persons other than those involved in computer operations?

6 Are the results of the control total procedures reviewed and approved by an independent responsible official?

File continuity – manually checked

7 Is the total of the items on file regularly manually reconciled to an

independently established total on a suitably timely basis (e.g. by agreement to a manual control account)?

8 Is the brought forward total on the computer control report manually checked to the carried forward total of the key data to ensure that the correct generation of the file is used?

9 Are there adequate procedures to investigate and correct differences disclosed by the reconciliation and, if applicable, the check of the brought forward total?

10 Is the reconciliation of totals and, if applicable, the check of the brought forward total, either performed or checked by persons other than those involved in computer operations or in maintaining the manual control total?

11 Is the investigation and correction of differences performed or checked by persons other than those involved in computer operations or in maintaining the manual control total?

12 Are the results of the control total procedures reviewed and approved by an independent responsible official?

File continuity – other controls

13 Are user procedures adequate to identify the use of the wrong version of the file and are appropriate actions taken to correct any errors identified?

14 Do the user procedures operate so that all errors would be identified on a suitably timely basis?

15 Are there adequate procedures to investigate and correct those errors?

16 Are the user procedures either performed or checked by persons other than those involved in computer operations?

17 Are the results of the user procedures reviewed and approved by an independent responsible official?

File continuity at the detailed level

File details – management information

18 Is there management information which is relevant to the control of the details on the file? Describe the control procedures and identify

the key data covered. Identify the audit objectives (completeness, accuracy, existence) affected by the control technique.

19 Is operating information prepared on a regular basis (e.g. summaries, exception reports, overall reconciliations or performance indicators)?

20 Where these operating reports depend on comparisons to forecasts, budgets, prior periods, other departments or divisions, or industry statistics, are there appropriate procedures to ensure that the comparative figures were prepared on the same assumptions and that differences in assumptions and conditions are highlighted and explained (e.g. changes in business, organisation, accounting systems or policies, unusual events or different periods)?

21 Where these operating reports depend on comparisons to forecasts, budgets, prior periods, other departments or divisions, or industry statistics, are there appropriate procedures to ensure that the correct comparative figures have been accurately obtained and compared?

22 Are these operating reports prepared at a sufficient level of detail to pick up all significant errors in the financial accounting data?

23 Are the analyses performed using financial accounting data or if the analyses are prepared using the operational systems and data (e.g. items evaluated at standard cost) is this operational data reconciled to the financial accounting data?

24 Are there written explanations of all significant results, variances and exceptions?

25 Are these explanations independently reviewed and the causes of major exceptions properly investigated?

File details – matching

26 Are there matching controls which are relevant to the control of the details on the file? Describe the control procedures and identify the key data covered. Identify the audit objectives (completeness, accuracy, existence) affected by the control technique.

27 Does the design of the matching process ensure that all mismatched items are appropriately reported (e.g. cash is matched to sales invoices by invoice number rather than being allocated against the oldest invoice for a customer)?

28 Is a report of all items outstanding for an unreasonable length of time

or a suitable aged analysis of all items on the file prepared at appropriate intervals (e.g. receiving memoranda, unmatched cash)?

29 Are there adequate procedures to investigate and, if necessary, correct all clearing transactions rejected as mismatches (e.g. purchase invoices outstanding not matched to receiving memoranda, unmatched cash)?

30 Are there adequate procedures to investigate and, if necessary, correct long outstanding items (e.g. receiving memoranda outstanding, long outstanding invoices)?

31 Are all corrections arising from investigation of mismatches and long outstanding items approved by an independent responsible official?

File details – independent comparisons

32 Are there independent comparisons which are relevant to the control of the details on the file? Describe the control procedures and identify the key data covered. Identify the audit objectives (completeness, accuracy, existence) affected by the control technique.

33 Are the records independently compared, at appropriate intervals, to the physical assets (e.g. inventory) or third party evidence (e.g. loan certificates or suppliers' statements) providing an adequate basis for rechecking the completeness and accuracy of the recorded data?

34 Are these comparison procedures adequate to identify possible errors or omissions in the data on file?

35 Are there adequate procedures to investigate and, if necessary, correct any differences disclosed?

36 Does the comparison provide sufficient coverage of data on the file (i.e. the proportion, by number and value, of items on the file checked in this way)?

37 Are the results of the procedures for comparison to physical assets or third party data, identified above, reviewed and approved by an independent responsible official?

File details – other controls

38 Are there other controls which are relevant to the control of the details on the file? Describe the control procedures and the key data covered. Identify which audit objectives (completeness, accuracy, existence) are affected by the control technique.

39 Where the controls are based on reviews of exception reports does the design of the process to identify exceptional items ensure that all exceptional items are appropriately reported?

40 Are the exception reports prepared or are the other procedures performed at appropriate intervals?

41 Are there adequate procedures to investigate and, if necessary, correct all exceptional items identified in exception reports or by the other procedures?

42 Are all corrections arising from investigation of exceptional items or items identified by other procedures approved by an independent responsible official?

Asset Protection

Custody of assets

1 Are there adequate procedures over the custody of assets between their receipt and their initial recording (e.g. receipt of goods into a secure area)?

2 Are assets protected from unauthorised access, use and misappropriation (e.g. locks, safes, guards, warehouse and site security)?

3 Are all assets movements supported by adequate written authorisations?

4 Are the persons responsible for the custody of assets, or for authorising their movement, persons other than those who maintain the related accounting records?

Security of recorded data

5 Review the answers to the data file security section of the IT CART. Are the procedures adequate to ensure the security of significant data relating to assets susceptible to theft?

Completeness of Input

Matching

Matching to data on a key file

1 Review the sections of the CART completed for the key file and key

data against which matching takes place. Are there adequate controls to ensure that the data on the file is complete?

Matching to other data

2 Identify the control file used for matching to ensure completeness of input (e.g. goods received notes file used for matching to purchase invoices).

3 Are the procedures for setting up and maintaining expected transactions on the control file adequate to ensure that the matching process could ensure completeness of processing?

4 Are all changes and deletions (before matching) to the control file of expected transactions approved by an independent responsible official?

All matching

5 Is the matching process adequate to form a basis for identifying all unmatched transactions?

6 Is the matching process adequate to identify duplicates and other mismatched transactions?

7 Is a report of long outstanding transactions or an aged analysis produced at regular intervals?

8 Are there adequate procedures to investigate and, if necessary, correct all long outstanding items?

9 Are there adequate procedures to investigate and, if necessary, correct all duplicates, mismatches and rejections?

10 Are all corrections arising from reports of long outstanding or mismatched items approved by an independent responsible official?

Batching

11 Are there adequate controls to ensure that all transactions are recorded?

12 Are there adequate controls to ensure that all transaction documents are included in a batch?

13 Are there controls to ensure that all batches are input to the computer and accepted once and only once?

14 If predetermined control totals are input and agreed by the computer to the accumulation of individual items accepted, is adequate evidence of this check printed out?

15 Are predetermined control totals agreed manually with the total of accepted items accumulated and printed out by the computer?

16 Are there adequate procedures to investigate and, if necessary, correct missing and duplicate transactions disclosed by the above controls?

17 Are there adequate procedures to investigate and, if necessary, correct rejected items?

18 Are all necessary corrections approved by an independent responsible official?

Sequence checking

19 Are there adequate procedures to ensure that all transactions are recorded on a serially numbered document?

20 Is the method used for checking the numerical sequence appropriate (e.g. does it cater for changes in sequence and more than one sequence running at a time)?

21 Is a print-out of missing documents produced at regular intervals (e.g. weekly) or is a list of missing documents prepared regularly from the manual sequence check?

22 Does the sequence check ensure that all recorded transactions are reported if rejected?

23 Are there adequate procedures for investigation and, if necessary, correction of missing, duplicate or rejected transactions?

24 Are any necessary corrections approved by an independent responsible official?

One for one checking

25 Is there a control to ensure that all transactions are recorded?

26 Are there controls to ensure that all documents are submitted for processing (e.g. by checking against retained copy, or by manual sequence check)?

27 Are there controls to ensure that all transactions are input to the computer once and only once?

28 Is the method used in the program for the production of the print-out appropriate (e.g. does it contain details of all items that have been written to the file)?

29 Are there adequate procedures to investigate and, if necessary, correct missing, duplicate and rejected transactions identified by the one for one checking?

30 Are necessary corrections approved by an independent responsible official?

Accuracy of Input

Matching

1 If matching is used as the principal control to ensure the accuracy of input of any of the key data, list the key input fields and describe the control procedure.

2 Is there adequate reporting of mismatches?

3 Is there adequate reporting of forced matching (e.g. by terminal operators overriding mismatches)?

4 Is there adequate reporting of automatic processing despite significant discrepancies reported (e.g. write-offs outside certain tolerances, large price variances)?

5 Are all changes (before matching) to the control file approved?

6 Are there adequate procedures to investigate and correct differences or exceptions identified by matching controls?

7 Are any necessary corrections approved by an independent responsible official?

Batching

8 If batching is used as the principal control to ensure the accuracy of input of key data, list the key input fields covered by the batching process and describe the control procedure.

9 Are there controls to ensure that the data is accurately recorded prior to input?

10 Are predetermined control totals input and agreed by the computer with the accumulation of individual items accepted and, if so, is adequate evidence of this check printed out, or are they agreed manually to the total of accepted items accumulated and printed out by the computer?

11 Are there adequate procedures to investigate and correct differences, exceptions or rejections identified by the batching control?

12 Are any necessary corrections approved by an independent responsible official?

One for one checking

13 If one for one checking is used as the principal control to ensure the accuracy of input of key data, list the key input fields covered by the checking process and describe the control procedure.

14 Is the method used in the program for the production of the print-out appropriate (e.g. does it contain details of the key fields of items that have been written to the file)?

15 Are there adequate procedures to investigate and correct differences disclosed by one for one checking?

16 Are any necessary corrections approved by an independent responsible official?

Edit checks

17 If edit checks are used as the principal control to ensure the accuracy of input of key data, list the key input fields covered by the edit checks and the type of edit check.

18 Considering the significance of the data are the edit checks adequate to ensure the accuracy of the data?

19 Where operators are permitted to override edit checks are all uses of the override identified on override reports?

20 Are all differences and exceptions noted by the edit checks reported on exception reports?

21 Are there adequate procedures to investigate and correct differences or exceptions identified by the edit checks and override reports?

22 Are necessary corrections approved by an independent responsible official?

Authorisation of Transactions

Matching

1 Specify the key data used for authorisation by computer matching.

2 Review the answers to the CART for the data used to provide authorisation. Are there adequate controls to ensure that the stored data accessed in the matching process is complete and accurate?

3 Review the answers to the CART for the data used to provide authorisation. Are there adequate controls to ensure that the stored data accessed in the matching process is itself authorised?

4 Review the answers to the IT CART for Data File Security in relation to the data used to provide authorisation. Are there adequate controls to ensure that the stored data accessed in the matching process is secure?

5 Are reported failures to match investigated and, if necessary, corrected?

6 Are necessary corrections approved by an independent responsible official?

Manual authorisation

7 Are there controls to ensure that transactions are properly authorised by an independent responsible official?

8 Are there controls to ensure that no unauthorised alterations are made to authorised transactions?

9 Where applicable, is supporting documentation cancelled or suitably controlled to prevent subsequent re-use?

Selective authorisation

10 Are the procedures for identifying items needing approval adequate to identify all such transactions and print them on an exception report?

11 Are there controls to ensure that the transactions on the exception report are properly authorised by an independent responsible official?

12 Are there controls to ensure that no unauthorised alterations are made to the authorised transactions?

On-line authorisation

13 Are the procedures for identifying items needing approval adequate to identify all such transactions and route them to a file pending review?

14 Are there controls to ensure that the transactions on the file are properly authorised by an independent responsible official?

15 Are there controls to ensure that no unauthorised alterations are made to the authorised transactions?

16 Review the answers to the Data File Security section of the IT CART. Are the passwords which are used to release transactions from the file adequately controlled?

17 Review the answers to the Data File Security section of the IT CART. Do the passwords which are used to release transactions from the file reflect the appropriate authority limits?

18 Where applicable, is supporting documentation cancelled or suitably controlled to prevent subsequent re-use?

Generation of Data/Transactions

Generation of data

1 Identify the event that causes the transaction to be generated (e.g. input of a parameter such as a date, attainment of a condition such as the stock level falling below the re-order level), the key data used as a basis for the generation, and the programmed procedures that perform the generation.

2 For the key data outlined above, review the answers to the appropriate file and transaction sections of the CART. Are there adequate controls to ensure that the key data used as a basis for the generation of data is:

(a) complete and accurate;

(b) where applicable, authorised and kept secure?

3 For the programmed procedure that generates the data, if user controls are relied on to check the accuracy of the generation process, are these controls adequate?

4 Are there adequate controls to ensure that all:

(a) parameters relevant to the generation process are accurately input;

(b) generation runs are performed?

5 Are there adequate procedures to investigate and correct any differences or exceptions identified by the controls over the completeness and accuracy of generation?

6 Are the necessary corrections reviewed and approved by an independent responsible official?

Update of Data onto Files

Calculating

1 Is there any standing data, in addition to the transaction data input, used or referred to in processing? Identify the data involved. Ensure that the controls over the relevant files and transactions have been assessed.

2 Review the answers to the appropriate file and transaction sections of the CART for the standing data used in processing. Are there controls to ensure that the standing data used is complete and accurate and, where applicable, authorised and kept secure?

3 Where operators can override standing data (e.g. special pricing, credit limit overrides) are all uses of the override reported?

4 Is the method used in the program for performing calculations appropriate?

5 Are there adequate procedures to investigate and correct differences and exceptions reported, including reports of overrides of standing data?

6 Are any necessary corrections approved by an independent responsible official?

Input controls

7 Do input controls ensure completeness or accuracy of update to any file(s) updated by this transaction? Specify completeness and/or accuracy and identify the files and the key data elements.

8 Do the input controls adequately cover update to the files identified? Specify the control relied on.

User controls

9 Are there user controls over completeness or accuracy of update to any file(s) updated by this transaction? Specify completeness and/or accuracy and describe the control procedures. Identify the files and the key data elements covered by the user controls.

10 Are there adequate controls to ensure all transactions update the files?

11 If user controls are relied on to check the accuracy of update, are the user controls adequate?

12 Are there adequate procedures for investigation and correction of differences or exceptions identified by the control over update for completeness?

13 Are there adequate procedures for investigation and correction of differences or exceptions identified by the control over update for accuracy?

14 Are any necessary corrections approved by an independent responsible official?

Programmed procedures

15 If reliance is placed on IT controls to ensure the proper update of the files, review the IT CART. Are there controls to ensure that the programmed procedures continue to operate properly?

File Conversion

Standing data transfers

1 Are there adequate controls to ensure that standing data transferred from the old system to this file was:

(a) completely transferred;

(b) accurately transferred;

(c) if applicable, kept secure (preventing unauthorised changes)?

Transaction data transfers

2 Are there controls to ensure that transaction data from the old system was:

(a) completely transferred;

(b) accurately transferred;

(c) if applicable, kept secure (preventing unauthorised changes)?

Set-up of new data

3 Are there controls to ensure that new data, not present on the previous system, has been calculated or otherwise obtained and:

(a) completely set up;

(b) accurately set up (specify key data of accounting significance);

(c) authorised?

Final approval

4 Were the final results of the conversion process approved (e.g. review and sign-off of above procedures)?

IT CART

Implementation Controls

Systems developed in-house

Overall management of system development

1 Is performance against implementation plans monitored and are

excessive variances identified and suitably investigated (e.g. by a steering group)?

2 Are the following people involved to an adequate extent in the key stages of the design, implementation and final approval of new systems:

(a) users;

(b) relevant data processing personnel;

(c) others (e.g. quality assurance)?

Design of systems

3 Are there controls to ensure that the design of systems (i.e. wholly internal designs or tailoring for packages) is appropriate to the organisation's accounting and control requirements (e.g. user and data processing personnel review and approval of specifications, prototyping)?

4 Is the documentation of systems and programs of a sufficient standard to provide a basis for future maintenance?

5 Are the following prepared and issued as part of the systems documentation:

(a) operating procedures;

(b) back-up requirements;

(c) user clerical procedures?

Design and programming standards

6 Are appropriate design and programming standards enforced to ensure that:

(a) new systems interact correctly with existing systems;

(b) programs interact correctly with system software (e.g. appropriate options specified, appropriate response to errors detected by the system software);

(c) adequate control features are built into new systems?

7 Is there adequate supervision of the programming of new systems?

Testing

8 Are programs and systems adequately tested as regards:

(a) the methods of testing used;

(b) the scope of testing?

9 Are the testing procedures performed or checked by persons other than those involved in writing the programs?

10 Are the testing procedures adequate to prevent any unauthorised coding from being inserted into programs during development?

11 Are modifications to specifications and programs identified during the design and development process:

(a) approved;

(b) tested to the same degree as the originals?

12 Are new systems subject to an adequate live test period (e.g. parallel or pilot running)?

Cataloguing

13 Is the transfer of new programs from test to production status formally approved by:

(a) users;

(b) relevant data processing personnel;

(c) others (e.g. steering group, quality assurance)?

14 Are there controls to ensure that:

(a) the versions of programs taken into all production libraries are the current tested and approved versions (e.g. by use of program library software);

(b) the correct versions are updated to all relevant operational libraries (e.g. source and object, different locations);

(c) no unauthorised changes can be made to the authorised programs between the time they are tested and approved and the time they are catalogued (e.g. transfer to intermediate secured library immediately after testing)?

Vendor supplied systems

Specification and selection of packages

(The following questions assume that only minor modifications are made in-house to vendor supplied systems. Where more extensive changes are made, questions 1 to 14 on in-house systems should be answered.)

15 Are there controls to ensure that:

(a) the systems and options selected meet the organisation's accounting and control requirements (e.g. statement of requirements prepared and approved by users and data processing personnel, trial periods);

(b) any modifications required to adapt standard packages to these requirements have been identified, clearly specified and approved by users and data processing personnel?

16 Does the contract with the vendor:

(a) provide for adequate support for the package over its expected useful life, including any necessary changes required by legislation and business developments;

(b) allow the organisation to continue to use the package in the event of the vendor becoming insolvent, or indemnify it if the vendor proves not to have adequate title to sell/lease software originally produced by a third party?

Testing and implementation of packages

17 Are new systems adequately tested (e.g. parallel or pilot running)?

18 Are the following people involved to an adequate extent in the implementation of the system, including final approval where appropriate:

(a) users;

(b) data processing personnel;

(c) others (e.g. quality assurance)?

System Maintenance Controls

In-house maintenance

Completeness of changes

1 Are there controls to ensure that:

(a) all requests for system amendment are considered for action;

(b) all approved requests are implemented on a timely basis (e.g. entry in a register and investigation of outstanding changes)?

Validity of changes

2 If modifications are made to existing systems during the year, are there adequate procedures to ensure that systems, operations and clerical documentation is properly updated?

3 Is there adequate involvement in and approval of system modifications by:

(a) users, to ensure that the modifications are appropriate;

(b) relevant data processing personnel (e.g. chief programmer, operations manager, database support, network controller)?

Testing

4 If modifications are made to existing systems during the year, are there controls to ensure that modifications are properly tested?

5 Are the testing procedures performed or checked by persons other than those involved in writing the programs?

6 Are the testing procedures adequate to prevent any unauthorised coding from being inserted into programs during their modification?

Vendor maintained packages

Validity and testing

7 If vendors make modifications to existing systems during the year, are there controls to ensure that:

(a) the modifications are appropriate to the users' requirements;

(b) the amended systems are adequately tested;

(c) systems, operations, back-up and user documentation is appropriately updated?

8 Is there adequate involvement in, and approval of, modifications made by vendors by:

(a) users;

(b) relevant data processing personnel;

(c) other (e.g. quality assurance)?

Cataloguing

9 In respect of both in-house maintained and vendor maintained

software, is the transfer of amended programs from test to production status formally approved by:

(a) users;

(b) relevant data processing personnel;

(c) others (e.g. steering group, quality assurance)?

10 Are there controls to ensure that:

(a) the versions of programs taken into all production libraries are the current tested and approved versions (e.g. by use of program library software);

(b) the correct versions are updated to all relevant operational libraries (e.g. source and object, different locations);

(c) no unauthorised changes can be made to the authorised programs between the time they are tested and approved and the time they are catalogued (e.g. transfer to intermediate secured library immediately after testing)?

Back-up and recovery of programs

11 Are there adequate controls to ensure that:

(a) programs taken into production are also copied and stored (e.g. in a disaster store) such that the current, authorised versions will be used as a basis for future maintenance and disaster recovery;

(b) production program libraries are regularly backed up, together with a record of changes between back-ups?

12 Are there controls to ensure that program libraries are recovered properly after a failure and that no errors are introduced by the recovery process?

13 If immediate modifications are made to programs during emergencies are there controls to ensure that the changes are correctly made and approved (e.g. by retroactively applying system development and maintenance procedures for programs)?

Program and Data File Security Controls

In practice, separate CART sections are used for program and data file security controls. They are combined here in view of the similarity of the questions asked.

Software Access Controls

1 List the software options (e.g. library package, passwords, security package, blocking of terminal capabilities) used to prevent unauthorised access to:

(a) the system;

(b) program libraries/data files;

(c) programs/data elements.

2 Is there an adequate combination of software procedures and manual action to:

(a) prevent unauthorised accesses and report and investigate persistent attempts to bypass the access controls; or

(b) report and investigate unauthorised accesses?

3 Are there adequate controls over:

(a) assigning access rights to appropriate individuals in the organisation;

(b) granting and revoking authorised access on the system (e.g. user-IDs or passwords);

(c) allocating and withdrawing special facilities from users (e.g. ability to use certain utilities, higher levels of clearance in a hierarchy);

(d) protecting the security tables stored on the system which are used by the system to verify authenticity (e.g. password control files, communication control tables can be one-way encrypted)?

4 Where passwords (or other codes) are used to identify individuals to the system as authorised users, are there adequate procedures to ensure that the passwords are:

(a) periodically changed;

(b) kept secret (e.g. not written down or displayed on screen);

(c) not easily guessed;

(d) cancelled for terminated or transferred employees?

5 Are there adequate procedures to ensure that the ability to use the following access control functions is itself restricted to appropriate staff with no other incompatible duties:

(a) granting or changing system identities (3(b));

(b) granting or changing the ability to use special facilities (3(c));

(c) changing passwords or other identification codes (4)?

6 Are there adequate procedures to prevent unauthorised public access via dial-up (e.g. use of dial-back, dial-up access restricted to non-confidential information)?

7 Are the procedures in 1 to 6 above subject to adequate supervision by a responsible official?

Physical access controls

8 Are there controls to restrict physical access to the following:

(a) terminals;

(b) computer room;

(c) hardware outside the computer room (e.g. network switchgear, modems) where unauthorised peripherals could be attached;

(d) communications lines (e.g. cables should be sealed in ducts outside the hardware area to prevent tapping or reading by service equipment);

(e) other (specify)?

Note: Questions (c) and (d) evaluate controls to prevent sophisticated frauds being committed by tapping private networks. Unacceptable exposure in this area is likely to occur only for sensitive networks such as bank fund transfer systems.

9 Are there adequate controls over:

(a) granting and revoking the means of permitting physical access (e.g. key, security badge, combination number);

(b) where applicable, unissued physical access permits, badges or keys?

10 Is the person responsible for controlling physical access in 9 above independent of programming, system software and accounting control functions?

11 Are the procedures in 8 to 10 above subject to adequate supervision by a responsible official?

Off-line programs and data

12 Where programs and data, including back-up copies, are physically controlled:

(a) are there adequate records to identify programs/data uniquely (e.g. external labels);

(b) are there controls over the issue and return of programs/data files:

(i) to and from the physical library;

(ii) to and from the store to be used for recovery in the event of a disaster;

(iii) to and from the installation;

(c) do the storage methods prevent the unauthorised removal of programs/data?

13 Is the librarian function performed by a person independent of computer operation and programming responsibilities?

14 Are the procedures in 12 and 13 above subject to adequate supervision by a responsible official?

Utilities

15 If utilities or other special programs can be used to change application programs/data by bypassing normal software access restrictions:

(a) are there adequate procedures to identify all programs with this special status;

(b) is the ability to use such programs restricted to appropriate, authorised personnel;

(c) are there adequate controls to log and report the use, or attempted use, of such programs and for a review of such reports by a responsible official to determine and investigate unauthorised access?

Bypassing of normal access controls

16 Where it is necessary to bypass normal security and access controls (e.g. emergencies or maintenance of program libraries by outside software support, such as vendors, through dial-up):

(a) is there appropriate authorisation before or after the event;

(b) are there adequate controls to:

(i) ensure that security is subsequently reinstated;

(ii) prevent or report and investigate unauthorised changes to data?

User programming

17 Where users are permitted to use utilities or high level programming languages which can change data:

(a) are there controls either to prevent the unauthorised use of this facility or to report and investigate unauthorised use, or attempts to use it;

(b) are there controls to report or prevent unauthorised use of programs written by an authorised user?

Division of duties

18 Are there adequate controls to prevent:

(a) computer operators, schedulers, data input staff and other operations personnel from gaining access to program documentation and development libraries;

(b) development personnel from gaining access to the computer operations area;

(c) systems implementation personnel responsible for the cataloguing function from gaining access to program documentation and development libraries, and from entering the operations area or performing computer operations functions?

Computer Operations Controls

Scheduling

1 Are there controls to ensure that:

(a) proper schedules of jobs/programs are prepared;

(b) jobs/programs are run in accordance with the schedules;

(c) any departures from the schedules are documented and approved?

Job set-up and execution

2 Are there adequate procedures for:

(a) setting up batch jobs;

(b) loading on-line application systems;

(c) loading system software?

3 Are there controls to prevent or detect and investigate unauthorised changes to approved job set-up instructions?

4 Are there controls to ensure that control statements and parameters used in processing are in accordance with the approved procedures (e.g. independent check of run instructions, review of output JCL listings)?

5 Is there appropriate written approval, including user involvement where appropriate, of:

(a) variations in parameters and control statements that may affect the way a batch job or an on-line system runs (e.g. dates, currency rates, period end routines);

(b) departures from authorised set-up procedures (e.g. use of programs from a test library for production)?

6 Are the procedures in 2 to 5 above subject to adequate supervision by a responsible official?

Use of correct data files

7 Are there controls to ensure that:

(a) the correct data files are used (e.g. software label checking, generation data sets, use of a tape management system, user check of volume/serial numbers, controlling manual overrides which bypass label checking);

(b) where applicable, all volumes of a multi-volume file are used (e.g. software checking of file and volume labels);

(c) exceptions are reported and investigated (e.g. where all volumes of a multi-volume file were not used)?

Operator actions

8 Are there controls over:

(a) initial loading and subsequent use of system software, including amendments to parameters while the system is running (e.g. re-allocation of physical/logical terminals, changes to logging options, changes to program libraries);

(b) the execution of application programs;

(c) compliance with other standard operating procedures?

9 Is there adequate identification and reporting of:

(a) system failures;

(b) restart and recovery;

(c) emergency situations;

(d) other unusual situations?

10 Are operator actions in the event of the incidents in 9 above reviewed for appropriateness and to ensure that the results of processing were not adversely affected (e.g. review of logs and incident reports, daily problem meeting)?

11 Is there appropriate supervision of operators at all times, including shifts outside the normal working period?

Logs of activity

12 Where manual or automated logs are relied upon for recording system or operator activities, are there adequate controls over the completeness and accuracy of these logs?

13 Are changes made to logs (or to the method of logging), appropriately authorised?

14 Are the logs adequately reviewed and unusual situations investigated?

15 Are the results of the investigation and correction of unusual situations and resulting operator actions reviewed and approved by a responsible official?

Note: Where operators have access to utility programs which can be used to change application programs/data by bypassing normal software access restrictions answer question 15 of the program and data file security section.

Back-up and recovery of data

16 Are there adequate controls to:

(a) back-up and store independently copies of all data at appropriate intervals;

(b) log or save activity so that the status of data files at the time of failure is known?

17 Are there controls to ensure that data files are recovered properly after a processing failure and that no errors are introduced by the recovery process?

18 If modifications are made to data after failures or during emergencies (e.g. use of utilities to correct transmission errors), are there adequate procedures to ensure that the changes are made correctly and approved (e.g. by retroactively applying user controls over adjustments)?

19 Is there adequate user involvement to ensure that proper recovery from failures takes place (e.g. notification to users by the data processing department that major recoveries have taken place)?

20 Are the procedures in 16 to 19 above subject to adequate supervision by a responsible official?

System Software Controls

Technical Support Organisation

1 Are staff employed in the technical support function only on the basis of either:

(a) thorough enquiry into the validity of references; or

(b) assessment of the integrity of the individual in the course of earlier duties in the organisation?

Implementation

The questions assume that, in each area, organisations make use of vendor supplied software packages. If such software is developed internally, the auditor should enquire in more detail into the design, development and maintenance of the software, using the implementation and systems maintenance sections of the CART, as appropriate.

2 Are there controls to ensure that system software packages, options, and fixes selected are appropriate to the organisation's requirements?

3 Are there controls to ensure that the tailoring of system software by the technical support group is:

(a) designed to meet the organisation's requirements;

(b) reviewed or otherwise tested prior to implementation;

(c) documented to a sufficient standard to provide a basis for subsequent maintenance?

4 Is new system software, including any tailoring, subjected to an adequate live test to ensure that it does not adversely affect existing applications or system software functions?

5 Are the following prepared and issued as part of the system software documentation:

(a) operating procedures;

(b) back-up requirements and disaster store/emergency plan procedures?

6 Are the following people involved to an adequate extent in the implementation of new or amended system software, including final approval:

(a) technical support management;

(b) computer operations management;

(c) other relevant data processing personnel (e.g. network manager, database administrator);

(d) users, where applicable?

Security and back-up

7 Are system software program libraries and files (e.g. logs, control tables) protected against unauthorised access?

8 Are there controls to prevent system software programmers from gaining access to the computer operations area, data files, and application programs?

9 Are there adequate procedures to ensure that system software libraries are backed up regularly together with a record of changes between back-ups?

10 Are there controls to ensure that system software libraries are recovered properly after a processing failure, and that no errors are introduced by the recovery process?

11 If modifications are made to system software after failures or during emergencies, are there adequate procedures to ensure that the changes are made correctly and approved (e.g. by retroactively testing or authorising the change)?

Questions 1 to 11 deal with the implementation and security of all system software. The remainder of this section is divided into questions on each major function of system software. The auditor should answer the relevant questions in each area where he wishes to place reliance on controls.

Operating systems

Vendor maintenance
Questions 12 to 15 should be answered if the operating system is maintained by vendors.

12 Are there controls to ensure that modifications (e.g. fixes) are appropriate to the installation's requirements (e.g. analysis of vendor announcements by a responsible official, approval by a competent official)?

13 Are there controls to ensure that the modifications function as expected (e.g. testing, review of software update log)?

14 Are there controls to ensure that operating documentation and the record of modifications are properly updated?

15 Are the following people involved to an adequate extent in the above procedures, including final approval of changes:

(a) technical support management;

(b) computer operations management;

(c) other relevant data processing personnel (e.g. data processing manager);

(d) users, where applicable?

Internal maintenance
Questions 16 to 19 should be answered if modifications or enhancements are made to the operating system by the organisation's staff.

16 Are there controls to ensure that modifications or enhancements are appropriate to the installation's requirements (e.g. analysis of vendor announcements by a responsible official, approval by a competent official)?

17 Are modifications subjected to adequate testing to ensure that they do not adversely affect existing application or system software functions?

18 Are there controls to ensure that operating documentation and the record of modifications are properly updated?

19 Are the following people involved to an adequate extent in the above procedures, including final approval of changes:

(a) technical support management;

(b) computer operations management;

(c) other relevant data processing personnel (e.g. data processing manager);

(d) users, where applicable?

Database management systems

Questions 20 to 27 should be answered if a database management system (DBMS) is in use.

20 Is there a database administrator and/or a database administration function?

21 Are there controls to ensure that all modifications and fixes to the DBMS:

(a) are appropriate to the installation's requirements;

(b) function as expected (e.g. review of subsequent operations or other testing);

(c) are recorded, and operating and other documentation is properly updated?

22 Are logical views of the database (e.g. sub-schemas):

(a) adequately documented;

(b) allocated by the database administrator only to authorised users;

(c) allocated such that ownership of data elements is clearly defined?

23 Have DBMS logging options been selected such that, in the event of failures, the database can be recovered without loss or corruption of data?

24 Is the integrity of the internal pointers and indices periodically verified?

25 Are any database integrity failures identified in 24 above investigated and appropriate corrective action taken?

26 Is the database periodically reviewed:

(a) to identify redundant (duplicate) information;

(b) to ensure that any duplicated information is consistent (e.g. that employee data duplicated in both payroll and personnel systems is identical)?

27 Are the procedures in 21 to 26 above subject to adequate supervision by a responsible official?

Telecommunications and networks

If telecommunications and/or network facilities are present, answer appropriate questions from 28 to 34 below.

28 Is there a network or telecommunications support and control function?

29 Are there controls to ensure that all modifications and fixes to the telecommunications and networking software:

(a) are appropriate to the installation's requirements;

(b) function as expected (e.g. review of subsequent operations or other testing);

(c) are recorded, and operating and other documentation is properly updated?

30 Are network facilities:

(a) adequately documented;

(b) allocated by the network manager only to authorised users?

31 If confidential or sensitive information is transmitted through public carrier networks (e.g. by leased line), are suitable protection methods used to prevent or detect unauthorised access to transmissions, either as a part of the carrier's security or by independent methods (e.g. use of encryption)?

32 Are there adequate software checks, either by the installation or as part of the carrier's service, to detect and correct transmission errors?

33 Is the network sufficiently resilient to compensate for the following without significant degradation of security or of service to the users:

(a) communications line failures;

(b) partial network failures (e.g. when one computer fails)?

34 Are the procedures in 28 to 33 above subject to adequate supervision by a responsible official?

Security software

Questions 35 to 38 should be answered if software access control is present.

35 Is a responsible official independent of computer operations, systems development and system software in charge of security?

36 Are there controls to ensure that all modifications and fixes to the security software:

(a) are appropriate to the installation's requirements;

(b) function as expected (e.g. review of subsequent operations or other testing);

(c) are recorded, and operating and other documentation is properly updated?

37 Have the appropriate options in relation to logging and reporting of access and violations been selected?

38 Are there controls to ensure that:

(a) the security software protection can be removed only by appropriately authorised personnel (e.g. the security officer in 35 above);

(b) when the software protection has been removed, other access controls prevent the unauthorised modification of programs and data files (e.g. software protection removed only when all on-line services are down and physical access procedures can be relied on)?

Personal computer facilities

Questions 39 to 42 should be answered if personal computing facilities are provided to users, usually management, to assist them in their work. Such facilities would normally comprise programming and report generation capability.

39 Is there a central information centre responsible for:

(a) selecting, providing, and supporting user programming facilities;

(b) monitoring the proportion of total computing resources utilised by user computing;

(c) provision of training to users?

40 Are there controls to ensure that all modifications and fixes to user programming aids:

(a) are appropriate to the installation's requirements;

(b) function as expected (e.g. review of subsequent operations or other testing);

(c) are recorded, and operating and other documentation is properly updated;

(d) are drawn to the attention of users, when applicable?

41 If programs developed by individual users/user groups are either proposed for wider distribution or produce files or reports for use by other users/user groups, are such programs subjected to a quality assurance review to ensure that:

(a) there is a clear written description of the program objectives;

(b) the programs correspond to the descriptions in (a);

(c) documentation of the programs is adequate to provide a basis for subsequent maintenance;

(d) there are clear written operating procedures?

42 Are there controls to prevent or detect unauthorised change, whether accidental or deliberate, to programs or data used for personal computing?

5

Evaluation of Controls: Application Controls

Introduction

5.01 In this chapter and Chapters 6, 7 and 8 the detailed control considerations in computer systems that are relevant to the auditor and how they can be evaluated using the CART questionnaire described in Chapter 4 are considered. Application controls are dealt with in this chapter and IT controls in Chapters 6, 7 and 8. During the discussion in this chapter reference may usefully be made to the questions included in Appendix A to Chapter 4. This chapter is written from the point of view of the auditor rather than those concerned in the design of systems. As a result, it should not be viewed as a statement of either all, or the best, control techniques that should be used for any particular system. However, there are certain overall design concepts which it may be helpful to discuss, before considering the controls in detail.

Design Concepts

Control structure

5.02 The control structure adopted for each application should take account of the whole sequence of processing from the time that transactions occur, through each stage of processing and recording the transactions in master files to the production and use of output from the system, including both screen based and printed output. In particular, the system of control should include control procedures carried out as a result of the receipt of information output from the system, for example, the investigation of reported exceptions.

5.03 In the past it has often been the practice for much of the processing of a transaction to be carried out manually, with the computer involved in only a part of the processing such as the recording of the completed transaction in a computerised ledger. The present trend is for the computer to carry out much more of the processing. Frequently transactions are input to the computer at a very early stage using terminals, with most of the subsequent processing and recording performed by the computer. In some cases transactions are input to computer terminals as they occur, without being recorded beforehand on any document. In such systems a substantial number of control features which would be difficult or time-consuming to carry out manually are incorporated within computer programs, for example edit checks. However, in these circumstances, where the greater part of processing and controls rely on the computer, it is essential that controls are designed as an integral part of the system rather than being added later as an after-thought, or as a result of external pressure, for example from an auditor.

5.04 Once the requirements of the whole system of control for any application have been established, it becomes necessary to see how these can be satisfied, bearing in mind the wide range of control techniques available and the differences which exist in complexity, efficacy and expense. In particular, allowance can often be made for a control weakness at one point by the inclusion of an appropriate control at another stage in processing. The object is to ensure that the overall system of control is effective.

Standards of control

5.05 When designing a system of control, it is often difficult, on the one hand, to ensure that no vital control has been omitted and, on the other hand, to avoid controls for their own sake. In particular, consideration has to be given to the real purpose of each control and a balanced judgement made between the cost of operating the control and the risk of any loss that might be experienced if it were omitted.

Types of data to be controlled

5.06 The distinction between **standing data** and **transaction data** has already been made in Chapter 3. In general, an error in a single item of transaction data will have limited effect, whereas an error in standing data, which may be used in the processing of many transactions, may have more far-reaching effects. It is therefore usual for higher standards of control to be appropriate for standing data than for transaction data.

5.07 The different data fields within a record may also vary in the degree to which standards of accuracy and extent of checking are important. Transactions will normally contain some data which requires to be converted into financial terms, for example the quantity of an item sold, and some which is only included for reference purposes, for example a customer order number. Although a higher standard of accuracy may usually be appropriate for the financial data than for the data included for reference purposes only, reference data can also be of major importance, as is discussed later in this chapter.

5.08 The factors set out in paragraphs 5.06 and 5.07 need to be taken into account by the auditor in his evaluation of internal control in order to ensure that any recommendations he makes to management are both desirable and practicable.

Application Controls

5.09 Application controls can be defined as all those controls and procedures designed to ensure that data on files is properly maintained between transaction updates (**file controls**) and that valid transactions, and only valid transactions, are processed and recorded completely and accurately in the accounting records (**transaction controls**). They can be conveniently considered under the following headings which correspond, where appropriate, to the main groupings of questions in the CART:

- File continuity.
- Asset protection.
- Completeness of input.
- Accuracy of input.
- Authorisation of transactions.
- Computer-generated data.
- Update of data onto files.

Except where specifically mentioned, the considerations are similar for both standing and transaction data.

File continuity

5.10 Controls over the continuity of stored data are designed to ensure that, once data is updated to a file, the data remains correct and current on the file. Control may be exercised at both the file total level and over the details stored on the file. The CART includes separate questions for each of these levels.

File continuity at the total level

5.11 File continuity controls at thc total level are designed to ensure that:

(a) The file carried forward from one update process is the file brought forward to the next update process.

(b) In the event of a processing failure the file can be promptly recovered to its proper state.

5.12 In computer systems there may be several versions of a file in existence and controls are needed to ensure that the correct version is used for updating. In addition, failures in processing and recovery therefrom may introduce errors into the data. The most effective control technique to achieve (a) and (b) above is normally the reconciliation of control totals of the data on the file. The reconciliation of independently maintained control totals to an accumulation of items in a file is illustrated in Figure 42.

5.13 The total of items in the file may be reconciled to a manually maintained control account. The way in which such a control would work is described in the section on updating controls (paragraph 5.93). Alternatively, the control total can be maintained and checked by the computer in the following manner:

(a) Totals of items processed through the normal, authorised system should be accumulated at the time or before the principal input control is exercised. These totals should be added to a control total stored in a computer file.

(b) Periodically the items on the file to be controlled should be added up, and their total compared to the control total by the computer.

(c) The computer should print out adequate evidence to prove to the users that reconciliation has been achieved satisfactorily. This should include the control total brought forward from the previous reconciliation, the total of items processed since then, the final control total and the accumulated total of items on the file.

(d) The brought forward totals should be checked manually to the carried forward totals on the previous report. This is necessary because a programmed reconciliation will not normally identify that the opening balance is the same as the closing balance when the last reconciliation took place, and

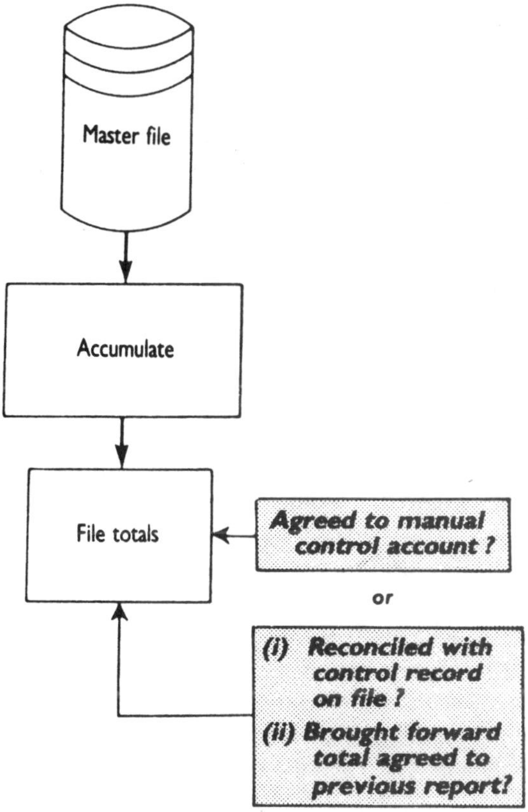

FIG. 42. Reconciliation of file totals (para. 5.12)

unauthorised processing and resulting alterations to control totals may have occurred. These reconciliation procedures are illustrated in Figure 42.

5.14 A programmed reconciliation of control totals will provide protection against the loss of data under most circumstances. However, as with the manual reconciliation of control totals, it will not detect alterations which do not change the control total. An example of this is where the control total is the total value of all balances in a ledger and the alteration has the effect of transferring an amount from one account within the ledger to another. Furthermore it will not detect an alteration to the data where a corresponding change has been made to the control total. A simple example of this occurs when both data and control totals have been amended by processing an unauthorised transaction. Protection against these sorts of risks must be provided by other controls, for example, controls over continuity of the details on the file and over protection of assets.

5.15 The frequency of file reconciliation procedures will depend largely on the nature of processing. Where file updating is by direct access methods, particularly in real-time systems, reconciliation procedures are likely to be carried out periodically, either when the data on the discs is reorganised or using a special program designed for the purpose. The latter method is the one normally used where the data is organised on files using database techniques. When file updating is sequential, usually in on-line or batch systems, it will be normal for reconciliations to be carried out during each processing run because all records are read and can easily be accumulated.

5.16 The reconciliation of control totals outlined in the preceding paragraphs should be applied to files containing transaction data and standing data. For files of transaction data the value balance on the account usually forms the basis for the control. For files of standing data the control may be based on the more important data fields, such as prices and interest rates, or even on the total number of items on the file. For example, the total number of employees on a payroll file adjusted for new starters and leavers might be used, or the total number of suppliers' accounts on a suppliers' masterfile. Such a control would also assist in protecting against computer fraud since the addition of unauthorised employees or suppliers and the generation of computer produced payments to them is a known form of fraud in computer systems.

5.17 Where the reconciliation of control totals is not carried out it may be that other controls performed by users will ensure continuity of the totals on the file. For example, the matching of cash received to unpaid accounts receivable might be adequate to disclose errors if continuity of processing was disrupted. Finally, computer operations controls over the loading and processing of computer files may be adequate to ensure continuity of files at the total level. These controls are discussed in paragraphs 8.25 to 8.32 of Chapter 8.

5.18 The CART includes separate questions for control reconciliations performed by the computer and those performed manually. The questions for computer reconciliations are as follows:

"*1. Is the total of items on file regularly reconciled by computer to an independently established total on a suitably timely basis (e.g. by computer agreement to a control record)?*

2. Is the computer control total stored on an independent control file, so that any use of an incorrect file or loss of data from the file would be detected?

3. Are all differences reported?

4. Are there adequate procedures to investigate and correct differences disclosed by the reconciliation?

5. Is the investigation and correction of differences performed or checked by persons other than those involved in computer operations?

6. Are the results of the control total procedures reviewed and approved by an independent responsible official?"

5.19 The following questions regarding other user controls that ensure the continuity of file totals are asked in the CART:

"*1. Are user procedures adequate to identify the use of the wrong version of the file and are appropriate actions taken to correct any errors identified?*

2. Do the user procedures operate so that all errors would be identified on a suitably timely basis?

3. Are there adequate procedures to investigate and correct those errors?

4. Are the user procedures either performed or checked by persons other than those involved in computer operations?

5. Are the results of the user procedures reviewed and approved by an independent responsible official?"

File continuity at the detailed level

5.20 File continuity controls at the detailed level may assist in detecting:

(a) Errors in the recorded data arising from inaccuracies in the recording and processing of transactions.

(b) Omissions or the failure to initiate and record all transactions.

(c) The processing of transactions that should not have been recorded, for example, duplicate items.

(d) Data that is no longer current or that requires some action to be taken, for example, overdue accounts receivable or excess inventory.

5.21 The presence of these controls at the detailed level is desirable in the internal control structure. Where they are present and effective they may provide the auditor with considerable assurance about the reliability of the balances on the file and enable work on other controls to be reduced. However, the possible control techniques will vary significantly according to the nature of the file and application, and such controls may not detect all of the above conditions. This does not necessarily result in a control weakness but implies that greater reliance is being placed on control totals, transaction controls and data file security controls.

5.22 Techniques that may constitute controls over the continuity of details on a file include:

- Reviews of management information.
- Matching.
- Independent comparisons with physical assets or third party evidence.

Reviews of management information

5.23 The detailed review and follow up of reports by line managers may provide assurance about the balances on a file. To be effective as a control over details on a file the technique must operate at a detailed level. Examples are the detailed review by a credit controller of an accounts receivable aged analysis and the review by a departmental manager of a detailed report by product line of sales and inventory. For such controls to be effective the management information reviewed must itself be reliable and there must be suitable follow up of the results of the reviews.

5.24 The CART includes the following questions on reviews of management information:

"*1. Is there management information which is relevant to the control of the details on the file? Describe the control procedures and identify the key data covered. Identify the audit objectives (completeness, accuracy, existence) affected by the control technique.*

2. Is operating information prepared on a regular basis (e.g. summaries, exception reports, overall reconciliations or performance indicators)?

3. *Where these operating reports depend on comparisons to forecasts, budgets, prior periods, other departments or divisions or industry statistics, are there appropriate procedures to ensure that the comparative figures were prepared on the same assumptions and that differences in assumptions and conditions are highlighted and explained (e.g. changes in business, organisation, accounting systems or policies, unusual events or different periods)?*
4. *Where these operating reports depend on comparisons to forecasts, budgets, prior periods, other departments or divisions or industry statistics, are there appropriate procedures to ensure that the correct comparative figures have been accurately obtained and compared?*
5. *Are these operating reports prepared at a sufficient level of detail to pick up all significant errors in the financial accounting data?*
6. *Are the analyses performed using financial accounting data or if the analyses are prepared using the operational systems and data (e.g. items evaluated at standard cost) is this operational data reconciled to the financial accounting data?*
7. *Are there written explanations of all significant results, variances and exceptions?*
8. *Are these explanations independently reviewed and the causes of major exceptions properly investigated?*"

Matching

5.25 The technique of matching transaction data to data stored on files is a common control technique in computer systems. It frequently forms part of the controls over the processing of transactions and may assist in achieving the control objectives of completeness and accuracy of input and updating and the authorisation of transactions. The technique is illustrated in detail in the section on completeness of input (paragraph 5.37). Where the control involves the clearance of open items on a file by matching with external evidence the technique may also provide considerable assurance that the details on the file are reliable.

5.26 An example may be the matching of cash received from customers with open items on an accounts receivable file. The regular receipt and matching of cash to open items will reveal errors in the details on the file, and the absence of significant errors provides some assurance on the reliability of the details on the file. The control would in any case be identified when evaluating transaction controls but it is helpful to identify it separately as a control over file details in view of the fact that it may provide the auditor with significant assurance about the account balance. It will only do this if the evidence matched is received from an external source. Matching two internal items would not provide such assurance although it might still form an effective detailed control over transactions. Effective control will also require the follow up of outstanding and mismatched items.

5.27 The following questions regarding matching controls over file details are included in the CART:

"*1. Are there matching controls which are relevant to the control of the details on the file? Describe the control procedures and identify the key data covered. Identify the audit objectives (completeness, accuracy, existence) affected by the control technique.*

2. Does the design of the matching process ensure that all mismatched items are appropriately reported (e.g. cash is matched to sales invoices by invoice number rather than being allocated against the oldest invoice for a customer)?

3. Is a report of all items outstanding for an unreasonable length of time or a suitable aged analysis of all items on the file prepared at appropriate intervals (e.g. receiving memoranda, unmatched cash)?

4. Are there adequate procedures to investigate and, if necessary, correct all clearing transactions rejected as mismatches (e.g. purchase invoices outstanding not matched to receiving memoranda, unmatched cash)?

5. Are there adequate procedures to investigate and, if necessary, correct long outstanding items (e.g. receiving memoranda outstanding, long outstanding invoices)?

6. Are all corrections arising from investigation of mismatches and long outstanding items approved by an independent responsible official?"

Independent comparisons with physical assets or third party evidence

5.28 The independent comparison of records on the file with physical assets or third party evidence may provide significant assurance to the auditor concerning the reliability of the balances on the file. An example of comparison to physical assets is the counting of inventory items and checking of the results against inventory balances as recorded on the file. Third party evidence which could be compared to records on a file could include such things as suppliers' statements and investment confirmations from a bank. A common control for standing data is the regular cyclical checking of the data on file with independent source data. To be effective as a control the comparisons would need to be made at suitably frequent intervals and to cover a sufficient proportion of the items on the file. Procedures to investigate and correct differences revealed by the comparisons would also be required.

5.29 The CART includes the following questions on the independent comparison of file details with physical assets or third party evidence:

"*1. Are there independent comparisons which are relevant to the control of the details on the file? Describe the control procedures and identify the key data covered. Identify the audit objectives (completeness, accuracy, existence) affected by the control technique.*

2. Are the records independently compared, at appropriate intervals, to the physical assets (e.g. inventory) or third party evidence (e.g. loan certificates or suppliers' statements) providing an adequate basis for rechecking the completeness and accuracy of the recorded data?

3. Are these comparison procedures adequate to identify possible errors or omissions in the data on file?

4. Are there adequate procedures to investigate and, if necessary, correct any differences disclosed?

5. Does the comparison provide sufficient coverage of data on the file (i.e. the proportion, by number and value, of items on the file checked in this way)?

6. Are the results of the procedures for comparison to physical assets or third party data, identified above, reviewed and approved by an independent responsible official?"

Asset protection

5.30 It is important that the assets represented by the balances on files are suitably protected. There are two aspects to such asset protection, as follows:

(a) Custody of assets. Assets should be physically secure and asset movements should only take place when they are properly approved and recorded.

(b) Data file security. Security over stored data must be sufficient to prevent misappropriation of assets or manipulation of financial data through unauthorised access to data files.

5.31 Asset custody is relevant where the account balance represents a physical asset, such as cash, inventory and investments. Asset custody controls also depend upon an adequate division of duties. Data file security is relevant where there is sensitive information or data, such as price files, the manipulation of which could result in the loss of assets. Data file security is considered in detail in Chapter 7.

5.32 The CART includes questions on the custody of assets and a cross reference to the data file security section of the IT CART The relevant questions are as follows:

"*1. Are there adequate procedures over the custody of assets between their receipt and their initial recording (e.g. receipt of goods into a secure area)?*

2. Are assets protected from unauthorised access, use and misappropriation (e.g. locks, safes, guards, warehouse and site security)?

3. Are all asset movements supported by adequate written authorisations?

4. Are the persons responsible for the custody of assets, or for authorising their movement, persons other than those who maintain the related accounting records?

5. Review the answers to the data file security section of the IT CART. Are the procedures adequate to ensure the security of significant data relating to assets susceptible to theft?"

Completeness of input

5.33 It is important that all transactions are input to the relevant master files. This requirement is referred to as the completeness of input. It should not be confused with the accuracy of input which is dealt with in paragraphs 5.48 to 5.60. The reason for the distinction is one of convenience in that different techniques are often used to control, on the one hand, completeness and, on the other, accuracy. Completeness means simply all the transactions, whereas accuracy is concerned with the data of each transaction. It follows from this definition that the controls that ensure the resubmission of rejected data relate to completeness.

5.34 In practice, there is a number of control techniques by which the completeness of input is usually controlled. In the following paragraphs the various control techniques – computer matching, computer sequence check, batch totals and checking of print-outs – are outlined, together with examples of the relevant questions in the CART.

Selecting the controls on which to place reliance

5.35 The auditor will often find that more than one technique for ensuring completeness of input is in use for particular transactions. For efficiency, he will wish to place reliance on only one technique. He will normally choose the one that is the most effective and whose functioning he can confirm in the most efficient manner.

Computer matching

5.36 This technique, which is illustrated in Figure 43, consists of the computer matching data on transactions input with information held on master or pipeline files. Outstanding items, being those that have not yet been matched, are reported for manual investigation. As examples, the computer might match input of time worked with an employees' master file and identify and report employees with duplicate or no input, or the computer might match suppliers' invoices input with a pipeline file of goods received details and periodically report outstanding goods received records. In these examples the matching process is an effective control over the completeness of input of time worked and suppliers' invoices. This technique is more practicable in real-time and on-line systems than batch systems because of the greater opportunity to match the input with up to date master or pipeline files during editing.

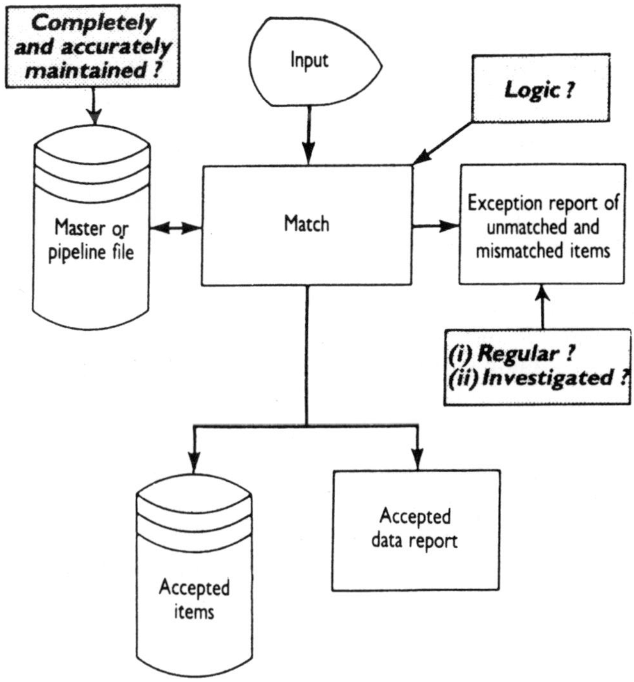

FIG. 43. Computer matching (para. 5.36)

5.37 For this control technique to be effective, the following user controls and programmed procedures must be present:

(a) There must be adequate controls over the file holding details of items to be matched. This will usually be achieved by a regular agreement of file totals with an independent control account.

(b) All adjustments to the data on file should be properly authorised, for example cancelled orders in a sales order processing system.

(c) The method used in the program for matching must be logically sound. In general more than one field of data should be matched, for example both document number and quantities where goods received details are matched with suppliers' invoices.

(d) There must be adequate manual procedures to follow up outstanding and mismatched items. If reports contain a cumulative list of outstanding items, control over investigation work is rendered easier.

5.38 It may be that the file to which transactions are being matched is an important financial file over which the auditor has already assessed file controls. The CART includes a question to refer the auditor to the relevant file controls section of the CART where controls over completeness of data on the file will have been evaluated. Alternatively, the file used in the matching process may be of less financial significance so that the auditor will not have considered it efficient to assess the controls over the file in detail. The completeness of input section of the CART includes separate questions to address controls over the file used for matching in these circumstances. Questions are also included on the matching process itself and the reporting and follow up of outstanding and mismatched items. The CART asks the following questions on matching:

"*Matching to data on a key file*

1. *Review the sections of the CART completed for the key file and key data against which matching takes place. Are there adequate controls to ensure that the data on the file is complete?*

Matching to other data

2. *Identify the control file used for matching to ensure completeness of input (e.g. goods received notes file used for matching to purchase invoices).*

3. *Are the procedures for setting up and maintaining expected transactions on the control file adequate to ensure that the matching process could ensure completeness of processing?*

4. *Are all changes and deletions (before matching) to the control file of expected transactions approved by an independent responsible official?*

All Matching

5. *Is the matching process adequate to form a basis for identifying all unmatched transactions?*

6. *Is the matching process adequate to identify duplicates and other mismatched transactions?*

7. *Is a report of long outstanding transactions or an aged analysis produced at regular intervals?*

8. *Are there adequate procedures to investigate and, if necessary, correct all long outstanding items?*

9. *Are there adequate procedures to investigate and, if necessary, correct all duplicates, mismatches and rejections?*

10. *Are all corrections arising from reports of long outstanding or mismatched items approved by an independent responsible official?*"

Computer sequence check

5.39 This technique, which is illustrated in Figure 44, consists of the computer checking the numbers on transactions input and reporting missing and duplicate numbers for manual investigation. This technique is appropriate in real-time, on-line and batch systems.

5.40 For this control technique to be effective, the following user controls and programmed procedures must be present:

(a) There must be procedures to ensure that all transactions are recorded on a standard serially numbered form. Control should exist over the issue of the forms so that a limited number of series are in use at any time.

(b) The method used in the program for checking the numerical sequence must be logically sound. In considering the method, the following points should be borne in mind:

(i) Changes in sequence must be catered for. This can be achieved by the input of parameters (see paragraph 8.13) containing the numbers to be checked or by setting up a file containing a table of all numbers which have been issued.

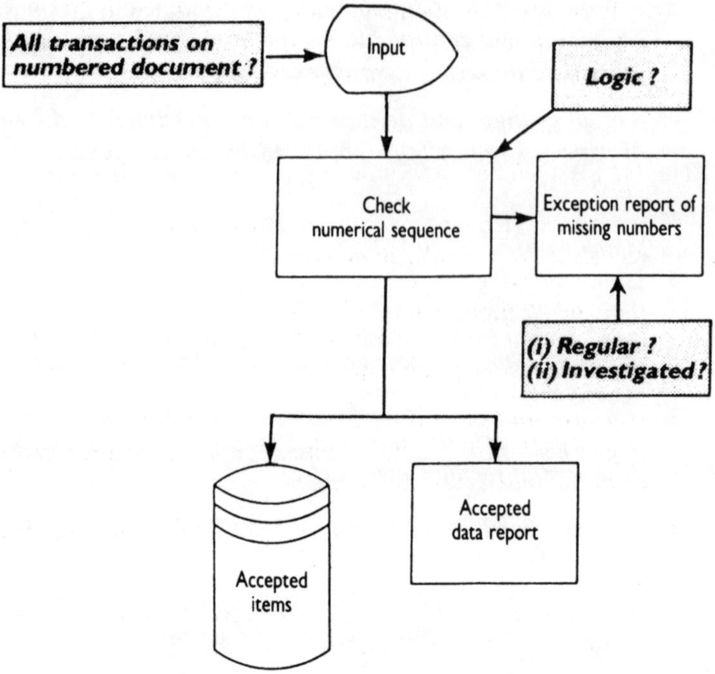

FIG. 44. Computer sequence check (para. 5.39)

Alternatively, the computer may report a change in sequence when it cannot find, say, ten consecutive numbers.

(ii) More than one sequence running at the same time must be catered for. The techniques will be similar to those employed for changes in sequence.

(iii) Where parameters are used to identify the first and last sequence numbers, there should be a check to ensure that the first number in a sequence follows on from the last number of the previous sequence.

(iv) Duplicate numbers should be identified and reported. If a table file of numbers (see (b)(i) above) is maintained, duplicates from earlier runs can easily be identified. If there is no table, duplicates can only be identified if they fall between the numbers of the parameters input.

(c) Reports of missing and duplicate numbers must be produced frequently to enable prompt follow-up action to correct the error. If reports are not frequently and regularly produced, an error in the sequence logic may not be identified.

(d) There must be adequate manual procedures to investigate missing and duplicate numbers. If a cumulative list of outstanding items is reported, control over investigation work is rendered easier.

5.41 The CART includes the following questions on sequence checking:

"*1. Are there adequate procedures to ensure that all transactions are recorded on a serially numbered document?*

2. Is the method used for checking the numerical sequence appropriate (e.g. does it cater for changes in sequence and more than one sequence running at a time)?

3. Is a print-out of missing documents produced at regular intervals (e.g. weekly) or is a list of missing documents prepared regularly from the manual sequence check?

4. Does the sequence check ensure that all recorded transactions are reported if rejected?

5. Are there adequate procedures for investigation and, if necessary, correction of missing, duplicate or rejected transactions?

6. Are any necessary corrections approved by an independent responsible official?"

Batch totals

5.42 The use of batch totals is a common control technique in batch systems but is seldom used in real-time or on-line systems. In batch systems the technique is found in two basic forms:

- A suitable total for the batch is established manually and recorded in a register. The batch is input and the computer accumulates and prints out the batch total. The total on the print-out is manually agreed with the total recorded in the register. This form of the technique is illustrated in Figure 45.

- The batch total is established manually and input with the batch. The computer accumulates the batch total and compares it with the total input. The computer prints out whether totals are agreed or disagreed. Where totals disagree, the batch is normally rejected. This form of the technique is illustrated in Figure 46.

5.43 In order to ensure completeness of input, a document count will normally suffice as the minimum level of batch total required. If more than one transaction appears on certain of the documents, a transaction count will be necessary. In practice, batch totals are often based

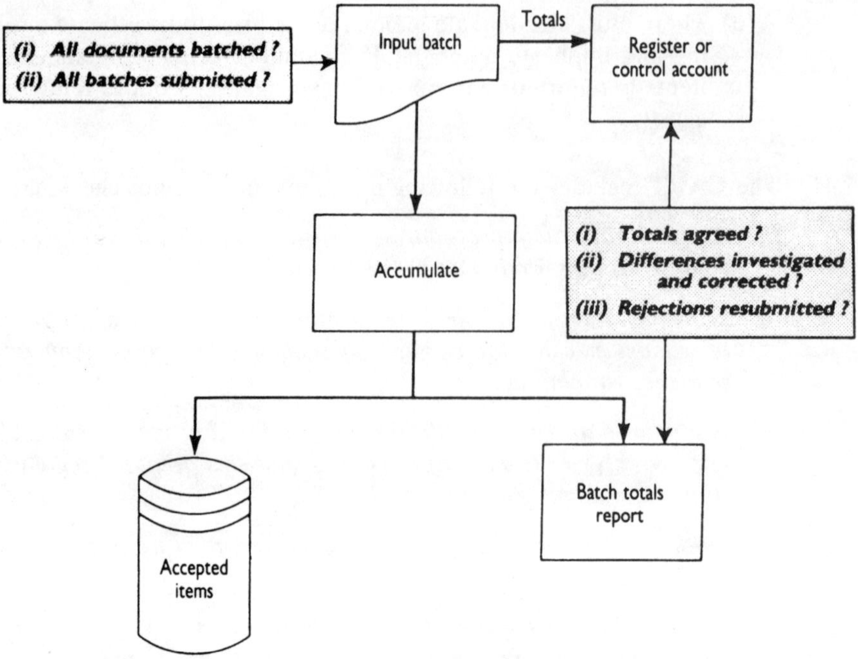

FIG. 45. Manual agreement of batch totals (para. 5.42)

on an important data field, such as value or quantity, and this is equally effective.

5.44 The use of batch totals is only effective as a control technique for completeness from the time that the documents are batched. For this technique to be fully effective it is therefore necessary for there to be adequate controls to ensure that:

(a) all documents are batched; and

(b) all batches are presented for processing.

These requirements will often be met by checking the sequence of numbered documents or batches.

5.45 The following questions on batch totals are asked in the CART:

"*1. Are there adequate controls to ensure that all transactions are recorded?*

2. Are there adequate controls to ensure that all transaction documents are included in a batch?

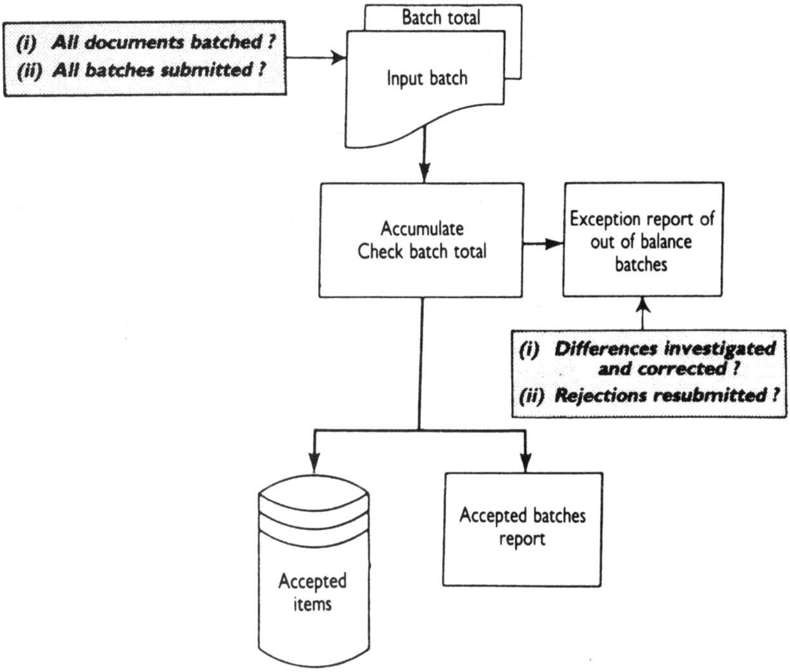

FIG. 46. Computer agreement of batch totals (para. 5.42)

3. *Are there controls to ensure that all batches are input to the computer and accepted once and only once?*

4. *If pre-determined control totals are input and agreed by the computer to the accumulation of individual items accepted, is adequate evidence of this check printed out?*

5. *Are pre-determined control totals agreed manually with the total of accepted items accumulated and printed out by the computer?*

6. *Are there adequate procedures to investigate and, if necessary, correct missing and duplicate transactions disclosed by the above controls?*

7. *Are there adequate procedures to investigate and, if necessary, correct rejected items?*

8. *Are all necessary corrections approved by an independent responsible official?*"

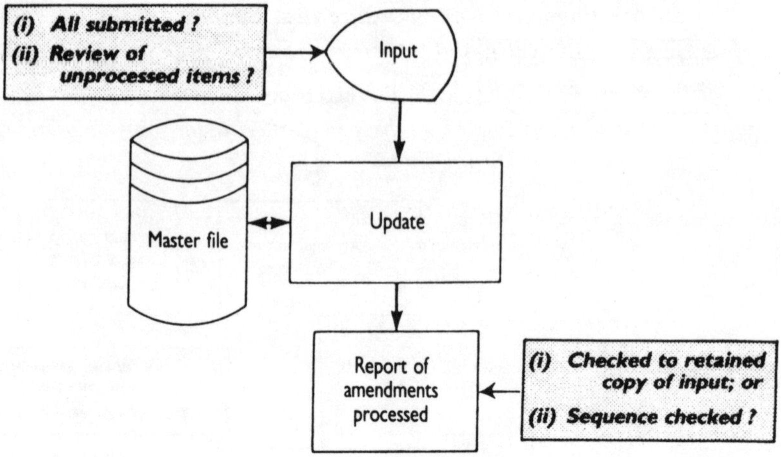

FIG. 47. Checking of print-outs (para. 5.46)

Checking of print-outs

5.46 This technique, which is illustrated in Figure 47, consists of the checking of individual input documents with a detailed listing of items processed by the computer. When relying on this technique, it is necessary to ensure that all documents are included for processing. This is usually achieved by:

(a) retaining a copy in the originating department of all documents to be processed (the print-out is then checked with the retained copy); or

(b) checking the sequence of input documents or using document counts.

Checking of print-outs is a particularly effective control. It is, however, time-consuming and costly. It is thus normally only used as a technique to control the input and updating of standing data amendments and important accounting adjustments such as write-offs. It is particularly appropriate in batch and on-line systems.

5.47 The CART includes the following questions on checking of print-outs:

"*1. Is there a control to ensure that all transactions are recorded?*

2. Are there controls to ensure that all documents are submitted for processing (e.g. by checking against retained copy, or by manual sequence check)?

3. *Are there controls to ensure that all transactions are input to the computer once and only once?*
4. *Is the method used in the program for the production of the print-out appropriate (e.g. does it contain details of all items that have been written to the file)?*
5. *Are there adequate procedures to investigate and, if necessary, correct missing, duplicate and rejected transactions identified by the one for one checking?*
6. *Are necessary corrections approved by an independent responsible official?"*

Accuracy of input

5.48 It is important to ensure that data is accurately input to the computer. For these purposes input includes the input of data into the computer by means of a terminal or by any of the other methods described in Chapter 3. In some systems it may also include the transcription of data from one document to another and its conversion into machine readable form, for example the transcription of invoices onto input forms and the keying of these to disc. Accuracy of input can only be achieved if all data fields of accounting significance are adequately controlled. The requirement for control is greater at the input stage than during processing, because it is unusual for data to become corrupted once it is in the computer.

Data fields to be controlled

5.49 Initially, it is necessary for the auditor to establish the data fields that require to be controlled and the degree of control that is necessary. In this context, it has to be recognised that it may not be practicable to achieve an exhaustive degree of control over all data fields. The identification of the data fields that require a high degree of control is not necessarily obvious. All "financial" data fields are important, that is to say either value fields or fields that will enter into a calculation of value such as hours or quantities. In addition, certain "reference" data fields will be important. These may include reference numbers, dates and indicators.

Reference numbers

5.50 The accuracy of reference numbers of personal accounts, inventory lines and general ledger codings will be important to ensure that correct accounts are updated. The accuracy of reference numbers of inventory lines will also be important to ensure that pricing is properly carried out.

Dates

5.51 The accurate input of dates can be important in many circumstances. Dates held as standing data may initiate the computer accounting process. Examples of dates used in this manner include the date stock is to be reported for counting, the date of credit sale agreements and when repayment instalments are due and, in relation to utilities, the date on which a customer's meter is to be read and thus, a set time thereafter, a bill is to be raised. Failure to input accurately dates of this nature may lead to loss of revenue or the failure to carry out control procedures. Dates input as part of transactions may also be important, as, for example, in the case of sales or inventory transactions where computer ageing of customers' and inventory balances is relied on or, in the case of suppliers' invoices, where the computer is programmed to generate cheques on specified dates.

Indicators

5.52 The accurate input of indicators can also be important. An indicator is a field on a data record, the content of which determines how a transaction is to be treated by the application programs. Often the type or sign (i.e. positive or negative) of a transaction is identified by means of an indicator and an error in its input could lead to the opposite effect to that intended. For example, in wages and salaries systems it is common for a similar form to be used for those starting and leaving employment, the distinction being made by a different indicator for a starter and a leaver. Indicators can also be important from a control point of view as, for example, where a stock item is defined as high security stock and is input with an indicator so that the program selects it for count more frequently.

Control techniques

Use of completeness controls

5.53 Some of the techniques by which accuracy of input is achieved are similar to those used for completeness of input. These are computer matching, which checks the accuracy of the fields that are matched, checking of print-outs, directed to the accuracy of the fields examined, and batch totals, directed to the accuracy of the fields totalled and agreed. These techniques may be used singly to achieve both completeness and accuracy or separately to achieve accuracy with another technique being used for completeness.

Edit checks

5.54 Except for checking of print-outs, it is unusual for the techniques outlined in paragraph 5.53 to control all important data fields and use will probably be made of programmed procedures to check the accuracy of other data fields, usually during input. These procedures are normally called "edit checks". There are often several checks and considerable scope is available if care is taken at the program specification stage. The different types of edit checks are considered in paragraphs 5.56 and 5.57.

5.55 The opportunity for editing is usually greater in real-time and on-line systems where input data can often be comprehensively matched with master files. This process can be extended where the files are organised as a database, and more data is available for matching. For example, a sales invoice which could, in a simple batch system, only be compared with a constant for size, could, in a database, be compared with the previous experience of sales to the customer concerned.

5.56 *Format checks, screen checks, existence checks and check digit verification*: these can be described as follows:

- **Format checks.** These test the format of input records and ensure, for example, that all data fields are present and contain alphabetic or numeric characters, as appropriate. Checks of this nature will usually be required for operational reasons and may be helpful to the auditor to ensure that reference data such as dates and indicators are present.

- **Screen checks.** There are a number of techniques in use where data is input by terminal. These include operator scrutiny before data is processed by the computer whereby the operator is required to strike a key before processing can continue; the provision by the computer of information for the operator to check against data to be input, for example, the computer providing the customer name upon input of the customer reference number when inputting cash receipts; the entering and checking of hash totals of items input on a particular screen; and the pre-formatting of screens to minimise the possibility of operator error.

- **Existence checks.** These test reference numbers with previously established lists of valid numbers held on a file or in the program. They can be useful in ensuring that only valid general ledger codes are input.

- **Check digit verification.** Using this technique the program carries out a mathematical test on reference numbers which enables it to identify most incorrectly transcribed numbers.

In real-time and on-line systems when master files are on-line, the validity of data such as reference numbers can usually be more effectively checked by matching with the master file records at the input stage, thus reducing the importance of these checks. The effect of format checks, screen checks, existence checks and check digit verification is to identify errors as early as possible in the processing cycle. If the checks were not present, the errors would emerge at the updating stage when it was found that items could not match with a record on the relevant master file.

5.57 *Reasonableness checks and dependency checks*: these can be briefly described as follows:

- **Reasonableness checks.** These are checks to test whether the data is reasonable in relation to a standard or previous input. The standard is held on a file or in the program and can be used where it is possible to define a standard against which the data input can be compared. Examples are hours worked, quantities shipped and interest rates. In cases where a standard is not appropriate, it may be practical to compare data input with previous input. Examples are units consumed in utilities and prices of goods purchased.

- **Dependency checks.** These are checks to test whether the content of a data field is logically possible in relation to other data fields on the same transaction or on a file. Considerable ingenuity can be exercised in devising tests of this nature which can provide a strong control over the accuracy of the fields concerned. Examples are that requests for final bills, in utilities, must have an up-to-date meter reading present, shipments of refrigerated goods must include a charge for refrigerated transport, and hire purchase agreements must have a valid start date.

Reasonableness and dependency checks are likely to be of particular importance since they are often applied to the data fields, such as indicators, that it is difficult or impracticable to control in any other manner.

Verification of conversion and scrutiny of output

5.58 In many older batch systems it used to be common to verify conversion by carrying out the operation a second time. However, reliance on verification of keying has diminished rapidly as it becomes easier and cheaper to identify conversion errors by the use of the edit checks described in paragraphs 5.56 and 5.57. Where fields cannot be subjected to these tests, verification of keying can still be an element of control. However it is a relatively weak technique since it will not reliably detect errors which are caused by ambiguity in handwritten characters. As an alternative, it may be practical to carry out a manual scrutiny of output to obtain a degree of satisfaction that data has been input accurately. Reliance on a scrutiny of this nature would probably only be reasonable where the fields concerned were less important, for example those used in a geographical analysis of sales.

Selecting the controls on which to place reliance

5.59 In practice the auditor is likely to be confronted with a combination of the controls outlined in paragraphs 5.53 to 5.58. From these he will seek to identify the controls on which to place reliance. In general he will ascertain whether suitable controls exist in the order outlined above, that is he will see first whether the completeness controls ensure accuracy of input. As regards data fields not controlled in this manner, he will enquire into the edit checks and any other programmed procedures. He will also need to bear in mind, as indicated in paragraph 5.49 that it may not be possible to provide complete assurance as to the accurate input of every data field, particularly as regards transaction data.

5.60 Questions in the CART on matching, batching and checking of print-outs are similar to those in the completeness of input section and are included in Appendix A to Chapter 4. The following questions on edit checks are included in the CART:

"1. *If edit checks are used as the principal control to ensure the accuracy of input of key data, list the key input fields covered by the edit checks and the type of edit check.*

2. *Considering the significance of the data are the edit checks adequate to ensure the accuracy of the data?*

3. *Where operators are permitted to override edit checks are all uses of the override identified on override reports?*

4. *Are all differences and exceptions noted by the edit checks reported on exception reports?*

5. *Are there adequate procedures to investigate and correct differences or exceptions identified by the edit checks and override reports?*

6. *Are necessary corrections approved by an independent responsible official?*"

Authorisation of transactions

5.61 Having considered the controls over the input data, it is next appropriate to consider the controls that ensure that the data being processed is authorised. It is essential that only valid data is written to master files, printed on reports and incorporated in the accounting records. Thus all data should be appropriately authorised or checked. In many cases the checking procedure will be similar to that used in a non-computer system, as, for example, when goods received notes are checked with the physical goods or shipping documents are checked with goods shipped.

5.62 There are, however, the following important features in authorising data in computer systems:

(a) In some cases the ability of the program to test precisely aspects of an item's validity is such that manual authorisation may no longer be required, for example matching hours worked by employees with the employees' master file and rejecting duplicate input.

(b) Data is often authorised at the time it is input to the computer rather than at the time the resulting accounting output is produced.

(c) Instead of authorising all data prior to input or after processing, the computer may be programmed to identify and report defined items for manual authorisation, for example excessive overtime. Items passing the programmed checking procedures are not specifically authorised.

(d) Data is sometimes input to the computer before authorisation, but the system will not update it until it has been reviewed and authorised on-line through a terminal using a special password.

(e) Data is not authorised at all in the conventional sense. Users are allocated individual identities and the system software contains rules that restrict the users' ability to process transactions.

The significance of these differences is discussed in the following paragraphs.

Programmed authorisation

5.63 The computer can be programmed to test precisely an item's validity. The computer either accepts or rejects the item. This occurs where the program can match input with the data on a master file, for example matching hours worked by employees with an employees' master file and rejecting duplicate input, or matching with a pipeline file, for example matching suppliers' invoices with a file of purchase orders and goods received details and rejecting invoices where there is no record of order or receipt of goods. In these cases the computer test is so conclusive as to the specified aspects of validity that manual authorisation may be unnecessary. For this form of checking to be effective there must be adequate controls over the data against which the input is matched, the matching process must be logically sound, and the mismatched items must be investigated and if necessary corrected. Programmed checking of validity is illustrated in Figure 48.

5.64 The following questions on authorisation by computer matching are asked in the CART:

"1. *Specify the key data used for authorisation by computer matching.*

2. *Review the answers to the CART for the data used to provide authorisation. Are there adequate controls to ensure that the stored data accessed in the matching process is complete and accurate?*

3. *Review the answers to the CART for the data used to provide authorisation. Are there adequate controls to ensure that the stored data accessed in the matching process is itself authorised?*

4. *Review the answers to the IT CART for data file security in relation to the data used to provide authorisation. Are there adequate controls to ensure that the stored data accessed in the matching process is secure?*

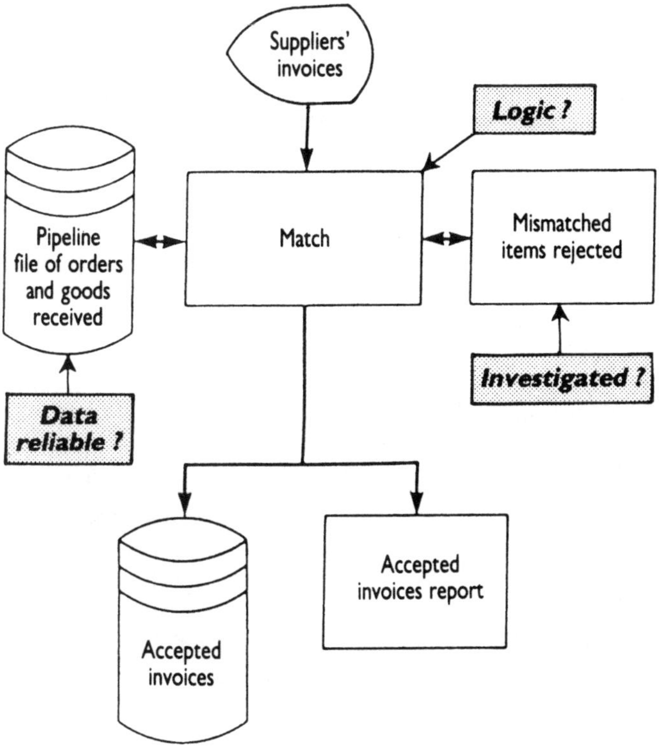

FIG. 48. Programed checking of validity (para. 5.63)

5. *Are reported failures to match investigated and, if necessary, corrected?*

6. *Are necessary corrections approved by an independent responsible official?"*

Manual authorisation

5.65 The technique of manual authorisation of transactions by a suitable responsible official is still an important control technique in computer systems. As in manual systems, where supporting documentation is reviewed as part of the authorisation process then this documentation should be cancelled or controlled in order to prevent it being re-used in support of further transactions.

Timing of authorisation

5.66 In computer systems, the authorisation of data at the time of input, rather than when the resulting accounting output is produced, occurs both with standing data and with transaction data. For example, sales prices will be authorised when they are written to the file, but thereafter the price will not normally be authorised when sales invoices are produced; credit given to customers will be authorised at the time the claim is input and not when the credit note is produced. Where data is authorised at the time of input, it is important to ensure that the authorisation remains effective and that changes cannot be made after authorisation and during the subsequent processing.

5.67 In some cases the controls for completeness and accuracy will indicate the presence of unauthorised data. For example, processed output is sometimes checked in detail with authorised input by one for one checking of standing data amendments, or input is matched with authorised data held on file, such as goods received details matched with a file of purchase orders.

5.68 In other cases specific procedures will be required. These will normally consist either of authorising the data after control for completeness and accuracy of input has been established, for example by authorising items after they have been recorded on serially numbered documents, or of checking that all items have been authorised after control has been established, for example by checking that all items on serially numbered documents have been authorised. These procedures are illustrated in Figure 49.

Selective authorisation

5.69 Manual authorisation on a selective basis is relied on where the com-

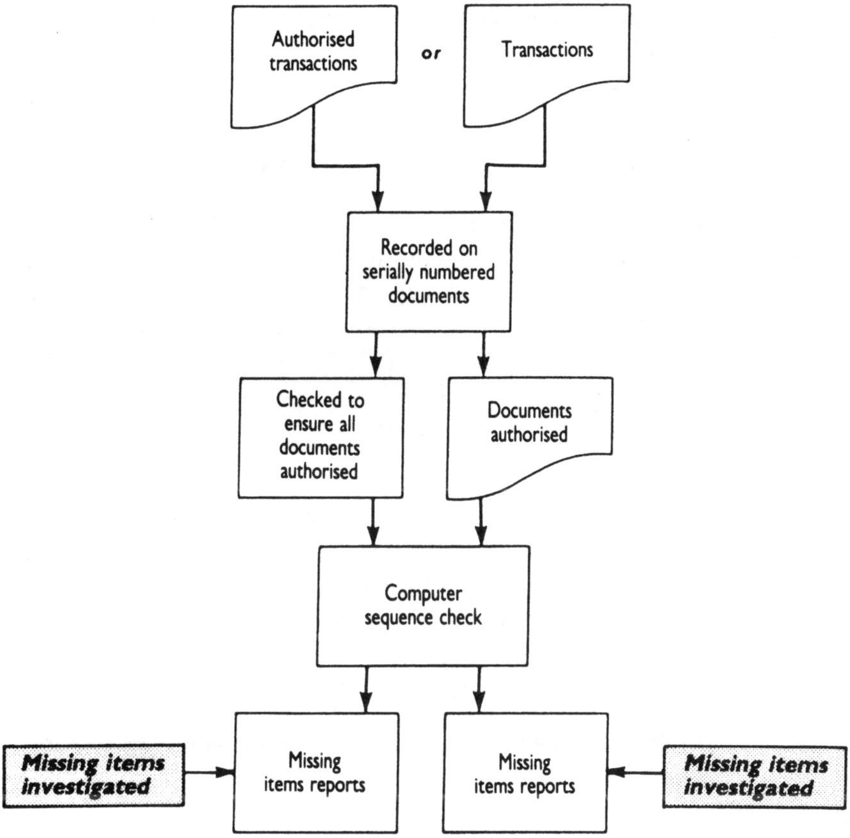

FIG. 49. Timing of authorisation (para. 5.68)

puter is programmed to identify and report defined items for manual authorisation. This will involve the program matching the input with a constant in the program, for example matching hours worked with a standard, and reporting excessive overtime, as illustrated in Figure 50. For this form of authorisation to be effective, the constant must be appropriately fixed, the matching process must be logically sound and the items reported as exceptional must be authorised as acceptable or not.

5.70 The following questions on manual authorisation are included in the CART:

"*1. Are there controls to ensure that transactions are properly authorised by an independent responsible official?*

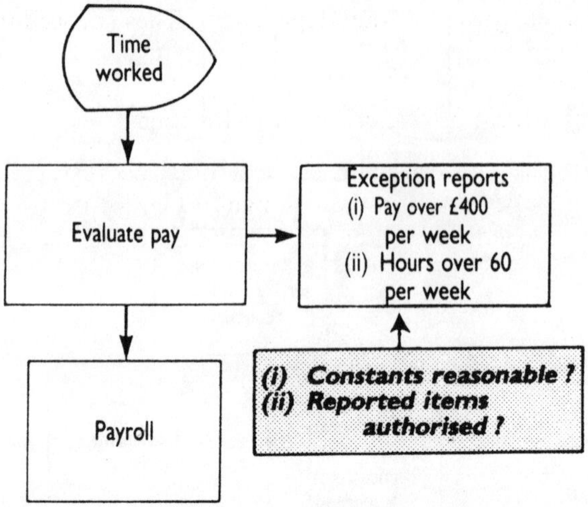

FIG. 50. Selective authorisation (para. 5.69)

2. *Are there controls to ensure that no unauthorised alterations are made to authorised transactions?*
3. *Where applicable, is supporting documentation cancelled or suitably controlled to prevent subsequent re-use?*

Selective authorisation

4. *Are the procedures for identifying items needing approval adequate to identify all such transactions and print them on an exception report?*
5. *Are there controls to ensure that the transactions on the exception report are properly authorised by an independent responsible official?*
6. *Are there controls to ensure that no unauthorised alterations are made to the authorised transactions?*"

On-line authorisation

5.71 On-line authorisation occurs where the computer stores the unapproved transactions in a pipeline file or flags them as unapproved. The authorising officials are given special passwords which allow them to display these transactions and change their status to approved, and the computer will prevent any attempt to update them to the master files until this has been done. For example, purchase invoices may be input as unapproved invoices as soon as they are received, and authorised later by the relevant department. These procedures are illustrated in Figure 51.

5.72 For this form of authorisation to be effective:

(a) The authorising passwords must be restricted to the officials empowered by the company to authorise transactions. Special procedures will be required to deal with the occasional absence

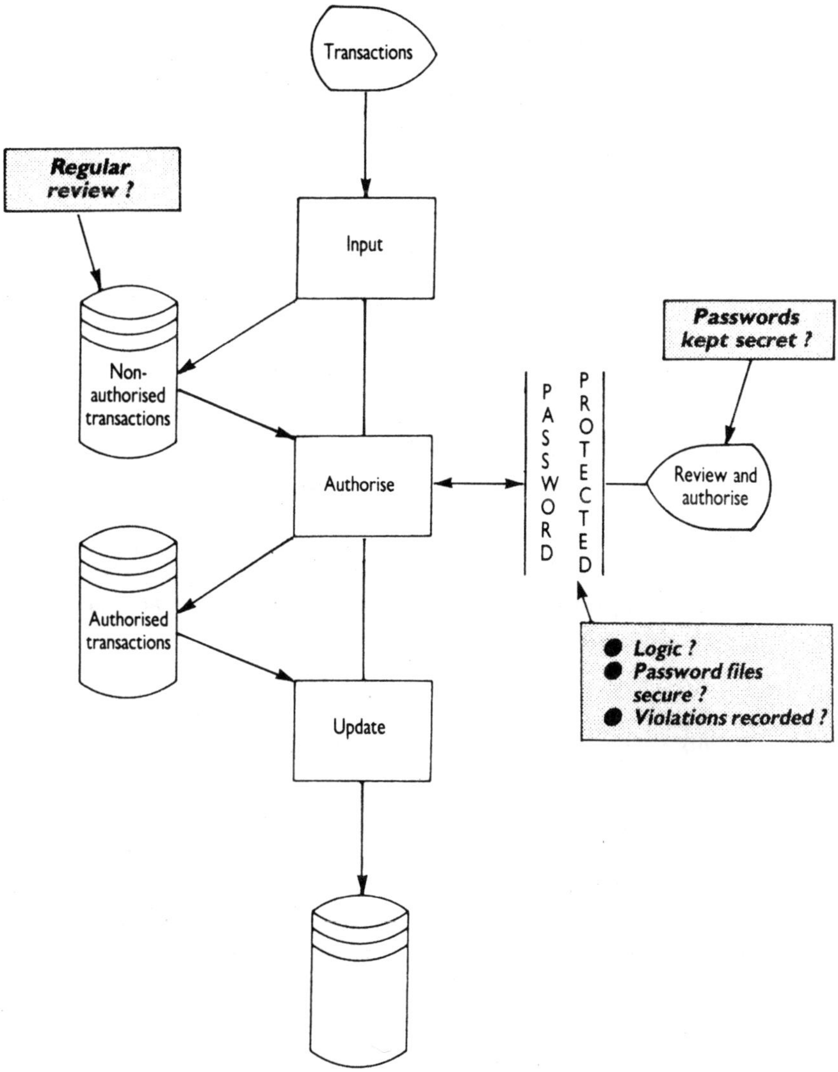

Fig. 51. On-line authorisation (para. 5.71)

of these officials without resulting in the disclosure of their passwords.

(b) The method used in the program to check the passwords of people attempting to authorise transactions must be logically sound.

(c) The password system must remain secure so that it is not possible for an unauthorised person to obtain access to the file of passwords. This will require adequate IT controls over the password system as described in Chapter 7.

(d) The password system should record attempted violations of the system.

(e) The file of non-authorised transactions should be reviewed regularly for old items, and any such items should be investigated and cleared.

5.73 The CART asks the following questions about on-line authorisation:

"*1. Are the procedures for identifying items needing approval adequate to identify all such transactions and route them to a file pending review?*

2. Are there controls to ensure that the transactions on the file are properly authorised by an independent responsible official?

3. Are there controls to ensure that no unauthorised alterations are made to the authorised transactions?

4. Review the answers to the data file security section of the IT CART. Are the passwords which are used to release transactions from the file adequately controlled?

5. Review the answers to the data file security section of the IT CART. Do the passwords which are used to release transactions from the file reflect the appropriate authority limits?

6. Where applicable, is supporting documentation cancelled or suitably controlled to prevent subsequent re-use?"

User authorities

5.74 In many large installations, all transactions processed pass through a security "umbrella". This is provided by special security software which resides permanently in the system, sitting between the application programs and the operating system. Common security packages of this nature are RACF, ACF2, and TOP SECRET. When implementing this software, rights are allocated to individual users and groups of users which specifically allow defined users to read, write, alter or delete items on the file as appropriate. The tables of users, rights and data elements are held in the system as the "security profiles".

5.75 Users are allocated individual passwords. When a user logs on to a system through a terminal, he is asked for his individual password. The system compares the password with the security profiles to see if the attempted access is valid, i.e. if the user is permitted to carry out the action proposed. Thus authorisation of individual transactions is no longer carried out, the validity of transactions relying not on authorisation but on pre-defined rules.

5.76 For such systems to be effective the following steps must be taken:

(a) The appropriate options must be selected in the security software. In practice this is complicated and it is an area where companies will often seek advice from the computer audit specialist.

(b) The security profiles must be carefully established so that the maximum independence of duties is maintained.

(c) Responsibility for ownership of data must be defined to appropriate persons.

(d) Security profiles must be kept secure and confidential.

(e) Passwords must be sensible, kept secret and be changed at regular intervals.

(f) Attempted violations should be recorded and investigated.

5.77 Since security software tends to be applied to all transactions, data files and program libraries, the detailed questions are asked in the IT CART. The use of passwords and security software packages to control access to programs and data is considered further in Chapter 7 which deals with program and data file security.

Computer-generated data

5.78 The circumstances in which the computer may initiate data have been outlined in paragraph 3.37. The computer can be programmed to initiate data under specified conditions in one of the following ways:

(a) The processing of a transaction may create a specified condition. For example, the processing of a stock issue reduces stock below minimum level and a purchase order is produced. In these cases the condition is normally recognised by a comparison with standing data, for example the minimum stock level. This form of generation of data is likely to be most common where data from many different sources can be matched and compared, normally the case when the files are organised as a database.

(b) A signal that triggers the initiation of a transaction may be input. For example, the input of a date will lead to the production of cheques for all suppliers' invoices dated prior to a certain date; the input of a stage of production reached will generate the appropriate charges to work in progress; the input of a requisition code will generate a listing of the components to be issued.

5.79 If data is to be generated by the computer completely and accurately in the circumstances outlined in paragraph 5.78 the following features, which are illustrated in Figure 52, are necessary:

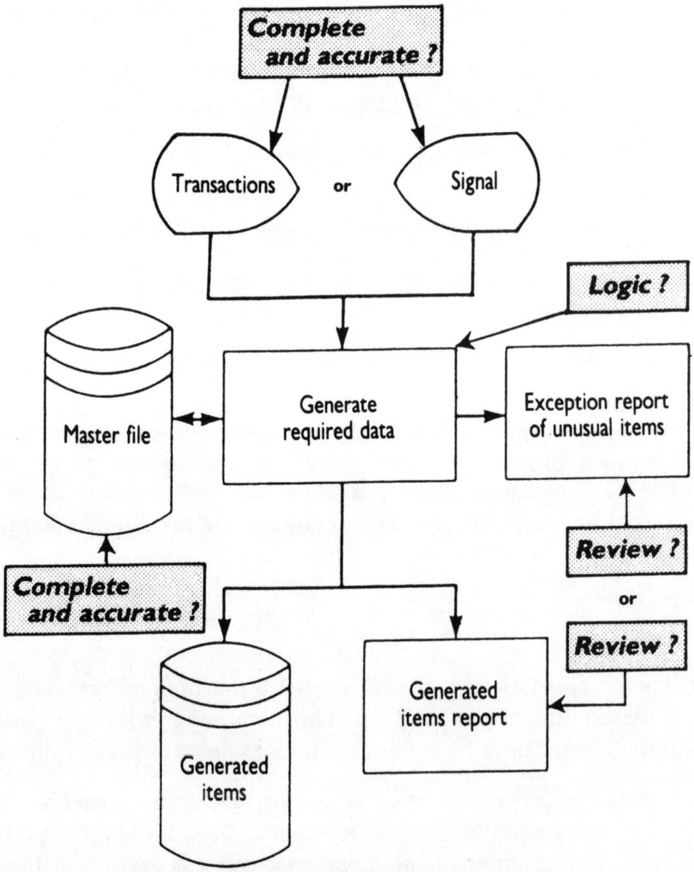

FIG. 52. Computer-generated data (para. 5.79)

- The signals, such as dates, or stage of production reached, that trigger the generation of data must be input completely and accurately.
- The steps carried out by the program in generating the data must be logically sound. The first step will consist of identifying the data, for example, in the case of cheque payments, invoices dated prior to the date signal or, in the case of purchase orders, stock items where the present balance is less than minimum stock level. Further steps will include producing a document, such as a cheque or purchase order, and accumulating the value of transactions generated (purchases, payments) to create a control total.
- The standing data referred to, such as the minimum stock level, or providing the basis of the generated data, such as re-order quantity or a parts explosion, must be reliable. This involves all the controls over the amendment and maintenance of standing data on the file because, unlike manual systems, the standing data is not likely to be manually checked on the generated documents.

5.80 The CART includes the following questions on computer-generated data:

"*1. Identify the event that causes the transaction to be generated (e.g. input of a parameter such as a date, attainment of a condition such as the stock level falling below the re-order level), the key data used as a basis for the generation and the programmed procedures that perform the generation.*

2. For the key data outlined above, review the answers to the appropriate file and transaction sections of the CART. Are there adequate controls to ensure that the key data used as a basis for the generation of data is:
(a) complete and accurate;
(b) where applicable, authorised and kept secure?

3. For the programmed procedure that generates the data, if user controls are relied on to check the accuracy of the generation process, are these controls adequate?

4. Are there adequate controls to ensure that all:
(a) parameters relevant to the generation process are accurately input;
(b) generation runs are performed?

5. Are there adequate procedures to investigate and correct any differences or exceptions identified by the controls over the completeness and accuracy of generation?

6. Are the necessary corrections reviewed and approved by an independent responsible official?"

Updating

5.81 Following input, data will be processed by the application programs and updated to the relevant files. Processing may include the performance of calculations on the data and summarisation and categorisation of data and these processes are described in the following paragraphs.

Calculating

5.82 For computer calculating to be effective the following features, which are illustrated in Figure 53 are necessary:

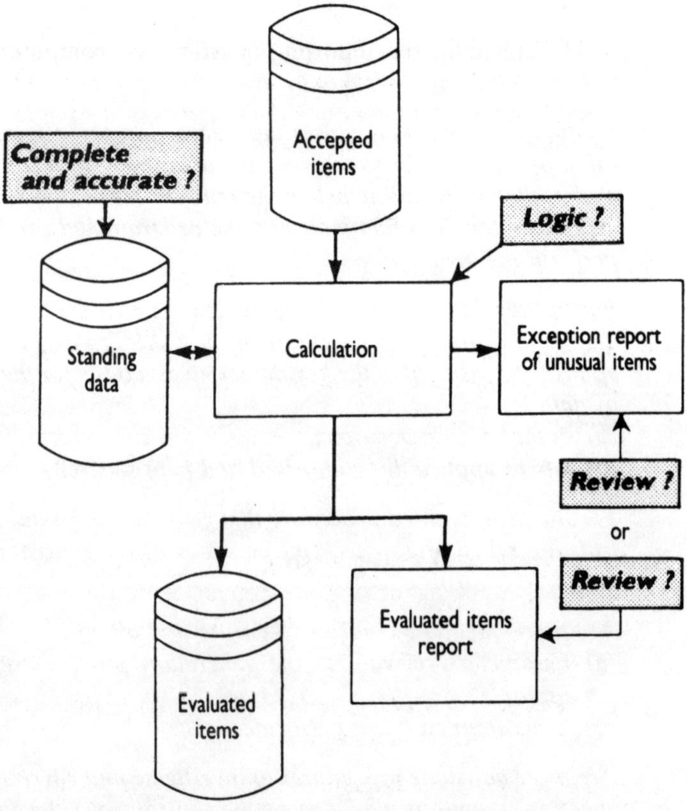

FIG. 53. Calculating (para. 5.82)

(a) The standing data referred to, such as prices or rates of pay, must be reliable. This involves all the controls over the amendment and maintenance of standing data on the file because, unlike manual systems, the standing data normally will not be manually checked on the accounting documents.

(b) The method used in the program to carry out the calculation must be logically sound.

(c) There should be some check on the accuracy of the calculations. This usually takes the form of a manual review of exceptions, such as excessive wages, produced and reported by the computer, or a manual review of the results of the calculations.

5.83 The following questions on calculating are included in the CART:

"*1. Is there any standing data, in addition to the transaction data input, used or referred to in processing? Identify the data involved. Ensure that the controls over the relevant files and transactions have been assessed.*

2. Review the answers to the appropriate file and transaction sections of the CART for the standing data used in processing. Are there controls to ensure that the standing data used is complete and accurate and, where applicable, authorised and kept secure?

3. Where operators can override standing data (e.g. special pricing, credit limit overrides) are all uses of the override reported?

4. Is the method used in the program for performing calculations appropriate?

5. Are there adequate procedures to investigate and correct differences and exceptions reported, including reports of overrides of standing data?

6. Are any necessary corrections approved by an independent responsible official?"

Summarising and categorising

5.84 Summarising and categorising are conveniently considered together. To be effective the following features, which are illustrated in Figure 54, are necessary:

(a) The codes on which summarisation and categorisation are based must be correct and accurately input.

(b) There must be adequate controls over the summarisation. This will normally be achieved by the use of control totals as described in paragraphs 5.92 to 5.100.

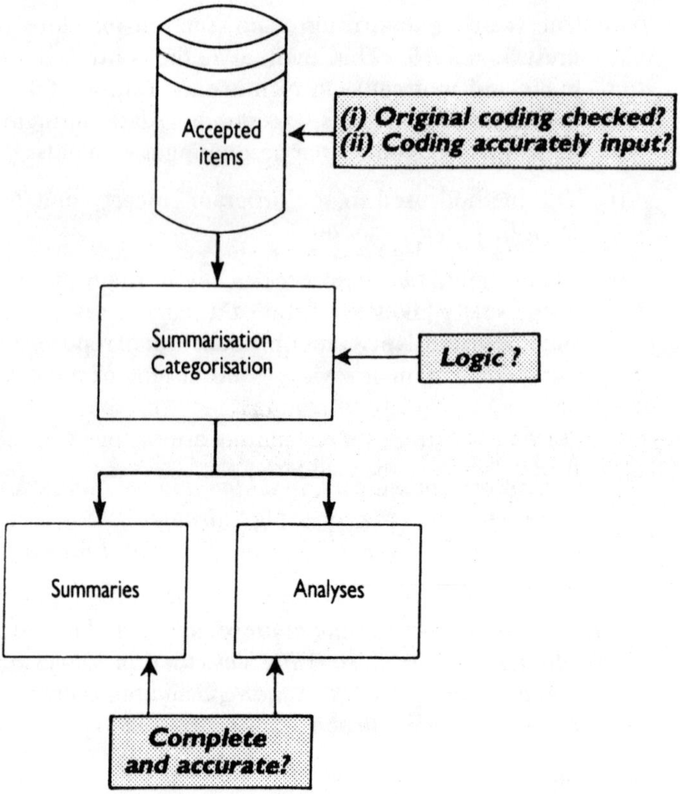

FIG. 54. Summarising and categorising (para. 5.84)

(c) The basis on which the program carries out categorisation must be sound.

Controls over summarising and categorising are dealt with by the CART questions on accuracy of input and on updating.

Completeness of updating

5.85 Control over the completeness of updating to a master file is normally achieved in one of three ways:

(a) By relying on the control over completeness of input.

(b) By the reconciliation of control totals.

(c) By the reconciliation of account balances.

Reliance on the control over input

5.86 In order that the control over completeness of input can be relied upon to control completeness of updating to a master file, it is necessary that the updated data within the master file is used as a basis for the control. This will normally, though not always, be the case when the input control takes place after updating. The circumstances in which this type of control may be found, and the special considerations applicable to each circumstance are discussed below.

5.87 In real-time systems transactions are updated at the time that they are input and therefore the input control will normally control updating. For example, in a money market dealing system, where deals are updated immediately, the computer may be programmed to check the sequence of deal numbers on the deals master file at the end of each day. This would prove both completeness of input and completeness of updating to the deals master file since the deals whose sequence is checked have already been updated.

5.88 However many real-time systems only update the most important files immediately since real-time update places considerable demands on computer resources. In the example quoted above it may be that deals are subsequently updated weekly to the general ledger master file. The sequence check would not control the updating of the general ledger which might be controlled by the reconciliation of account balances discussed below.

5.89 The auditor should also be aware that some on-line systems appear to the user to be real-time systems even though transactions are stored on a pipeline file after input and updated later in batches. Such a system might set a flag on the appropriate master file record to indicate that a transaction is awaiting update to that account. If there are any enquiries on that account before updating takes place the computer is programmed to refer to the pipeline file to establish and display the up to date position, so that it appears to the user that all transactions are updated immediately when in fact they are not.

5.90 The completeness of input control can also be relied on to control completeness of update where the transaction to be updated is matched to a record already held on the master file resulting in the update of a status flag within that record, and where the input control consists of a review of a report of records whose status has not been updated (unmatched records). A common example of this is a sales system in which the sales order master file is used as a basis for despatching, invoicing and updating the sales ledger and these operations are recorded within the system by setting flags within the appropriate sales order record. The most common control over the completeness of input of despatches in such a system would be the review of a report of orders not yet despatched as determined by reference to the despatch flag on the order file. This would control completeness of both input and updating of despatches to the orders file.

5.91 Another situation in which the completeness of input control can be used is that of the simpler batch and on-line systems, where data is updated to the master file in the form in which it was input with little or no intervening processing. Examples might be the update of standing data, or the update of cash receipts to the sales ledger. In such systems the input control is often the detailed checking of data from a report of items updated to retained copies of source documents, or the agreement of batch totals to a report of items updated. Provided that the report used as a basis for the control is known to have been produced by reading the master file itself, such a control would also control updating.

Reconciliation of control totals

5.92 Where the input control cannot be used to control updating, the most common updating control is the reconciliation of control totals of items input to totals of items updated. This technique works best when items are processed and updated in batches since totals can conveniently be established over each batch. It is likely to be used in most on-line or batch systems, particularly those where significant computer processing takes place between input and updating and where updating results in the addition of new records to a file or a change to financial data held in an existing record. Control totals will also be used in many real-time systems in respect of any files which are not updated immediately.

5.93 The reconciliation of control totals works as follows:

- Control totals are established over the data to be controlled at the time that or before the input control is applied to it. Commonly the totals are reported by the program used for the purpose of the input control. The totals to be used will depend on the circumstances but will normally be totals of the most significant field or fields, for example values or stock quantities. Care must be taken to ensure that the totals are established at the time that or before the input control is exercised, as if they are not there is a possibility that data could be lost or corrupted in the intervening period.

- The control totals are stored, either in a control record on a computer file or in a manual register or control account outside the computer system.

- When the data is updated to the master file the totals of items updated to the file are checked to the totals which have been carried through from the input stage. This can be carried out either manually using totals reported by the computer, or by a programmed procedure which uses totals stored in a control record and reports the result. Any differences are investigated and appropriate action is taken on them.

5.94 Where calculations are performed on the data or where data is amended in any way the control totals may need to be changed. For example, where invoices are calculated from goods despatched a new control total of invoice values might need to be established to replace a total of quantities. In such cases it is important that the new totals are accumulated before or at the same time as the existing totals are checked. A similar procedure should be followed where several types of transactions are merged or summarised, such as where invoices, credit notes and adjustments are merged before posting to the sales ledger.

5.95 It is preferable to agree the totals carried through processing to the overall change in the totals of all items on the file as calculated by comparing the opening and closing balances. They can also be agreed to totals accumulated during updating, but in this case the reconciliation is less comprehensive and significant reliance is placed on a programmed procedure to report correctly the totals of items updated.

5.96 Where the totals are checked by a programmed procedure it is important that adequate evidence of its operation is printed out. This normally means that the totals used in the reconciliation should be reported rather than a simple narrative comment that reconciliation has been achieved. Reliance is placed on the programmed procedure to reconcile and report the totals correctly, and on the secure storage of the totals in the control records.

5.97 The reconciliation of control totals by a programmed procedure using a control total stored on a control record in a computer file is illustrated in Figure 55.

5.98 Although most suited to controlling the processing of transactions in batches, control totals are also used to control the processing of transactions individually in real-time and on-line systems. In this case transactions are logged on a transaction file as they are input. Transactions update the master file or database either in real-time or in batch mode, possibly overnight. The totals written to the transaction file are recorded in a control record held on that file or separately, and

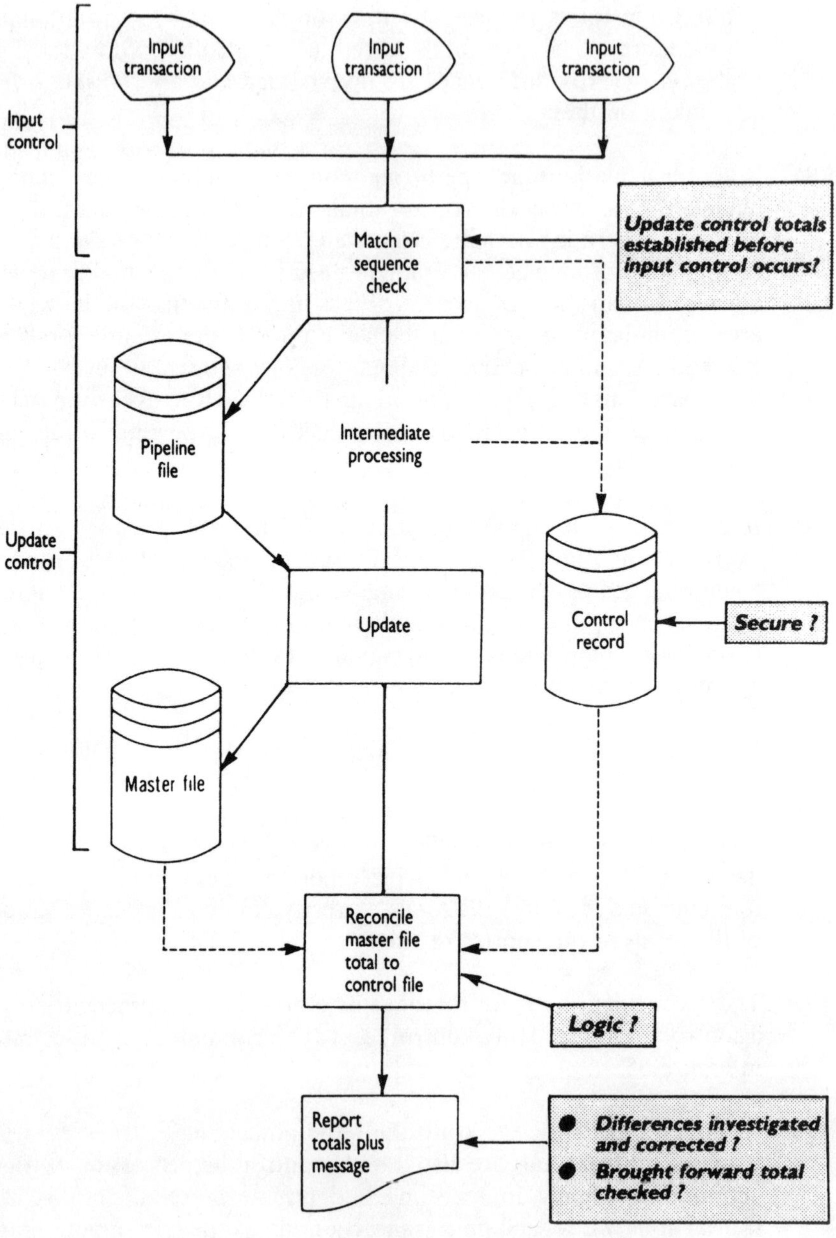

FIG. 55. Computer reconciliation of update control totals (para. 5.97)

this total is then agreed with the movements shown by the control record on the master file or database, which is built up cumulatively as each item is updated to the file. Periodically the individual items on the master file or database are balanced with the control record to establish that individual items are written properly to the file as well as amending the control record.

5.99 Where volumes of transactions and data stored are very large, it is good practice to maintain several different control totals, for example, totals of different transaction types or totals of segments of the file. The reasons for this are first that any differences are contained within a manageable volume, and secondly that the processing overhead in reconciling the file or database items to the control record can be performed in a continuous cycle so as not to be too disruptive. In database systems, separate control records can be maintained to coincide with logical files so that the reconciliation of individual items to the control record will establish that all key pointers have been set up on the individual items.

Reconciliation of account balances

5.100 Where the same data is updated to more than one master file, reconciling a suitable control total from one file to another can ensure that the same data has updated all the files. For example, in a sales system which updates the stock ledger immediately on input, the completeness of input control may ensure completeness of update of the stock ledger. Reconciling the stock ledger balance to the balance on a stock control account in the general ledger would then control completeness of update of the cost of sales entries to the general ledger.

Updating controls in distributed processing systems

5.101 In distributed processing systems where data is transmitted between separate computers control can be, and frequently is, established over updating by treating the system as a whole applying the techniques already discussed. However, the auditor may also find separate controls over the transmission of data from one computer to the other. For example, the update control in a real-time sales order processing and stock system running on a minicomputer in a branch may be the same as the input control. The transactions may then be transmitted overnight to the sales ledger system running on a computer at the company's head office, with control totals used to control subsequent updating within the sales ledger system. A separate control would be needed to ensure that all transactions are transmitted to the head office.

5.102 The control over the transmission of the data may be the use of control totals – usually a different control total from that used elsewhere in the system. For example, a hash total might be used of all data transmitted which might include data from other systems such as payroll and purchases. Alternatively the sending computer may assign sequential numbers to transactions and the receiving computer may check the sequence of numbers. Other techniques are also possible, although these two are common ones.

Rejections

5.103 The data input for processing in a computer system will often contain incorrect items, but, unlike non-computer systems, it is not normally possible or practical to investigate and adjust each incorrect item as it occurs during processing. In real-time and on-line systems incorrect items are most commonly identified during input when editing is carried out of both the transaction itself for format and reasonableness, and by matching against the master files. In batch systems incorrect items are also frequently identified at the updating stage since transactions are not normally matched with master files until this stage. The incorrect data has to be either rejected from the processing or transferred to a suspense file within the computer system. For example, cash which cannot be matched to a specific open item on a customer account in an on-line accounts receivable file is often posted to an unmatched cash suspense account.

5.104 Detailed procedures are required for the prompt investigation, correction and resubmission of rejections and items held on suspense files. It may also be necessary to adjust previously-established control totals.

5.105 The speed of correction of rejections may be important in real-time and on-line systems where input data is matched with master files. If rejections are left uncorrected, the master files will not be up to date when the validity of subsequent input is checked. This would be of particular importance where, for example, cash requests are matched with a customer's overdraft balance. Speed of correction may also be important where database file organisation is used, since several users may depend on common input and not all may be aware of outstanding rejections.

5.106 As regards rejections at the input stage, the auditor, being concerned with the principal controls, will normally only need to rely on specific rejection procedures where the agreement of control totals forms the principal completeness control over input or updating. This is because, where computer matching, computer sequence check or checking of print-outs is the control on which he has chosen to rely, rejections will usually continue to be identified as items that are unmatched, missing or unprocessed and the investigation of these items will reveal any breakdowns in rejection procedures. This is not the case where batch totals form the principal control because it is not always the case that the computer will store and continue to report details of rejected items or batches.

5.107 The nature of the monitoring of the rejection procedures will depend on whether the totals are checked manually or by the computer. If the totals are checked manually, there will be a register and rejections must be recorded therein when the control totals are adjusted. If the totals are checked by computer, there will be no previously-established total and no record of the adjustment. Thus, in these cases, there is less evidence of the volume of rejections and a greater reliance on the supervision of the detailed procedures for dealing with rejections.

Accuracy of updating

5.108 Accuracy of updating for some data fields may be achieved by the same techniques used for completeness of updating. Examples are computer matching, which checks the accuracy of the fields that are matched, checking of print-outs, directed to the accuracy of the fields examined, and batch totals, directed to the accuracy of the fields totalled and agreed. To be effective as a control over updating the control should take place after updating has occurred. For example, batch totals should be agreed to a report of the total updated to the file, and print-outs used for one-to-one checking should be produced after update.

5.109 The reconciliation of control totals and of account balances described in paragraphs 5.92 to 5.102 will also be effective in confirming the accuracy of the fields subject to totalling or reconciliation. In some cases the scrutiny of output produced from processing may confirm the accuracy of update. For example, the scrutiny of a listing of cheque payments to suppliers and of remaining supplier balances may provide evidence that payments have been properly updated to the supplier master file. Unless the scrutiny is at a detailed level it is likely to be a relatively weak technique.

5.110 It is unlikely in practice that the auditor will find specific controls over the accuracy of update of all significant fields. Reliance is often placed on the operation of programmed procedures to update data accurately once it has been input to the computer. Where the auditor is concerned about accuracy of update in these circumstances, he will have reference to the IT controls over the programmed procedures as recorded on the IT CART.

5.111 The following questions on controls over updating are included in the CART:

"Input Controls

1. *Do input controls ensure completeness or accuracy of update to any file(s) updated by this transaction? Specify completeness and/or accuracy and identify the files and the key data elements.*
2. *Do the input controls adequately cover update to the files identified? Specify the control relied on.*

User Controls

3. *Are there user controls over completeness or accuracy of update to any file(s) updated by this transaction? Specify completeness and/or accuracy and describe the control procedures. Identify the files and the key data elements covered by the user controls.*
4. *Are there adequate controls to ensure all transactions update the files?*
5. *If user controls are relied on to check accuracy of update, are the user controls adequate?*
6. *Are there adequate procedures for investigation and correction of differences or exceptions identified by the control over update for completeness?*
7. *Are there adequate procedures for investigation and correction of differences or exceptions identified by the control over update for accuracy?*
8. *Are any necessary corrections approved by an independent responsible official?*

Programmed Procedures

9. *If reliance is placed on IT controls to ensure the proper update of the files, review the IT CART. Are there controls to ensure that the programmed procedures continue to operate properly?"*

File creation

5.112 When new computer applications are implemented, it is necessary to ensure that the opening standing and transaction data is completely and accurately set up on the new files. This can arise when manual systems are transferred to a computer or when a computer system is changed. Depending upon the significance of the application and the degree of assurance provided by his other audit procedures, the auditor may decide to evaluate and test the controls over the conversion process.

5.113 Data set up on the new system may be transferred from a previous system or be new data required by the new system but not present in the old system. For example, when implementing a more sophisticated inventory system new data on re-order levels and time intervals between inventory counts may be required for each inventory line. Sometimes specific computer programs will be written to transfer data from a previous computer system to a new one and sometimes data will be manually input to the new system. Computer programs used for this purpose will often not be subject to the full range of IT controls over development in view of their limited usage and purpose. Instead reliance is more usually placed on specific checks on the data on the new system. These may include checking of control totals with the old system, detailed reviews of the data on the new system or detailed cross checking of data with the old system.

5.114 In some cases the operation of controls within the new application may be expected to detect errors in the opening data, if such controls are adequate and sufficient time after set-up is available to allow any conversion errors to be disclosed by this means. For example, in an invoicing and accounts receivable system, the sending of statements to customers and follow up of queries and unpaid items may identify incorrect initial allocation of balances between customers, while exception reports of excess charges may detect material errors in the set up of prices. In general, controls within the new application will be more effective in detecting errors in transaction data than in detecting errors in standing data. This is because standing data is commonly only subject to control at the time it is input rather than each time it is used.

5.115 The CART includes the following questions on the transfer or set up of data in a new file:

"*Standing data transfers*

1. *Are there adequate controls to ensure that standing data transferred from the old system to this file was:*
   - *(a) completely transferred;*
   - *(b) accurately transferred;*
   - *(c) if applicable, kept secure (preventing unauthorised changes)?*

Transaction data transfers

2. *Are there controls to ensure that transaction data from the old system was:*
   - *(a) completely transferred;*
   - *(b) accurately transferred;*
   - *(c) if applicable, kept secure (preventing unauthorised changes)?*

Set-up of new data

3. Are there controls to ensure that new data, not present on the previous system, has been calculated or otherwise obtained and:
(a) completely set up;
(b) accurately set up (specify key data of accounting significance);
(c) authorised?

Final approval

4. Were the final results of the conversion process approved (e.g. review and sign off of above procedures)?"

Division of duties

5.116 The effectiveness of internal control will be influenced by whether there is adequate division of duties in the performance of accounting procedures and related internal controls. Such division of duties will consist of arrangements that reduce the risk of error and that limit the activities of individuals to ensure that the opportunity to misappropriate assets or conceal other misrepresentations in the financial statements is restricted. In general, the division of duties required is that:

- those persons carrying out or checking controls should be independent of computer operations;
- controls relating to standing data should be carried out or checked by persons other than those who deal with the related transaction data;
- separate persons should perform or check the controls relating to input and updating, and those carried out on the control account;
- the reconciliation of control accounts with the subsidiary records should be performed or checked by persons other than those maintaining the control account.

5.117 The term *computer operations* includes the functions of system design, programming and computer operating. However, it excludes the people who carry out the day-to-day input and enquiry functions, such as user departments, even though they may use computer terminals to carry out this work. The CART does not seek to include separately all of the detailed questions which could be asked relating to division of duties. Rather, the auditor should consider when answering the questions in the CART whether there is an adequate division of duties in the performance of the controls and he should take this into account in deciding whether the controls taken overall are adequate for his purposes.

Supervision

5.118 In order to ensure that controls are carried out effectively, the results of their operation should be subject to review and approval by a responsible official. The CART includes a number of questions relating to such supervision. An example relating to correction of long outstanding or mismatched items identified as part of a matching control for completeness is given in paragraph 5.38, and is as follows:

"*Are all corrections arising from reports of long outstanding or mismatched items approved by an independent responsible official?*"

Summary

5.119 Application controls can be defined as all those controls and procedures designed to ensure that data on files is properly maintained between transaction updates (file controls) and that valid transactions, and only valid transactions, are processed and recorded completely and accurately in the accounting records (transaction controls). The detailed control requirements and techniques are conveniently divided between file continuity, asset protection, completeness of input, accuracy of input, authorisation of transactions, computer-generated data, update of data onto files and file creation.

5.120 Important control considerations regarding these matters can be summarised as follows:

(a) File continuity. It is important to ensure that, once data is updated to a file, it remains correct and current on the file. File continuity controls may operate over the total of balances on the file or over the detailed items recorded on the file and the CART includes separate questions for each of these levels.

(b) Asset protection. Controls to protect assets include both direct controls over asset custody and movements, and controls over the security of data stored on files, which seek to prevent misappropriation of assets or manipulation of data through unauthorised access to data files.

(c) Input. Completeness of input is dealt with separately from accuracy of input. The distinction is made because different techniques are often used to control completeness (i.e. all the transactions) and accuracy (i.e. the data of each transaction). There are various control techniques that may be used and the CART is designed to enable the auditor to identify the principal user controls and programmed procedures on which he may wish to place reliance.

(d) Authorisation of transactions. Checking and authorisation in computer systems introduces new considerations of timing, on-line authorisation, access controls, and whether the checking and authorisation is programmed or manual.

(e) Computer-generated data. The computer itself may be programmed to generate data either following the input of a signal or by the processing of a transaction creating a specified condition. The completeness, accuracy and validity of the generated data will depend on the effectiveness of controls over all of the data used in the generation process and the correct operation of the process itself.

(f) Update of data onto files. Following input, data will be processed by the application programs and updated onto files. Control over the completeness and accuracy of updating may be ensured by the controls over input. Where this is not the case, there may be separate controls over update, and in some cases reliance may be placed on programmed procedures, particularly to ensure the accuracy of update of specific fields of data.

(g) File creation. When new applications are implemented, the auditor may wish to satisfy himself, during the audit of the accounting period in which the files were initially created, that the opening transaction and standing data was completely and accurately set up on the new files.

6

Evaluation of Controls: Information Technology (IT) Controls (1)

Introduction

6.01 In this chapter and Chapters 7 and 8, the detailed control requirements and techniques relating to IT controls that may be relevant to the auditor, and how they are evaluated using the CART described in Chapter 4, are considered. This chapter is concerned with implementation controls and certain general points regarding the evaluation of IT controls. Program and data file security controls, computer operations controls and system software are dealt with in Chapters 7 and 8. The discussion in these chapters, as in Chapter 5, is from the point of view of the auditor rather than those concerned in the design of systems of control. As a result, it should not be viewed as a statement of either all, or the best, control techniques that should be used in any particular installation.

6.02 The discussion of IT controls in this chapter and Chapters 7 and 8 is relevant to computer installations of all sizes. However, in recent years there has been a dramatic growth in the use of small computer systems for accounting purposes, and the particular nature of IT controls in the small computer installation is discussed further in paragraphs 13.23 to 13.53 of Chapter 13 "Small Computer Systems".

Method of Evaluation

IT CART

6.03 The questions regarding IT controls are asked separately in the IT CART. Where the procedures for the implementation, security and operation of computer systems are the same for all systems for which the auditor wishes to rely on IT controls, the IT CART can be completed once for the computer installation as a whole. However where the procedures vary from one system to another the IT CART may need to be completed separately for each different set of procedures.

6.04 The IT CART is arranged in six parts:

- Implementation controls for new systems.
- System maintenance controls.
- Computer operations controls.
- Program security controls.
- Data file security controls.
- System software controls.

The first four parts relate to the controls necessary for the effective operation of programmed procedures. The fifth part relates to the protection and maintenance of data on files. The last part concerns the effective operation of system software, and is relevant when controls identified in the other five parts rely on procedures carried out within the system software. For example, a software program library and software label checking are likely to be relied on as part of the controls over program security and computer operations respectively.

6.05 As noted in paragraph 4.31, the application controls CART includes a column to record whether programmed procedures are relevant to the operation of each control which is carried out. The completion of this column will give an indication of the importance of programmed procedures, and therefore of the IT controls, to the overall system of control. The application controls CART also includes a number of specific cross references to the IT CART, including the data file security section, and examples relating to asset protection, authorisation and update controls are given in paragraphs 5.32, 5.64, 5.73 and 5.111.

6.06 Even in those cases where he decides not to place reliance thereon, the auditor may wish to evaluate the IT controls from time to time so that he can report to management any weaknesses that come to his attention during the evaluation. This approach is particularly desirable in the case of IT controls since modern computer systems normally place considerable reliance on the IT controls over programmed procedures and data files, and weaknesses can lead to widespread operational inefficiency and to the risk of loss to the business.

6.07 In paragraphs 6.12 to 6.106, and in Chapters 7 and 8, each of the six parts in the IT CART is discussed, together with the considerations to be taken into account in answering the questions. The complete IT CART is included in Appendix A to Chapter 4. Before discussing the

IT CART some general comments regarding the effect of the size and organisation of the computer department on the IT controls are made in paragraphs 6.08 to 6.11.

Organisation of the Computer Department

6.08 An important general factor relating to the evaluation of IT controls will be the structure of the computer department. The organisation of the work and staff in the department will depend largely on the extent of computer processing, the number of staff employed in the department and the control techniques used. In general, the larger the department the greater will be the need to install strong controls with formal supervision in order to ensure the effective development, security and operation of computer systems. At the same time, in a larger department there will be greater opportunities for such controls because of the greater supervision and division of duties which is possible and the more sophisticated control-related software, such as access control software, which is available on the larger computers.

6.09 The organisation chart of a typical large installation is shown in Figure 56, although the precise structure will vary from department to department. In a department of this size, which might include about two hundred staff, there is not only functional segregation of duties between operations and systems development but segregation of duties within these functions. For example, system development is distinct from technical support and control over data is separate from the scheduling and operation of the computers. A considerable degree of formal organisation is also possible within functions. Thus, within the operations function, the work of data control, scheduling and processing is carried out by separate groups. In an installation of this size the auditor should find a comprehensive set of IT controls, many of which will be software-based, and full disciplines, both as regards segregation of duties and supervision.

6.10 The organisation chart of a typical medium-sized installation is shown in Figure 57. A department of this size, which might include about thirty staff, will provide a functional segregation of duties between operations and systems development and might, as in the illustration, include a small technical support team. However, the formalisation within functions is less well-developed than in a larger installation. For example, in the illustration shown a single manager or supervisor is responsible for systems development and the database. Staff in each function are likely to be less restricted in the duties they may carry out. The auditor should find an adequate set of IT controls, with less

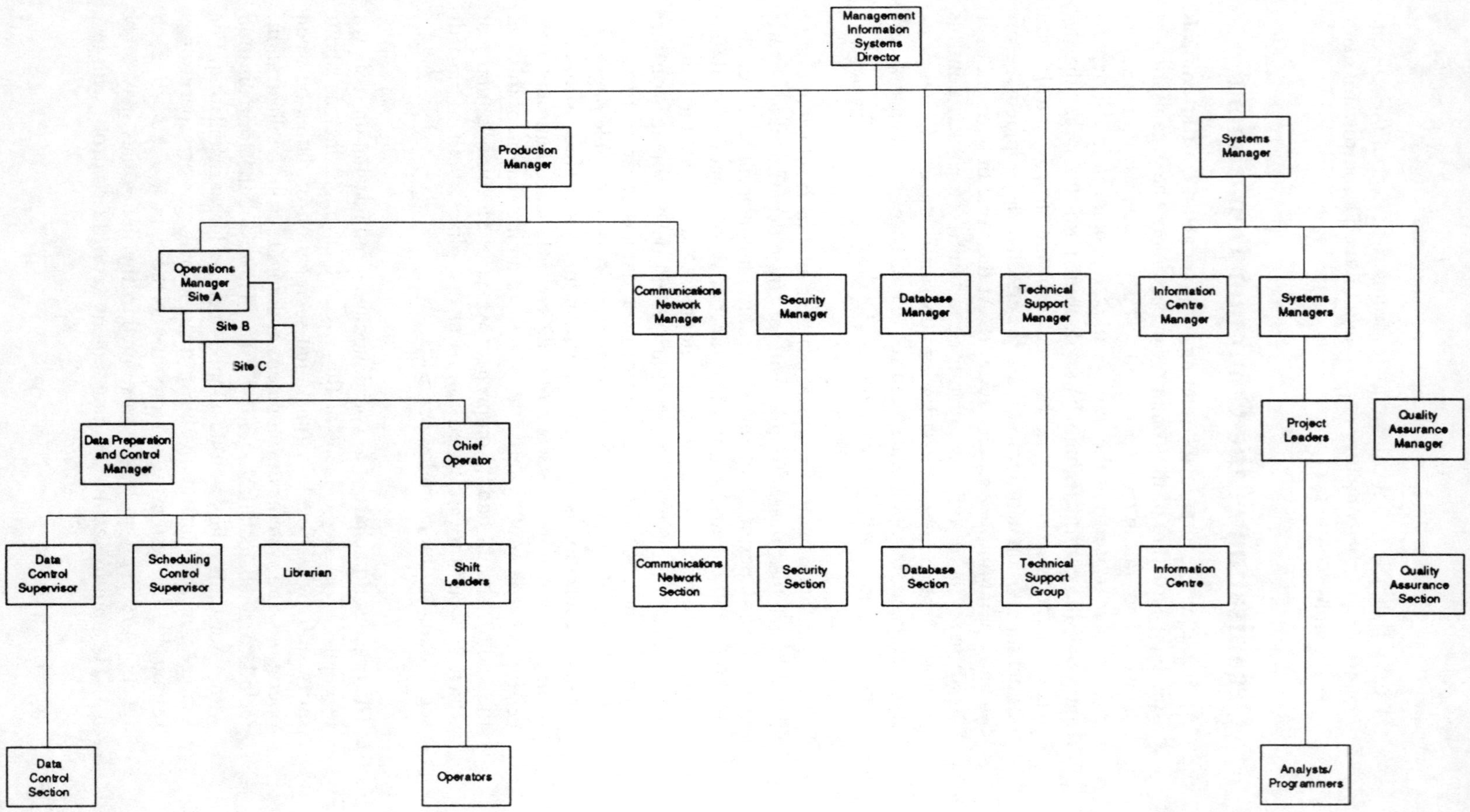

FIG. 56. Organisation chart – large installation (para. 6.09)

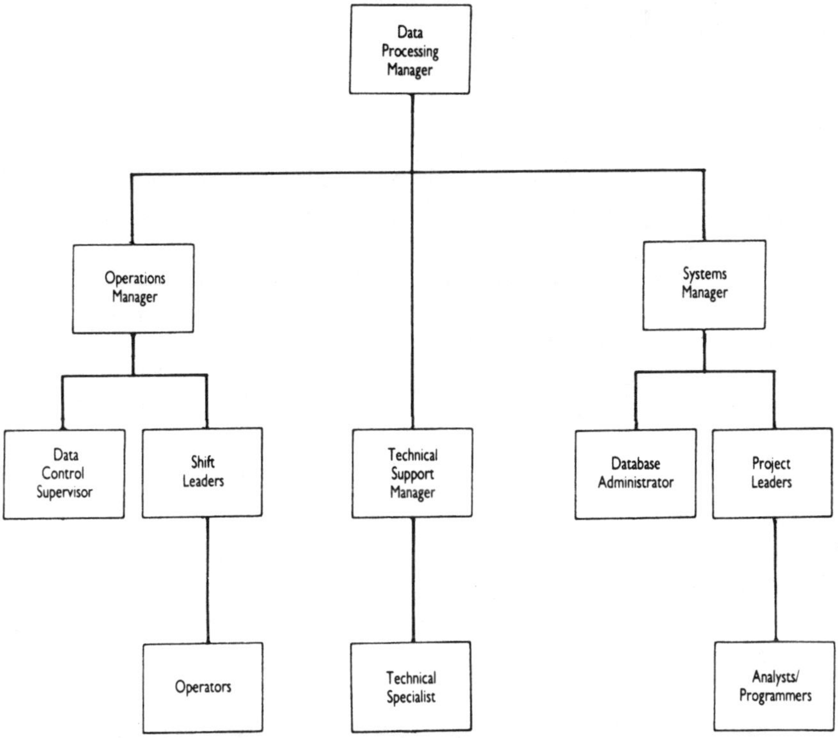

FIG. 57. Organisation chart – medium-sized installation (para. 6.10)

reliance on software procedures than in the larger installation. He should also find some disciplines, although the supervisory function is likely to be concentrated in the hands of fewer people.

6.11 In the smaller installations, an example of which is shown in Figure 58, which may comprise only about five staff, there is unlikely even to be the broad functional segregation of duties between operations, program maintenance and data control, since the manager will be responsible for all these functions. Likewise, there can be little supervision, since the manager will be undertaking much of the work himself. Installations of this size will normally buy software packages rather than writing their own systems, although they may, as shown, employ a programmer to carry out minor modifications to purchased software. Certain basic IT controls will need to be present, such as the procedures for selecting packages and controlling their amendment, and the auditor should be able to place a degree of reliance on these. However, the supervision and division of duties will necessarily be very

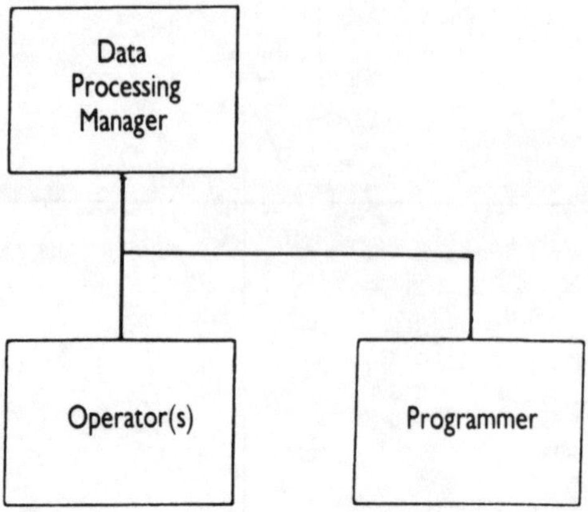

FIG. 58. Organisation chart – small installation (para. 6.11)

limited. Particular considerations relating to IT controls in the smaller computer installation are dealt with in Chapter 13 "Small Computer Systems".

Implementation Controls for New Systems

6.12 Implementation controls for new systems are concerned with the suitability of the proposed system and the effective implementation of the proposed programmed procedures in the production programs. By **production programs** are meant those versions of the application programs which are actually used to process accounting data. They include what are termed **source** programs (programs as written by the programmers in a high level language such as COBOL) and **executable** programs (programs translated into machine code which can be executed directly by the computer). **Application programs** mean the programs unique to the particular accounting application. They do not include the operating system, which is considered under system software.

6.13 Although the auditor may decide not to rely on the implementation controls over the introduction of new systems when no new systems of major financial significance have been introduced in the period under audit, it is still beneficial for him to participate in the implementation procedures in order to provide an additional service to clients by bringing any deficiencies to their attention in time for remedial action to be taken. It is thus good practice, even where he does not intend to rely thereon, for the auditor to be requested to evaluate implementation controls applicable to the introduction of new systems.

6.14 The work undertaken by the company between the initial study of feasibility and the successful implementation of a computer system is usually substantial. During this period the user's requirements are progressively translated from an overall statement of intent into a detailed system specification, the necessary programs are either purchased or designed and written, the system is tested, the data files and manual procedures are set up and the programs are catalogued in the computer's production program library. The process of implementing a system is illustrated diagrammatically in Figure 59.

6.15 The controls required over the implementation of a system will depend on whether the system is developed in-house by the company, or purchased as a package from a software house. The implementation controls required in each case are dealt with in detail below. Where a system is purchased as a package and then subjected to substantial in-house modification by the company, controls will be required over both the purchase of the package and the subsequent in-house development work.

Systems developed in-house

6.16 In order to implement a system successfully it is necessary to ensure that the design of the system is in accordance with the requirements of the business, that the system is technically sound, that it will work satisfactorily and that it is catalogued properly in the production library. Controls are needed in the following areas:

- Overall management of system development.
- System specification.
- System design and programming standards.
- Testing.
- Cataloguing.

Overall management of system development

6.17 The overall management of a development project is important to the company for reasons of operational efficiency and effectiveness. It is also important to the auditor because it influences the environment in which IT controls operate. Of particular significance to the auditor is the control over the scheduling and cost of system development since any slippage against budgets or time schedules is likely to put pressure on the company to cut corners. Under these circumstances the auditor will need to pay greater attention to ensuring that the controls over

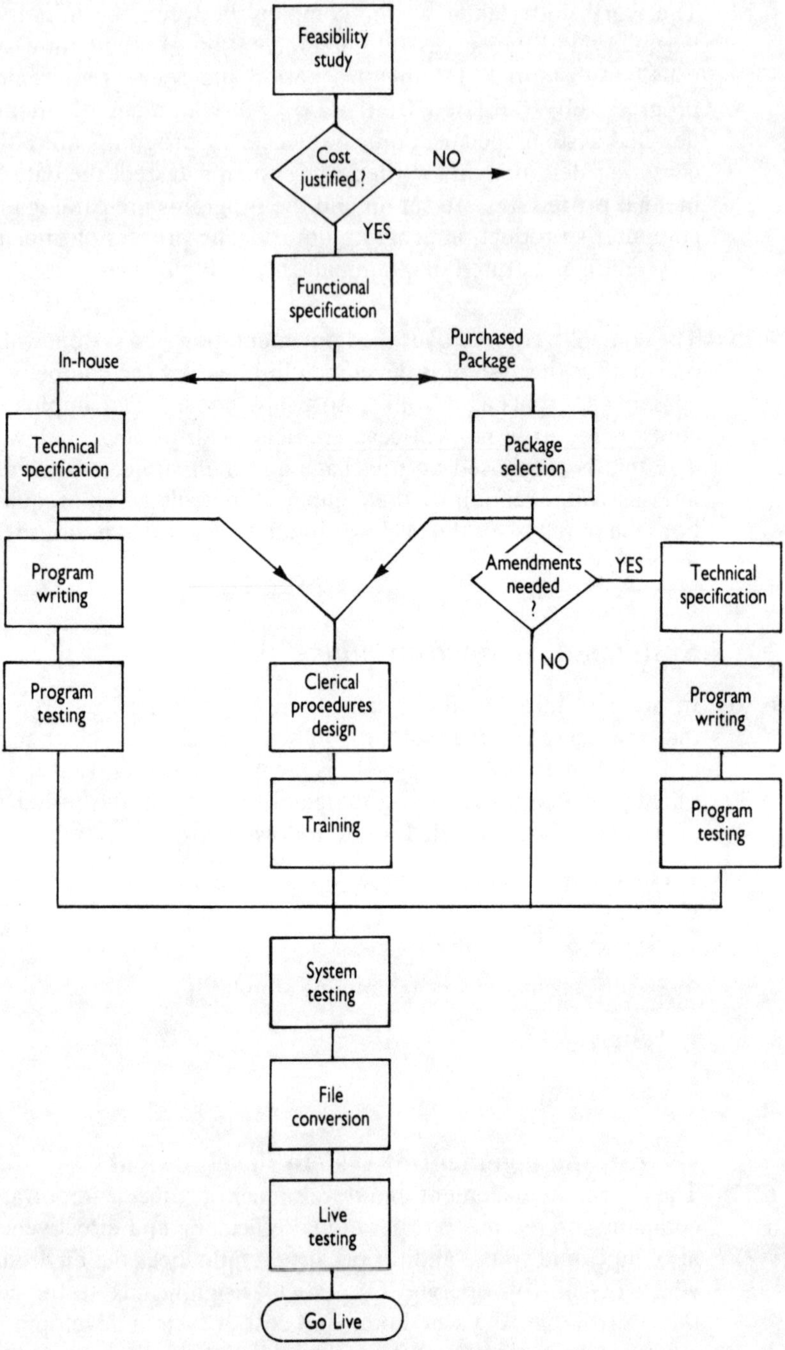

FIG. 59. Implementation of a computer system (para. 6.14)

the specification, design, testing and cataloguing of the system are effective.

6.18 In large or medium-sized organisations, the development of a new system is usually a major project requiring considerable time and resources and the co-ordination of a large number of different tasks carried out by many people. These need to be controlled to ensure that all parts of the project are completed on schedule and within the financial limits authorised. Overall responsibility for the project is usually given to a steering committee made up of senior management from both user and computer departments. Control is usually achieved by the use of detailed timetables and budgets. It is important that actual performance is monitored against these. Any differences will need to be investigated and the overall plans adjusted where necessary. Frequently a software package is used to analyse the relationships between the tasks making up the project and assist in allocating resources and tasks in the best way. Software can also be used to record actual performance, report differences from planned performance and to adjust the plans accordingly.

6.19 In addition it is essential for all the departments with an interest in the new system to be closely involved in its design, testing and implementation. These should normally include user departments, the data processing department (in respect of its technical soundness, compatibility with other systems and operational aspects) and a quality control department or responsible official on behalf of management (in respect of the standard of design, testing and documentation). Their involvement should include assistance in the detailed work of design, testing and documentation and, as appropriate, the review and approval of results. The implementation of the new system should be finally authorised by all interested departments to ensure that they are satisfied with it and prepared for its implementation.

6.20 The main problem usually arises in respect of the involvement of user departments in the development of systems. Frequently it is difficult to find users from all interested departments who are both sufficiently knowledgeable about their department's requirements and prepared to spend sufficient time helping to ensure that these are incorporated into the system. However in the long run it will normally pay management to ensure that such users are made available, if necessary by re-scheduling their other responsibilities, since if this is not done the system is more likely to be unsatisfactory.

6.21 The following questions regarding the management of the development process are included in the CART:

"*1. Is performance against implementation plans monitored and are excessive variances identified and suitably investigated (e.g. by a steering group)?*

2. Are the following people involved to an adequate extent in the key stages of the design, implementation and final approval of new systems:
(a) users;
(b) relevant data processing personnel;
(c) others (e.g. quality assurance)?"

System specification

6.22 The specification of a system is the process of defining the way in which the system must work if it is to meet the requirements of its users and of the business. This is often a time-consuming and difficult process. There is a need for careful control to ensure that all users' requirements are properly defined and incorporated, that any conflicts between them are resolved and that the resulting overall design is technically sound. During this process the auditor will be particularly concerned with the programmed procedures which he has determined as having accounting or control implications.

6.23 There are two common methods of specifying systems. The traditional method is the preparation of written system specifications by means of discussions between the data processing department and all other departments who will be affected by the new system. More recently, as a result of improvements in programming languages, it has become practical to create **prototype systems** for user departments to try out, and to refine the design through a series of such prototypes until considered satisfactory. This has the advantage of increasing the effectiveness with which users can ensure that the system will meet their requirements.

Computer aided software engineering

6.24 Recent years have seen the development of "computer aided software engineering" (CASE) tools to assist and partially automate the development and maintenance of computer systems. These tools, which utilise computer programs, incorporate formal principles of design and analysis, in some cases adapted from engineering disciplines. They are intended to enable systems to be developed faster than would be possible using existing techniques and to a higher quality, thus necessitating less maintenance. The tools may apply to any stage of development including requirements definition, analysis, design, generation of program code, testing and implementation management. Where the tools are integrated and cover more than one stage of development, they would normally transfer information from stage to stage automatically. In practice most users at present are using CASE tools in some phases of development and not in others. CASE tools are sometimes used with a "repository" which is a special type of database used to store all the information required to create and maintain computer systems. A repository can store graphic information as well as the more usual forms and the items stored are referred to as "objects". For example, the repository may store data models which can be used in any system development. The repository does not necessarily need to be used in conjunction with CASE tools.

Traditional specification methods

6.25 Under the traditional method of system design it is normally necessary to prepare two types of system specification – **functional specifications** (sometimes called outline specifications or statements of user requirements) and **technical specifications** (sometimes called detailed specifications or programming specifications).

6.26 **Functional specifications** describe the way in which the system is required to work from the point of view of its users. They will normally include specifications for screen layouts, report layouts, and the way in which each type of transaction should be processed by the system. They will be used as a basis for the users to review and agree to the proposed design, and for the design of appropriate clerical procedures for running the system. They should be written in such a way that the user departments can review them effectively. Further work should not proceed until the functional specifications have been properly examined and approved by all departments affected by the system, which will normally include:

(a) all relevant user departments, as regards whether the design meets the organisation's requirements;

(b) the data processing department, as regards the technical soundness and practicality of the design; and

(c) departments such as database administration and network control who are charged with ensuring that the system is compatible with other aspects of the organisation's data processing systems.

6.27 **Technical specifications** describe the detailed design of the programs and data files needed to implement the system and the interrelationships between them. They should be written in such a way that the programming work can be both carried out and supervised effectively. Detailed programming should not proceed until the technical specifications have been reviewed and approved by senior data processing officials to ensure that they are technically sound and consistent with the functional specifications.

6.28 The quality of the functional and technical specifications is of major importance when it subsequently becomes necessary to make program changes, since it is difficult to design the changes unless there is an accurate, comprehensive and easily understood record of the existing design. It is therefore important that the quality of the specifications themselves is adequately reviewed and approved. Furthermore, it is important to ensure that the specifications are kept up to date following any changes to the design of the system, either during its initial development or when it is subsequently amended. All amendments to the specifications should be reviewed and approved to the same extent as the originals.

6.29 The specifications discussed above can take many forms. For example it is common nowadays for some of the documentation of individual programs to be included in the source programs themselves by means of comment statements which serve only as description for the reader. Similarly many database management systems maintain records of the contents and usage of data items held within the database. In such cases some parts of the original technical specification of a system may be duplicated in the programs when these have been written, although a full specification is still necessary to control their development.

Prototype systems

6.30 The use of prototype systems as an aid to system design has become practical following the development of powerful, high level programming languages which enable such systems to be set up quickly and cheaply. In this system design technique, which is commonly known as **prototyping**, a skeleton system is set up which is sufficient to enable the users to form a clear impression of the final form of the proposed system. This may comprise anything from dummy screen layouts and reports to a relatively complete system depending on the complexity of the system and the clarity with which its requirements are already known. The users then experiment with the prototype and the design of the system is refined through a series of such prototypes until it has been approved by all the relevant departments. The complete system can then be programmed either using the same high level language or, since some such languages are relatively inefficient in their use of the computer, in a traditional programming language.

6.31 Prototyping should be viewed as an aid to the efficiency and effectiveness of the users' examination of system design. At some stage it is still necessary to produce a definitive specification of the system for final approval by the user departments, the data processing department and, where appropriate, other departments such as the database administration and network control departments. These specifications are also needed as a basis for the subsequent amendment of the system. The high level programming languages used to set up the prototype systems may be capable of producing part of the necessary specifications in the form either of high level source programs, where these are easily understood, or of reports describing the system.

Operating instructions

6.32 In addition to preparing system and program specifications, it is also necessary to prepare documentation describing for computer operators and user departments how they should operate the system. This will cover operating procedures (the use of terminals and the running of programs), back-up procedures and clerical procedures within user departments. These topics are considered in more detail in Chapter 8. Operating instructions are best prepared at the same time as the system specification since their preparation and review may disclose flaws in the design of the system which would cause operational or clerical difficulties if not corrected.

CART questions

6.33 The following questions concerning the design of in-house systems are asked in the CART:

"*1. Are there controls to ensure that the design of systems (i.e. wholly internal designs or tailoring for packages) is appropriate to the organisation's accounting and control requirements (e.g. user and data processing personnel review and approval of specifications, prototyping)?*

2 Is the documentation of systems and programs of a sufficient standard to provide a basis for future maintenance?

3. Are the following prepared and issued as part of the systems documentation:
(a) operating procedures;
(b) back-up requirements;
(c) user clerical procedures?"

System design and programming standards

6.34 The design of systems is likely to be better, and their subsequent amendment easier, if appropriate system design and programming standards were used in their development. **Structured programming** techniques make programs easier to understand and minimise the effect of changes to one part on another by breaking the functions of a program down into discrete, easily understood parts and segregating these into separate sections of coding. **Naming conventions** can also be used for programs, procedures and data items to assist in understanding them later. For example, a series of programs producing reports in an accounts receivable system may be named ARREPO1, ARREPO2 etc. to assist in identifying their purpose.

6.35 Suitable design and programming standards are also needed to ensure that the new system interacts correctly with existing systems and with the system software. The interaction with existing systems is normally only a concern when several systems share a database, or common data files. Standards will be needed which describe controls and checks which should be applied by each system updating information to a shared database or shared data files, for example edit checks on the format of data and its consistency with other data already in the database. The descriptions and meanings of data within the database should be defined centrally so that each system interprets them correctly. Normally these standards will be the responsibility of a separate database administrator.

6.36 The interaction of programs with system software normally takes the form of system software procedures used within programs to carry out standard tasks; for example to read or write to a file or database, or to transmit or receive data through a telecommunications network. Standards are needed to ensure that:

(a) the correct use is made of control facilities within system software, for example logging or security facilities when updating a database;

(b) appropriate action is taken by the application program whenever an error is detected by the system software, for example when the program tries to read a record which does not exist in a database.

6.37 Finally design and programming standards are necessary to ensure that new systems can be effectively controlled. The standards should ensure that appropriate control-related programmed procedures are built in, for example edit checks, sequence checks and programmed reconciliations of control totals.

6.38 Effective supervision is important in the development of systems in order to ensure that the work of the many people involved, who will possess different degrees of skill and experience, is carried out to an adequate standard. In large and medium-sized organisations it is usually necessary for this to be formalised to enable those ultimately responsible for the system to ensure that adequate supervision has been applied at each stage. In many organisations part of the detailed supervision is assigned to a separate quality control department which, for example, checks that programming and testing has been completed by all the necessary departments and that design and programming standards have been met. However, the existence of such a function does not lessen the requirement for quality to be built in at all stages of the development process, and detailed day to day supervision by experienced data processing staff is necessary to ensure that the work of less experienced staff is technically sound and achieves the required quality.

6.39 The following questions regarding design and programming standards are asked in the CART:

"*1. Are appropriate design and programming standards enforced to ensure that:*
(a) new systems interact correctly with existing systems;
(b) programs interact correctly with system software (e.g. appropriate options specified, appropriate response tó errors detected by the system software);
(c) adequate control features are built into new systems?

2. Is there adequate supervision of the programming of new systems?"

Testing

6.40 Testing of in-house systems should be carried out in three distinct stages: program testing, system testing and live testing.

Program testing

6.41 Program testing consists of checking the logic of individual programs against their specifications. The principal methods used are **desk checking** and **test data**. Test data, when used for audit purposes, is described in Appendix B to Chapter 9. When it is used for program testing it is common to employ a special program, frequently known as an animator, which enables the programmer to run his program against the test data one instruction at a time and examine the contents of working storage after each instruction. Desk checking corresponds to the audit testing technique of program code analysis described later in Appendix D to Chapter 9. Desk checking is more effective if carried out by someone other than the programmer who wrote the program since another person is less likely to repeat any logical misconceptions made by the original programmer.

System testing

6.42 System testing consists of checking that the logic of the various individual programs links together to form a system in line with the requirements of the detailed system description. The principal technique used is **test data**. When test data is used for system testing, there is a need to extend the variety of transactions designed beyond those that are representative of normal transactions. This is because the purpose of the test data is to test exhaustively the logic of the programs in the system as they affect individual transactions. It is thus desirable that the test data is devised by a combined team of programmers and analysts, advised as necessary by the relevant user departments. The results should be carefully scrutinised and the test data should be rerun, and the system redesigned as necessary, until all logical failures are corrected. Formal procedures are required to decide on any amendments to be made to the programs as a result of problems identified by the system testing, and to monitor their successful change. System testing should be performed or checked by persons other than those responsible for the detailed programming, and should be adequate to detect any unauthorised procedures inserted into the system during development.

6.43 System testing should also include testing by the eventual users of the system, often known as **user testing**. The purpose of this is to enable the users to satisfy themselves that their requirements have been implemented in the system correctly. It usually consists of the use of extensive test data which can conveniently be derived from the company's real transactions, thus enabling the users to ensure that the system will cope with actual operational data.

Live testing

6.44 Before committing the accounting records of the company to a new system, the system should normally be tested under operational conditions. The purpose of this is to ensure that it can cope with operational workloads and to detect any problems which will be encountered in using it under operational conditions. It also enables the clerical procedures and controls to be tested. The principal techniques used are parallel running and pilot running.

6.45 **Parallel running** means operating the new system in parallel with the existing system and comparing the results obtained from the two systems with a view to identifying and investigating differences. There are difficulties in using parallel running for these purposes, for example the cost of double processing and the difficulty of comparison when the results of the new system are not identical to, or are additional to, those of the existing system. For these reasons pilot running is often favoured. Nevertheless, when it is practicable, parallel running constitutes the best method of testing the system thoroughly.

6.46 **Pilot running** means introducing the system initially for only a small portion of the relevant records, for example those of one branch or department, whilst continuing to use the old system for the remainder. The results of using the system are examined in detail to ensure that it is reliable, and as it proves itself reliable it takes over progressively more of the records from the old system until eventually the old system can be discontinued.

6.47 When a new system is to be tested on live accounting records it is important that the system is as reliable as possible before this takes place and that all departments affected by it are ready to cope with any resulting problems. The live trial should not normally take place until all the relevant departments have given their approval.

CART questions

6.48 The following questions in relation to testing are asked in the CART:

"*1. Are programs and systems adequately tested as regards:*
(a) the methods of testing used;
(b) the scope of testing?

2. Are the testing procedures performed or checked by persons other than those involved in writing the programs?

3. Are the testing procedures adequate to prevent any unauthorised coding from being inserted into programs during development?

4. Are modifications to specifications and programs identified during the design and development process:
(a) approved;
(b) tested to the same degree as the originals?

5. Are new systems subject to an adequate live test period (e.g. parallel or pilot running)?"

Cataloguing

6.49 **Cataloguing** is defined as the procedures necessary to bring the tested programs into operational use and includes both manual and software procedures. Cataloguing procedures are illustrated in outline in Figure 60.

6.50 The most important manual procedures are those necessary to ensure that testing and documentation are satisfactorily completed before the programs go into production, and that the manual procedures for the new or changed system are ready in both the user and data processing departments. There will need to be a formal manual procedure to instruct the transfer of the new or changed programs, at an appropriate

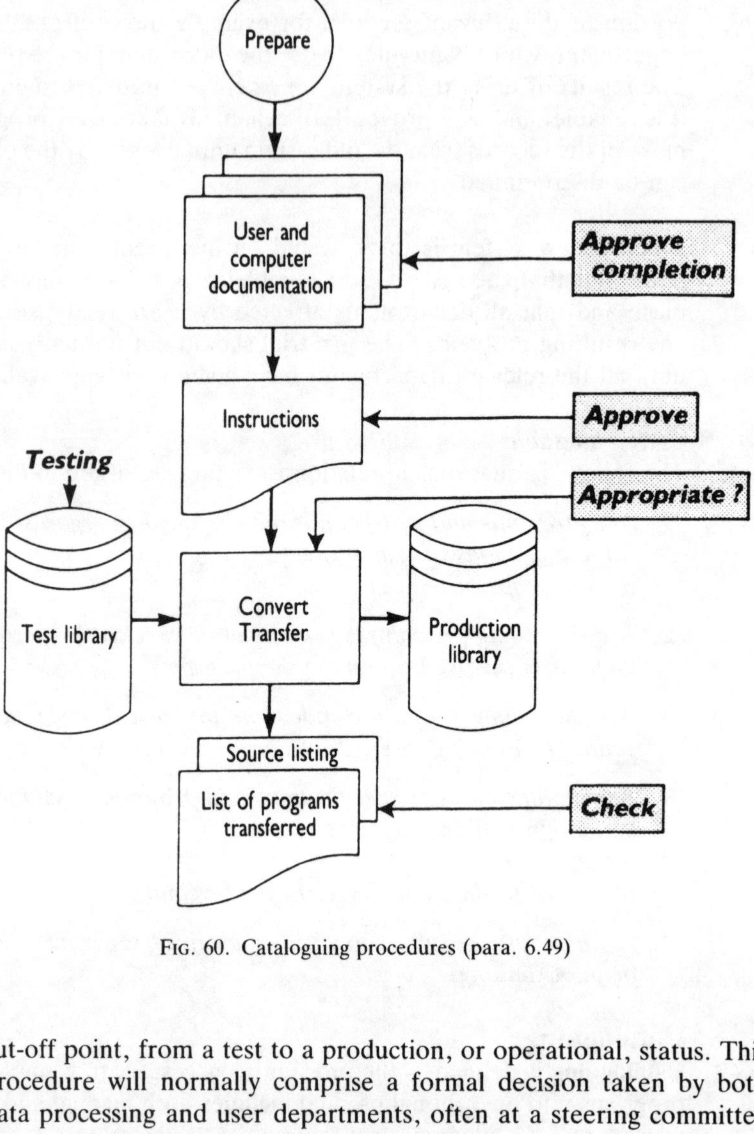

FIG. 60. Cataloguing procedures (para. 6.49)

cut-off point, from a test to a production, or operational, status. This procedure will normally comprise a formal decision taken by both data processing and user departments, often at a steering committee meeting. A procedure of this nature is necessary in order to enable all departments, particularly user departments, to transfer to the new procedures in an orderly manner. The decision to transfer the programs to a production status should thus only be taken on formal evidence of the satisfactory completion of system testing and live testing, and the completion of all the necessary system documentation, for example program documentation, operating instructions and user department procedure manuals. The auditor will not normally need to concern himself with the software which processes amendments or compiles amended source programs in the test library since errors should be identified through the testing procedures. These matters will, however, be of concern to the client.

6.51 The software procedures relating to cataloguing are those which transfer the new programs from test to production status and convert them into a form which can be executed in normal production processing. They may include:

(a) the copying of programs from a separate test library to a production library;

(b) the changing of security codes, database sub-schemas or job control statements used by the program from those which give access to test files or test databases to those which will give access to the company's live data;

(c) the conversion of source programs into executable form by means of a compiler, and the linking of new programs with existing programs, possibly using a link editor;

(d) the deletion of previous versions when programs are changed, or the labelling of different versions of the same program so that the latest version can be distinguished.

6.52 During program development or maintenance many different versions of a program will be created as errors are discovered and corrected. Procedures will be needed to ensure that the final version of the program can be identified when testing is complete so that the correct version can be taken into production. Similarly earlier generations of production programs may be maintained on production libraries and in back-up libraries, and there will be a need to identify these so that the correct version can always be used. Commonly different versions of programs are identified by version numbers and dates. These can be applied manually, but in many modern systems program library software automatically sets up dates and version numbers.

6.53 In addition there will normally be several different copies of the current version of a program, often in different forms. For example there will be both source programs and the equivalent executable programs. Copies of both of these will exist in both the production library and in back-up libraries for use if the production library becomes damaged or corrupted. There may also be copies of the same programs at different computer installations in a distributed processing system. Controls will be needed to ensure that source and executable programs are the same, and that the correct, authorised version of the program is held on each library including back-up libraries, so that all processing is carried out using the correct version and so that no unintentional changes are introduced when system maintenance is carried out using source programs or when back-up libraries are used to recreate production libraries.

6.54 The techniques which can be used for this purpose include:

(a) recompiling source programs whenever the program is transferred to a production library to ensure that the executable program is the same as the source program;

(b) checking version numbers of source programs on different libraries;

(c) where some production libraries hold only executable programs, including program version numbers within the machine code of executable programs, and using software to check these;

(d) using special programs to compare different versions of programs directly with each other, or to produce a hash total from the coding of programs for comparison with the hash total relating to a master copy.

6.55 In addition it will be necessary to ensure that no unauthorised changes are made to authorised programs before they are transferred into production libraries. This is normally done by transferring new programs into a secure library immediately after final testing, from where they are later transferred to a production library. The security controls required over program libraries are considered in Chapter 7.

6.56 In some systems programs are held off-line. This may occur either in old systems with inadequate on-line program library facilities or as a particularly strong security measure where the programs themselves are sensitive or carry out sensitive functions. In the case of old systems, manual controls will be needed to ensure that different versions of programs are adequately identified and the correct versions are used in production and held in back-up libraries. In more modern systems, manual controls may also be used where the number of programs held off-line is small. However, it is common for program library software to be used to keep records of the location of programs and to check that the correct programs are loaded for use or copied for back-up purposes.

6.57 The following questions regarding cataloguing are asked in the CART:

"*1. Is the transfer of new or amended programs from test to production status formally approved by:*

(a) users;
(b) relevant data processing personnel;
(c) others (e.g. steering group, quality assurance)?

2. *Are there controls to ensure that:*
   (a) the versions of programs taken into all production libraries are the current tested and approved versions (e.g. by use of program library software);
   (b) the correct versions are updated to all relevant operational libraries (e.g. source and object, different locations);
   (c) no unauthorised changes can be made to the authorised programs between the time they are tested and approved and the time they are catalogued (e.g. transfer to intermediate secured library immediately after testing)?"

Systems purchased as packages

6.58 Packages are systems developed by computer manufacturers or software houses for the more common and widely used applications such as payroll, sales, purchases and general ledger. The facilities available within each package are fixed, but the purchaser can frequently select between the available facilities and vary the way in which they are used by means of parameters specified when the system is first set up. For example, a company buying a sales ledger package might be able to specify whether it wanted to apply prompt settlement discounts, if this facility was available within the package, and to set the discount rates applicable.

6.59 The company which purchases a package has no control over its development. Thus instead of detailed controls over the specification, design and testing of the package there should normally be procedures to select a package which best meets the requirements of the users and can be relied upon to work satisfactorily under operational workloads and conditions. These will typically include defining the users' requirements sufficiently clearly, usually in the form of a statement of requirements, and reviewing the actual performance of the package in use by other companies. In addition there should normally be procedures for testing and implementing the system.

6.60 Implementation controls in respect of systems purchased as packages are therefore required in the following areas:

- Specification and selection.
- Implementation and testing.

The specification and selection of packages

6.61 Where a package is purchased from a software house or computer manufacturer, it will be necessary to ensure that the package will meet the requirements of the users. This is normally achieved by preparing a statement of requirements describing the facilities required and the volume of data to be processed. The available packages are then assessed to determine which is most suitable, taking into account the facilities they provide and the volume of data they are capable of processing. The statement of requirements serves to enable the wishes of several users to be combined in a logical way and reviewed. It can then be used to communicate the requirements to potential suppliers and as a checklist in assessing alternative packages.

6.62 The preparation of a statement of requirements is similar to the preparation of a functional specification for an in-house system. The considerations regarding the involvement of all user departments and the review and approval of the specifications are equivalent. The only significant difference is the usage to which it will be put. Instead of being used as a basis for preparing a technical specification and subsequently programs, the statement of requirements will be used to compare the different available packages and select the most appropriate.

6.63 Packages need to be compared carefully with the statement of requirements in order to identify any changes which must be made in order to meet the company's requirements. There is a strong argument for leaving a package unchanged wherever possible, since this will reduce the risk of introducing errors into tested programs and will allow the company to take full advantage of the assistance provided by the suppliers, including any future improvements to the package that they may introduce.

6.64 However, in some cases a package may have to be modified where the best available package fails to meet important requirements. If this is done in-house, the control considerations already discussed in respect of the design and development of systems apply in the same way to the design and development of the modifications to a package. If modifications are made by the supplier then the company will need to specify its requirements clearly and carry out additional testing to ensure that the modifications have been properly made.

6.65 The selection of a package must take into consideration the possibility that amendments may have to be made to it in future to correct program errors or to cater for changing requirements. For example, payroll systems, which are often bought as packages, have to be modified regularly to take account of changes in tax legislation.

6.66 The maintenance of a package is normally the responsibility of its suppliers unless the purchaser has made substantial modifications to it. It is necessary to assess the quality of the maintenance service provided. For example, it should normally provide for all future improvements to be made available, for amendments to be made at the users' request on reasonable terms and for a guarantee of continued support of this nature for the foreseeable future. Furthermore it should allow for the users of the package to make alternative arrangements for maintenance should the suppliers fail to meet their maintenance obligations for any reason, for example if they cease trading. It is common for the users to have a right to the source coded and technical documentation supporting the package if this happens, so that maintenance can be carried out in-house or by another software company. Where the purchaser has made amendments, he will normally have to assume some responsibility for future maintenance.

6.67 Finally when selecting a package there should be procedures to ensure that it will work satisfactorily under expected operating conditions and workloads. The auditor is principally concerned that the package functions correctly from an accounting and control point of view. However management will wish for reasons of operational efficiency to consider factors such as the incidence of other program errors that may have no accounting implications, the speed and efficiency of processing, and the acceptability of screen or report layouts. The procedures in force to ensure that a package works satisfactorily will normally be a combination of reviewing the experiences of other users of the package and testing the selected package in actual operation at the company's offices, prior to its acceptance.

6.68 A review of the experiences of other users of a package is probably the best way in which the prospective purchaser can satisfy himself, prior to signing the contract, that the package will be satisfactory. It involves visiting other users, observing the operation of the package and questioning management and staff about every aspect of the package. These include the facilities which it offers, its freedom from program errors, its speed and efficiency, how easy it is to use and the quality of the support provided by the supplier both during installation and thereafter.

6.69 Care should be taken to ensure that the most appropriate users are visited. The amount of useful information that the company can obtain from another user will depend on a number of factors including:

(a) the extent of the other user's experience with the package;

(b) the degree of similarity between the nature and size of the business of the prospective purchaser and the other user;

(c) whether the other user uses the package in the same way as intended by the prospective purchaser.

6.70 The following questions are asked in the CART regarding the specification and selection of packages and the availability of maintenance for them:

"*1. Are there controls to ensure that:*

(a) the systems and options selected meet the organisation's accounting and control requirements (e.g. statement of requirements prepared and approved by users and data processing personnel, trial periods);

(b) any modifications required to adapt standard packages to these requirements have been identified, clearly specified and approved by users and data processing personnel?

2. Does the contract with the vendor:

(a) provide for adequate support for the package over its expected useful life, including any necessary changes required by legislation and business developments;

(b) allow the organisation to continue to use the package in the event of the vendor becoming insolvent, or indemnify it if the vendor proves not to have adequate title to sell/lease software originally produced by a third party?"

The implementation and testing of packages

6.71 Where packages are modified extensively in-house, the control considerations for implementation and testing will be the same as those relating to the in-house development of new systems. The CART directs the reviewer to answer, in respect of the modifications, the questions relating to the in-house development of new systems. This section relates to the testing and implementation of a package which is not modified in-house, or where any in-house modifications are superficial, for example minor changes to screen or report layouts.

6.72 The testing of purchased packages can be considered in two parts:

(a) a review of the experiences of other users of the same package;

(b) independent testing of the installed package by the purchaser.

6.73 A review of the experiences of other users, as discussed in paragraphs 6.68 and 6.69, will assist not only in determining whether the package will meet the purchaser's requirements but also in ensuring that the package has been properly tested and is reliable in practice. In assessing the degree of reliance which can be placed on the experience of other users of the package, it is necessary to take into account any changes which have been made to the package recently. These may have been either to correct errors or to add new features to the package. However it is possible that they have introduced new errors which the other users have not yet detected. This may be because the other users have not received the latest version of the programs, or simply because sufficient time has not yet elapsed for all the errors to be discovered.

6.74 It is always important for the purchaser to carry out his own tests when a package is installed, even if the programs themselves have been extensively tested by other users. At the very least this is necessary to ensure that the installed equipment works properly and that the programs and files have been set up correctly. However when a major system is implemented it is usually desirable to test the programs themselves. The reason for this is that most packages are complex, allowing for different users to use them in different ways, and it is quite likely that no other users are using the package in exactly the same way as is proposed. Furthermore most major packages undergo regular changes which may introduce errors that take time to detect and correct.

6.75 The testing of a package by its purchaser corresponds to the user testing and live testing of a system developed in-house. Judgement must be exercised as to the extent of testing required in the light of the assurance gained from other users and the extent to which any program errors would be detected by user controls.

6.76 As with systems developed in-house, the implementation of a package requires the active participation of user departments, data processing departments and management, perhaps represented by a quality assurance department; for example, to ensure that appropriate clerical procedures are implemented. These control considerations have already been discussed in the section on testing in-house systems in paragraphs 6.40 to 6.47.

6.77 The following questions are asked in the CART regarding the testing and implementation of purchased packages:

"*1. Are new systems adequately tested (e.g. parallel or pilot running)?*

2. *Are the following people involved to an adequate extent in the implementation of the system, including final approval where appropriate:*
   (a) users;
   (b) data processing personnel;
   (c) others (e.g. quality assurance)?"

System Maintenance Controls

6.78 System maintenance is the term used to describe the changing of a system after it has been implemented, either to correct errors in it or to reflect the changing requirements of users. Where the auditor places reliance on programmed procedures he will need to satisfy himself that their operation has not been adversely affected by program and system changes. Where his audit strategy is to place reliance on IT controls he will normally evaluate and test the controls over system maintenance for this purpose.

6.79 The controls required over system maintenance are similar in many respects to those for new systems. For example similar controls are needed to ensure that changes are correctly designed, adequately tested and properly catalogued. However there are two additional control considerations for system maintenance.

6.80 First, for practical reasons, there should be a procedure to ensure that all valid requests for changes are accounted for and promptly effected. This is important to the company for operational reasons. It is also important to the auditor because, where he is relying on the controls over changes, it is essential that required changes are made promptly and completely, as well as effectively, since other controls will not necessarily identify an ongoing deficiency which the change was designed to eliminate.

6.81 Second, system maintenance controls must also cover the emergency procedures which the company adopts to enable it to recover from processing failures. In such an emergency there is often not time for the normal controls to be applied, and control must therefore be established retroactively. The purpose of controls in this situation is to ensure that errors are not introduced into production programs or data files during the recovery procedures. They need to cover both the recovery of programs destroyed accidentally and the procedures for making emergency amendments to programs when errors are discovered during production processing.

6.82 Controls over system maintenance are therefore required in the following areas:

- Completeness of changes.
- Validity of changes.
- Testing.
- Cataloguing.
- Back-up and recovery.

There will be differences in the control techniques depending on whether system maintenance is carried out internally by the company or, in respect of a purchased package, by the supplier of the package. Controls will be considered first for system maintenance carried out internally, and then for modifications made by the suppliers to a package. System maintenance procedures for internal program changes are illustrated in Figure 61. The controls in respect of cataloguing have already been described in paragraphs 6.49 to 6.57 and will therefore not be covered here.

In-house maintenance

Completeness of changes

6.83 In order to ensure that all approved requests are processed, and the changes to programs implemented, there will need to be a procedure to account for all changes. This can conveniently take the form of checking the sequence of serially pre-numbered documentation or by entering change forms in a manual or computer register. Outstanding changes requests should then be reviewed regularly by a responsible official in the data processing department.

6.84 The following question regarding completeness of changes is asked in the CART:

"*Are there controls to ensure that:*
(a) all requests for system amendment are considered for action;
(b) all approved requests are implemented on a timely basis (e.g. entry in a register and investigation of outstanding changes)?"

Validity of changes

6.85 It is important that only valid changes are made. Normally the request to change a program will come to an analyst from a user department or the computer operations staff. Requests for the changes should be appropriately approved before work on them begins. The seniority of

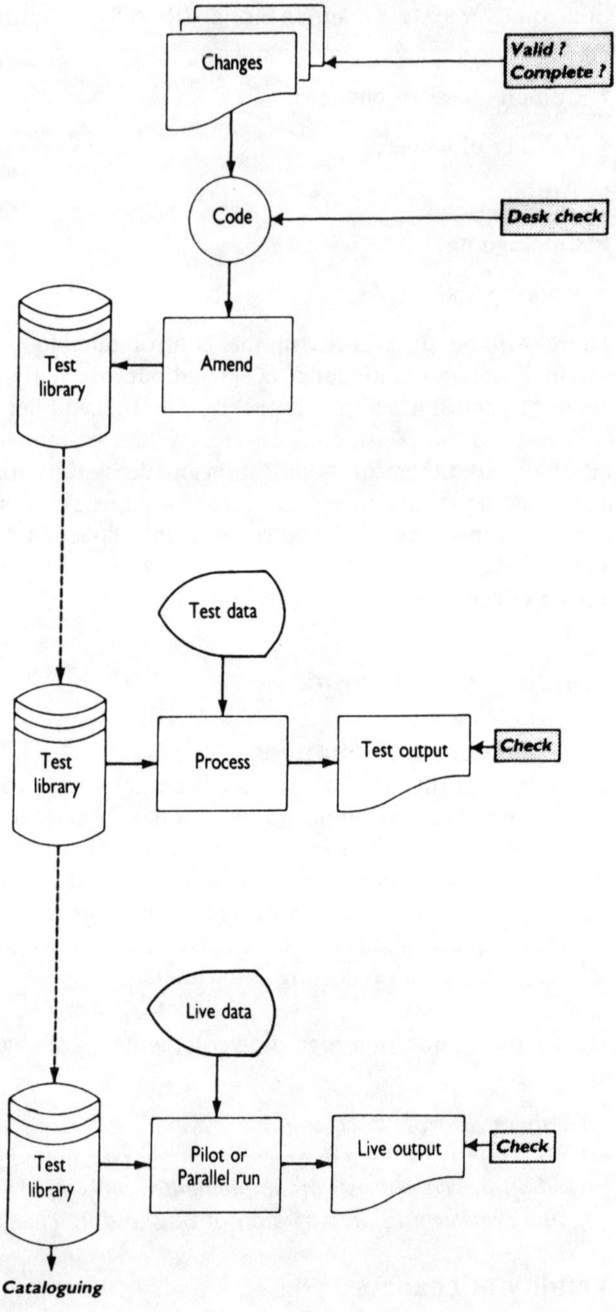

FIG. 61. Internal program change procedures (para. 6.82)

the person responsible for approving the request for a change will often depend on the importance and cost of implementing the change and the strength of other controls. For example, if the request is for a change to the print format of a relatively unimportant report, a lower level of approval would be called for than if the change was to the method of evaluation of inventory. In smaller installations, the most senior persons may need to approve all requests. This is largely a matter of common sense and the precise arrangements to be made will depend on the circumstances. In general it would be expected that a reasonably senior official would authorise all requests for change and, at the time, indicate the level of further supervision and approval required. In order to assist this procedure it is desirable to use standard forms for requests to change programs.

6.86 In addition there must be controls to ensure that changes are designed in accordance with the requirements of all users, and of those responsible for the control and operation of the system. As with new systems it is important to ensure that changes are reviewed by any user departments affected by them, although the amount of review necessary in each case will depend on the importance of the change.

6.87 Similarly, as with new systems, the change will need to be reviewed by the data processing department to ensure that it is technically sound, that it will not adversely affect other systems, and that it makes correct use of system software and shared resources such as databases. Thus it may need to be reviewed, as appropriate, by the database administrator, the network controller and the management of the data processing department.

6.88 Finally the change must be documented to the same standard as a new system. This involves updating system specifications, program specifications, operational procedures and clerical procedures to reflect the change to the original system. There should be a review to ensure that the documentation has been updated satisfactorily. This could be the responsibility either of a quality control department or of a responsible person in the management of the data processing department. Where old systems with inadequate documentation are being maintained, it may be possible to use "reverse engineering" software tools which analyse the source code and produce documentation in the form of design diagrams.

6.89 The following questions regarding validity of changes are asked in the CART:

"*1. If modifications are made to existing systems during the year, are there adequate procedures to ensure that systems, operations and clerical documentation is properly updated?*

2. Is there adequate involvement in and approval of system modifications by:

(a) users, to ensure that the modifications are appropriate;

(b) relevant data processing personnel (e.g. chief programmer, operations manager, database support, network controller)?"

Testing

6.90 The testing procedures for new systems, including program testing, system testing and parallel or pilot running were discussed in paragraphs 6.40 to 6.47 and the same principles apply to the testing of changes. Regard should be had to the quality of the existing documentation, since the design of the change will be based thereon; if the documentation is deficient, there is a chance that the change will be incorrectly designed and testing should therefore be increased. Likewise, the degree of testing applied will depend on the scope of the change. For example, a change to a print program concerned with a single data file might require only superficial testing by means of test data. Changes affecting important calculations, for example new payroll deductions, or special summer bonuses, might also involve system testing, using a comprehensive variety of test data, to test all programs in the system containing the changed program. This would protect against the dangers of unforeseen side effects. Where the changes are major, or affect other suites of programs, it might also be desirable to adopt parallel or pilot running in order to prove the changes against operational volumes of data. The change may also affect user controls and these may require to be tested if the change to user procedures is significant.

6.91 The following questions regarding testing are asked in the CART:

"*1. If modifications are made to existing systems during the year, are there controls to ensure that modifications are properly tested?*

2. Are the testing procedures performed or checked by persons other than those involved in writing the programs?

3. Are the testing procedures adequate to prevent any unauthorised coding from being inserted into programs during their modification?"

Back-up and recovery

6.92 Controls are required over the emergency procedures which the company designs to enable it to recover from processing failures. These must cover two eventualities:

(a) the re-creation of programs which have been accidentally destroyed, for example by an operator error;

(b) the emergency amendment of programs when an error is discovered during production processing. Often in such cases the normal system maintenance controls cannot be applied immediately because of the need to correct the system as quickly as possible.

6.93 In order to ensure that program libraries can always be restored if necessary, the company will need to create back-up copies of its programs and of its system and program documentation. Normally there should be several such copies, including copies stored in a separate "disaster store" where they will not be damaged by an event such as a fire in the computer room or off-line program library. Procedures will also be needed to restore the normal program libraries from the back-up copies should this be necessary.

6.94 The creation of back-up copies of programs and the establishment of recovery procedures will be necessary for operational reasons. The auditor's primary concern in this respect is to ensure that the correct, authorised versions of programs are recovered should the back-up copies need to be used, and that no errors are introduced into these programs in the process. Such errors could be introduced either because the back-up libraries contained the wrong versions of programs, or because of an error in the recovery procedures, for example the failure to copy all the necessary programs correctly.

6.95 When an error is discovered in a program during production processing it will normally be necessary to correct it before processing can continue. It is often necessary to correct the program as quickly as possible to minimise the delay experienced by the users. This usually means that the normal system maintenance cannot be applied. Special controls will be necessary to ensure that errors are not introduced in the program as a result. The usual method is to apply the normal authorisation, testing and cataloguing controls retroactively. There will need to be a completeness control to ensure that all emergency modifications are authorised and tested retrospectively, and also procedures for correcting data files should the tests reveal errors in the program.

6.96 The following questions regarding back-up and recovery are asked in the CART:

"1. Are there adequate controls to ensure that:

(a) programs taken into production are also copied and stored (e.g. in a disaster store) such that the current, authorised versions will be used as a basis for future maintenance and disaster recovery;

(b) production program libraries are regularly backed up, together with a record of changes between back-ups?

2. Are there controls to ensure that program libraries are recovered properly after a failure and that no errors are introduced by the recovery process?

3. If immediate modifications are made to programs during emergencies are there controls to ensure that the changes are correctly made and approved (e.g. by retroactively applying system development and maintenance procedures for programs)?"

Modifications made by suppliers of packages

6.97 Modifications made to packages by suppliers will normally fall into one of two categories; regular changes made in the normal course of developing the package and emergency modifications to correct errors discovered during its use. Emergency modifications will normally take place at the installation which discovered the error, in order to allow processing to continue. The control implications for emergency modifications to packages by suppliers are the same as those relating to emergency system changes made internally by a company, and have already been dealt with.

6.98 Regular changes will normally be made by the suppliers at their own installation with the intention of improving the package or keeping it up to date. The supplier will normally have a system for recording amendments suggested by users and ensuring that these are considered for action and, if appropriate, incorporated in the package. However the user company will have no control over this. The user company may not have any need to maintain or control back-up copies of programs since the supplier can usually supply new copies if needed. However the user will normally wish to do so as a matter of operational convenience to minimise the delay in restoring programs if this is necessary. Finally the controls required over cataloguing at the user installation are greatly simplified because users receive only the final, completed versions of programs, and usually receive these at long intervals in the form of new releases of the complete package, incorporating a number of modifications.

6.99 The user company will need to ensure that any amendments made to a package are in accordance with its own particular requirements. It is important that it receives and reviews an adequate specification of all changes. This should take place if possible before the changes are implemented by the supplier, since if changes were made which were undesirable from the company's point of view it might be forced to continue to use an older version of the package. It would then risk the gradual loss of the supplier's support for the out of date version, and it might also be unable to take advantage of future, more desirable, changes. There are therefore considerable advantages in a continuing involvement in the supplier's system maintenance plans. This is also useful to the supplier since it keeps him more in touch with the needs of his customers.

6.100 The user company will also need to ensure that any modifications are adequately tested and documented. It will have little control over the supplier's testing and documentation, but it should ensure that it tests the modifications to an appropriate extent and reviews the adequacy of revised documentation. The extent of testing will depend on factors such as the extent and significance of the changes and on the quality of testing which appears to have been carried out by the supplier. The company should also ensure that the documentation provided by the supplier to enable it to understand and operate the package has been adequately updated, and it will need to update the documentation of clerical procedures, including back-up copies, itself where necessary.

6.101 The following questions regarding the maintenance of packages by their suppliers are asked in the CART.

"*1. If vendors make modifications to existing systems during the year, are there controls to ensure that:*
- *(a) the modifications are appropriate to the users' requirements;*
- *(b) the amended systems are adequately tested;*
- *(c) systems, operations, back-up and user documentation is appropriately updated?*

2. Is there adequate involvement in and approval of modifications made by vendors by:
- *(a) users;*
- *(b) relevant data processing personnel;*
- *(c) other (e.g. quality assurance)?*"

Summary

6.102 IT controls are intended to ensure that programmed procedures are developed, implemented, maintained and operated correctly, and that data files and programs are stored correctly without unauthorised amendment. This book considers IT controls from the point of view of the auditor. For this purpose they are divided into six sections: implementation controls for new systems, system maintenance controls, computer operations controls, program security controls, data file security controls and system software controls. This chapter deals with implementation and system maintenance.

6.103 Questions regarding IT controls are asked separately in the CART in the IT controls section. The application controls CART includes a column to identify the relevance of programmed procedures to each control, and specific cross references to the IT CART, including the program and data file security sections.

6.104 The purpose of implementation controls is to ensure that new systems are designed and implemented correctly. Where systems are developed in-house, controls will be required in the areas of overall management, system specification, system design and programming standards, testing and cataloguing.

6.105 Where an externally-developed package is purchased the company will have less control over design and testing, but selection procedures will be needed to ensure that the system meets the company's requirements and works satisfactorily. Provision must also exist for the future maintenance of the package, either by the supplier or internally by the company. Where a package is modified internally a combination of selection procedures and controls over system development will be needed.

6.106 Controls over internal system maintenance will need, as with new systems, to cover the design, testing, documentation and cataloguing of system changes. They must also cover the completeness of dealing with requested changes and the controls to prevent errors from being introduced by the recovery process which follows system failures. Where packages are maintained by the suppliers it is important to review proposed modifications to ensure that they are in accordance with the company's requirements.

7

Evaluation of Controls: Information Technology (IT) Controls (2)

Introduction

7.01 In this chapter the detailed control requirements and techniques relating to program and data file security controls and how they are evaluated using the CART described in Chapter 4 are considered. The other elements of IT controls (implementation controls, computer operations controls and system software) and certain general points regarding the evaluation of IT controls are considered in Chapters 6 and 8. The discussion in this chapter, as in Chapters 5, 6 and 8, is from the point of view of the auditor.

7.02 The auditor is interested in program security controls because of their effect on the reliable operation of programmed procedures, whereas his concern with data file security is to ensure that data stored on computer systems is properly maintained and adequately secured. In spite of the differences in the nature of the auditor's interest, these two subjects are, in the main, dealt with together in this chapter in view of the similarity of the control techniques employed. From the point of view of the computer system there is little intrinsic difference in the way in which programs and data are stored in magnetic form and the methods by which access to these magnetic records may be controlled. The audit considerations relating to program and data file security are expanded upon in paragraphs 7.03 to 7.11, and differences in the detailed control considerations are highlighted where relevant throughout the chapter.

Program Security Controls

7.03 Program security controls are those controls designed to ensure that unauthorised changes cannot be made to the production programs that process accounting data. They do not include the controls over normal program change procedures, which have already been considered under implementation controls. Program security will be of particular concern to the auditor in respect of those programs in which an unauthorised change might benefit the person making the change, for example in systems processing wages and cash payments.

7.04 Program security controls will be needed for programs both while in use and while held off-line. **Programs in use** are defined as programs which can be accessed through the system, either by operators processing jobs or through terminals. **Off-line programs** are those held away from the computer, normally in a physical library. A **physical library** is defined as a self-contained area dedicated to the holding of programs and data files when not in use.

Data File Security Controls

7.05 Data file security controls are those controls designed to ensure that unauthorised changes cannot be made to data. The auditor may wish to place reliance on data file security controls to reduce the risk of misappropriation of assets or manipulation of financial data by unauthorised access to data files. Data file security as part of asset protection controls is discussed in paragraphs 5.30 to 5.32. The auditor may also wish to rely on data file security controls where the operation of other application controls is dependent upon data file security. An example is the dependence of authorisation controls using passwords on effective data file security, as discussed in paragraphs 5.71 to 5.77. The need to place reliance on data file security controls has increased with the growing sophistication of computer systems. In real-time and on-line systems, for example, data is frequently stored in a database and made available to many users through terminals. In such systems, traditional reconciliation procedures will often be carried out less frequently than would be necessary to provide timely identification of unauthorised changes, and management increasingly places reliance on data file security controls to protect the data.

7.06 The particular concern where input is through terminals, as in real-time and on-line systems, is to protect against the entry of unauthorised input which will subsequently be updated on the database or data files. The attempt to input this unauthorised data would often be made outside the normal input streams.

7.07 This input of invalid data might be of either transaction data or standing data. Invalid transaction data would normally be a complete transaction either to add to a balance, such as a supplier's invoice, or to alter the effect of a transaction already recorded, for example a credit note to match a sales invoice. Invalid standing data might be a complete record, such as a fictitious supplier's account, or a field, such as rate of pay or interest rate. The potential to alter fields is usually increased where files are on-line and records can be displayed at terminals.

7.08 Unauthorised access to details of the data on the system may also be important. The obtaining of information in this way might facilitate subsequent unauthorised input. In addition, the information obtained might reduce the value of a subsequent control. For example, the counting of stock would be less effective if the counter could enquire by means of a terminal as to the balance before making the count.

7.09 Although the principal reason why the auditor may be concerned with data file security controls is to ensure that no unauthorised changes can be made to data, it should be remembered that there are other important reasons why the company should establish suitable controls. These reasons include operational factors such as the need to protect data from being accidentally overwritten or destroyed and against copies of data being taken and the information being used to the company's disadvantage. In addition, as regards data related to living individuals, the Data Protection Act requires that appropriate security measures are taken against unauthorised access to, or alteration, disclosure or destruction of personal data. The Data Protection Act is dealt with in Chapter 16, "Computer Security".

7.10 Controls will be required for data both while in use and while held off-line. **Data in use** is defined, in a similar manner to programs in use, to include data which can be accessed through the system, either by operators processing jobs or through terminals. Data in use thus includes both data permanently loaded on disc storage and available for enquiry or updating as in real-time and on-line systems and tapes or discs which have been loaded for a specific processing run but are otherwise stored off-line as in batch systems. Data organised as a database would normally be in the former category. **Off-line data files** are those held in a physical library.

7.11 Data in real-time and on-line systems requires permanent protection, particularly against access from terminals. Control is required during periods of normal production processing and while non-production tasks are being undertaken, such as during maintenance or testing. In batch systems, where the files have been loaded for a specific processing run, the problem is limited to controlling the action of operators during the particular run. Controls to protect programs and data from unauthorised access by operators are dealt with in Chapter 8 as part of operations controls.

Control Techniques

7.12 The principal areas which should be subject to control are as follows:

- Programs and data files in use.
- Off-line programs and data.
- Utilities.
- Bypassing of normal access controls.
- User programming.

The control techniques which may be applied to achieve control over program and data file security in each of the above areas are discussed in detail in the remainder of this chapter.

Programs and data files in use

7.13 The control techniques for programs and data files in use are software access controls and physical access controls. These techniques are discussed below and are illustrated in Figure 62.

Software access controls

7.14 In recent years there has been a rapid growth in real-time and on-line systems which, as well as processing accounting data, have become an integral part of all aspects of the operation of a business. Such systems commonly use databases and make information available to a very broad range of users throughout the organisation, for example, from clerks in a sales department accepting orders based on stock availability and customer credit ratings shown on a terminal, to senior management accessing sales and performance statistics on a screen. In such real-time and on-line environments, more users are able to gain access to systems where large quantities of sensitive data are stored, and it has become increasingly difficult for users to exercise sufficient manual procedures to control all aspects of processing data. This has led to emphasis being placed on the internal controls operating within the data processing installation over program and data file security.

7.15 Many of these controls are incorporated into the system software. Communications software for transaction processing in real-time and on-line environments, and database packages, commonly include password facilities as described below. A source program library package

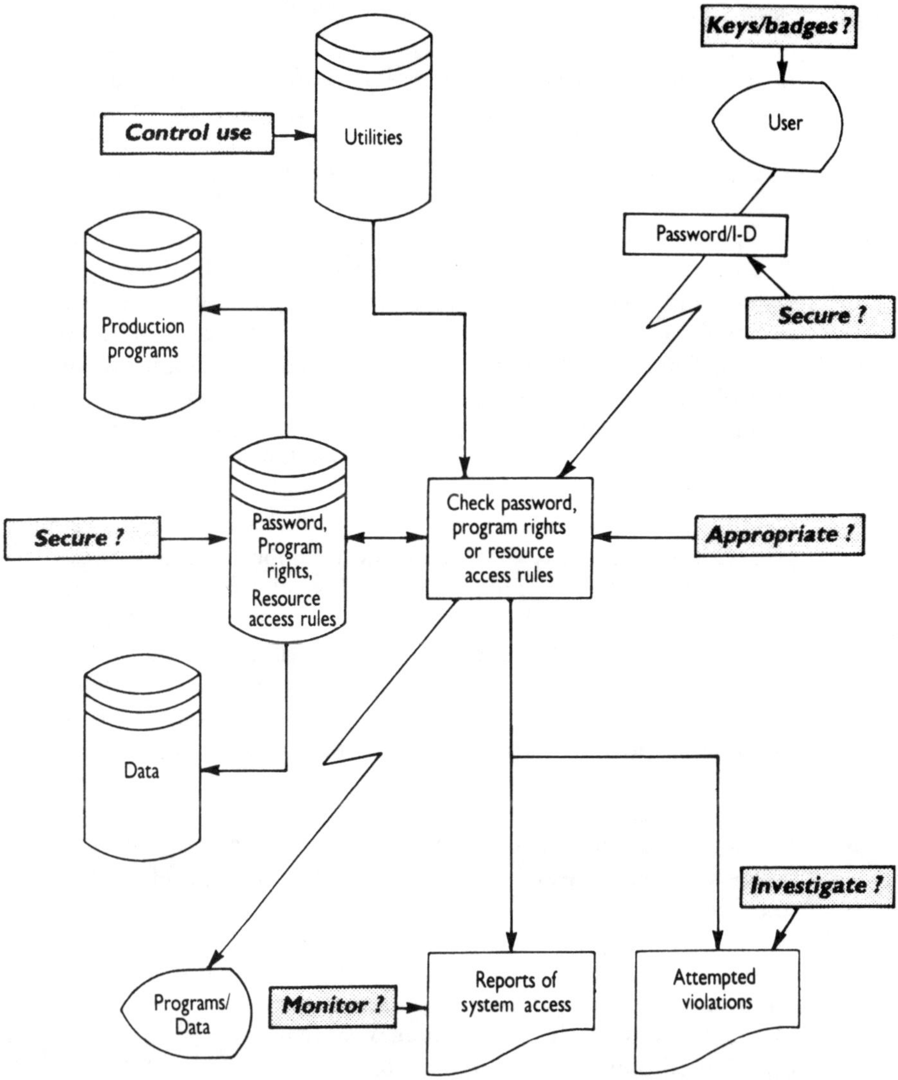

FIG. 62. Program and data file security controls – on-line programs and data (para. 7.13)

may well possess security features such as the recording of version numbers of each program or the ability to secure production programs from alteration. Specific security packages have been developed to enhance protection of programs and data, particularly in real-time and on-line database systems. Such packages are discussed in more detail in paragraphs 7.25 to 7.30.

Passwords

7.16 In both simple and complex systems it is normal for the system software to provide protection by only allowing a terminal to be activated if a valid identification has been input by the potential user and recognised by the program. This identification is normally called a password.

7.17 The password is often used in conjunction with a user identification. The user identification is input by the user when first accessing the system, and a request is then made by the system for input of the user's personal password to verify that the user is authorised to access the system. The user identification can be used for administrative and control purposes. For example, it is often used to record the usage of system resources for each user, perhaps for internal charging purposes. Frequently the user identification includes information which determines the system resources to which the user has access. The user identification may relate to a specific individual thus providing a greater level of security than the password alone, or it may be used to cover a group of related individuals with similar processing needs. In this latter case, the user identification will be known to all members of the group, so that it provides relatively little security as regards people outside the group, while each member of the group will have a unique individual password. Such an arrangement might be used, for example, to provide all members of a credit control department with access to the same processing options and to enable the system to record the total usage of resources by the department. Thus while the user identification may commonly be known to a number of users, the password should always be kept confidential and should relate to an individual user.

7.18 In simpler systems, the use of the appropriate password may enable the user to obtain, by report or on screen, any record on the file and to input any data. In more complex systems, the password system can be used both to limit users to specified terminals and data and to limit terminals to specific files. Thus, for example, in the case of an accounts receivable file, one password might permit the display or input of name and address data while another password might be needed to display or input credit limits. At the same time, only certain terminals might accept the second password needed to display or input credit limits. Attempted violations should be recorded, printed out and investigated promptly. In these complex systems, the password is often used in conjunction with a software security package, and this is discussed in more detail in paragraphs 7.25 to 7.30. Further considerations on passwords are set out below under the following headings:

- Design of passwords.
- Control of passwords.
- Communications and networks.

Design of passwords

7.19 Care should be taken in the design of passwords. If the passwords are logically related, for example by straightforward sequence numbering plus a fixed prefix such as SALES010, SALES020, SALES030, to access the accounts receivable ledger, and each password accesses different data on the file, terminal operators may be able, by trial and error, to obtain access to data fields which should otherwise be inaccessible to them. In general, passwords should not be too short or easily guessable, and the use of a mixture of alphabetic and numeric characters within passwords will increase their security.

Control of passwords

7.20 There will need to be suitable controls over the design, maintenance and issue of passwords. Password tables should be controlled, issued and amended by staff independent of computer operations and terminal usage. This activity is often monitored by internal audit.

7.21 Procedures are necessary to ensure that passwords cannot be obtained by unauthorised staff. For this reason details of passwords should not be printed on the terminal at the time they are input and the system should "log-off" a terminal after a limited number of failed attempts to input a password or after a limited period of inactivity. Password tables stored in the computer should preferably be held in unintelligible code form. It is also advisable to change the passwords periodically, and they should be revoked immediately when staff leave or transfer.

Communications and networks

7.22 Where dial-up facilities are provided so that remote users may access the system through telephone lines, it is particularly important to ensure that there are adequate password controls. In addition, control may be assisted by restricting dial-up capabilities to less sensitive functions and by arranging that when dial-up access occurs, the system will dial back the authorised user rather than permitting immediate access. For networks where particularly sensitive data is transmitted, security can be further enhanced by encryption of data before it is transmitted, and by authentication routines which enable the recipient of data to ensure that a message is authentic by the inclusion of control and identification data within it.

Databases

7.23 In addition to the features outlined above with regard to passwords, it is necessary, where database organisation is used, to control the rights of the various production programs to access or modify the data on files. In database systems each application program has an associated sub-schema held on the database library. This defines the logical view of the database for the particular application program, that is, which fields of information the program has access to. The database software is also used to define what can be done with each field, for example read only, change, delete, or change and delete.

7.24 Without a sub-schema a program cannot access the database. This restriction is usually of significance in database systems because of the greater amount and variety of data potentially available to application programs. Control of the sub-schemas is thus an important aspect in restricting unauthorised access to data in such systems. The original specification, and subsequent control, of sub-schemas is one of the functions of database administration. Control usually includes the reporting and investigation of attempted unauthorised accesses.

Security packages

7.25 In the more complex real-time and on-line environments which commonly use databases for data storage, sophisticated security packages have been developed to assist in providing adequate program and data file security. Such packages act as an interface between users and defined resources to provide a mechanism by which data sharing and processing can take place in a controlled environment. Defined resources include programs, data and transactions.

7.26 The software assists security by providing control over the users who may access the system, the resources within the system that each user may access and the access authorities, or how each user may access those resources. This is accomplished by defining rules within the software that determine each user's authority and the restrictions over each resource. The rules may be specific for each user and resource or more general, for example, granting most users read access to a particular resource. The quality of the rules specified will have a direct effect on the adequacy of the security afforded by the package. Typically resources have an "owner" who may determine the extent to which his resource is to be shared. The controls associated with a security package are discussed in the following paragraphs.

7.27 Initially access to the system will be controlled by providing users with a unique identifier or user-ID which together with a password will determine whether access is granted. The considerations related to passwords set out in paragraphs 7.16 to 7.21 are equally relevant here. Once access to the system has been gained the user has access only to those resources for which access has been specifically granted to him within the rules. The level of access to a resource may also be controlled, typically sub-divided between read, update and ability to create or delete programs or data.

7.28 Controlling access to a system is on its own insufficient to provide an adequate level of control. Therefore, the following additional considerations are also appropriate:

(a) Individual accountability. The security system should be able to associate each job or transaction with the person or department initiating the job. Provision is made for each user to have a unique identifier which enables the tracing of all attempted and unauthorised accesses to a particular individual. However, it should be noted that a user may be assigned more than one identifier each with different attributes.

(b) Auditability. It is normal practice for the package to produce regular reports of who accessed what data. Often, the package will have a report writing capability which can be used to generate the information needed for an adequate audit trail. Special reports will also be available to assist in the maintenance of the security system.

7.29 Such a complex and sophisticated security system requires software specialists and security officers to control its implementation and day-to-day operation. The function of the security officer is normally to perform maintenance functions and to ensure that the security provided by the package is not compromised by the lack of adequate follow-up and monitoring procedures. The systems software specialist is normally assigned to provide technical support to the package. It is normal practice to appoint a security administrator to monitor the activities of the security officer and technical support staff.

7.30 A security package on its own will not provide adequate program and data file security. It is necessary that there should be adequate manual procedures for follow up and monitoring of the operation of the package, and also that its interaction with other elements of the system software such as communications software, the database and the operating system is considered. The package may be implemented so that certain functions within the system are able to bypass it, and typically there will be powerful attributes within the package giving access to the rules tables which should be carefully controlled by the security officer.

CART questions

7.31 The following questions regarding software access control are asked in the CART:

"*1. List the software options (e.g. library package, passwords, security package, blocking of terminal capabilities) used to prevent unauthorised access to:*
   (a) the system;
   (b) program libraries/data files;
   (c) programs/data elements.

2. Is there an adequate combination of software procedures and manual action to:
   (a) prevent unauthorised accesses and report and investigate persistent attempts to bypass the access controls;
   or
   (b) report and investigate unauthorised accesses?

3. Are there adequate controls over:
   (a) assigning access rights to appropriate individuals in the organisation;
   (b) granting and revoking authorised access on the system (e.g. user-IDs or passwords);
   (c) allocating and withdrawing special facilities from users (e.g. ability to use certain utilities, higher levels of clearance in a hierarchy);
   (d) protecting the security tables stored on the system which are used by the system to verify authenticity (e.g. password control files, communication control tables can be one-way encrypted)?

4. Where passwords (or other codes) are used to identify individuals to the system as authorised users, are there adequate procedures to ensure that the passwords are:
   (a) periodically changed;
   (b) kept secret (e.g. not written down or displayed on screen);
   (c) not easily guessed;
   (d) cancelled for terminated or transferred employees?

5. Are there adequate procedures to ensure that the ability to use the following access control functions is itself restricted to appropriate staff with no other incompatible duties:
   (a) granting or changing system identities (3(b));
   (b) granting or changing the ability to use special facilities (3(c));
   (c) changing passwords or other identification codes (4)?

6. Are there adequate procedures to prevent unauthorised public access via dial-up (e.g. use of dial-back, dial-up access restricted to non-confidential information)?

7. *Are the procedures in 1 to 6 above subject to adequate supervision by a responsible official?*"

Physical access controls

7.32 In addition to controlling access to programs and data by suitable software procedures, there should also be adequate physical control over access to computer resources. The degree of control required, as with software controls, will depend upon the sensitivity of the processing which is taking place. For example, security will be of greater importance in a banking network used for electronic funds transfer than in a stock system providing physical balances to warehouses. Physical control of programs and data files stored off-line in libraries is dealt with in paragraphs 7.40 to 7.49 below.

7.33 Access to the computer room itself should be controlled so that only those staff who require to be there are able to enter. This includes operations staff and, on occasions and under supervision, system software staff for system maintenance purposes. Such access may be controlled by magnetic security badges, combination locks, keys or by intrusion detection systems. In sensitive installations similar control may be necessary over access to hardware such as network switching and communication lines outside the computer room.

7.34 Control can also be assisted by restricting physical access to terminals and by requiring the use of an appropriate key or badge to activate the terminal. The growth in real-time and on-line systems has, however, made it increasingly difficult to exercise effective physical control over access to terminals. Software can be of assistance by limiting the function of specific terminals. For example, terminals in a warehouse may be restricted to accessing physical stock records. Such software controls may be used in conjunction with physical controls, so that particularly sensitive functions are restricted by software to a few terminals and access to these is subject to good physical control.

7.35 It is important to remember that such controls are only effective if applied at all relevant times including the normal working day and outside working hours. Where keys or badges are used there will need to be a method of accounting for issues to staff so as to ensure that they are only used by authorised staff. Granting and revoking the means to physical access should be under the control of a sufficiently senior member of staff, and unissued keys or badges should also be physically controlled.

7.36 A particular method of physical control over programs in distributed systems is to distribute only executable versions of programs to the various processing locations. Denying physical access to the source code helps to ensure that no unauthorised amendments are made to the programs and that the versions in use at different locations remain consistent.

7.37 Unlike data, programs do not normally require to be changed frequently and, where it is not practicable to establish software or physical controls over programs, it may be possible to employ alternative techniques. One such technique is to compare the production programs with independently controlled copies on a regular basis. These copies and the software carrying out the comparison would normally be held either in a permanently supervised physical library or at a remote location. The comparison would often be carried out by the internal audit department who might have custody of the comparison software. This technique can be particularly effective in distributed systems where remote locations are only issued with executable versions.

7.38 In smaller installations, the periodic running of test data by responsible officials may be a practical method to ensure that unauthorised changes have not been made.

7.39 The following questions regarding physical access controls are asked in the CART:

"*1. Are there controls to restrict physical access to the following:*
(a) terminals;
(b) computer room;
(c) hardware outside the computer room (e.g. network switchgear, modems) where unauthorised peripherals could be attached;
(d) communications lines (e.g. cables should be sealed in ducts outside the hardware area to prevent tapping or reading by service equipment);
(e) other (specify)?
Note: Questions (c) and (d) evaluate controls to prevent sophisticated frauds being committed by tapping private networks. Unacceptable exposure in this area is likely to occur only for sensitive networks such as bank fund transfer systems.

2. Are there adequate controls over:
(a) granting and revoking of the means of permitting physical access (e.g. key, security badge, combination number);
(b) where applicable, unissued physical access permits, badges or keys?

3. Is the person responsible for controlling physical access in 2 above independent of programming, system software and accounting control functions?

4. *Are the procedures in 1 to 3 above subject to adequate supervision by a responsible official?*"

Off-line programs and data

7.40 Where programs and data are held off-line, they should be subject to physical library controls whereby they are securely held, only issued on appropriate authority and promptly returned. With the growth in real-time and on-line systems, much of the storage of programs off-line will comprise back-up copies, and both these and program documentation should be protected to avoid unauthorised personnel obtaining a detailed knowledge of the contents of the programs. Back-up copies of programs should be securely held in a library, or outside the installation, and should only be issued to the operations staff on the authority of a responsible official.

7.41 Data is commonly held off-line, since even in real-time and on-line systems there is frequently some batch processing, perhaps overnight. In addition, there is also a need to store back-up copies of on-line files or databases. The particular threat against data held off-line is that it may be removed for unauthorised purposes. The control features that protect off-line programs and data are discussed below under the headings of physical custody and library records.

Physical custody

7.42 In order that off-line programs and data may be secure from unauthorised access there should be a lockable storage area, separate from the computer room, preferably supervised by a full-time librarian responsible for the issue, receipt and security of all programs and data. Where the installation is not large enough to warrant a full-time librarian, a member of the control staff should have similar duties. Access to the library should be restricted to staff authorised to obtain and deliver programs and data. Off-site storage will need to be similarly secure.

7.43 Where batch processing is carried out there will need to be procedures so that files are only issued for authorised processing. This means that processing schedules should be prepared giving details of the files required for processing. Schedules should be prepared for all applications and be approved by a responsible official. Librarians should be instructed only to issue the appropriate files on production of an authorised processing schedule. The authority of a responsible official should be necessary for the issue of any file unsupported by a processing schedule, including transfers to off-site storage.

7.44 Files issued for processing should not be removed from the operations area. Physical control of files in issue will normally be the responsibility of the operations manager or chief operator. Further protection may be afforded by the follow up of files recorded as in issue for an unreasonable length of time.

Library records

7.45 Each removable storage device should be allocated a unique identity number which should be permanently recorded on the device. A record of devices can then be maintained as a means of accounting for and controlling both programs and data files issued from the library and those created during processing. The record of devices and files can be maintained either by the system software or manually.

7.46 Where the records are maintained by computer, the details of all devices will be input and held on the computer by the system software, commonly a file management package. During batch processing, the system software will also record, as it processes the files, the name, version number and date created on the file on each device. With this information the system software can produce the processing schedules indicating the devices to be issued. After processing, the computer will produce an updated register of devices, on the basis of which the librarian can check the return of devices issued. The system software will also produce a schedule of files processed. This can be checked by the librarian to ensure that only devices required for processing, as indicated by the processing schedule, have been used.

7.47 Where the records are maintained manually, they will normally take the form of a register of devices on which is recorded the name, version number and date created of the program or data on each device. This information will also be attached to the device itself. Issues of devices should be recorded in the register by the librarian together with the purpose for which they have been issued, as indicated on the processing schedule in the case of batch processing. Some of these devices will be holding data required for processing, such as master files of standing data. Others will be devices holding data which is no longer required, as, for example, a tape of last month's stores issues. The librarian should ensure that devices holding confidential data which is no longer required are purged before release. The register of devices should be reviewed on a daily basis and any devices outstanding for longer than the requisite period should be followed up.

7.48 In addition to accounting for devices in this manner, it is desirable that in a batch processing environment, the details of files in the library should be independently compared with those created during processing, as indicated on the processing schedule or reported on the system log. This control is particularly important where there is no independent librarian.

CART questions

7.49 The following questions regarding off-line programs and data are asked in the CART:

"*1. Where programs and data, including back-up copies, are physically controlled:*

(a) are there adequate records to identify programs/data uniquely (e.g. external labels);

(b) are there controls over the issue and return of programs/data files:

(i) to and from the physical library;

(ii) to and from the store to be used for recovery in the event of a disaster;

(iii) to and from the installation;

(c) do the storage methods prevent the unauthorised removal of programs/data?

2. Is the librarian function performed by a person independent of computer operation and programming responsibilities?

3. Are the procedures in 1 and 2 above subject to adequate supervision by a responsible official?"

Utility programs

7.50 In most computer systems there are general purpose programs, often known as **utility programs**, which can amend data files, programs or spooled input and output directly. These programs are often necessary to correct programs and data after a processing failure, and normally leave no trace of their use in the files or programs amended. They must therefore be particularly tightly controlled to ensure that their inappropriate use, either during recovery from a processing failure or at any other time, does not have adverse effects on production data or programs. These controls are normally a combination of preventative controls, such as password restrictions on the use of utility programs, or the holding of the programs off-line with specific authorisation for usage, and detective controls, such as the reporting, investigation and retrospective authorisation of all usage.

7.51 In database systems, it is important to control the use of utilities which may give access to the physical database when it is not under the control of the DBMS, for example when the DBMS is undergoing maintenance. To make a meaningful change in this way it is first necessary to ascertain the physical nature of the database, in particular the relationship between the various data elements contained in the schema. It is therefore important that unauthorised access is not allowed to the schema or its related documentation. The original specification, and subsequent control, of schemas is one of the functions of database administration.

7.52 The following question regarding the use of utilities is asked in the CART:

"*If utilities or other special programs can be used to change application programs/data by bypassing normal software access restrictions:*
(a) are there adequate procedures to identify all programs with this special status;
(b) is the ability to use such programs restricted to appropriate, authorised personnel;
(c) are there adequate controls to log and report the use, or attempted use, of such programs and for a review of such reports by a responsible official to determine and investigate unauthorised access?"

Bypassing of normal access controls

7.53 Occasionally it may be necessary to bypass the normal security and access controls over programs and data. Examples of where this may occur are in emergency situations such as processing failures where data may need to be amended to correct transmission errors, or where access is given through dial-up to an external software vendor to enable him to maintain programs. In such cases there will need to be controls to ensure that such actions are authorised, that security is subsequently reinstated and that unauthorised actions are prevented, or reported and investigated.

7.54 The following question concerning the bypassing of normal security and access controls is asked in the CART:

"*Where it is necessary to bypass normal security and access controls (e.g. emergencies or maintenance of program libraries by outside software support, such as vendors, through dial-up):*
(a) is there appropriate authorisation before or after the event;
(b) are there adequate controls to:
(i) ensure that security is subsequently reinstated;
(ii) prevent or report and investigate unauthorised changes to data?"

User programming

7.55 A more recent development has been for users to be given the ability to write programs to generate reports, typically using utilities or high level fourth generation languages. Such facilities enable users to access data and to produce reports tailored to their own needs. In some cases only extracts of a main database may be made available to users while in others live data may be accessed. Security issues arise since there may well be large numbers of physically dispersed users with such facilities, and sensitive data may well be involved. The risks may include both loss of confidentiality and unauthorised changes to data. It is therefore necessary to ensure that adequate security is implemented using the techniques outlined in this chapter. These will include such things as passwords, limiting the functions to certain terminals, physical controls over access and reviewing reported usage of such facilities.

7.56 The following question regarding user programming is asked in the CART:

"*Where users are permitted to use utilities or high level programming languages which can change data:*
(a) are there controls either to prevent the unauthorised use of this facility or to report and investigate unauthorised use, or attempts to use it;
(b) are there controls to report or prevent unauthorised use of programs written by an authorised user?"

Division of duties

7.57 In order for the controls described in this chapter to be effective, it is necessary that there should be an adequate division of duties within the computer installation so that the activities of staff within each major function such as operations are restricted to that function. With sufficient technical skill and detailed knowledge of their contents, operators can make changes to production programs. Protection against this possibility is normally provided by a suitable segregation of duties whereby the operators cannot obtain a detailed knowledge of the programs. Similarly, those responsible for the development and maintenance of programs should not be able to gain access to the production version of a program or to the computer operations area. Where a separate program library group exists with responsibility for cataloguing programs and maintaining program libraries, then staff in this group should not be able to access program documentation and development libraries or to access the computer operations area. In addition to an adequate division of duties, there should be adequate supervision within each main function so that the work of junior staff is supervised and controlled by more senior staff.

7.58 The following question concerning division of duties is asked in the CART:

"*Are there adequate controls to prevent:*
- *(a) computer operators, schedulers, data input staff and other operations personnel from gaining access to program documentation and development libraries;*
- *(b) development personnel from gaining access to the computer operations area;*
- *(c) systems implementation personnel responsible for the cataloguing function from gaining access to program documentation and development libraries, and from entering the operations area or performing computer operations functions?*"

Summary

7.59 Program security controls are designed to ensure that unauthorised changes cannot be made to the production programs that process accounting data. In conjunction with suitable controls over computer operations, they provide the auditor with assurance that key programmed procedures continue to operate properly. Data file security controls are designed to ensure that unauthorised changes cannot be made to data stored on computer systems and they complement more traditional application controls over data files. The increase in real-time and on-line systems has resulted in access to programs and data via networks of terminals being available to many users and has placed increasing emphasis on program and data file security controls. This trend is likely to continue and security features will become of increasing importance to management and auditors.

7.60 Programs and data need to be subject to security both while accessible on the system and while held off-line. In real-time and on-line systems programs and data are normally held on the system. Off-line storage will then be restricted to any batch processing carried out together with back-up copies of programs and data. In batch systems, data and less frequently programs are held off-line and loaded onto the system for processing.

7.61 The main techniques to ensure security of programs and data held on the system comprise software access controls and physical access controls. Software access controls include passwords, specific security packages to protect programs and data, and features of database, communications and library software. Physical access controls include controls over access to the computer room itself, to terminals and to other hardware outside the computer room such as communications lines. Controls over programs and data held off-line comprise physical custody controls over the storage of the magnetic media and library controls to record the movement of storage devices. Such controls should apply to programs and data stored in the computer installation and to storage off-site for back-up purposes.

7.62 It is necessary to control the usage of utility programs which can amend programs and data directly and procedures should be laid down to ensure that security is adequate when normal access controls are bypassed, for example during an emergency. Users are increasingly being given access to high level programming languages or utilities to produce their own reports, and the usage of these powerful tools should be subject to control. Finally, as in the case of user controls, there should be adequate division of duties and supervision if program and data file security controls are to be fully effective.

8

Evaluation of Controls: Information Technology (IT) Controls (3)

Introduction

8.01 In this chapter the detailed control requirements and techniques relating to computer operations controls, and system software, and how they are evaluated using the CART described in Chapter 4 are considered. The other elements of IT controls (implementation controls and program and data file security controls), and certain general points regarding the evaluation of IT controls, were considered in Chapters 6 and 7. The discussion in this chapter, as in Chapters 6 and 7, is from the point of view of the auditor.

Computer Operations Controls

8.02 Computer operations controls are those controls designed to ensure that the programmed procedures are correctly and consistently applied during the processing of accounting data. They thus include controls to ensure that programs are run at the right time and in the right sequence, the correct programs are run in the correct way, the correct data files are used in processing, operator actions during normal processing are correct, and the procedures which the company adopts to recover from any processing errors or failures are appropriate. The way in which programs are run, and the relevant controls, are considered in the following paragraphs under the headings:

- Scheduling.
- Set-up and execution.
- Use of correct data files.
- Operations software and computer operating.
- Recovery from processing failure.

8.03 Distinction is made between on-line systems and batch systems since control considerations arise at different points and the control techniques employed are likely to differ. As regards operations controls, real-time and on-line systems, as defined in Chapter 3, are considered to be similar. Both types of systems permit users to run programs from terminals, the only significant distinction being that in on-line systems certain of the updating may be carried out periodically in a batch processing mode. The controls over operations in on-line systems discussed in the following paragraphs are therefore also applicable to real-time systems.

8.04 The main distinction between on-line and batch systems in relation to computer operations control is the extent to which the running of programs is controlled centrally by the computer operators. Many of the programs making up an on-line system can be run by users from their terminals, and are typically called into operation by pressing a single key to select one of several programs displayed in a menu on the screen. All the files required for processing will already be on-line. A special program, interfacing to or forming part of the computer's operating system, handles the allocation of resources to each user in an on-line system. In the following paragraphs this program is called the **on-line monitor**.

8.05 By contrast, batch systems are normally run by specialist computer operators who are responsible for scheduling and controlling the running of programs. They do this by using commands, often called **job control statements** or **job control language** (JCL for short). These commands instruct the operating system to run particular programs, in a particular sequence, using particular files. They may also include instructions to control, for example, the rewinding of magnetic tapes and the setting of system options such as error reporting methods and the destination of output. In an on-line system JCL would usually be used to instruct the computer to run the on-line monitor, but not to run programs under the control of the on-line monitor.

8.06 Many of the controls discussed in the following paragraphs depend on either programmed procedures within the system software (for example the on-line monitor or a program to print a log of operator actions) or on data files containing operational information (for example a log written to a disc file, or a control file used to schedule processing). Reliance on computer operations controls therefore usually involves reliance also on controls over the implementation and security of system software and, in some cases, the security of data files.

Scheduling

8.07 In most systems there is a need to ensure that processing takes place at the appropriate time and in the correct sequence. For example, customer statements must normally be produced at the end of each financial period, and it may be important that the program which produces them is run after all transactions for the period have been updated but before any matched transactions are deleted. Similarly it is necessary to ensure that back-up copies of accounting files are made regularly.

8.08 In on-line systems much of the processing takes place on-line, under the control of the users. Most programs process one transaction or request, or at most a handful. The system is designed so that they can be run at any time convenient to the user, and hence scheduling control considerations do not arise. However in all on-line systems there are likely to be procedures which take place periodically, for example printing reports, calculating interest on loans, or transferring matched transactions from an on-line master file to a history file. It is in respect of these that scheduling control considerations arise.

8.09 In an on-line system the control techniques employed for periodic procedures depend on whether they are run under the control of the on-line monitor or not. In many on-line systems, usually those designed for larger computers, the periodic procedures will be run by specialist computer operators, and the controls are likely to be the same as those for batch systems discussed below.

8.10 However in many on-line systems, particularly in smaller installations with no separate computer operations department, the periodic procedures will be controlled by the on-line monitor in the same way as all other procedures. Ease of use will be maximised so that the whole system can be operated by user departments, and controlled automatically to ensure as far as possible that the correct programs are run in the right sequence. This can be done in two ways:

(a) The system can be made as automatic as possible. For example, all the end of day reporting, back-up and housekeeping procedures might be contained in one program (or in a sequence of programs run automatically by a master program) which the user runs by selecting a single option from the main menu displayed on his terminal by the on-line monitor.

(b) The system can keep a record of programs which have been run in a control file, and, when a request is made to run a program, check this to ensure that the right programs are run in the right sequence. For example, it might not allow customer statements to be printed before all transactions in the pipeline files have been updated, it might ensure that daily reports and back-ups have been run before allowing itself to be closed down at the end of the day.

8.11 In a batch system, control is typically established over the programs run by the operators by means of processing schedules showing the sequence of programs to be run and approximate timings. These may be maintained manually or be kept on a computer file. They should be prepared by reference to system documentation for each system showing the time constraints and sequences of processing applying to each system. There must be suitable review and approval of the schedules, and of any departures therefrom, to ensure that they are appropriate. After processing has taken place, a log showing when each program was run must be compared with the authorised schedules and any differences investigated to ensure that they have not resulted in errors. In large organisations there may be a separate scheduling department responsible for preparing schedules and checking processing against them. In smaller organisations this function may be carried out by the shift leaders or operators and supervised by the operations manager.

8.12 The following question regarding scheduling is asked in the CART:

"*Are there controls to ensure that:*
(a) proper schedules of jobs/programs are prepared;
(b) jobs/programs are run in accordance with the schedules;
(c) any departures from the schedules are documented and approved?"

Set-up and execution

8.13 The controls required over the set-up and execution of programs are those which ensure that the correct programs are used in the correct way. They are illustrated in outline in Figure 63. The way in which programs are used is controlled by:

- The on-line monitor (in an on-line system) or the job control statements (in a batch system).
- **Parameters** containing variable information. The most common parameters are dates, which may be used for example in the generation of cheques, the ageing of accounts receivable balances or the dating of transactions updated to a file. Other parameters may be used to indicate whether program steps only used periodically, such as the production of statements, should be activated.

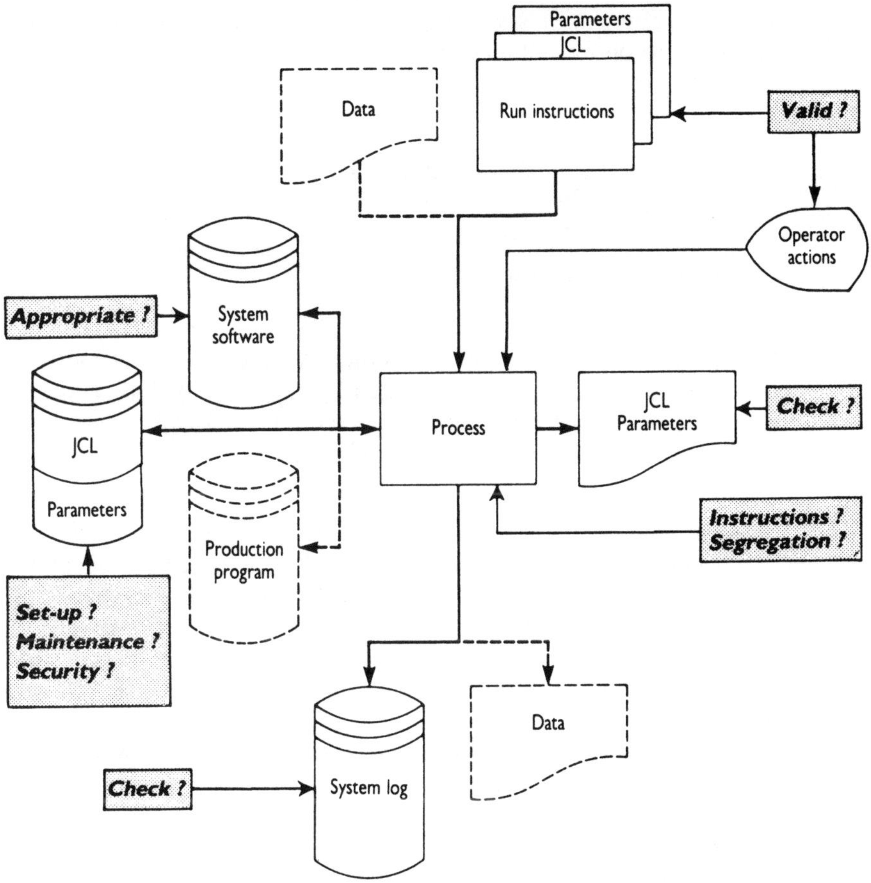

FIG. 63. Set-up and execution (para 8.13)

8.14 On-line systems are normally loaded once at the beginning of the day or session, after which all control over the running of each transaction processing program is delegated to the on-line monitor. Set-up and execution controls are therefore usually relevant only at the start of the day or session, and again at its end when periodic procedures are run. In respect of the periodic procedures some control may also be delegated to the on-line monitor, although there are still likely to be variable parameters input manually which need to be controlled. In batch systems, set-up and execution controls are relevant to each program run.

8.15 The control techniques employed in both on-line and batch systems are likely to be a combination of:

- Manual checking against set-up instructions.
- Reliance on controls over the set-up and maintenance of files of job control statements.
- Reliance on controls over the set-up and maintenance of parameter tables or control files.

8.16 Set-up instructions should be maintained for each manually controlled procedure within each system. These should give details of the job control statements and parameters to be used, and of any other actions necessary in setting up and executing the programs.

8.17 Set-up instructions will be prepared and updated as part of the system development and maintenance procedures discussed in Chapter 6. Care must be taken to ensure that they are complete and correct, and that they are kept up to date whenever the system is changed. To this end they should be checked and approved as part of the system development and maintenance controls. Care must also be taken to protect them from unauthorised changes. A record should be kept of any changes made, their purpose and the authority for them. Set-up instructions should be reviewed regularly by a responsible official to verify that they are up to date and any changes are valid.

8.18 Each time programs are run there should be controls to ensure that the job control statements and parameters are in accordance with the instructions. Usually this is achieved by checking the job control statements and parameters reported on a computer-produced log of processing. In an on-line system, only a limited number of job control statements and parameters will be input manually, and these can be checked easily by a responsible official.

8.19 In a batch system the volume of job control statements and parameters is likely to be much higher. In larger installations a separate data control department may exist to check the results of processing, including a check that the correct job control statements and parameters were used. It is important that the log is sufficiently compact to enable a meaningful review to be carried out, and this means that it must be selective in the information which it reports. Where the normal computer logs do not permit selective reporting, it may be possible to use a separate program to identify and report the relevant information.

8.20 In most batch systems, job control statements are stored in a file on disc. This will normally be set up when the related programs are implemented and maintained as part of the program maintenance procedures. Reliance is then placed on the controls over the set-up, maintenance and security of job control statements, and when they are used in operational processing it is only necessary to check that the appropriate file of job control statements was used.

8.21 The controls over the set-up and maintenance of job control statements are likely to be the detailed checking and authorisation by a responsible official when a new or amended program is catalogued. Security controls are likely to be similar to those over programs stored on disc, and it is only necessary when considering job control statements to establish that the same controls apply.

8.22 Application programs can also carry out checks on parameters, for example to ensure that dates are valid and reasonable in relation to the current date recorded in the system. However, in many systems the application programs can obtain parameters automatically from a control file set up at an earlier date, thus reducing the volume of parameters to be checked at each processing run. The most common example of this is the use of an accounting calendar stored on disc which is used to determine when to run periodic procedures such as month end reports. Controls are then necessary over the set-up of the calendar file, for example the checking of the details by a responsible official, and over its security thereafter.

8.23 The controls in force must allow also for variations from authorised job control statements and parameters. These may be necessary to overcome processing problems, for example to use programs from a test library when those in the production library are corrupted. Where departures are made from authorised procedures, variations should be reviewed and approved by responsible officials to ensure that the results are nevertheless satisfactory. Controls should include a review by a data processing official who is familiar with the design of the system and the implications of any departures from normal processing. They should also include a close review by user departments of the results of processing.

8.24 The following questions regarding the set-up and execution of programs are asked in the CART:

"*1. Are there adequate procedures for:*
(a) setting up batch jobs;

(b) loading on-line application systems;
(c) loading system software?

2. Are there controls to prevent or detect and investigate unauthorised changes to approved job set-up instructions?

3. Are there controls to ensure that control statements and parameters used in processing are in accordance with the approved procedures (e.g. independent check of run instructions, review of output JCL listings)?

4. Is there appropriate written approval, including user involvement where appropriate, of:
(a) variations in parameters and control statements that may affect the way a batch job or an on-line system runs (e.g. dates, currency rates, period end routines);
(b) departures from authorised set-up procedures (e.g. use of programs from a test library for production)?

5. Are the procedures in 1 to 4 above subject to adequate supervision by a responsible official?"

Use of correct data files

8.25 In many cases use of the correct data files will be ensured by the normal updating and continuity controls discussed in Chapter 5. However, particularly as regards those files that contain tables referred to in processing, for example the list of numbers where sequence checks are used, specific controls over the use of the correct file will be required.

8.26 Controls over the use of the correct data files can take the following forms:

(a) reliance on the on-line monitor in an on-line system;

(b) programmed checking of file labels and retention dates; and

(c) reliance on a database management system.

8.27 In an on-line system, the files needed by users during the day must be continuously on-line. The on-line monitor normally takes control of the necessary files when the system is loaded at the start of the day. When users need access to data for enquiry or input purposes, the on-line monitor ensures that they use the appropriate files, and controls the use of files so that different users do not conflict (e.g. one user amending a record while another is reading the same record). Reliance is thus placed on the on-line monitor to ensure that all users have access to the correct on-line data files. Separate controls will still be necessary in respect of other files used in periodic processing.

8.28 Programmed checking of file labels is used mainly where files are held off-line and loaded by the operators for use. Although there will be manual controls over the data files at the time of issue from the physical library to job set-up, the auditor will usually rely on the system software to ensure that the correct files are loaded. Each file held on a device will include a header label containing such information as the file name and the version number. If a file is so large as to require more than one device, the header label will also include a sequence number to identify the part of the file concerned.

8.29 When the file is loaded for processing, the details on the header label are checked. Additional protection can be achieved in the case of batch systems by the use of retention periods. When a file is created, the system software adds to the header label the current date and the number of days for which the data is to be retained. The system software will not accept the file for processing until the expiry date of the retention period has been reached. Any operator override of these controls should be reviewed. Additional manual checks may also be required where the programmed checking is not as comprehensive as that outlined above.

8.30 Where programmed label checking is used, the software can only check that the file in use corresponds to that defined either in the program or in the related job control statements. Controls are therefore required to ensure that the program or job control statements specify the correct data file or sub-schema. These are normally checked by a responsible official as part of the controls over program cataloguing and the set-up of job control statements, since at that time the file required will be changed from a test file to a production file.

8.31 Where a database is in use, reliance is placed on the database management system to control and organise the access to data. It does this in accordance with the sub-schemas used by each program. Some reliance can be placed on the testing procedures during program development. However, additional controls must be present when programs are catalogued in the production program libraries, since this will usually involve changing the sub-schemas from those for the test database to those relevant to the production database.

8.32 The following question regarding the use of data files is asked in the CART:

"*Are there controls to ensure that:*

(a) the correct data files are used (e.g. software label checking, generation data sets, use of a tape management system, user check of volume/serial numbers, controlling manual overrides which bypass label checking);

(b) where applicable, all volumes of a multi-volume file are used (e.g. software checking of file and volume labels);

(c) exceptions are reported and investigated (e.g. where all volumes of a multi-volume file were not used)?"

Operations software and computer operating

8.33 The procedures which organise and control the activity involved in computer processing will be exercised partly manually and partly by software. In on-line systems and the more advanced batch systems, the procedures are mainly carried out by software and the manual functions are then restricted to actions required or requested by the software. There is an increasing trend in more sophisticated systems to simplify manual operator activity and restrict the need for operations personnel, for example, by using software to suppress the reporting of less important systems activity which might otherwise require manual scrutiny by operators. The principal control considerations are that the system software used is reliable and that the manual procedures do not, by error or otherwise, interfere with, or affect, normal processing.

8.34 The main system software used is generally known as the operating system. An operating system usually consists of a series of program modules. The principal module is variously known (depending upon the particular computer manufacturer) as the control module, supervisor, monitor, or executive. In its simplest form, the control module is a program, permanently resident in the computer while it is in operation, which supervises the running of the application programs. The control module supervises the operation of the subsidiary program modules, transferring control of the computer to them as and when required. Examples of the more common subsidiary program modules are those used to carry out file handling procedures, to control multiprogramming (where used), to control spooling systems (where used) and to control the manipulation of data.

8.35 In advanced systems, further system software is used which has to interface with the operating system. For example, where remote terminals are used, data communications software is necessary to handle the transmission of data to and from the terminals. In database systems, the DBMS is necessary for the processing of data on the database. The facilities of reading and writing included within the DBMS work in conjunction with the file handling module of the operating system.

8.36 One area in which operator actions can affect processing, even in on-line systems where their control over application programs is minimal, is in the loading and running of system software. System software is usually controlled, both when it is set up and during subsequent processing, by means of system parameters. These contain variable information such as which terminals are to be allowed access to the system, which program libraries are to be used, where printed output is to be directed, or what events are to be reported on computer-produced logs of processing.

8.37 Another area where operators have control over processing is in the actions taken following a processing failure when the operators will normally be responsible for taking initial corrective action and restarting the system. In some cases it may be necessary for a technician or systems analyst to operate the computer in order to diagnose and correct the problem. When the normal systems are not running, many of the controls built into them will also not function. In these circumstances it is particularly important that the actions of operators, or of other people operating the computer in order to correct a problem, are recorded and reviewed to ensure that no error has been introduced into programs or data files during the process. In recovering from a processing failure it may well be that utility programs which can amend data files or programs directly, often with no trace, will be used. The particular considerations in respect of data files are covered in paragraphs 8.45 to 8.50.

8.38 The controls over the manual procedures will depend largely on the nature of the system and the size of the installation. They will normally comprise a combination of procedures designed both to prevent and detect error. The preventative procedures usually include the provision of operating instructions and the establishment, where practicable, of a suitable division of duties. The measures to detect error will be based on reviews of operator activity.

8.39 Operator procedures should be based on a framework of standing instructions. These instructions should deal with the operation of the computer and its peripheral equipment, the actions to be taken in the event of machine or program failure and the records to be kept. The standing instructions, when combined with the run instructions, should provide rules for each step that may need to be taken by operators. A responsible official, such as the operations manager, should periodically review the operating instructions and confirm that they remain up to date. Evidence of compliance with operating instructions should be included in the review of processing referred to in paragraph 8.41.

8.40 In the larger installations it is likely that more than one operator will be present during processes and there will thus be opportunities to rotate duties. In addition, the work of operators may be supervised during processing by a chief operator or shift leader. In smaller installations it will be less practicable to provide for a segregation of duties and more emphasis will need to be given to a review of operator actions during processing.

8.41 The review of operator actions will be based on a computer-produced report or, less frequently, a manual report. The system software will usually record on file details of all activity during processing. The details on this file, defined as the **system log**, can be printed out for review. Unusual activity such as hardware malfunction, re-runs and abnormal endings and the resulting operator actions can thus be investigated. However, it should be borne in mind that the information recorded on these logs is voluminous and technical in nature, and a full review is thus often impracticable. Manufacturers' software may be available, or system software may be designed, to analyse the entries and report items of particular interest as an aid to their investigation.

8.42 Where, as in some smaller installations, the system software does not produce a log in sufficient detail to review unusual activity, or where it is not practicable to review the system log, the review of unusual activity may be based on a fully manual report or a part computer and part manual report. For example, the system software may generate details of time spent on the jobs processed and the operators may enter thereon details of the causes of differences from scheduled times. It would normally only be possible to place reliance on a fully manual log where there was adequate division of duties or supervision in the computer room during the processing to which it related.

8.43 The system log should be reviewed by a responsible official or by someone other than those responsible for job set-up or computer operations. Particular attention should be paid to evidence of:

(a) operators overriding system software checks, for example, by overriding retention periods on data files;

(b) actions taken between the time of a processing failure and the resumption of normal processing;

(c) any reported usage of utility programs; and

(d) the changing of system parameters in such a way as to affect production processing.

The person carrying out the review should establish that the report is complete for the period under review and follows on from the previously reviewed system log. This control can be conveniently based on the use of sequentially prenumbered stationery.

8.44 The following questions in respect of computer operating are asked in the CART:

Operator actions:

"*1. Are there controls over:*

(a) initial loading and subsequent use of system software, including amendments to parameters while the system is running (e.g. re-allocation of physical/logical terminals, changes to logging options, changes to program libraries);

(b) the execution of application programs;

(c) compliance with other standard operating procedures?

2. Is there adequate identification and reporting of:

(a) system failures;

(b) restart and recovery;

(c) emergency situations;

(d) other unusual situations?

3. Are operator actions in the event of the incidents in 2 above reviewed for appropriateness and to ensure that the results of processing were not adversely affected (e.g. review of logs and incident reports, daily problem meeting)?

4. Is there appropriate supervision of operators at all times, including shifts outside the normal working period?

Logs of activity:

5. Where manual or automated logs are relied upon for recording system or operator activities, are there adequate controls over the completeness and accuracy of these logs?

6. Are changes made to logs (or to the method of logging), appropriately authorised?

7. Are the logs adequately reviewed and unusual situations investigated?

8. *Are the results of the investigation and correction of unusual situations and resulting operator actions reviewed and approved by a responsible official?*
Note: Where operators have access to utility programs which can be used to change application programs/data by bypassing normal software access restrictions answer question 15 of the program and data file security section."

Recovery from processing failure

8.45 When a processing failure occurs, special procedures must be adopted to ensure that data files are not corrupted. Errors can be introduced by direct corruption of data during the processing failure, in which case it is necessary to restore data from back-up files. For this purpose it is necessary that back-up copies of data files are created regularly. The frequency of backing up files is a matter of operational convenience, bearing in mind the risk that in the event of a processing failure it may be necessary to repeat all processing since the last back-up. It is common for errors to be introduced because the failure occurred in the middle of processing, when some data files had been partly processed. Care must be taken to restart processing at the correct point. Usually it will be necessary to restore the data files using back-up copies to their status at a particular, known point in processing and restart from that point.

8.46 The more commonly used methods of recovery in real-time, on-line and database systems are based on the logging of information as each transaction is processed. The information logged is the details of each transaction and of the file record being accessed. This information is used in the recovery process in the following manner:

- When logging takes place of the existing contents of each file or database record which is to be accessed by a transaction, before it is processed by that transaction ("before image") – if a failure occurs which affects only the transaction and record being processed the file or database can be restored to its previous correct state by reinstating the "before image" record of the affected record. If a more serious failure occurs, the before image log records are used to overwrite their corresponding file or database records to a point before the corruption occurred. This technique is variously known as *backing out*, *point of failure recovery*, or *roll back*.
- When logging takes place of the contents of the file or database record after it has been processed by a transaction but before the new information is physically written ("after image") – the file or database is dumped at intervals and, in the event of a processing

failure, recovery is achieved by taking the last dump and processing the after image records for transactions since that dump. This technique is normally known as *roll forward*.

8.47 It is one of the functions of the DBMS to monitor the database as processing takes place and to detect any logical damage to the database (for example, incorrect or missing linkages; incorrect record counts). Often the DBMS will automatically put into effect the recovery procedures described above to correct logical damage to the database. The Database Administrator will control this function.

8.48 In an on-line system, a processing failure which involves restoring data files to an earlier back-up copy may mean that users have to repeat all recent input. There must be procedures to ensure that users are aware of this, know what data needs to be reinput, and reinput it completely. This may take the form of a notification from the data processing department to users of the time after which all input has been lost, together with a report of updated transactions to enable users to find out which have been lost, and user controls over the completeness of reinput.

8.49 In a batch system procedures should include a facility for restarting at an intermediate stage of processing programs terminated before their normal ending or before completing the processing of a transaction. This procedure prevents the whole run having to be reprocessed. The technique used is known as checkpointing and involves the recording ("dumping") of the contents of memory at various stages during processing. In the event of the program terminating it may be restarted at the previous checkpoint. Such procedures are generally not suitable for real-time, on-line and database systems since dumps need to be taken very frequently and the machine time requirement tends to become prohibitive.

8.50 The following questions regarding the back-up and recovery of data files are asked in the CART:

"*1. Are there adequate controls to:*
- *(a) back-up and store independently copies of all data at appropriate intervals;*
- *(b) log or save activity so that the status of data files at the time of failure is known?*

2. Are there controls to ensure that data files are recovered properly after a processing failure and that no errors are introduced by the recovery process?

3. *If modifications are made to data after failures or during emergencies (e.g. use of utilities to correct transmission errors), are there adequate procedures to ensure that the changes are made correctly and approved (e.g. by retroactively applying user controls over adjustments)?*

4. *Is there adequate user involvement to ensure that proper recovery from failures takes place (e.g. notification to users by the data processing department that major recoveries have taken place)?*

5. *Are the procedures in 1 to 4 above subject to adequate supervision by a responsible official?*"

System Software

8.51 At various points in this chapter, and in Chapters 6 and 7, reference has been made to system software. System software was defined in Chapter 2 as those programs on whose functioning the auditor may wish to place reliance although they do not process accounting data. System software is relevant to the auditor because it assists in the control both of the programs that process accounting data and of the data files.

8.52 The system software that may be of relevance to the auditor, and which has been referred to earlier in this chapter and in Chapters 6 and 7, includes the programs relating to:

(a) Cataloguing (paragraph 6.49).

(b) Software access controls (paragraphs 7.14 to 7.31).

(c) Program comparison (paragraph 7.37).

(d) Library records (paragraph 7.46).

(e) Supervision of application programs (paragraphs 8.04 to 8.06 and 8.34).

(f) File handling/DBMS (paragraphs 8.34 to 8.35).

(g) Data communications (paragraph 8.35).

(h) Reporting of operations (paragraph 8.41).

(i) Use of correct data files (paragraphs 8.26 to 8.31).

(j) Recovery from processing failure (paragraphs 8.45 to 8.50).

The system software section of the CART contains general questions on controls over system software, together with specific questions for the more significant functions of system software with which the auditor might be concerned, for example the DBMS.

8.53 Having identified those software procedures on which he wishes to place reliance, the auditor will be concerned that they are appropriate, have been properly implemented and maintained and are kept secure. The considerations to be taken into account in evaluating the appropriateness of the software procedures have been outlined earlier. In this section the controls over the implementation, maintenance and security of system software as a whole and over some specific system software functions are considered.

Implementation and maintenance

8.54 The controls required for the successful implementation of system software are substantially similar to those required for the implementation of application programs.

8.55 Where system software is designed by a technical support group within the company, or software supplied from outside is altered, the procedures for system design, outlined in Chapter 6, should be followed. Where system software is supplied from outside by manufacturers or software houses, normally the only work required of the company will be the selection of the software and, where appropriate, of options in the software. The procedures described in Chapter 6 for the selection and implementation of packaged systems will be relevant in this case.

8.56 Any changes made by the company to the implemented software will need to be controlled in the manner outlined in Chapter 6. In the case of software, particularly operating systems, supplied by the manufacturers, improvements and modifications will be made from time to time. These modifications will be introduced in the form of new programs received from the manufacturers or by amendments to the existing programs, usually made by the manufacturer's systems engineer.

8.57 When new or amended system software has been loaded, i.e. copied to a disc permanently on-line to the computer, it should be tested to ensure that it performs as intended. Where the software is used with application programs, for example the operating system, tests would normally involve the running of the software with proven application programs so that any anomalies which may occur can be identified as resulting from the system software. This approach will also be important where application programs require modification in order to be compatible with the revised operating system, for example when the company is introducing a database structure for data files, using a DBMS.

8.58 Where the software is unrelated to the running of application programs, for example the software producing the report of operations and file set-up, the proper functioning of the software, and the inclusion of the appropriate options, may be confirmed by a review of the system-generated output.

8.59 The controls over the copying of the tested software onto the installation's library should follow, as appropriate, the procedures for the cataloguing of application programs outlined in Chapter 6.

Security

8.60 Controls, similar to those outlined in Chapter 7 for the security of programs, should be used to ensure that unauthorised changes are not made to system software either while in use or when held off-line.

8.61 One additional consideration arises in respect of the security of system software. The security of application programs can be controlled primarily through the use of system software (e.g. access control software) and by an adequate segregation of duties within the system development department. However adequate security controls over system software are more difficult to achieve. The system software support department is smaller and their work is highly specialised, and hence more difficult to review. In addition access control software is inoperative when the system software is deactivated for maintenance, providing unrestricted access to data. Furthermore the system software support department is needed particularly in emergencies when there are processing failures or in implementing changes to system software. It is at these times that a formalised system of control is difficult to apply without inhibiting the work of the system software support department.

8.62 Thus there is a greater risk that system software will be subject to unauthorised amendment. Where security from unauthorised amendment is relevant therefore, it is necessary to place reliance on other factors which act to reduce the risk. The main precaution which a company should take is the use of suitable personnel policies to ensure as far as possible the reliability of system software personnel. It should always take up references for new system software staff, or evaluate staff internally before transferring them to the system software department. When staff leave, they should be transferred out of the system software department and prevented from gaining access to the computer as soon as notice is given on either side. In addition to sound personnel policies the work of system software support staff should be closely supervised by the head of the group or by an appropriate person if the department is small.

8.63 The questions asked in the CART in respect of the implementation and security of system software are similar to those asked in respect of application programs and are included in the IT controls section of the CART in Appendix A to Chapter 4. One additional question is asked, which is not similar to those for application programs:

"Are staff employed in the technical support function only on the basis of either:
(a) thorough enquiry into the validity of references; or
(b) assessment of the integrity of the individual in the course of earlier duties in the organisation?"

Database administration

8.64 The size and complexity of databases often leads to the appointment of specific personnel responsible for all aspects of database administration. These personnel are often collectively called the database administrator (DBA). Their tasks might include the design and maintenance of the schemas and sub-schemas, the maintenance of the DBMS and related software and liaison with users, other computer department staff and outside suppliers. Certain important integrity controls relating to the database may be undertaken by the DBA. These have already been mentioned at the appropriate places in Chapters 6 to 8 and include:

(a) review of new systems for compatibility with the database (paragraphs 6.26, 6.35 and 6.36);

(b) documentation of the database (paragraph 6.29);

(c) review of program changes for impact on the database (paragraph 6.87);

(d) control of schemas and sub-schemas (paragraphs 7.24 and 7.51);

(e) back-up, logging and recovery procedures in respect of the database (paragraph 8.46).

In addition the DBA may be responsible for maintenance controls over data on the database and for maintenance of the database management software itself.

8.65 The DBA may thus combine responsibility for procedures and controls which, in conventional systems, would normally be carried out by separate people. When these procedures and controls are combined to a significant extent in the DBA, it is important, in order to preserve an appropriate division of duties, that the DBA is restricted from unsupervised access to computer facilities or operation of the computer and cannot initiate transactions.

Telecommunications, networks and distributed systems

8.66 Where data is transmitted from one installation to another, there will normally be a separate telecommunications or network support department. This will be responsible for maintaining the communications software and for allocating communications facilities to users of computer installations. The same considerations apply to the implementation and maintenance of communications software as to other parts of the system software.

8.67 The auditor's primary concern is to ensure that the transmitted data is received completely and accurately, and that communications facilities are not used to make unauthorised alterations to data or programs stored at any installation. The company will also wish for operational reasons to ensure that confidentiality is maintained in respect of sensitive information transmitted through the system.

8.68 As regards the completeness and accuracy of transmission and reception the auditor will normally rely on controls over completeness and accuracy of input and updating as described in Chapter 5. In addition, to enable errors to be corrected promptly and the communications network to operate efficiently, there will normally be software checks built into the communications software to ensure the correct transmission of messages. For example, the receiving computer can transmit the data it receives back to the sending computer, which then checks it against the data originally sent. This is commonly known as "echo checking". Where public data communication lines are used similar controls are normally provided by the carrier (the owner of the communication lines). Control over the input of unauthorised data is normally achieved by the use of physical and software access controls as described in Chapter 7, including checks built into the communications software.

8.69 In the event of a failure within the network, either a processing failure at one of the linked computers or the failure of a communication line, the controls over recovery from processing failure at each site, already described in paragraphs 8.45 to 8.50, should ensure that there is no corruption of production data or programs at any site. However the company may implement special controls which will allow the network to continue to function as effectively as possible in the event of a failure of one component in the network.

Personal computing

8.70 In many organisations there are, in addition to the main computer systems, facilities provided to users to enable them to carry out minor tasks themselves. These facilities may be provided using microcomputers or terminals connected to a larger computer installation. Typically there will be a department responsible for training users, providing technical assistance where necessary and co-ordinating the development of programs so as to avoid wasting resources. Users are normally provided with facilities to write programs, possibly using a program generator or general purpose data manipulation package, and to devise and run computer models using special modelling packages.

8.71 The auditor's concern in respect of personal computing facilities relates to the development by users of programs or models which are used to process accounting data. Controls are particularly important when programs or models developed by one user are passed to other users, since the recipients are likely to place reliance on them without being aware of any limitations or shortcomings in their design.

8.72 In general, user controls will be the most practical way of controlling data processed by such means, since the volume of such data is likely to be low. However where user controls are not relied upon, implementation, security and operations controls will be needed. The control considerations have already been discussed in Chapters 6 and 7, and in the current chapter.

8.73 The control techniques will be simpler because of the more informal nature of the development process. A quality control function should be exercised to ensure that:

(a) programs are properly designed and tested;

(b) there is a clear, written description of the objective of each program and the method of using it;

(c) there is adequate documentation to enable maintenance to be carried out subsequently;

(d) authorised versions of programs are kept secure from unauthorised amendments.

8.74 There will also need to be controls over any standard software, for example programming aids or modelling packages, which are supplied to users. These will be similar to those already described for system software.

Summary

8.75 Computer operations controls are designed to ensure that programmed procedures are correctly and consistently applied during the processing of accounting data. Control must be exercised over job scheduling to ensure that processing takes place at the appropriate time and in the correct sequence, over the set-up and execution of jobs so as to ensure that the correct programs are used in the correct way, to ensure that the correct data files are used, to ensure that the actions of operators are correct and to enable recovery to be made from processing failures without corruption of programs or data.

8.76 There are significant differences between real-time and on-line systems and batch systems in regard to computer operations controls. For real-time and on-line systems many of the programs can be run by users selecting options from a menu, and programs and data files are continuously available on the system. A program called the on-line monitor handles the allocation of resources to each user. In batch systems programs are normally run by specialist computer operators using job control statements to initiate processing. Data files are separately loaded onto the system for the particular execution.

8.77 Implementation controls, program and data file security controls and operations controls are frequently dependent on the operation of system software. System software does not itself process accounting data but it is of relevance to the auditor because it assists in the control of both the programs that do process accounting data and of the data files. The importance of system software to the auditor has increased with the growing complexity of computer systems. In particular, the expansion in on-line networks frequently involving access to a database has meant that database software, communications software and security software are increasingly of relevance in assessing the controls over computer systems.

9

Testing Controls and the Response to Weaknesses

General Approach

Purpose and scope

9.01 Where the auditor decides to carry out an extended assessment of controls as part of his audit strategy, he will need to carry out tests to satisfy himself that the controls have operated effectively and continuously throughout the period under audit. In general, the auditor will seek to perform the minimum amount of testing necessary to provide the degree of assurance that he requires on the operation of the controls.

9.02 The auditor obtains direct and indirect evidence of the effective operation of controls from many aspects of his audit work and, in deciding the extent of testing which is necessary, he should take into account all other relevant work he has performed. Where an audit has been carried out in earlier years the auditor will have knowledge of the previous operation of the business, of overview and possibly extended assessments of controls and of substantive testing performed in earlier years. Where the results of this work were satisfactory the auditor should take this into account in deciding the extent of testing necessary in the current year. He will have gained further information from the work performed to determine the audit strategy and to evaluate controls in the current year.

9.03 Specifically, the auditor will have reviewed the overall control environment in determining his audit strategy, as discussed in Chapter 2. Where this is favourable it will provide the auditor with a significant degree of assurance that application controls subject to the environment are effective. Where he wishes to satisfy himself as to the effective operation of programmed procedures, the auditor will normally evaluate and test the IT controls. The extent of testing of the application controls will be a matter for judgement in each case taking into account all of the above factors. The auditor should be able to be selective in deciding which systems and controls to test and should not need to test every control on which he wishes to rely, provided the results of his tests and his work on the control environment and IT controls are satisfactory. This is because assurance on the consistency of operation of controls and programmed procedures in the applications will be provided by the work performed on the control environment and IT controls.

Documentation of testing

9.04 The tests carried out on the controls will be documented using the "tests" column of the CART which was illustrated in Figure 41 in Chapter 4. In this way the tests are related directly to the controls. The following details should normally be recorded, using supporting working papers where there is insufficient space on the CART:

(a) the name and job title of the person with whom the procedure was discussed, or who was observed carrying out the procedure;

(b) the date of the discussion or observation;

(c) details of the discussion, observation, evidence examined or other tests carried out;

(d) the level and spread of tests;

(e) an indication that the work has been completed, usually the initials of the person completing the work, and the date of its performance.

Types of tests

9.05 The auditor performs tests of controls in order to ensure that they operate effectively, and this encompasses two elements, as follows:

(a) the control must be appropriately designed to achieve its objective;

(b) the control must operate as prescribed. The person carrying out control procedures should understand how to perform them and be diligent in doing so.

9.06 The techniques used to obtain evidence for the extended assessment of controls are:

- **Observation and enquiry**, i.e. the viewing of the actions of employees in their work environment and the making of specific enquiries of management and staff, for example, observing the physical inspection of goods received.
- **Examination of evidence**, i.e. the inspection of records, documents, reconciliations and reports for evidence that a control has been properly carried out, for example, the inspection of signatures or initials on a supplier's invoice evidencing that the invoice has been matched with a goods received note.
- **Reperformance**, i.e. the repeating, either in whole or in part, of the same work processes as those performed by the company's employees or a computer program, for example, the actual matching by the auditor of a supplier's invoice with the corresponding goods received note, in order to obtain assurance that the evidence seen on the supplier's invoice actually represents work done.

9.07 The auditor's objective is to obtain sufficient evidence to support his conclusions and to obtain that evidence in the most efficient manner. He may well concentrate his tests on observation and enquiry together with examination of evidence and limit reperformance to cases where the other techniques do not provide sufficient assurance that the control is operating effectively.

Observation and enquiry

9.08 Where the auditor is performing tests based on observation and enquiry he must ensure that the procedures followed are sufficiently comprehensive to establish the effectiveness of the controls. When relying on observation the auditor should bear in mind the possibility that the observed control may not be performed when he is not present. He should also make any enquiries he considers necessary to support and amplify his observations; for example, where details of goods received are to be entered on a sequentially numbered document, he should enquire as to the effect of part deliveries, backlog of work and abnormal deliveries on the procedure observed.

9.09 In making enquiries, the auditor should be alert to vague or glib answers and to apparent inconsistencies. For example, if the control is a sales manager's review and investigation of a report of invoices with unusually high or low gross margins, merely asking the sales manager whether discrepancies are investigated will be inadequate. Appropriate questions to ask might cover the following aspects of the procedure:

(a) how the items on the report are investigated;

(b) whether all items are investigated;

(c) how it is ensured that every report is received;

(d) whether every report is investigated;

(e) whether there are particular situations to which attention is directed;

(f) how long the review takes;

(g) how the investigation of the report is evidenced and approved;

(h) whether there were any periods in which the reports were not reviewed; and

(i) who reviews the reports in the absence of the normal reviewer.

Examination of evidence

9.10 Evidence examined may include written explanations, clearance marks or other indications of performance on a copy of a report or document used in the control procedures. In the case of the report referred to in paragraph 9.09, the auditor would examine the report for evidence of review and corrective action taken. Absence of evidence is often indicative that the control is not operating as prescribed. The auditor may find it helpful to make corroborative enquiries of persons other than those performing the controls.

Reperformance

9.11 Reperformance tests are time consuming to perform and the auditor is likely to restrict the extent of his reperformance work as far as possible. Sometimes the operation of a control if of such significance that he will need to obtain further evidence of its effective operation, because there would be a risk of significant misstatement if it were not operating properly. For example, a control designed to ensure the completeness, accuracy and authorisation of the update of a standing data file of interest rates in a bank might be so significant to the accuracy of interest charged to customers that the auditor would wish to gain additional evidence that the control is operating as prescribed.

9.12 The extent of reperformance required is a matter of judgement. Normally, where the auditor does decide to reperform a control he will only need to do so to a limited extent, perhaps once or twice. Where reperformance is performed it should be remembered that it is the control which is being assessed and not the existence or accuracy of specific transactions. For this reason it is not necessary to select high value items for testing or to select different types of transactions. Where the auditor concludes that he will need to carry out extensive reperformance of controls to gain the required assurance, he should consider whether it is still efficient to make an extended assessment of control. The internal auditor may have as his objective the detailed testing of controls in the system and he may therefore perform more extensive reperformance tests.

9.13 In order to assist in assembling a programme of tests which is appropriate to the system being tested, and to ensure standardisation in the tests carried out, specimen tests can be provided for many of the common control techniques. Specimen tests to assist in testing the more common controls are set out in Appendix A to this chapter and are referred to where considered helpful in the paragraphs below. The tests should be tailored in each case to fit the precise characteristics of the system. The specimen tests include reperformance tests although, as noted in paragraph 9.12, the external auditor is unlikely to perform extensive reperformance.

The Approach in Computer Systems

The nature of tests in a computer system

9.14 As in non-computer systems, the purpose of tests of controls is to provide evidence as to whether or not an internal control procedure is being operated as planned. However, because of the changes in controls discussed in the previous four chapters, there are often differences in the techniques used.

9.15 The techniques for testing controls in computer systems can be further considered under the following headings:

- Supervision and division of duties.
- User controls.
- IT controls.
- Programmed procedures.

Supervision and division of duties

Supervisory controls

9.16 Tests of the supervisory controls will be largely based on the examination of evidence. The primary evidence examined will be the signature or initials of the person exercising the supervision on the relevant documents or records, for example, in the case of user controls, on a rejection or exception report indicating that all items have been satisfactorily dealt with or, as regards IT controls, on a program change form indicating that testing has been properly carried out. Particular attention should also be given to other evidence, such as internal memoranda indicating the disposition of unsatisfactory documents or records which have been queried as a result of the supervisory control. Where appropriate, the auditor will also wish to confirm that the material submitted to the supervisor was, prima facie, suitable to enable a satisfactory review to be carried out, for example, in the case of program testing, that details of the test data and the results were submitted to the supervisor. The auditor may also be able to observe the application of the supervisory control to transactions being processed or reports being prepared at the time of his visit.

9.17 Complete reperformance of a supervisory control will often not be possible, partly because the auditor does not have the knowledge and experience of the supervisor concerned, and partly because the nature and extent of the checks carried out by the supervisor may be at his discretion and may not be clearly evidenced. Reperformance is therefore usually limited to the inspection of the supporting documentation that should have been seen, together with evidence of prior checks as required by the company's procedures.

9.18 As a practical matter, it is frequently more efficient to use the same transactions to carry out tests of supervisory controls and the underlying user controls. The existence of errors in the application of the underlying user control that were not detected by the supervisor may indicate that the supervisory control is not being applied effectively, and to this extent a test of the underlying user control can serve the same purpose as a reperformance test of the supervisory control.

Division of duties

9.19 The tests of division of duties are normally carried out by the examination of signatures and initials on documents and records, and observation and enquiry. It is not usually possible to carry out satisfactory reperformance tests on controls of this nature.

9.20 In the case of user controls, the auditor will, for example, review signatures and initials on reconciliation and exception reports to confirm that the persons carrying out the user controls were independent of computer operations, that is to say those responsible for the functions of system design, programming and computer operating. He might, in addition, visit the departments concerned and verify by observation that the independence referred to above was being maintained at the time of his visit.

9.21 As regards the division of duties in IT controls, for example, between those involved in system development and maintenance, computer operating and custody of data files, the auditor will wish to examine the computer department organisation charts, written procedures and job descriptions and confirm that they provide for adequate division of duties both during and outside the normal working day. He can also visit the data processing department and the computer room and observe that this division of duties existed at the time of his visit. In addition, he may, where possible, examine work schedules, time reports, operator logs, evidence of access rights and similar documentation to confirm that the names of individuals performing duties are consistent with the written procedures.

Tests of user controls

9.22 In the majority of cases no particular difficulties are likely to be experienced because visible evidence of the controls is normally available. For example, the review of a computer-produced report of the result of a control total reconciliation, or the action taken on an exception report, are frequently noted on the relevant reports.

9.23 Increasingly, however, in advanced systems control procedures are carried out on-line and the evidence that they have been carried out exists only within computer files. For example, purchase invoices may be input to the system before authorisation and reviewed on-line via a terminal by authorising officials. In order to authorise invoices for payment, the officials input a payment code, known only to them, which is stored in the purchase ledger file and causes the system to generate a cheque at the next payment point. The payment codes on file can be examined by the auditor, possibly using a computer program, and used as evidence of the control procedure. He will also need to satisfy himself as to the operation of the programmed procedures which ensure that the payment codes are valid and if so update them to the purchase ledger file, and the data security controls which ensure that payment codes cannot be updated or amended on the files except through the proper, authorised procedure.

9.24 Where reperformance tests are being performed and there are large volumes, it should be noted that complete reperformance may not be practicable. For example, where control is exercised by the reconciliation of the total of a large number of batches with a subsequent total produced by the computer, reperformance of the establishment of the initial total might consist of checking the additions of a sample of batches and tracing the selected batch totals to the control register.

9.25 Tests of controls comprising physical procedures normally consist of observation of, and enquiry about, the procedures in force together with a review of documentation. As regards control, for example over the security of unissued cheques, the auditor will wish to observe that such cheques are under adequate physical controls and that proper procedures are laid down for access to the cheques.

Tests of IT controls

9.26 Where IT controls are to be relied upon, the auditor will need to carry out tests on the manual control procedures and also to test a sample of the relevant system software procedures that are relied upon. He will decide how many, and which, system software procedures to test in the light of the results of his tests on the other IT controls.

9.27 Testing of those IT controls that are carried out manually will include examination of evidence, observation and enquiry, and possibly reperformance. Many of the tests will be similar to those for testing user controls, for example the review of computer-produced reports. Other tests will be similar to those carried out in non-computer systems, such as those on the completeness controls over program changes. Certain tests as, for example, those on the testing procedures are unique to testing IT controls. Examination of evidence is particularly important because, in many cases, reperformance is not an appropriate technique. This is so, for example, where the auditor is testing the adequacy of documentation, such as system descriptions and operating instructions.

9.28 Where, as is normally the case, IT controls depend on system software procedures the auditor must also carry out tests to satisfy himself as to the appropriateness of the system software procedures. These tests will be similar in nature to those on other manual IT control procedures. In general, the external auditor will be able to gain sufficient assurance regarding controls over system software from observation and enquiry and examination of evidence, particularly since much of the software is standard in nature and supplied by external vendors.

9.29 The internal auditor may wish to carry out more detailed tests of system software and the external auditor may do so as an additional service to management or where a particular system software procedure is of great importance. Where it is decided to perform detailed tests on system software, various techniques are available to test the appropriateness of system software procedures. The technique selected will depend on the nature of the procedure being tested. For example, in testing the cataloguing procedures the use of audit test data and program code analysis may assist in establishing that new or changed programs function properly, thus confirming that they were satisfactorily catalogued. The use of audit test data and program code analysis is considered in greater detail later in this chapter (paragraphs 9.41 to 9.43).

9.30 Computer programs have been developed to assist in, and render more effective, the testing of system software procedures. These include:

(a) programs which examine the company's production programs and, by comparing them with independently controlled copies, assist in confirming that authorised changes have been properly made or that unauthorised changes have not been made. Examples of such programs which compare the executable and source versions of the client's production programs with independently controlled copies are illustrated in Figures 64 and 65;

(b) programs which will analyse and report defined items on the system files which the auditor can then compare with the client's report produced by a system software procedure. An example of such a program is illustrated in Figure 66 (page 287).

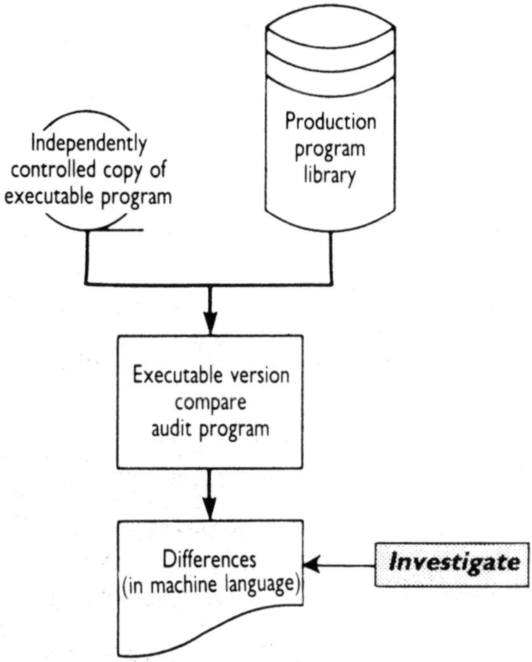

FIG. 64. Audit examination of executable programs (para. 9.30)

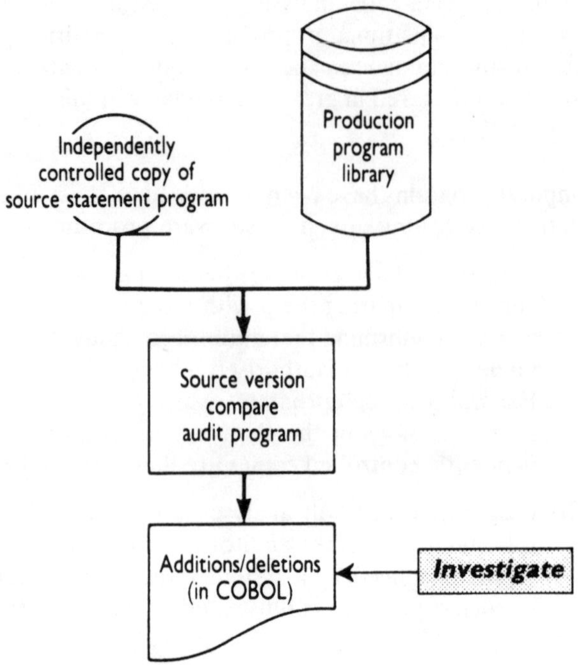

FIG. 65. Audit examination of source statement programs (para. 9.30)

9.31 The auditor may wish to place reliance on those system software procedures which ensure the security of a system from unauthorised access. Tests may include:

- The auditor attempting to gain access to protected data files or programs using invalid passwords. Before doing so he should gain permission from the client to undertake such a test and consider the consequences both if the controls should operate properly and if they should fail to operate.
- Review of reports of access violations or attempted unauthorised access for follow up action.
- Use of computer programs to interrogate security tables or system logs to produce reports which can be compared to the client's reports and reviewed to ensure that access rules are reasonable.
- Discussion, observation and review of documentation to confirm that the access controls implemented by the system software appear satisfactory.

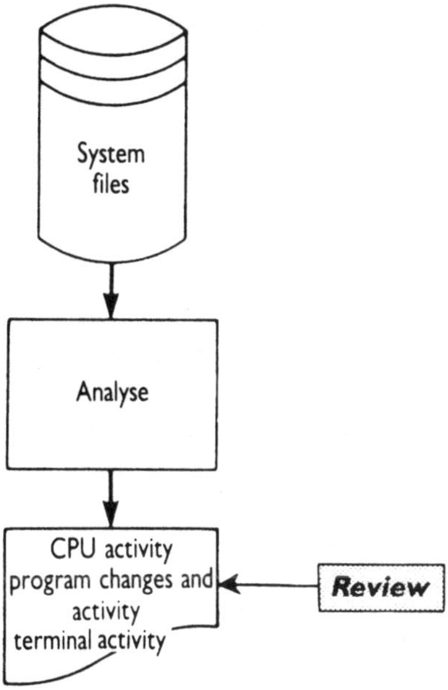

FIG. 66 Audit analysis of system files (para. 9.30)

Direct tests of programmed procedures

9.32 Direct tests of a programmed procedure are tests designed to confirm that it has operated correctly. Normally the external auditor will not find it efficient to test directly the operation of a large number of programmed procedures as part of his audit strategy. However, he may carry out direct tests on significant programmed procedures whose continued and proper operation is essential to the effectiveness of user controls on which he wishes to place reliance when:

(a) his audit strategy is to place no reliance, or only partial reliance, on IT controls; or

(b) his tests on IT controls reveal weaknesses which prevent him from relying wholly on IT controls; or

(c) the programmed procedures are of such importance that, despite the reliance he is able to place on the relevant IT controls, he judges it necessary to obtain further assurance as to the continued and proper operation of the programmed procedures.

In addition where the auditor carries out tests of implementation controls, he may gain some assurance on the operation programmed procedures during his tests.

9.33 Although direct tests of programmed procedures are substantive in nature, they are normally performed in conjunction with tests on user controls. Consequently it is convenient to consider them in this chapter rather than in that on substantive tests.

9.34 Direct tests of programmed procedures are normally carried out by reperformance because it is not possible to test their proper operation conclusively by examination of evidence. However, the examination of print-outs, such as lists of missing items, will often provide prima facie evidence that a programmed procedure has continued to operate properly. This examination of evidence will normally be carried out as part of the testing of user controls, for example while testing the investigation of the missing items reported.

9.35 The principal techniques available to test programmed procedures include manual tests, the use of audit test data, program code analysis and simulation using computer audit programs. The choice of technique is often governed by whether there is loss of visible evidence.

Loss of visible evidence

9.36 It is a feature of computer processing that the results of processing may not be printed out in detail. In the absence of such a print-out, the operation of programmed procedures cannot be tested by conventional means. There are three ways in which this difficulty can arise. First, totals and analyses may be printed out without supporting details, thus rendering it impossible to check the total or analysis. The second situation, although common, is less obvious. Where exception reports and rejection listings are produced, it is often impossible, by reference to the reports or listings, to establish that all items which should have been reported or rejected have been properly treated. Thirdly, the control procedure may be carried out entirely through a computer terminal with no evidence being printed out, as for example when data is edited during input and errors are displayed on the screen for the operator to correct immediately instead of being reported on an edit listing.

9.37 These three types of situation have traditionally been covered by the phrase "loss of audit trail". However, this term is unfortunate in that it implies that the means to check results by conventional tests should be available to auditors and the failure to incorporate this in the system is a matter for criticism. This is not true; what matters is the adequacy of the controls. If the failure to print out constitutes a weakness in control as, for example, if the contents of suspense files were not regularly printed out, the system is deficient and the auditor is correct to draw this to the attention of the company. But if the failure to print out does not represent a weakness, the auditor should normally be able to devise alternative techniques to test the operation of the programmed procedures if he wishes to test them. For these reasons the term **visible evidence** is used in this book in preference to "audit trail".

Manual tests

9.38 Manual tests can be carried out of programmed procedures where full visible evidence of the programmed procedure is available; for example, where a complete listing of sales invoices is provided, it can be added up to confirm the sales total or, where debtors' statements show all transactions on individual accounts, postings thereto can be checked. Tests will consist of repeating the work that the program carried out and verifying that the results are the same.

9.39 Manual tests can also be carried out where full visible evidence is not provided by the system, but can be created in one of the following ways:

- working on current data before it is sent for processing by the computer, for example manually checking the validity of product codes on despatch notes in order to test a programmed validity check;
- selecting a small number of items from those submitted for processing and processing these in a separate run, for example processing a small number of purchase invoices separately to allow the purchase analysis to be checked;
- simulating a condition which will produce a report if the programmed procedure is working properly, for example altering an item on an input document so that it fails to match correctly with data in a pipeline file, or withholding a document so that it is reported as missing (this approach requires careful planning and the agreement of the client);
- requesting a special print-out of items processed, for example a listing of sales invoices included in a sales total produced by the computer.

9.40 Where visible evidence of the operation of a programmed procedure neither exists nor can be created, and the appropriate condition cannot be simulated, it is not possible to carry out manual tests.

Audit test data

9.41 This technique, which is illustrated in Figure 67, consists of devising fictitious data and predicting the results that should be obtained if the programmed procedures operate properly. The data is processed against the client's operational programs and the actual results are

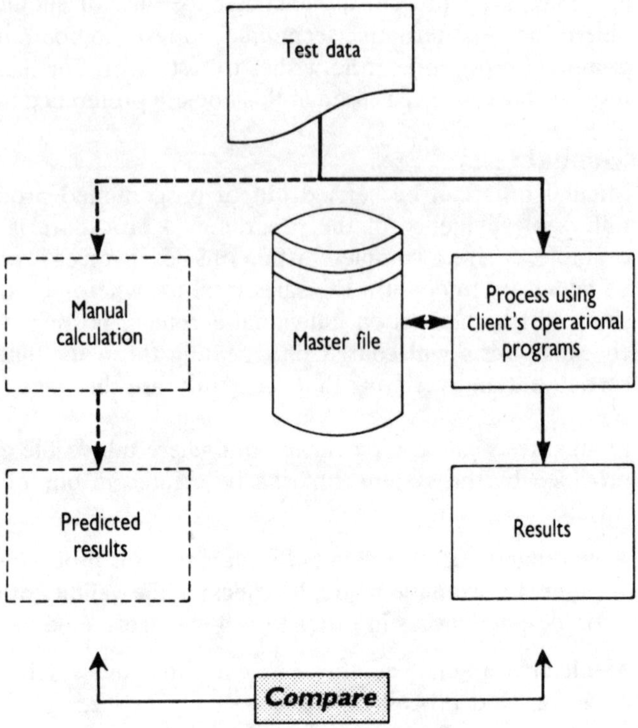

FIG. 67. Audit test data (para. 9.41)

checked against the predicted results. This technique is normally used where there is incomplete evidence available of how the procedure operated and manual tests are either impracticable or inefficient. Audit test data is usually designed to test the operation of several programmed procedures within an application, for example by processing fictitious orders to produce invoices, sales totals and entries in inventory and accounts receivable ledgers. In this case, although it may remain possible to test some of the programmed procedures by manual tests, for example calculations, it will often be more efficient to test them by the use of test data.

9.42 There are important practical considerations when audit test data is used and these are dealt with in Appendix B to this chapter. Two illustrations of the use of audit test data are set out in Appendix C.

Program code analysis

9.43 Program code analysis comprises the examination of source listings of operational programs to determine that the relevant programmed procedures are present and are logically coded. The technical skill required to perform program code analysis is high, as the auditor needs to be familiar with the program language used. The auditor must verify that the coding on the source listing that he is examining is the same as that contained in the operational program which is used for processing. The considerations to be taken into account, and procedures to be followed, when using program code analysis, are discussed in Appendix D to this chapter. Program code analysis is illustrated in Figure 68.

Use of computer programs

9.44 The auditor usually makes use of his own computer programs to assist in the carrying out of substantive tests. The use of programs in this manner is described in Chapter 10 "Substantive Tests" and Chapter 11 "The Use of File Interrogation Software". However, the auditor can also use his own computer programs to assist in testing programmed procedures. This use of programs is often referred to as **simulation**. There is no fundamental difference between the audit use of computer programs as a substantive test and as a test of a programmed procedure. The main distinction is that, when used for simulation, the objective of the auditor's program is to check that the company's program is operating correctly by checking and agreeing

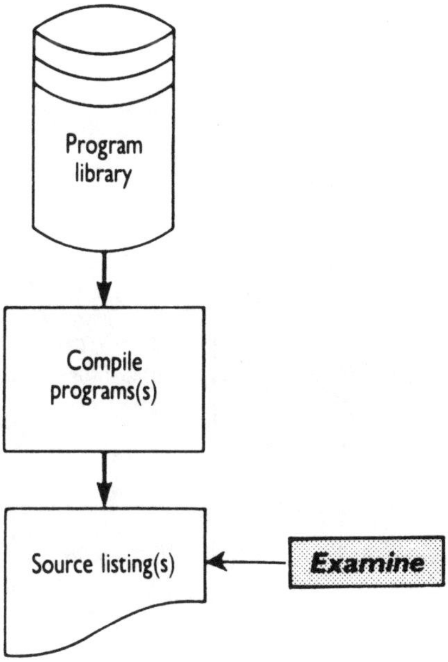

FIG. 68. Program code analysis (para. 9.43)

figures prepared by the company's program. When used as a substantive test, the program is also used to provide the auditor with information from the files, over and above that produced by the company, that will be helpful in his audit.

9.45 Examples of the use of a computer audit program as a method of testing programmed procedures include reading a sales invoicing file to verify the production of the sales analysis, reading a file of numbered goods received notes to verify the production of a missing numbers report, and reading a file of stock movements to verify the production of a stock evaluation and analysis report. As the auditor is primarily concerned with those parts of the program that comprise the programmed procedures, it is often unnecessary to duplicate exactly the precise and complete logic of the client's program. The auditor's program may thus be less complicated than that of the client. The use of computer programs for simulation is illustrated in Figure 69.

9.46 One of the practical problems of simulation is that it is often difficult to short-cut the logic of a complex client program. In attempting to do so, the auditor may arrive at different figures from the client and

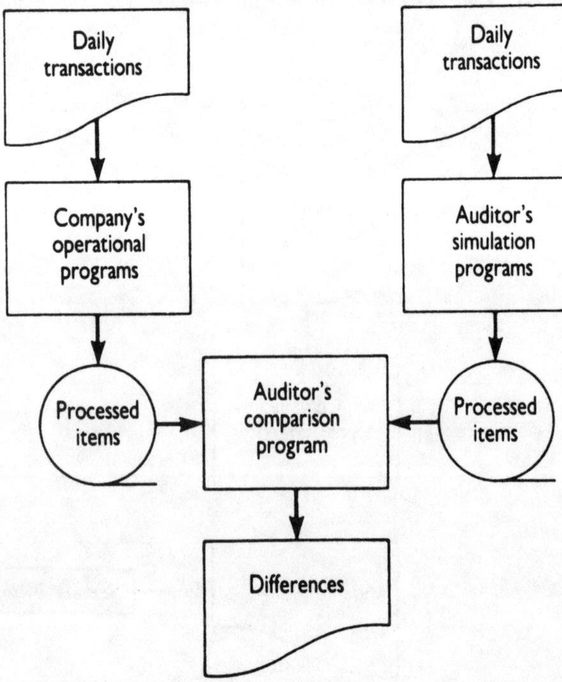

FIG. 69. Use of computer programs for simulation (para. 9.45)

have to spend time correcting his program logic or carrying out a reconciliation. Simulation can thus involve considerable set-up costs, although once set up the programs can usually be run relatively cheaply. For this reason it is only likely to be appropriate when the auditor needs to place substantial reliance on his direct tests of important programmed procedures, for example where the programmed procedures directly generate major items of revenue such as interest in a bank, and where little or no reliance is to be placed on IT controls.

9.47 As an extension of his tests, the auditor may wish to include checks in his program so that he can indicate to the company what would be the effect of introducing particular procedures; for example, if sales orders had been tested for credit, bad debts of a quantified value might have been avoided. This work goes beyond the normal statutory audit requirements and seeks to identify areas where the company can improve its system. It is therefore in the nature of operational auditing.

Extent of testing

9.48 It is not possible to provide hard and fast rules for determining the extent of testing as this is, in each case, a matter for judgement by the auditor in the light of all relevant factors. Factors which the auditor will take into account include the importance of the control or procedure and the risk that the auditor's observation of controls and the responses to his enquiries may not provide reliable evidence on the continued and proper operation of controls. His assessment of this risk will be based on the quality of answers received to enquiries and whether such answers appear sound and credible. Where the auditor judges the risk of erroneous or misleading answers to his enquiries to be low he may decide to restrict his examination of evidence to only one operation of the control. Where the auditor judges the risk of misleading answers to be higher, he will increase the extent of his testing.

9.49 The importance of the control or procedure will largely depend on the effect of a breakdown in it. If a breakdown could lead to material misstatement the auditor would be particularly concerned about the control or procedure. As a general rule breakdowns in controls over standing data will often be more far-reaching than breakdowns in controls over individual transactions. Breakdowns in controls over completeness will often be more serious than breakdowns in control over accuracy or validity of individual transactions, since items that should be present, but which have been omitted during processing will be difficult to identify. The auditor may also gain some assurance on the operation of a particular control from his tests of other controls and his other audit procedures, and he will take this into account in deciding the extent of his testing.

9.50 The auditor will also need to consider whether he needs to obtain specific evidence that controls operated continuously throughout the period by spreading the tests of controls. The auditor's observation and enquiry tests should be sufficiently thorough to enable him to draw a conclusion as to whether controls have operated effectively and continuously up to the date when the observation and enquiry were carried out. Control procedures carried out by the client, for example supervisory procedures, may provide evidence of the continuous operation of the underlying manually performed control procedures. Certain controls are cumulative, for example the review of a report of outstanding goods received notes where outstanding items continue to be reported until cleared. In such cases evidence that the control operated at a point of time will also provide evidence as to the operation of the control up to that point in time.

9.51 The auditor will need to gain assurance about the operation of controls in the intervening period between the date of his tests and the end of the financial period under examination. This may require him to spread his tests, but he may also be able to gain the required assurance from his work on the control environment and IT controls and his substantive tests.

The Response to Weaknesses in Control

9.52 The auditor's purpose in assessing the effectiveness of controls is to determine whether they support a conclusion that, for the relevant audit objectives, there is a low risk of material misstatement of the account balances or classes of transactions. The assessment will take into account not only the results of testing but also the assessment of the control environment, the knowledge of accounting systems and all other audit work performed up to that stage of the audit.

9.53 The absence of, or weakness in, individual procedures need not necessarily lead to a conclusion that the control procedures are not effective overall. The auditor should consider the effect of any significant control weaknesses encountered but should not give undue weight to individual or isolated weaknesses when drawing conclusions. In considering control weaknesses the auditor will seek to distinguish between those that are significant to his assessment of control effectiveness and those that are not. Weaknesses will be recorded on the CART and on supporting working papers. With the exception of wholly insignificant matters, weaknesses will normally be reported to the client.

9.54 In determining whether a control weakness is significant, the auditor will consider both the direct effect of the weakness and its implications for the overall assessment of control effectiveness. Depending on its nature, the weakness might have the following direct effects:

(a) the under or over-statement of an asset, or liability, in the balance sheet, with a corresponding effect on the profit and loss account;

(b) the failure to disclose a fraud in respect of which the loss has been written off in the profit and loss account;

(c) a misclassification of items, as a result of which there could be a failure to disclose an item properly in the financial statements.

9.55 The auditor will also consider the effect of the weakness on the control environment and the overall effectiveness of IT controls and application controls. Where the auditor has assessed the control environment as favourable he will be relying on this assessment for a significant degree of assurance that application controls subject to the environment are effective, and it is likely that his strategy will not involve testing every control on which he wishes to rely. If the weakness leads the auditor to conclude that the control environment is not favourable he will no longer be able to rely on it for this purpose. He should reconsider whether an extended assessment of controls is an efficient audit strategy, as he will need to perform additional tests of other application controls on which he wishes to place reliance.

9.56 Where there are weaknesses in IT controls, the auditor should consider whether these are so significant as to prevent overall reliance on the IT controls to ensure the continued and proper operation of programmed procedures or the security of programs and data files. Breakdowns identified in the operation of programmed procedures may also indicate weaknesses in the IT controls. Where there are weaknesses in application controls, the auditor will consider whether these are such as to suggest that application controls may in general be unreliable. For example, if the assessment of an application revealed that many controls procedures were not adhered to consistently in practice, this might suggest that a similar situation is likely to exist in other applications.

9.57 Where the auditor finds weaknesses that are significant to his assessment of control effectiveness, he will reconsider his audit strategy, and may conclude that it is no longer possible or efficient to rely on an extended assessment of controls. However, as noted above, he should avoid giving undue weight to individual weaknesses in making this decision.

Common Weaknesses in Computer Systems

9.58 Weaknesses often occur because of a failure to plan the controls adequately during the early stage of system development. This leads to the development of controls on an ad hoc and unstructured basis. In particular it is common, as indicated in paragraph 5.03, for the need to consider the entire system, both computer and non-computer, as a whole, to be overlooked; the manual controls are often not decided upon until the systems become operational. The need to reconsider existing manual controls when computer processing is introduced may also be overlooked.

9.59 The more common weaknesses include:

- The failure to establish controls over the continuity of standing data.
- The failure to recognise the need to control reference data.
- Ineffective authorisation procedures, particularly in relation to irregular input, such as adjustments.
- The failure to recognise the importance of supervisory controls.
- The failure to review the accuracy of computer-generated data, for example interest charges, by either reasonableness checks or overall total reconciliations.
- Unrealistic settings for the criteria in programmed reasonableness and dependency checks with the result that either too few or too many exceptional items are rejected or reported.
- The failure to establish a proper division of duties within the computer department between the functions of system analysts, programmers and computer operators.
- For small computer departments, inadequate supervision and division of duties.
- The failure to produce readily digestible reports of computer usage, such as exception reports of the usage of particularly sensitive facilities, in order that a meaningful review of computer operations can be carried out.
- The absence of control over access to program libraries, particularly as regards ensuring that only properly authorised amendments can be made.

- The failure to safeguard data files against access by unauthorised personnel.
- The failure to ensure that restrictions over the operation of the computer and access to data files are enforced at all times, particularly during evening and weekend shifts.
- Inadequate physical security over the data processing installation.

9.60 The more common breakdowns that are encountered during testing include:

- The failure to act promptly on exception reports.
- A build-up of uninvestigated rejections.
- A build-up of suspense items on files.
- Delays in the follow up of outstanding and overdue items, such as the despatch of reminder letters.
- The failure to carry out reconciliation procedures when under time pressure, following delays in processing.
- The low priority often given to cyclical checking of standing data.
- Inadequate protection of communication lines.
- Inadequate selection and testing of package applications.
- Inadequate procedures for the management of passwords.
- Failure to establish adequate control over end-user computing.
- Restrictions over the operating of the computer not enforced; in particular, programmers allowed to operate the machine unsupervised to test programs.
- A failure to review and approve records of computer usage sufficiently regularly.
- Program change reports not being adequately controlled and monitored.
- Creeping degeneration of distributed systems as a result of local program modifications.
- Amendments made to operational program libraries bypassing the normal control procedures and the requirement for authorisation.

- Password procedures not applied; in particular passwords not kept secret and not changed regularly.

Summary

9.61 As in non-computer systems, the purpose of tests of controls is to provide evidence as to whether or not an internal control procedure is being operated effectively. However, because of the changes in controls in computer systems, there are often differences in the techniques used for testing.

9.62 Tests of user controls and IT controls carried out manually are similar in nature to those in non-computer systems. There are a number of techniques available for testing directly the operation of programmed procedures and system software, where the auditor decides that this is necessary, including the use of test data, program code analysis and computer programs.

9.63 Where the auditor's tests reveal weaknesses in controls he should consider whether the weaknesses are significant to his overall assessment of the effectiveness of the controls. Where they are significant the auditor will need to reconsider his audit strategy, and particularly whether reliance on an extended assessment of controls is still feasible and cost-effective.

9: Appendix A

Specimen Tests

1 In this appendix there are examples of the specimen tests that may be used by the auditor in assembling his programme of tests.

2 The specimen tests have been prepared for testing user controls, programmed procedures and IT controls. They have not been designed to test every control but rather to provide a specimen for testing the more common computer related control techniques that are likely to apply in several cases in most applications. Tests for non-computer activities are not included. As stated in Chapter 9 care is needed to tailor the specimen tests to each particular situation.

3 The specimen tests include reperformance tests and direct tests of programmed procedures although, as noted in paragraph 9.12, the external auditor is unlikely to perform extensive reperformance or direct tests of programmed procedures.

Nature of Control	*Specimen Test*
Tests of user controls	
1 *Completeness and accuracy of input –* review of computer-produced reports.	(a) Examine computer reports and see: (i) evidence that reported items or batches (e.g. as outstanding, mismatched or missing) are being dealt with by persons with no incompatible duties; (ii) where appropriate, evidence indicating that the results of the procedures in (i) above have been reviewed and approved by a responsible official. (b) Reperform the clearance of reported items or batches by selecting cleared items or batches and checking that they were properly dealt with.
2 *Completeness and accuracy of input and updating –* manual agreement of pre-determined totals.	(a) (i) Examine the register/control account for evidence that the totals/balance are/is being regularly agreed, by persons with no incompatible duties, with the totals printed on the edit/update report. (ii) Examine evidence that discrepancies are being dealt with by persons with no incompatible duties. (iii) Where appropriate, examine evidence indicating that the results of the procedures in (i) and (ii) have been reviewed and approved by a responsible official. (b) Reperform the agreement of the totals by: (i) testing agreement of register/control account with the total printed out on the edit/update report; (ii) testing the additions of batches and of register/control account. (c) Reperform the clearance of discrepancies by selecting cleared items and checking that they were properly dealt with.

Nature of Control	*Specimen Test*
3 *Completeness and accuracy of updating* – manual agreement of computer-produced totals.	(a) (i) Examine computer reports or register for evidence that the computer-produced totals are being regularly agreed, by persons with no incompatible duties, with the totals printed out on the update report. (NOTE: take into account summarisation of totals or changes in the totals used.) (ii) Examine evidence that differences are investigated and dealt with by persons with no incompatible duties. (iii) Where appropriate, examine evidence indicating that the results of the procedures in (i) and (ii) have been reviewed and approved by a responsible official. (b) Reperform the agreement in (a)(i) above. (c) Where appropriate, reperform the clearance of reconciliation differences by selecting cleared items and checking that they were properly dealt with.
4 *Completeness and accuracy of updating* – manual review of programmed reconciliations.	(a) Examine computer reports and see: (i) that evidence of the reconciliation is examined by persons with no incompatible duties and suitable action taken on any differences; (ii) where appropriate, evidence indicating that the results of the procedures in (i) above have been reviewed and approved by a responsible official. (b) Where appropriate, reperform the clearance of reconciliation differences by selecting cleared items and checking that they were properly dealt with.
5 *Completeness and accuracy of input and updating* – checking of print-outs.	(a) Test the procedures designed to ensure that all source documents are recorded on an input document.

Nature of Control	*Specimen Test*
5 (*continued*)	(b) Examine records or files of source documents or retained copies of input documents and verify that there is no undue volume or value of unprocessed items. (c) (i) Examine update reports for evidence that the one for one checking procedures are being carried out. (ii) Reperform the checking by testing items on the update reports with the relevant original documents. (iii) Examine update reports or other evidence that differences are being investigated and corrected by persons with no incompatible duties. (iv) Reperform the clearance of differences by selecting cleared items and checking that they were properly dealt with.
6 *Accuracy of input* – verification of conversion.	(a) Examine evidence that the procedures for verification are being properly carried out. (b) Attend at the conversion department and observe that the fields required to be controlled for accuracy are being verified.
7 *Computer-generated data* – manual review.	(a) Examine computer reports and see: (i) that the data is being manually reviewed by persons with no incompatible duties and suitable action taken on any items requiring adjustment; (ii) where appropriate, evidence indicating that the results of the procedures in (i) above have been reviewed and approved by a responsible official. (b) Reperform the manual review of items by selecting items and checking by reference to source data that they were properly passed or adjusted.

Nature of Control	*Specimen Test*
8 *File continuity control* – manual control account.	(a) (i) Examine the control account for evidence that it is being regularly agreed to a print-out of total balances on the file by persons with no incompatible duties and suitable action taken in respect of any differences. (ii) Where appropriate, examine evidence indicating that the results of the procedures in (i) above have been reviewed and approved by a responsible official. (b) Reperform the agreement of the control account by: (i) testing the make-up of the control account; (ii) testing the agreement of the control account. (c) Where appropriate, reperform the clearance of differences by selecting cleared differences and checking that they were properly dealt with.
9 *File continuity control* – computer control record.	(a) Examine reports of computer reconciliations and see: (i) that evidence of the reconciliation is examined by persons with no incompatible duties and suitable action taken on any differences; (ii) where appropriate, evidence that the brought forward total appearing on the master file update report is agreed with the carried forward total on the previous report; (iii) where appropriate, evidence that the results of the procedures in (i) and (ii) above have been reviewed and approved by a responsible official. Where visible evidence of the reconciliation is available, reperform the control in (a)(ii) above by testing the agreement of brought forward and carried forward figures.

Nature of Control	*Specimen Test*
9 (*continued*)	(c) Where appropriate, reperform the clearance of differences by selecting cleared differences and checking that they were properly dealt with. (d) Where no evidence of the reconciliation exists, review the results of the tests of IT controls. Were the results of the tests of data file security controls satisfactory?
10 *File continuity control* – cyclical checking of standing data.	(a) (i) Examine computer reports or source data for evidence that detailed checking is being carried out by persons with no incompatible duties to the extent and frequency required and suitable action taken in respect of any differences. (ii) Where appropriate, examine evidence indicating that the results of the procedures in (i) above have been reviewed and approved by a responsible official. (b) Reperform the control by selecting items from the print-out which have been marked as checked and check them to source data. (c) Where appropriate, reperform the clearance of differences by selecting cleared differences and checking that they were properly dealt with.
11 *Timing of authorisation* – rechecking of authorised data after input controls established.	(a) Examine evidence that authorised data is rechecked by a responsible official after batch totals have been established or sequentially numbered documents raised to ensure that all authorised data is processed. (b) Reperform the rechecking by selecting current batches or serially numbered documents and verify with supporting documentation.
Direct tests of programmed procedures 12 *Computer matching.*	NOTE: Manual tests only are included Test the matching process by selecting items to be input and: (a) holding back until reported as missing; (b) altering relevant fields on documents and confirming that they are reported as mismatched.

Nature of Control	*Specimen Test*
13 *Computer sequence check.*	Test the sequence check by selecting documents from the current run and: (a) holding back until reported as missing; (b) arranging for documents to be converted twice and seeing that the duplicates are rejected.
14 *Computer batch totals.*	Test the computer agreement of batch totals by selecting current batches of documents and: (a) checking the additions and agreeing them to the batch headers; (b) altering the batch headers and checking that the batches are reported or rejected.
15 *Programmed procedures giving rise to rejection or exception reports:* (a) over the *accuracy of input and updating* (e.g. check digit verification, dependency tests); (b) over the *accuracy of calculations* (e.g. reasonableness test on wages giving rise to exception report of abnormal pay); (c) over the *continuity* of data stored (e.g. dependency tests giving rise to exception report of obsolete stocks; prices which have not moved for a given period).	Test the programmed procedure: (a) where full visible evidence is available, by checking by reference to appropriate data that items are correctly rejected or reported (e.g. where there are listings of both accepted and rejected items; where there is full print-out of the calculated data); or (b) by amending details on selected documents and seeing that these are correctly reported as invalid items or rejected.

Nature of Control	*Specimen Test*
16 *Computer-generated data.*	Test the generation of the data by: (a) checking by reference to source data that items were generated at the appropriate time; or (b) obtaining a special print-out of data generated and: (i) confirming by reference to source data that all data has been generated accurately; (ii) seeing that abnormal items are reported on the exception report.
17 *Computer calculating.*	Test the accuracy of calculations by selecting items from computer output and checking the calculations.
18 *Computer summarisation.*	Test that all accepted items are included in the total referred to, using one of the following methods: (a) where transaction listings are available, by verifying that all accepted items are on the listings and checking the additions; (b) where no transaction listings exist, by: (i) requesting a special print-out of transactions and carrying out the tests in (a) above; or (ii) arranging a special run and agreeing pre-calculated results (e.g. splitting a batch into two batches, one large and one small, calculating the results for the small batch and agreeing the results with the update reports).
19 *Computer categorisation and updating.*	Test the accuracy of postings to individual accounts by selecting items from appropriate source data and checking the postings.

Nature of Control	*Specimen Test*
IT controls I – *Common to several areas of IT controls*	
20 *Examination of documentation* (e.g. statements of requirements, system specifications, job set-up instructions, operating instructions, network diagrams, database descriptions).	(a) Examine documentation and confirm that: (i) it forms a suitable basis for the controls based thereon (e.g. approval of new programmed procedures, job set-up); (ii) it appears to be correct and up to date. (b) Select extracts from the documentation and confirm with the appropriate staff that they are understood and suitable for their purposes. (c) Where appropriate, select changes to the documentation and see that they have been reviewed and, where relevant, suitably approved by the appropriate persons.
21 *Completeness control over documents and computer-produced reports.*	(a) Examine registers, lists, annotations of reports or other evidence indicating that the sequence of numbered documents or reports and pages of reports (e.g. program change forms, system log reports) is periodically checked and anomalies investigated by staff with, where appropriate, suitably independent duties. (b) Where appropriate, examine evidence indicating that the results of the procedures in (a) above have been reviewed and suitably approved. (c) Reperform the control by selecting documents/reports and: (i) checking the sequence and, where appropriate, that all pages are present; (ii) obtaining satisfactory explanations for any missing or duplicate items; (iii) confirming that the client's procedures for dealing with cancelled or spoiled documents have been followed.

Nature of Control	*Specimen Test*
22 *Review of computer-produced reports* (e.g. listings from file management or security packages, console log and system activity analyses, database integrity check reports).	(a) Examine the computer reports and: (i) confirm that the reports identify unusual items (e.g. processing failures, database integrity errors) as a basis for control; (ii) see evidence that reported items have been investigated by staff with, where appropriate, suitably independent duties. (b) Where appropriate, examine evidence indicating that the results of the procedures in (a) above have been reviewed and suitably approved. (c) Reperform the clearance of reported items by selecting cleared items and checking that they were properly dealt with.
II – *New and modified software* 23 *Testing of application and system software* (new systems and modifications).	(a) Examine the results of testing of application/system software programs and confirm that the scope and method of testing was sufficiently comprehensive to test their functioning adequately. (b) In respect of selected programs reperform the testing, as appropriate, by: (i) examining the predicted results and checking the actual results with those predicted; (ii) reviewing program source listings for inclusion of the appropriate code; (iii) selecting a period from the parallel running and checking the results to the output from the previous system or, if applicable, selecting a part of the pilot run and checking the results to the system description.
24 *Final approval of application and system software* (new systems and modifications).	(a) Examine documentation for evidence of suitable final approval by officials with, where appropriate, no incompatible duties before cataloguing.

Nature of Control	*Specimen Test*
24 (*continued*)	(b) Examine available evidence of rejections or queries raised by the officials and of checks performed by them in giving final approval. (c) Reperform control by selecting a sample of documents examined in (a) above, and: (i) seeing that necessary supporting documentation (e.g. results of testing, operating instructions, user procedure manuals) appears to have been properly completed; (ii) reperforming any other steps that the officials are supposed to follow.
25 *Validity of changes to application and system software.*	(a) Examine a number of requests for changes to operational software and see that they have been approved by an appropriate official (e.g. the programming manager). (b) Select a number of the requests in (a) above and check to source memoranda to establish that there is an adequate reason for the change.
26 *Cataloguing.*	(a) Examine evidence of the cataloguing of new and modified programs and confirm that the procedures in place provide an effective control over the cataloguing process. (b) Where appropriate, reperform the cataloguing of new and modified software by: (i) obtaining a list of programs held on the library (e.g. by use of library analysis software) and checking that the new program is held thereon; (ii) checking the proper cataloguing of jobs run for audit purposes.

Nature of Control	*Specimen Test*
III – *Computer operations*	
27 *Reporting of jobs processed.*	(a) Examine evidence of the reporting of jobs processed and comparison with job schedules and confirm that it forms a suitable basis for the control of processing. (b) Where appropriate, examine evidence indicating that the results of processing and departures from normal processing have been reviewed and suitably approved. (c) Where appropriate, reperform the reporting of jobs processed by: (i) comparing with an authorised job schedule and accounting for differences; (ii) checking the proper reporting of jobs run for audit purposes; (iii) noting details of jobs prior to processing and checking their proper entry on the report.
28 *Reporting of incidents.*	(a) Examine evidence of the reporting of incidents during processing and confirm that it forms a suitable basis for control. (b) Where appropriate, examine evidence indicating that incidents are reviewed and corrective action approved by a responsible official. (c) Where appropriate, reperform the reporting of unusual incidents during processing by: (i) comparing entries on the report with those obtained by the auditor (e.g. by using system log analysis software); (ii) checking the proper reporting of any incidents (e.g. job failures) which occurred relating to jobs run for audit purposes.

Nature of Control	*Specimen Test*
29 *Batch system file set-up.*	(a) Examine evidence and confirm by discussion that there are procedures to check labels on tape files to ensure that the correct files are used. (b) Where appropriate, reperform label checking by: (i) noting details of files prior to set-up and checking their proper treatment; (ii) selecting invalid files and confirming that they are reported or rejected; (iii) checking the proper reporting of files processed by the auditor.
30 *Library records.*	(a) Examine evidence and confirm by discussion that there are effective library procedures to control the use of programs and files in processing and when transferred to back-up or disaster stores. (b) Where appropriate, reperform the maintenance of library records by: (i) comparing with an authorised job schedule and accounting for differences; (ii) checking the proper reporting of programs and files used in jobs run for audit purposes; (iii) noting details of programs and files prior to processing and checking that the records are properly updated; (iv) checking details of programs and files in back-up/disaster storage to those recorded by the library system.

Nature of Control	*Specimen Test*
IV – *Program and data file security*	
31 *Software access control.*	Examine the client's enforcement of security by: (a) confirming by discussion that there are suitable procedures for the staff responsible for security to permit new users to access the system and to delete users or change the capabilities of users, when appropriate; (b) confirming by discussion that where passwords are in use there are adequate procedures to ensure that they are changed periodically, kept secret and not easily guessed; (c) examining reports produced by the security system and confirming that the following are, where appropriate, reviewed and investigated at periodic intervals by staff with suitably independent duties: (i) the resource security profiles; (ii) communication control tables/database sub-schema allocations; (iii) attempted access violations. Test the security in force by, where appropriate: (a) reperforming the investigation of attempted violations by selecting investigated items and checking that they were properly dealt with; (b) with the client's permission and under suitable control, logging on under a master password and checking the security profiles of sensitive resources (including the mechanism for providing access, e.g. the password file itself); (c) listing control tables, for example, by means of software, and confirming that the actual allocations correspond to those provided by the staff responsible for security; (d) attempting to access resources belonging to one department under the passwords of others and ensuring that: (i) only appropriate accesses are permitted; (ii) failures appear on the reports of attempted access violations.

Nature of Control	*Specimen Test*
32 *Physical access control.*	Visit the computer department and off-site stores and verify that: (a) procedures are adequate to prevent unauthorised staff from gaining access; (b) when programs and data files are outside the secure area they are in the custody of authorised persons; (c) the record of data files/programs issued from the library shows that data files/programs overdue for return are being investigated by persons with suitably independent duties.
33 *Use of utilities.*	(a) Confirm by observation and examination of documentation that access to sensitive utilities which can be used to amend programs or data is restricted to authorised personnel. (b) Examine the log recording usage of sensitive utilities for evidence of review and approval by a responsible official. (c) Reperform the control by selecting uses of utilities from the log or by using system log analysis software and ensuring that the uses were for authorised purposes.

9: Appendix B

The Use of Audit Test Data

The Purpose and Scope of Audit Test Data

1 The principal purpose of audit test data is to test programmed procedures. It may also be useful in testing the effectiveness of such system software as cataloguing. Where information is produced by a program of the company at the year end only, as for example a sales analysis required to calculate a provision for warranties, test data can be used to test the programmed procedures concerned as part of the substantive testing.

2 Audit test data consists of fictitious data prepared by the auditor and processed against the company's operational programs. The results are compared with the results calculated manually by the auditor.

3 Audit test data should not be confused with the test data prepared by the company's data processing staff to test the operation of new programs. Such test data is more comprehensive in that it seeks to test every detailed aspect of the programs and often includes unrepresentative data in order to ensure that this will be recognised and treated appropriately by the computer. Audit test data is restricted to testing only particular programmed procedures on which the auditor wishes to rely. In addition, the data is designed to be as representative as possible of the actual data processed by the company. It is thus unusual to include unrepresentative data, as items of this nature would be unlikely to have a material effect on the financial statements.

4 Whenever audit test data is used, it is necessary to establish that the audit test data was run against the programs in current operational use. The procedures required for testing that the correct programs are used are outlined in paragraph 15.

5 Where it has been decided to use audit test data to test particular procedures, it is often practical and efficient to include tests on other procedures that could otherwise still be tested manually. When con-

sidering whether to include these extra tests, care must be taken to ensure the test data does not become too complicated and unwieldy.

Volume of Transactions

6 The number of transactions processed should be the minimum required to provide assurance of the correct functioning of the procedures to be tested. However, the variety of data chosen should be sufficient to represent each of the major types of transactions processed. For example, if the object of the test data is to test the correct production of a purchase analysis, it will be necessary to include transactions for each of the major types of purchases, for example inventory items, capital items and expense items.

7 As well as considering variety in terms of types of transactions it may be necessary to consider the size of the individual transactions processed in order to ensure that the programs treat different values in a similar manner. In that event, the volume of data processed must be high enough to enable a representative range of values to be covered.

8 Subject to the above considerations, the fewer transactions that are processed, the simpler and cheaper the test data exercise becomes. In addition, it is usually possible to use a transaction to satisfy more than one of the conditions required to be tested. This helps to reduce the number of transactions to be processed. It is helpful to use a matrix to indicate the master file records and transactions which will be used to test the various programmed procedures. In cases where a large volume of test transactions is required, or where only the later programs in a processing suite are of interest to the auditor, it may be cost effective to use a **test data generator** to produce the required transactions. Test data generators are software packages which can be used either to construct data to be used in the testing of application programs or to create dummy master files. The user describes the characteristics of the data required. The software then constructs test files containing the generated data and in addition gives the user a listing of the data that has been generated.

Methods of Running Audit Test Data

9 There are two methods of running audit test data which are termed "live" and "dead". Audit test data is classified as **dead** when the data is processed using the company's operational programs, but separately from the company's data, and using copies of master files or dummy files set up for the purpose. Audit test data is classified as **live** where

the data is processed at the same time as the company's data, using the actual master files. Usually specific records on the master files will be reserved or created for this purpose. This form of "live" test data is often called an **integrated test facility** (ITF).

10 There are advantages and disadvantages in both "live" and "dead" audit test data. The disadvantages of one method are, in general, the advantages of the other. In practice, the advantages of running "live" usually outweigh the advantages of running "dead".

11 The factors to be taken into account in making the decision whether to run "live" or "dead" are:

- possible processing difficulties;
- ease of achieving the audit objectives;
- complexity of developing the test data;
- confirmation that the correct programs are used;
- availability of computer time.

These factors are discussed in the following paragraphs.

Possible processing difficulties

12 When running "live", processing difficulties seldom arise and the auditor has the added advantage of knowing that the programs are being tested under normal operating conditions. Problems can arise running "dead" because of the need to handle small volumes of data, to create unusual data on master files, for example old data, and to force data through intermediate processing stages. Particular difficulties are usually encountered when trying to simulate a time span in two or three processing runs. When considering running test data in an on-line or real-time system, it may be impracticable to duplicate the company's whole system to run "dead" test data. In such systems, if the company does not possess a set of test files, "live" test data is the only practical approach.

Ease of achieving the audit objectives

13 Difficulties arise under this heading when running "live" which, in general, do not arise when running "dead". These difficulties are:

- The need to predict and avoid any side effects, for example the inclusion of fictitious inventory lines in a sales catalogue distributed to dealers.

- The testing of totals or analyses. As the test data is included with the actual data, it is not possible to predict what the totals will be. This can often be overcome by creating a dummy branch or department.

- Fictitious information may be included in the company's accounting records at the year end. This is usually acceptable if the value is immaterial. Alternatively, the auditor can insert further fictitious data before the books are closed to reverse the entries made as, for example in the case of sales systems, fictitious credit notes.

- The audit test data may have to remain in the system for a lengthy period to test ageing procedures effectively. In these cases the use of audit test data needs careful planning.

Complexity of developing audit test data

14 It is usually easier to develop data for "live" running because the system is being used in its normal way and it is only necessary to prepare the fictitious data. However, when running "dead", it is necessary to create dummy master files in addition to the test data.

Confirmation that the correct programs are used

15 When running "live", this factor does not arise, since the programs used are the company's actual programs; when running "dead", this assurance does not apply and specific tests are necessary to confirm that the correct programs are used. This can normally be achieved by comparing the name and serial number of the programs used with the system log for the most recent operational run. Where the IT controls have not been relied on, or where weaknesses or exceptions have been found, it will usually be advisable for the auditor to be present during the running of the audit test data, and it will be advisable for him to satisfy himself that no amendments have been made to the relevant programs. The latter might be achieved by examining system logs or by the use of program comparison techniques.

Availability of computer time

16 This factor does not arise when running "live", but can be important when running "dead", when it may often be difficult to obtain computer time. This is particularly so in on-line and real-time systems where the operational system must usually be halted to enable the test system to be run.

Procedures for Using Test Data

17 It is advisable to institute formal procedures for the use of audit test data for the following reasons:

(a) the complexity of the technique;

(b) the need for the company to be aware of and to co-operate with the auditor's plans;

(c) the possible side effects on the company;

(d) the different methods of operation;

(e) the need to build up a central pool of experience which can help in identifying suitable cases for using audit test data, designing objectives, preparing data and budgeting costs.

The procedures can easily be standardised and are considered below separately for the first year of use of audit test data, and for second and subsequent years of use.

First year of use

18 Programmed procedures will be identified in the CART and the auditor should consider whether the use of audit test data is the most effective method of carrying out tests. The auditor should look at all the programmed procedures in a system and make his decision on the basis of the alternative techniques available and the number of procedures that could be tested using audit test data. In general, the external auditor will test IT controls when he wishes to gain assurance on the operation of the programmed procedures, and he will only use test data where there are significant programmed procedures which he considers it necessary to reperform and which cannot be reperformed more efficiently by other means.

19 A **proposal for the use of audit test data** should be prepared, and then approved by the partner responsible for the audit. The proposal should state:

(a) the procedures to be tested by use of audit test data and why this is the most effective technique;

(b) whether the audit test data is to be run "live" or "dead" (if the proposal is that the audit test data should be run "live", a statement should be included of how any possible side effects are to be overcome. If the proposal is that the audit test data should be run "dead", an estimate should be included of the computer time expected to be required);

(c) brief details of the master file records to be created and the volume and variety of data to be processed (a matrix showing how the individual transactions will test the various programmed procedures should be attached);

(d) the budgeted costs of running the audit test data in the first year and in subsequent years;

(e) the effect of running the audit test data on existing audit tests;

(f) any expected practical difficulties, for example verifying the programs used when running "dead".

20 The principle of running audit test data should be agreed with the company. It is important for the company to be aware of the auditor's plans, particularly where "live" test data is used, so as to be sure that no unforeseen side effects take place. It is preferable to confirm any such arrangements made with the company in writing, specifying the objectives, the timing, the method of operation of the test data and any special facilities required, for example computer time.

21 The auditor is now in a position to devise and run the test data. He should prepare full working papers, including the predicted results and schedules of data to be processed. The programme of tests should be amended to take account of the tests carried out by the test data. The auditor should give adequate warning for the conversion of the test data, where this is required. It is good practice to check the input to avoid processing incorrect data.

22 When the results have been evaluated, a **report** should be prepared for those involved in the rest of the audit work. The report should contain:

(a) any alterations to the proposal;

(b) any deficiencies found in the programmed procedures tested;

(c) any difficulties encountered and suggestions for overcoming them;

(d) any suggestions for adding to the number of programmed procedures to be tested on future occasions;

(e) confirmation that the audit test data documentation is complete and up to date;

(f) the actual costs of preparing and running the audit data and the reasons for any variances from the budgeted costs.

Second and subsequent years

23 Much of the procedure will be similar in successive years. Instead of devising the audit test data afresh, the auditor will need to make such changes as are necessary to ensure that the data will not be rejected as invalid, for example revising the dates on documents. Care should be taken to ensure that the system has not changed or, if it has, that the audit test data is suitably amended. Proposals and reports should be prepared, but will only need to deal with changes from the previous year. The company should again be informed of the plans to use audit test data.

9: Appendix C

Examples of the Use of Audit Test Data

Example I – Payroll

The system

1 The company has 5,000 employees and maintains its payroll by computer. Starters, leavers and changes in standing data details are processed and checked manually each week. Hours worked are recorded on clock cards and input weekly.

2 In addition to calculating pay, producing the payroll and maintaining employees' earnings records, the computer provides the following reports:

(a) standing data amendments processed;

(b) employees for whom no clock cards were submitted;

(c) employees for whom more than one clock card was submitted (when this situation arises, all clock cards for these employees are rejected);

(d) clock cards with invalid employee numbers;

(e) employees for whom total hours worked are in excess of sixty hours;

(f) employees whose gross rate of pay is in excess of £200.00 per week;

(g) employees whose gross pay for the week (including overtime) is in excess of £300.00;

(h) general ledger posting tabulation.

The audit test data

3 The audit objectives to be achieved by running test data together with details of the data to be processed are set out on the matrix on pages 325 and 326.

4 The matrix consists of two parts:

(a) **Summary of data requirements.** The purpose of this summary is to show the number of items needed in the audit test data. As can be seen from the illustration, across the top are shown the details of the master file records required, in this case employees, and listed vertically are the details of the items to be processed, both standing and transaction data. These items are extended to show the master file records affected and enable, in the right hand column, a total to be shown of the data requirements. Thus, in this illustration, the requirement is ten opening master file records, eight standing data amendments and ten clock cards.

(b) **Data processed and procedures tested.** The purpose of this schedule is to show how the items processed test the procedures and thus achieve the objectives of the audit test data. The master file records remain stated across the top, although, as can be seen, the number that remain relevant to the test data reduces as items, such as leavers, are processed. The narrative in the vertical column now changes from items (as in the summary of data requirements) to the procedure being tested by the item. In order to keep the matrix simple, it is often helpful, after each group of tests, to restate the master file records still available for further tests. Examples of this technique can be seen after the tests on the procedures for amendments to standing data and after the tests on the procedures for the completeness and accuracy of the input of clock cards. It will be noted that, when the master file records are restated after the tests on the procedures for the completeness and accuracy of the input of clock cards, those that have no further use are no longer shown.

5 The levels of test suggested are purely for illustration purposes.

Summary of Data Requirements

	Test Employees 1	2	3	4	5	6	7	8	9	10	11	12	Total
Opening master file records													
Wages master file	–	–	*	*	*	*	*	*	*	*	*	*	10
Standing data amendments													
Starters	*	*											8 (for all six amendment rows)
Leavers			*	*									
Pay increase					*								
Change in tax code						*							
Additional deduction							*						
Previous deduction deleted								*					
Transaction data													
Clock cards	*	–	*	–	–	*	*	*	*	{ * *	*	*	10

Data Processed and Procedures Tested (1)

	Test Data Details 1	2	3	4	5	6	7	8	9	10	11	12	Total
Master file records set up and available for tests	–	–	*	*	*	*	*	*	*	*	*	*	10
Standing payroll data													
Completeness of writing amendments to the master file													
To verify that accepted master file amendments are reported on the amendments listing for checking against copies of authorised input documents													
Starters	*	*											2
Leavers			*	*									2
Pay increase					*								1
Change in tax code						*							1
Additional deduction							*						1
Previous deduction deleted								*					1
Accuracy of writing amendments to the master file													
To verify that all amendments as reported on the amendments listing are written to the correct employee record and included on the print-out of master file details	*	*	*	*	*	*	*	*					8
Master file records carried forward to transaction tests	*	*	–	–	*	*	*	*	*	*	*	*	10

Data Processed and Procedures Tested (2)

	Test Data Details 1	2	3	4	5	6	7	8	9	10	11	12	Total
Master file records available for tests	•	•	–	–	•	•	•	•	•	•	•	•	10
Payroll preparation													
Completeness of input..													
To verify that the following items are reported as exceptions:													
(a) employees for whom clock cards were not submitted;		•			•								2
(b) clock cards having invalid employee numbers;			•						•				2
(c) clock cards rejected due to duplicate employee numbers.										{ • •			2
Accuracy of input													
To verify that clock card hours in excess of 60 hours are reported as exceptions						•							1
Master file records and transactions available for further tests	•	–	–	–	–	•	•	•	–	–	•	•	6

Data Processed and Procedures Tested (3)

	Test Data Details 1	6	7	8	11	12	Total
Master file records and transactions available for tests	•	•	•	•	•	•	6
Accuracy of payroll processing							
To verify that the following are reported as exceptions:							
(a) employees whose total pre-tax pay exceeds £200.00 per week;			•				1
(b) employees whose total pre-tax pay exceeds £300.00 per week.		•	•	•			3
To ensure that gross pay, deductions and net pay are calculated accurately	•	•	•	•	•	•	6
To verify the accumulation of gross pay, deductions and net pay.	•	•	•	•	•	•	6
To verify that wages are correctly summarised on the nominal ledger posting analysis	•	•	•	•	•	•	6
To ensure wages paid and deductions are accurately posted to earnings records	•	•	•	•	•	•	6
Master file records and transactions present at the end of processing	•	•	•	•	•	•	6

Example II – Purchase Accounting

The system

1 Much of the accounting activity relating to purchases is processed on the computer. Initially purchase requisitions are input through terminals. Requisitions may be rejected for various reasons. Purchase orders are produced for accepted requisitions and the details written to an open orders file. Orders that fail certain reasonableness tests are reported for investigation but are not rejected. This may lead to the processing of purchase order cancellations. Overdue orders are also reported for investigation.

2 Details of goods received are input through the terminals and accepted if they match with the relevant outstanding order. They are deleted from the open order file and used to update the raw materials inventory and an open invoice file.

3 When received, invoices are input and matched with the open invoice file and posted to the accounts payable master file. Details of goods received not matched with invoices within a month are reported for investigation.

4 Cheques are produced by the computer according to rules held in the program.

The audit test data

5 The audit objectives to be achieved by running test data together with details of the data to be processed are set out on the matrix on pages 328 to 331.

6 The matrix is in the same format as that described in the first example. The only new feature is that shown to deal with situations where more than one item relates to a master file record or is necessary for a test. Thus, as can be seen on the "Summary of data requirements", although the auditor has decided that he requires thirty-one purchase requisitions for the various tests related to purchase requisitions, he decides he only needs three inventory file records and five accounts payable records for the relevant tests on the postings to the file. Likewise the thirty-one purchase requisitions can be assembled into six batches for the appropriate test. A further example can be seen in the "Data processed and procedures tested" schedule under the selection of items for payment test.

7 Postings to the general ledger have been ignored. The levels of test suggested are purely for illustration purposes.

Summary of Data Requirements

	Test Purchase Transactions																																	Total
	1	2	3	4	5	6	7	8	9	10	11	12	13	14	15	16	17	18	19	20	21	22	23	24	25	26	27	28	29	30	31	32	33	
Opening master file records																																		
Inventory master file	←						*						→	←				*			→	←					*				→			3
Suppliers' master file	←		*		→	–	←				*			→	←						*					→	←			*		→	*	5
Transaction data																																		
Purchase requisitions	*	*	*	*	*	*	*	*	*	*	*	*	*	*	*	*	*	*	*	*	*	*	*	*	*	*	*	*	*	*	*			31
Purchase requisition batch headers ..	←	*	→	← *	→	← *	→	← *	→	←								*								→	←		*		→			6
Purchase order cancellations										*	*																							2
Goods received notes												*	*	*	*				*	*	*	*	*	*	*	*	*	*	*	*	*			17
Suppliers' invoices													*	*	*	*							*	*	*	*	*	*	*	*	*	*		14

Data Processed and Procedures Tested (1)

	Test Data Details																															Total
	1	2	3	4	5	6	7	8	9	10	11	12	13	14	15	16	17	18	19	20	21	22	23	24	25	26	27	28	29	30	31	
Master file records set up and available for tests – Suppliers' master file	←		*		→	–	←				*			→	←					*						→	←		*		→	4
Transaction data input																																
Purchase requisitions	*	*	*	*	*	*	*	*	*	*	*	*	*	*	*	*	*	*	*	*	*	*	*	*	*	*	*	*	*	*	*	31
Purchase requisition batch headers	←	*	→	←*	→	←*	→	←*	→	←								*								→	←		*		→	6
Completeness of input and updating																																
To verify that batches of purchase requisitions are rejected if total disagrees with the total input on the batch header	*	*	*																													3
Accuracy of input and updating																																
To verify that a purchase requisition will not be accepted (and therefore the batch rejected) if:																																
(a) the stock code number is invalid;				*	*																											2
(b) the supplier number is invalid; or						*	*																									2
(c) the terminal operator does not indicate agreement of supplier's name per the requisition with the name displayed on the screen.								*	*																							2
To verify that an accurate purchase order is produced in respect of all requisitions accepted by the computer										*	*	*	*	*	*	*	*	*	*	*	*	*	*	*	*	*	*	*	*	*	*	22
To verify that an exception report is produced in respect of all orders where the anticipated price is:																																
(a) greater than £10,000;										*	*																					2
(b) greater than standard cost plus 10%; or												*	*																			2
(c) less than standard cost less 10%														*	*																	2
To verify that all orders printed are accurately included on the "orders printed" report										*	*	*	*	*	*	*	*	*	*	*	*	*	*	*	*	*	*	*	*	*	*	22
Record of unfulfilled commitments																																
To verify that purchase order cancellations are:																																
(a) reported; and										*	*																					2
(b) deleted from outstanding orders file.										*	*																					2
To verify that all orders which have been outstanding for more than 1 month are reported as exceptions																*	*	*														3
Outstanding orders carried forward for matching with goods received	–	–	–	–	–	–	–	–	–	–	–	*	*	*	*	–	–	–	*	*	*	*	*	*	*	*	*	*	*	*	*	17

Data Processed and Procedures Tested (2)

	Test Data Details 12	13	14	15	19	20	21	22	23	24	25	26	27	28	29	30	31	Total
Outstanding orders brought forward for matching with goods received	*	*	*	*	*	*	*	*	*	*	*	*	*	*	*	*	*	17
Accuracy of input and updating of goods received notes (GRN's)																		
To verify that program edit checks on accuracy of input are operating correctly by ensuring that:																		
(a) error message displayed and input not accepted if part number per GRN not included on the order number previously input;	*																	1
(b) error message displayed but GRN still accepted when goods received exceed goods ordered;		*																1
(c) a printed report is produced in respect of items in (b) above		*																1
To verify that orders matched with GRN's are deleted from the outstanding orders file and written to the outstanding invoices file	–	*	*	*	*	*	*	*	*	*	*	*	*	*	*	*	*	16
To verify that GRN's not matched with suppliers' invoices within one month are reported					*	*	*											3
GRN's carried forward for:																		
(a) matching with suppliers' invoices.	–	*	*	*	–	–	–	*	*	*	*	*	*	*	*	*	*	13
(b) updating of inventory records	–	*	*	*	*	*	*	*	*	*	*	*	*	*	*	*	*	16
Inventory master file records set up	← *	→	←		*		→	←				*					→	3
GRN's input during reperformance of goods received processing		*	*	*	*	*	*	*	*	*	*	*	*	**	*	*	*	16
Completeness of input and updating of inventory receipts																		
To verify that all GRN's input are included on the inventory update report. The total per this report is reconciled by the computer with the totals updated to the outstanding invoices file		*	*	*	*	*	*	*	*	*	*	*	*	*	*	*	*	16
Accuracy of input and updating of inventory receipts																		
To verify that individual inventory records are accurately updated in respect of goods received	← *	→	←		*		→	←				*					→	3

Data Processed and Procedures Tested (3)

	Test Data Details															Total
	13	14	15	22	23	24	25	26	27	28	29	30	31	32	33	
Suppliers' master file accounts set up and available for testing																
– nil balance									←	—	—	•	—	→		} 4
– negative balance															•	
– others	←	• →	←	—	—	•	—	→								
GRN s brought forward for matching with suppliers' invoices	•	•	•	•	•	•	•	•	•	•	•	•	•			13
Detailed checking of invoices and completeness and accuracy of input																
To verify that invoices will be rejected for investigation when they are compared with the outstanding invoices file if a match is not achieved in respect of:																
(a) purchase order number;														•		1
(b) supplier number;									•							1
(c) stock number;										•						1
(d) quantity received;											•					1
(e) price; and												•				1
(f) invoice total.													•			1
To verify that invoices are reported as exceptions if the invoice price is:																
(a) more that 5% greater than standard cost;					•	•										2
(b) more than 5% less than standard cost							•	•								2
Completeness and accuracy of updating																
To verify the computer reconciliation of total invoices accepted with the totals updated to the outstanding invoices file and the suppliers' master file	•	•	•	•	•	•	•	•								8
To verify that individual supplier's accounts are accurately updated	•	•	•	•	•	•	•	•								8
Cheque payments – selection of items for payment																
To verify that cheques are produced in respect of:																
(a) current balance outstanding when the prompt payment indicator is set; and	←	• →														1
(b) balance outstanding at the end of the previous month in respect of all other balances outstanding			←	—	—	•	—	→								1
To verify that cheques are not produced in respect of:																
(a) nil balances; and									←	—	—	•	—	→		1
(b) negative balances															•	1
To verify the computer reconciliation of total cheques printed with the amount updated to the suppliers' master file	←	• →	←	—	—	•	—	→								2
To verify that payee details are accurately printed on cheques and remittance advices	←	• →	←	—	—	•	—	→								2
Maintenance of the accounts payable file																
To verify that amounts outstanding on individual suppliers' accounts are accurately reported on the monthly creditors listing until such time as payment is made			←	—	—	•	—	→							•	2
Suppliers' master file accounts present at the end of processing	←	• →	←	—	—	•	—	↔	←	—	—	•	—	→	•	4

9: Appendix D

The Use of Program Code Analysis

The Purpose and Scope of Program Code Analysis

1 The principal purpose of program code analysis is to confirm the existence of programmed procedures in a program or series of programs. The programmed procedures to be confirmed will be those identified in the CART. Thus, a major use of program code analysis by the auditor is as a test of programmed procedures. It is a time consuming technique and the external auditor is likely to use it only rarely, when he wishes to test particularly important programmed procedures and more efficient techniques are not available. The technique may also be used by the auditor to obtain or confirm an understanding of the programs or parts of programs in the system. In these cases it may not be necessary to carry out all of the steps set out in this appendix.

2 For the technique to be effective, the auditor must either examine the code in object form, which is unlikely to be practicable, or confirm that the code he has examined in source statement form relates to the instructions in the executable programs. He will also need to be satisfied, either through his tests on IT controls or by direct tests such as the examination of system logs or the regular use of program comparison techniques, that the code he has examined is that used to process accounting data.

Method of Work

3 Program code analysis consists of four steps, which are discussed in the following paragraphs:

- Identifying the programs to be examined.
- Selecting the form of coding to be examined.
- Analysing the selected coding.

- Confirming that the coding examined is identical to that used to process accounting data.

Identifying the Programs to be Examined

4 It is first necessary to identify the programs or program modules which contain the programmed procedures whose existence it is desired to confirm by program code analysis. This can usually be done by reference to the company's system documentation. There will normally be a block diagram which sets out the logical sequence of programs within a system. It will then often be necessary to review the detailed specifications of individual programs in order to identify those containing the relevant procedures.

Selecting the Form of Coding to be Examined

5 The auditor will normally decide to examine the source statement program. In order to carry out this examination the auditor will require a knowledge of the source language used. Care is needed in selecting the version of the source statement program for examination. While listings which are held with the program documentation or print-outs of back-up security copies of programs may be easily obtained, they may not be up to date and the auditor, if he uses them, will need to confirm that they are identical to the source statement program from which the current operational program was compiled. It is thus usually preferable to obtain a print-out of the current source statement program. This is conveniently done by arranging to have the program compiled. The auditor can then request compilation options which may be useful in his analysis of the program, such as cross reference listings of data names and verb listings.

Analysing the Selected Coding

6 The need for the auditor to have a working knowledge of the relevant programming language has already been explained. Given this, the auditor can set out to analyse the source coding of the programs concerned. Most programmers recognise that understanding program logic for programs written by someone else is usually difficult. The auditor will find the work easier where the installation adheres to high standards of programming and program documentation. It is important to adopt a planned approach to the review of the coding. Starting from the first program statement and following the coding through line by

line to the last statement is unlikely to be an efficient or effective way to proceed.

7 In the following paragraphs a suggested approach to the detailed review of the selected coding is outlined. The approach is based upon three phases of work:

- obtaining an understanding of the files used by the programs being analysed and the data held thereon;
- analysing the logic of the relevant lines of coding;
- ensuring that the relevant lines of coding analysed are not bypassed or distorted by another part of the program or an entirely different program.

These matters are illustrated by reference to terms encountered in COBOL programming, since this is the most commonly used language.

8 Although analysing the selected coding will normally require a high degree of skill from the auditor, his job will almost certainly be made easier where the installation employs structured programming techniques. In such cases the logic of programs will be easier to follow because:

(a) programs developed in this way tend to be better structured;

(b) less use is made of GO TO statements and, in COBOL, more use made of PERFORM statements;

(c) IF statements tend to be concentrated into "decision" paragraphs in the programs.

9 The auditor's job will also be made easier if the installation makes extensive use of program generators, database QUERY languages or other very high level languages. Such languages use small numbers of very powerful commands to achieve results which would require lengthy programs if programmed in languages such as COBOL. For example, a COBOL program to report all debtors over £1,000, analysed by branch, might be several hundred lines long. The same report might be produced by the following coding if a report generator is used:

```
TABLE FILE SALES
PRINT NAME AND AMOUNT AND ACCOUNT-NUMBER
BY BRANCH
IF AMOUNT GREATER THAN 1000
ON BRANCH SKIP-LINE
END
```

Clearly such a program would be much easier for the auditor to analyse. However the use of such languages, while increasing, is not yet widespread. Furthermore they are not widely used in production programs which process large volumes of data, since at present most such languages result in inefficient processing. For the present they are used mainly for ad hoc reporting and for prototyping new systems.

Obtaining an understanding

10 Having obtained the source statement listings relating to the program he wishes to analyse, the auditor should first obtain an understanding of the files, records and data fields used and the manner in which they are used.

11 Obtaining such an understanding will normally involve a study of the source listings and associated program documentation to identify:

- **The data files used.** As a starting point the auditor will normally examine the SELECT clauses to identify all files used in the program and examine the OPEN and CLOSE statements in the procedure division to understand how the files are used in the program. These procedures enable the auditor to identify the function of each file, for example, input file, output file, input and output file.

- **The data records on each relevant file.** The auditor will normally examine the file description (FD) entries for each file. Where more than one data record is defined for a file, the auditor will need to understand the use of each data record in the program and assess its effect on the program steps being examined. Different data records are likely to have different logical paths through parts of the program.

- **The important data fields.** Important fields may be those recorded in file descriptions or working storage fields created by the programs. As well as gaining an understanding of the meaning of the contents of each field, the auditor will need to understand any complexities in respect of field definitions such as RE-DEFINES or RENAMES clauses in COBOL which enable the same data field to be interpreted by programs in different ways.

Where a data dictionary exists, useful information regarding the characteristics of the data may be obtained from the dictionary listing.

12 The auditor should also ascertain whether the program uses switches (either in the program or activated through the job control statements or console) to control program logic at run time. Switches may be used to "turn off" routines in a program which are only required periodically, such as month end procedures. If switches are used, the auditor should understand their use, as they may be important when he carries out his review of the detailed coding.

Analysing the logic

13 The first thing the auditor will wish to do is to identify the paragraph or paragraphs of coding which contained the detailed logic of the programmed procedures, for example the paragraphs in which the matching of despatch notes against sales orders is carried out or the paragraphs in which the program analyses suppliers' invoices. Such identification is not normally difficult and the required paragraphs can normally be identified quickly through the program documentation. Where documentation is poor, identification of the relevant paragraphs may take more time, as it will be necessary to scrutinise the source listing to identify the relevant paragraphs.

14 Having identified the relevant paragraphs of coding, the auditor may proceed to analyse their detailed logic. Most programmed procedures that the auditor wishes to analyse can conveniently be broken down into three elements, which can be called:

- COMPARISON – program statements which will compare data fields with other data fields or constants.
- CALCULATION – program statements which enable data to be manipulated according to normal arithmetic rules.
- WRITING – program statements which print data or output data on magnetic storage devices.

Each element would be made up of a number of program statements.

15 The order of the program elements is variable and a programmed procedure will normally incorporate more than one of the elements set out above. For example, where the program has been written to identify excess stocks based on data fields holding the monthly usage of each stock line for the previous twelve months, the programmed procedure would typically be structured to include the following elements:

(a) total the previous twelve monthly usage fields (CALCULATION);

(b) compare the total in (a) to the current stock balance (COMPARISON);

(c) calculate the value of excess stock by reference to the cost price, where the quantity on hand is greater than (a) (CALCULATION);

(d) total the value of excess stocks (CALCULATION);

(e) compare individual excesses to a constant to identify high value excess stocks (COMPARISON);

(f) print details of excess stocks (WRITING).

16 The detailed considerations that the auditor must take into account in analysing each element are set out below.

Comparison

17 Comparisons in COBOL programs are normally based upon the IF clause. IF clauses are used to make decisions governing the logical path that data will follow through the program. To the auditor, they are the most significant parts of the coding in the program he analyses.

18 The auditor should examine the IF clauses in the paragraphs of coding concerned and satisfy himself that:

(a) the test is a logically valid one to be carried out at that point, for example, where the test is to exclude records not required for further processing, that only logical exclusions are made;

(b) the correct data fields are used in the test, for example the correct price field is used in evaluating despatch details;

(c) the definition of each data field used in the test, as set out in the file description or in working storage, is such that the results of the test will be as predicted; this will normally involve examination of the definition of the fields used and consideration, in accordance with the rules of the programming language, of the likely results of the comparison;

(d) the paths directed for items passing and failing the test are valid. This will normally involve examining the destination of GO TO OR PERFORM statements which activate the next logical part of the coding.

Calculation

19 Calculation may involve statements such as ADD, MULTIPLY, SUBTRACT, DIVIDE, and COMPUTE. Again, the auditor can go through distinct stages to satisfy himself that calculations are correctly carried out. These will involve the auditor satisfying himself that:

(a) the calculation is a logically valid one to be carried out;

(b) the correct data fields are used in the calculation;

(c) the definition of each data field used as an operand in the calculation, as defined in the file description or in working storage, is such that the results of the calculation will be as predicted. The auditor should pay particular attention to field sizes and definitions to ensure that they are not likely to be exceeded during a calculation, that they will cope properly with both negative and positive data, and that data containing decimal points or pence is correctly dealt with.

Writing

20 Writing will normally involve outputting records to tapes or discs, or printing data on a printer device. In analysing the coding, the auditor will wish to ensure that:

(a) the correct data fields are moved to the records used for writing data;

(b) the definition of each field to be written, in particular its size, is consistent with the data being moved thereto;

(c) there are no program instructions, which will invalidly suppress the writing of items.

Interrelationship of elements

21 As well as considering the individual elements of comparison, calculation and writing dealt with above, the auditor will also wish to review the order of the elements to ensure that they are logically valid. Where the elements are incorporated into separate programs, the order of these programs should also be examined.

Ensuring that analysed coding is not bypassed

22 Having gone through the steps set out in paragraphs 13 to 21, the auditor will have examined several paragraphs of coding in the relevant program or programs. However, it is possible that the logic examined can be bypassed by coding in either:

- another part of the same program; or
- another program in the same system suite.

Another part of the same program

23 The auditor will need to follow the logic of the program backwards and forwards from the paragraphs he has analysed in detail and he

may find it helpful to obtain or prepare a flowchart of the program logic for this purpose. In so doing he will need first to ensure that the logic of the program provides that all relevant data items, and only those items, are directed to the paragraphs concerned and that the logic of subsequent paragraphs will not invalidate the earlier program steps, for example, by failing to direct all relevant items to the writing paragraph. He will also wish to ensure that the logical relationships between paragraphs he has analysed are correct.

24 Having established that the logic flow of data through the program is valid, the auditor will next wish to ensure that lines of coding elsewhere in the program do not incorrectly manipulate data fields used in the programmed procedure that he has analysed. To do this it is necessary to examine all lines of coding in the program that use the particular data fields. This examination can be carried out by scrutinising a cross-reference listing of the program. This listing, which may be produced on compilation, will show each data name and verb used in the program, together with the number of each line of coding in which each is used. Having identified the relevant data names, the auditor should check the validity of each line of coding in which they appear. It will be necessary to repeat the process for data names which are redefined versions of fields the auditor is interested in or group fields of which it is a member.

25 Finally, using the cross-reference listing the auditor will need to check the validity of the use of any verbs having the capacity to change data or program logic at run time. An example of such a verb is ALTER. Lines of coding using these verbs should be checked carefully. The programming standards of many installations prohibit the use of such verbs.

Another program in the same system suite

26 The extent to which other programs in the suite need to be examined will depend upon the circumstances in each case. The auditor will be concerned that the completeness and accuracy of data is not distorted by other programs in prior or subsequent processing. Where the auditor determines that the user controls will not detect distortion of data, he will normally adopt the following procedures:

(a) where the **completeness** of data could be distorted, check the logical flow of data through the relevant prior and subsequent programs. The auditor will direct his attention mainly to the IF, GO TO, PERFORM, and ALTER statements.

(b) Where the **accuracy** of data could be distorted, check the manipulation of the relevant data fields in prior and subsequent programs. The auditor will mainly direct his attention to the

ADD, SUBTRACT, MULTIPLY, DIVIDE, COMPUTE and MOVE statements. In advanced systems where a data dictionary exists, reference to the dictionary listing may enable the auditor to identify programs which access the relevant data fields.

Second and subsequent years

27 Once the auditor has analysed the programs in detail, in subsequent years it is normally only necessary to identify changes to those programs and analyse the effects of such changes. Complete re-analysis of the program will only be necessary where the program has been substantially rewritten.

28 The auditor can simplify considerably the task of identifying changes in source statement code from year to year if he is able to use a software package which will compare two versions of a source statement program and identify differences. The auditor would then proceed as follows:

(a) in the year in which he analyses the source statement code for the first time the auditor should obtain his own copy of the source statement program;

(b) in subsequent years, the auditor uses his source statement compare program to identify changes between the copy taken in (a) and the source statement version for the current operational program;

(c) the source statement compare program will highlight, for both old and new versions of the source, the additions, deletions and changes thereto and the auditor's review will be restricted to those changes;

(d) the auditor must then consider the effect of the changes on the unchanged parts of the program.

Confirming that the Examined Coding is Identical to that Used to Process Accounting Data

29 After he has examined the relevant coding in the source statement program, the auditor will need to confirm that the examined source statement program is in line with the operational program used to process data.

30 This confirmation can usually be obtained from the tests carried out on the program security controls. In the more advanced installations, where the auditor is most likely to use program code analysis, system software may ensure that the source and executable programs are in line and the auditor can often rely on tests on these procedures. The auditor will need to exercise care where changes can be made directly to executable programs by the use of utilities.

31 The auditor may, as an alternative, be able to make use of software to compare a compiled version of the examined source program with the executable program.

Administrative Procedures

32 It is desirable for the auditor to use administrative procedures on the lines suggested for audit test data in Appendix B to this chapter in order to control the use of program code analysis.

10

Substantive Tests

General Approach

Purpose and scope

10.01 **Substantive tests**, which are also called validation or verification procedures, have as their main objective the substantiation of account balances and other information contained in the balance sheet and profit and loss account and the related notes. In addition, substantive tests may complement tests of controls, since they provide further, though indirect, evidence as to whether the internal controls have continued to operate.

10.02 Substantive tests provide evidence that audit objectives have been satisfactorily achieved, and are therefore concerned with:

(a) Completeness, that is, that all assets, liabilities and transactions that should be included in the financial statements are included.

(b) Accuracy, that is, that recorded assets, liabilities and transactions are mathematically accurate, are based on correct amounts, have been allocated to the proper accounts, and have been accurately summarised and posted to the general ledger.

(c) The existence of assets and liabilities at the balance sheet date and that recorded transactions have occurred and are not fictitious.

(d) Cut-off, that is, that transactions are recorded in the correct period.

(e) The values attributed to assets and liabilities and the use of appropriate accounting measurement and recognition principles.

(f) The ownership of assets and the responsibility for liabilities.

(g) The appropriateness of the presentation and disclosure of items in the financial statements.

10.03 Substantive tests as applied to both the balance sheet and profit and loss account enable the auditor to determine whether the accounting policies of the entity are appropriate and have been consistently followed, and may reveal matters that have to be disclosed in the accounts as a result of professional or other requirements (e.g. the Companies Act 1985, Stock Exchange requirements and accounting standards).

Substantive test documentation

10.04 The auditor will need to make an appropriate record of the work to be carried out, partly to enable him to ensure that all the planned work takes place and partly to enable a reviewer to see whether the conclusions reached from the substantive tests are justified. A formal audit programme of substantive tests should be prepared and should include as a minimum:

(a) a description of the tests to be performed;

(b) identification of the levels of test;

(c) details of the evidence seen;

(d) details of any errors or exceptions noted during the performance of the work and of their disposition;

(e) an indication that the work has been completed (usually the initials of the person completing the work) and the date when it was carried out.

10.05 The general nature of substantive testing procedures is similar from company to company. Accordingly it is common for the auditor to develop specimen substantive tests for general use. The specimen tests will then be tailored to take account of the particular circumstances of the company and the particular testing techniques employed.

10.06 In order to illustrate the points made in this chapter, a typical section of an audit programme related to the substantive tests for trade accounts receivable is set out in Appendix A, together with an indication of the way in which the auditor might use computer interrogation programs to assist in carrying out the tests. Although the appendix only contains the substantive tests for trade accounts receivable, the same principles would apply to other sections of the audit programme. An example of the format of a programme is illustrated in Figure 70.

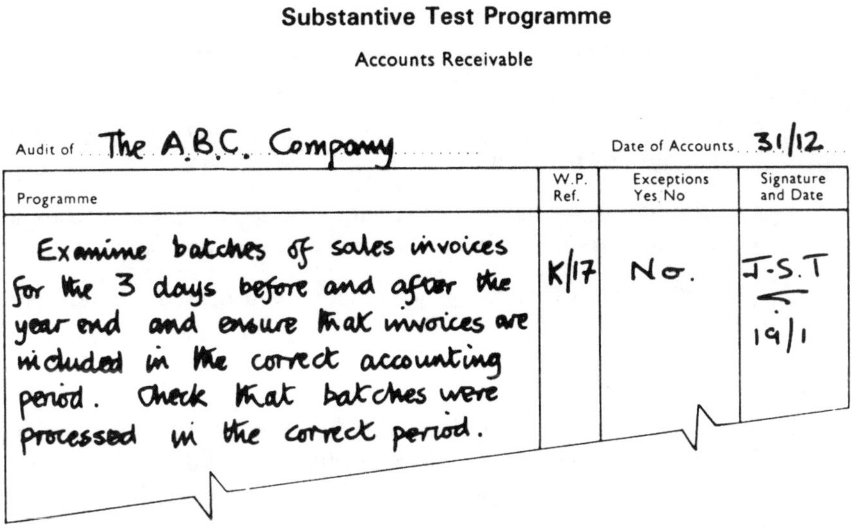

Substantive Test Programme

Accounts Receivable

Audit of The A.B.C. Company   Date of Accounts 31/12

Programme	W.P. Ref.	Exceptions Yes No	Signature and Date
Examine batches of sales invoices for the 3 days before and after the year end and ensure that invoices are included in the correct accounting period. Check that batches were processed in the correct period.	K/17	No.	J.S.T 19/1

FIG. 70. Substantive test programme – accounts receivable (para. 10.06)

The Nature of Substantive Tests

Types of substantive test

10.07 Substantive tests may be divided into two main categories:

- Analytical review.
- Tests of details.

Analytical review involves comparison of recorded amounts with expectations of what such amounts should be. **Tests of details** may involve direct tests of account balances or transactions, or more general procedures, such as a review of board minutes.

Analytical review

10.08 Analytical review procedures may be carried out as part of the preliminary work to determine the audit strategy, when the auditor is finally reviewing the financial statements or as part of the auditor's substantive testing. When performed as part of substantive testing, analytical review procedures will be more detailed and extensive than those performed at other stages of the audit.

10.09 The basic premise underlying the use of analytical review procedures is that relationships between data may be expected to exist and continue into the future unless changes occur. Such changes may result from changes in the business or in accounting methods, from unusual transactions or events, from random fluctuations or from misstatements. Effective analytical review comprises the following three elements:

- Developing an expectation of the recorded amount based on the relationships between data.
- Determining the amount of variation between the expectation and the recorded amount which is acceptable without explanation.
- Investigating variations which cannot be accepted without explanation.

Developing an expectation

10.10 To provide valid substantive evidence, the expectation developed should be such that, when compared to the recorded amount, it can reasonably be expected to highlight differences caused by significant errors. To achieve this the relationship on which the expectation is based must be plausible and the data used to develop the expectation must be reliable. A plausible relationship is one which can be explained logically either from its existence in previous years or from an understanding of the business. The auditor should not rely on a historical trend continuing unless he can explain why it should continue, and should not use a relationship which cannot be explained because this could lead to erroneous conclusions.

10.11 The auditor should consider the extent to which there are likely to be unpredictable fluctuations in the relationship since this will influence the efficiency and effectiveness of the review. The following matters should be borne in mind:

(a) relationships in a stable environment are more predictable than those in a dynamic or unstable environment;

(b) relationships for profit and loss accounts tend to be more predictable because they represent transactions over a period of time, whereas relationships for balance sheet accounts tend to be less predictable because a balance at a point in time might be subject to random or short term influences;

(c) relationships involving transactions undertaken at management's discretion, such as advertising expenditure, are usually less predictable.

10.12 The auditor must be satisfied that the data used to develop the expectation is reliable. The extent of evidence needed as to the reliability of information used in analytical review procedures will vary with the degree of assurance the auditor is seeking from the procedure. Where a variety of sources of information are used, the auditor will normally require less assurance of reliability in relation to each individual source than if only one source is used.

10.13 The auditor may be able to gain assurance as to the reliability of data by establishing either that the data is independent or that it has been audited. Data from sources external to the organisation is normally independent. This may not be the case, for example with industry statistics, where the client's data is included in the external data and represents a significant proportion of it. Data from internal sources can also be independent if it is derived from records maintained by persons who are not in a position to manipulate, directly or indirectly, the accounting records that affect the account balance or class of transactions being audited. For example, employment records kept by a personnel department may be independent of the payroll.

10.14 If internal data is not independent the auditor will need to consider the extent of testing necessary to satisfy himself as to its reliability. He will take into account knowledge obtained in previous audits, the results of the assessment of the control environment, accounting systems and internal accounting controls and the results of other substantive tests. Where these do not provide sufficient assurance the auditor may need to carry out specific tests to confirm the reliability of data used in analytical review procedures.

10.15 The auditor's expectation of what the recorded amount should be will normally be based on one or more of the following:

(a) Information used by management to monitor the business.

(b) Prior year amounts adjusted for known changes.

(c) Relationships between elements of financial data.

(d) Relationships between financial and non-financial data.

10.16 Management often uses key performance indicators and other management information to monitor the business and the auditor may well be able to use this information to develop an appropriate expectation. Where realistic budgets are prepared based on reliable data these can often be very helpful in developing the auditor's expectation since they represent management's expectation of current results based on known relationships between data. Budgets will not be helpful if they represent unrealistic targets. If management carries out analytical review procedures, using budgets or other management information, the auditor may assess the relevance and reliability of management's procedures as an alternative to performing detailed reviews himself.

10.17 There will often be a plausible relationship between the recorded amount and the prior period amount. For example, an expectation of monthly sales for the current year might be developed by adjusting prior year amounts for changes in the level of activity and price rises, in the absence of any known changes in the underlying relationships. An expectation may also be based on the relationship between elements of financial data or between financial and non-financial data. An example of the first would be an expectation of commission expense developed in relation to sales, based on the organisation's policies or the recorded relationship in the past. An example of the second would be an expectation of rental income developed in relation to square footage of property. In some instances income and expense items may be related to assets and liabilities and analytical review procedures on the income and expense accounts can be carried out at the same time as the related balance sheet accounts are tested. Examples of such relationships are dividends receivable and investments, interest payable and loans outstanding, and hire fees receivable and plant available for hire.

10.18 In general, the less precise the expectation the less possible it is to distinguish variations caused by material misstatements from random variations or those caused by the other changes referred to in paragraph 10.09. A less precise expectation reduces the effectiveness of the analytical review and decreases the assurance which can be obtained from it. It may also make the review less efficient since time may be spent investigating variations which have arisen from purely random fluctuations. The expectation can be made more precise by increasing the extent of disaggregation of data, by considering additional data which might affect the expectation or by examining relevant data in greater detail. For example, where annual payroll cost was being reviewed in relation to numbers of employees, precision might be increased by using monthly employee number statistics to develop a monthly expectation, by considering changes in the mix of grades of employee and by looking in more detail at the analysis of pay rises by grade.

Identifying variations which require investigation

10.19 The auditor should decide the amount of the variation between the recorded amount and the expectation which is acceptable without investigation. This should be an amount sufficiently small to detect potential misstatements which could be material either individually or when aggregated with other misstatements. Variations in excess of this amount indicate potential material misstatement and therefore require investigation. The acceptable variation will be a matter of judgement based on the following factors:

(a) Materiality.

(b) The size of the amount being audited.

(c) The effect of disaggregation.

(d) The precision of the expectation.

10.20 The acceptable variation for an entire account balance or class of transactions should not normally be set as high as the overall materiality level. This is because a variation which is equal to, or slightly less than, the materiality level could represent a material misstatement that has been offset by a fluctuation due to other factors. As the size of the account balance or class of transactions decreases, the acceptable variation should be decreased to allow for the possibility that non-material errors in several accounts might aggregate to a material amount.

10.21 The acceptable variation at a disaggregated level should generally be smaller than for an entire account balance or class of transactions, to allow for the fact that smaller misstatements in the disaggregated amounts might be material in aggregate. The acceptable variation will be lower where a more precise expectation has been developed since a variation will be more likely to represent a misstatement. For example, an estimate of interest expense might be expected to be very close to the actual amount if it were based on weighted average debt balances and interest rates. Consequently even a small difference might require investigation as a potential misstatement.

Investigating significant variations

10.22 Where there are differences in excess of the acceptable variation between the recorded amount and the expectation these must be investigated and evaluated. The auditor will seek to identify plausible reasons for the differences and should then corroborate these reasons and quantify their effect. The auditor should be alert for a consistent pattern of differences from the expectation which might indicate either a deficiency in the expectation or a misstatement in the recorded amount. For example, if the expectations of monthly balances were consistently less than the recorded amount, the reasons should be investigated even if the individual differences do not exceed the acceptable variations. Unexplained differences indicate an increased risk of misstatement.

10.23 In order to identify plausible reasons for differences requiring investigation, the auditor will reconsider relevant information about the client and may examine data in more detail or disaggregate it further. Explanations may also be identified from discussions with management and from reviewing management's investigation of variances from budgets or other fluctuations where these have been carried out.

10.24 The auditor should corroborate explanations for significant differences normally by examining documentation, extending his analytical review procedures or making independent enquiries. Examining documentation will normally be efficient when the difference is caused by a small number of unusual or infrequently occurring transactions, for example, major expenditure for a new advertising campaign. Extending analytical review procedures is appropriate when additional factors are identified which enable a more precise expectation to be developed. Independent enquiries might be made of other independent individuals within or possibly outside the organisation. For example, an explanation for an increase in advertising expense from the chief accountant might be substantiated by discussion with the marketing director. The auditor may also test detailed items to corroborate explanations. For example if an increase in sales is attributed to a general price rise the auditor might select items and compare prices before and after the change.

10.25 The auditor should attempt to quantify the portion of the difference for which explanations have been obtained in order to determine whether any remaining difference is material. If the auditor is unable to reduce the unexplained difference to an acceptable level by investigation he must conclude that the unexplained difference represents a misstatement and consider its effect on his audit. If a potentially material error is identified further investigation should be carried out by management and the auditor and adjustment made if necessary.

Tests of details

10.26 The nature of tests of details will vary depending on the account balance or class of transactions being examined but may include the following procedures:

- Observation and enquiry.
- Reperformance and recomputation.
- Confirmation.

- Physical inspection.
- Examination of documentary evidence.
- Review of minutes.
- Letters of enquiry to lawyers.

These techniques are described briefly in the following paragraphs.

Observation and enquiry

10.27 Observation and enquiry is normally used where management itself carries out specific procedures to validate financial information. Examples are observing stock counts, establishing by enquiry that regular reconciliations of debtors and bank balances are performed and reviewing with management the basis upon which provisions for bad debts, warranties or obsolete inventory have been made. When carrying out enquiries, the auditor should be alert for vague or glib answers and will normally wish to corroborate the results. In using observation the auditor should be aware that procedures may have been modified due to his presence. Observation and enquiry is normally combined with other tests of details.

Reperformance and recomputation

10.28 In many instances an account balance may represent the result of a computation or an accumulation of computations, for example depreciation of fixed assets. The testing of such an account balance often includes reperformance of the computation, either in detail or on an overall basis. Where judgement is the basis of a computation, reperformance of the computation should also include evaluating the reasoning process supporting the judgement in order to determine its propriety. For example, if the client's determination of the provision for doubtful debts, having regard to past experience, is based on a formula related to the age of the receivables, the auditor should evaluate the reasonableness of the formula as well as check the mathematical calculations.

Confirmation

10.29 Confirmation consists of obtaining verification of a fact or condition from a third party. This procedure is generally applied to items comprising an account balance, and commonly to accounts receivable balances. Confirmations obtained from persons who are independent of the client provide strong support for the existence, accuracy and rights and obligations audit objectives for the account balance. They often serve as the principal substantive test related to that account balance. Confirmations from parties that are not independent, for example of group balances from a related company, provide less assurance but may still be a useful supplement to other audit procedures.

Physical inspection

10.30 Inspection involves counting and/or examining the physical matter represented by items in the accounts, for example, cash or inventories. The procedures are often most cost effective when management performs them and the auditor combines his own inspection with observation and enquiry concerning management's procedures. In performing inspection procedures the auditor should be careful not to assume the role of valuer, lawyer or other expert outside the field of auditing. Sometimes the inspection procedure should be supplemented by a report by such outside experts.

Examination of documentary evidence

10.31 This will normally involve examining documents, on a test basis where appropriate, which support the existence or validity of a recorded item or balance. In examining documentation the auditor should consider whether there is evidence that the company's required approval procedures have been performed and whether any aspects of the transaction appear unreasonable, for example, a supplier's invoice not addressed to the client. The auditor should also consider what further steps are necessary to satisfy himself as to the authenticity of documentation if there are any signs of erasure or alteration, or if it is not in its original form, for example, because it has been copied. Documents generated by persons outside of the client are normally more conclusive than internal evidence.

Review of minutes

10.32 Reviewing the minutes of general meetings and of meetings of the board of directors and important committees enables the auditor to examine the members' or board's approval of significant corporate actions. This will enable him to determine whether significant decisions taken that affect or require disclosure in the financial statements have been dealt with properly. The auditor should ensure that copies of all relevant minutes have been provided to him.

Letters of enquiry to lawyers

10.33 Obtaining letters from the client's lawyers regarding legal matters provides the auditor with additional assurance as to active, pending or expected litigation.

Use of the Computer to Assist in Substantive Testing

10.34 The auditor can gain considerable improvements in both the effectiveness and efficiency of his substantive testing by using the computer to assist in his work. The most effective use of the computer for this purpose has been in the development of file interrogation software to interrogate data held on a client's system. In addition, in recent years, auditors have made increasing use of microcomputers to assist in a number of aspects of their substantive testing, including file interrogation software. Both of these techniques and other computer-assisted audit techniques are dealt with below under the following headings:

- File interrogation software.
- Microcomputer software.
- Resident code.
- Snapshot.
- Interactive enquiry software.
- Test data.

File interrogation software

10.35 Auditors, confronted with large files of accounting data, quickly found the idea of using file interrogation software attractive. Using such file interrogation programs offered several major advantages over manual work. First, the work is carried out much faster and more accurately by program. A typical program running on a medium size computer might review and classify around 50,000 accounts in five minutes and with much greater consistency than clerical work. Secondly, as a result, far more data can be reviewed. Invariably in manual auditing a compromise has to be struck between the volume the auditor would like to examine and the volume he can in practice examine. This leads in manual work to the use of sampling techniques of either a formal or informal nature. With a file interrogation program it is often possible to read the whole population in the time it would take an auditor to work out what the sample should be. Thirdly, less paper work is required and generated; it is only necessary to print out the results of the test or the items selected for investigation. Last, and most important, clerical audit time can be devoted to an examination of the items defined by the auditor as significant; in other words, the auditor can concentrate on what matters.

Scope of assistance

10.36 File interrogation can be used to assist substantive tests in the following ways:

- The **reperformance** of the company's procedures, for example reperforming the accumulation and ageing of accounts receivable.
- The **selection** of defined items in account balances for the purpose of **confirmation** or **examination**. The program can also assist in the confirmation work, for example by printing confirmation request letters.
- The production of **additional account analyses** and exception reports, for example an analysis of accounts receivable in relation to credit limits, or exception reports of excess stock based on past usage.

These tasks are illustrated in Figure 71 and discussed in the following paragraphs.

Reperformance

10.37 The reperformance of the company's procedures replaces work otherwise carried out manually. However, in most cases, the extent of reperformance will be much higher because all items will be accumulated,

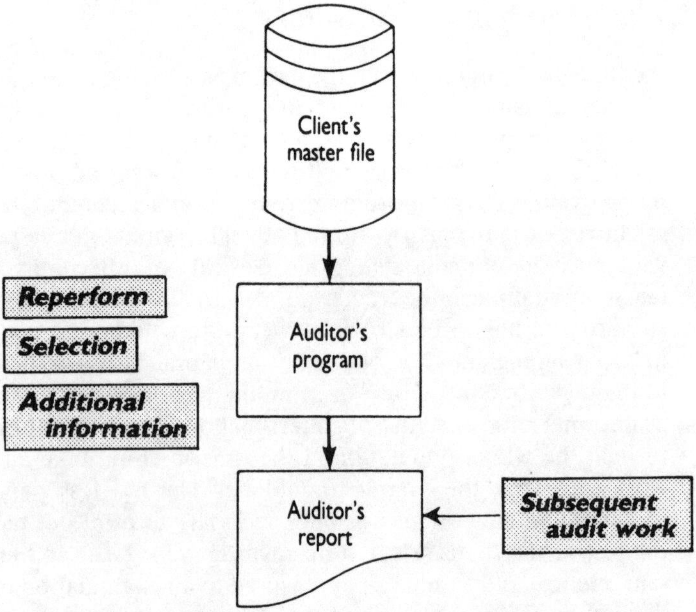

FIG. 71. Use of computer programs – substantive tests (para. 10.36)

calculated or analysed, whereas, using manual techniques, only a sample of items would normally be subject to reperformance tests. This improved testing will usually be most marked in respect of analyses as, for example, in ageing of accounts receivable and analysing inventories in relation to usage, which are often difficult to test adequately by manual means.

Selection

10.38 The selection of items for confirmation or examination replaces work otherwise carried out manually. Computer programs enable the auditor to review all the items on the file. This is an important feature, as in many modern computer systems the volume of data is so large that the auditor has considerable difficulty in establishing from a print-out that his selection of items is made from all accounts on the file. Depending on the nature of the program, it will be possible to obtain a statistical, systematic or random sample. The program will also probably be able to divide the items into strata for selecting the sample, for example debit balances greater than £1,000, credit balances greater than £500 and a systematic sample of items between these amounts.

Additional account analyses or exception reports

10.39 The production of additional information in the form of account analyses and samples of exceptional items to assist the auditor represents one of the most significant effects that computers can have on audit procedures. The review of all data on file and the production of suitable analyses enables the auditor to identify the areas where problems do, or do not, exist, as an aid to subsequent testing. For example, by ageing inventories according to his specified criteria, and by comparing balances with past and forecast usage, the auditor may be able to establish the materiality of old and excessive inventory and decide on the manual investigation that will be necessary.

10.40 File interrogation software usually enables the auditor to carry out more effective manual substantive tests than are possible by solely manual means. As illustrated in Figure 72, when programs are used, the auditor can decide on his detailed tests based on the results of a reading by the computer of all the data on the files. This enables him to form a view on materiality before any detailed testing of items is carried out. It must however be remembered that, except in those cases where the selection or analysis shows the population concerned to be immaterial, normal manual substantive tests will need to be carried out on the items reported or analysed by the computer program. In addition, the program can only read the data actually on the file and it will usually be necessary to establish by manual tests that

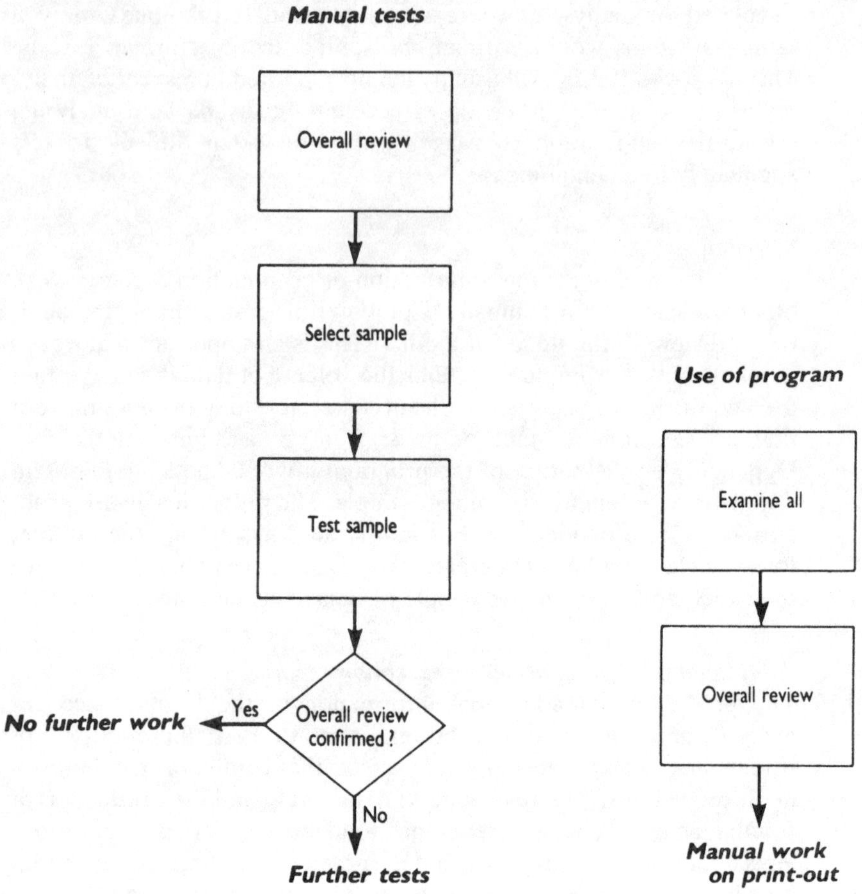

FIG. 72. Influence of computer programs on substantive tests (para. 10.40)

the file represents the total population, for example, by reconciling the total reported to an independent control account.

Procedures for using file interrogation software

10.41 There will need to be formal procedures, both to prepare the computer programs and to incorporate the use of the program into the substantive tests. These latter steps are particularly important in order to ensure that audit staff understand the relationship of the program to the manual procedures and, on the one hand, avoid unnecessary work and, on the other, understand, and do not overlook, the work required on the information produced by the program.

Preparation of the file interrogation software

10.42 There are various ways in which the auditor can set up or obtain suitable file interrogation software. These, together with the procedures to be followed in preparing, testing and executing software both in the first and subsequent years of use, are considered in Chapter 11 "The Use of File Interrogation Software".

Audit work on program results

10.43 It should not be overlooked that manual work, often of a high quality, will be necessary to interpret the information produced by the computer program and to decide on, and carry out, such subsequent investigation as is needed. The specific work to be done on the results, such as checking to the company's figures, and details of any further tests required, such as manual investigation, should be incorporated in the audit program.

Examples of uses of file interrogation software

10.44 The tasks undertaken by file interrogation software will depend on the audit requirements, the variety of information that is available on the relevant files and the auditor's ability to include his requirements in a program. Certain tasks, when appropriate, are usually included in all uses of programs. These include:

(a) Accumulating the balances or items on the file and reporting separate totals of debits, credits and nil balances and a net total of balances.

(b) Stratifying the balances or items on the file and selecting appropriate samples from all or selected strata for subsequent testing, for example for physical inspection.

(c) Sub-totalling the items making up each balance, comparing the sub-total with the balance and reporting those which disagree.

(d) Identifying, accumulating and reporting transactions dated after the cut-off date for the file.

The nature of the other tasks, which will consist in the main of the production of analyses and reports of specified items, will differ according to the application. The more common additional tasks are set out in the following paragraphs under the application concerned. In addition, illustrations of the use of file interrogation programs to assist in the substantive testing of accounts receivable and inventories are set out in Appendix B to this chapter.

Accounts payable

10.45 Typical tasks include:

- Stratifying the population.

- Matching subsequent period recorded payments against earlier period items and balances and identifying unmatched payments.
- Identifying old invoices or goods received documentation unmatched on the file.
- Identifying unusual transactions, for example large non-stock purchases for particular accounts codes.
- Identifying unusual standing data, for example accounts for inactive suppliers.
- Identifying accounts not reconciled to supplier's statement for a significant length of time.
- Identifying overpayments and other debit balances.
- Identifying the largest creditors to determine changing patterns of trade.

Accounts receivable

10.46 Typical tasks include:

- Analysing the balances or transactions into age categories. Often a more detailed analysis than that prepared by the company can be produced. Analysing by transaction type may produce useful information regarding payments on account and unmatched adjustments.
- Analysing the balances into strata by reference to the amount outstanding and reporting the largest individual balances on the file.
- Identifying balances in excess of credit limits, analysing them into strata by reference to the amount by which the credit limit is exceeded and computing the amount of excess over credit limits.
- Identifying accounts with unusual credit limits or no credit limits.
- Identifying unusual transactions, for example large sales near the year end or transfers between accounts.
- Identifying unmatched transactions, for example payments on account.
- Identifying unusual standing data, for example high discount rates.
- Selecting items for confirmation and printing appropriate confirmation requests. These items can be written to the file and replies can be matched. Information regarding outstanding items and second requests can then be produced.

- Comparing amounts outstanding at the balance sheet date with subsequent cash receipts, computing the amount remaining unpaid after a reasonable time and analysing the balances into strata by reference to this amount.

Inventories

10.47 Typical tasks include:

- Analysing the balances into age categories. This can be done by reference to the date of last receipt or last issue.
- Analysing the balances into categories of number of years' stock held. This can be done by reference to past or forecast issues or other production information. Often this information must first be calculated.
- Identifying balances in excess of maximum stock levels, analysing them into strata by reference to the extent by which the maximum stock level is exceeded and computing the extent of excess over maximum stock levels.
- Identifying items with unusual maximum stock levels or no maximum stock levels.
- Identifying items recorded as obsolete or damaged.
- Identifying items where significant scrap adjustments have been recorded.
- Identifying item with unusual prices, for example by comparing cost and selling prices, by range tests, or comparing current prices with previous prices. Sometimes it is possible to identify items for which the price has not been updated within a given period of time. Balances without prices may also be identified.
- Computing, where appropriate, the amount by which inventory valued at cost price exceeds inventory valued at selling price.
- Analysing the balances into age categories since date last counted.
- Identifying items that existed in the prior year's inventory but do not exist in the current year's inventory.
- Identifying balances with no physical location reference.

Work in progress

10.48 Typical tasks include:

- Analysing the balances into age categories.

- Identifying items where the full value of work done may not be recoverable. This can be achieved by:
  - identifying items whose actual costs exceed authorised or budgeted costs;
  - identifying items whose costs to date exceed fixed selling prices;
  - identifying items whose costs are not rechargeable to customers, such as warranty work;
  - selecting items for comparison of total expected costs to complete with realisable value.
- Identifying balances which include unusual items, for example adjustments.
- Identifying closed work in progress items not invoiced with a reasonable period of time.
- Identifying items which have been open for an unreasonable period of time.

Fixed assets

10.49 Typical tasks include:

- Calculating depreciation and checking the company's figure.
- Identifying fully depreciated assets and calculating what would have been the normal depreciation thereon.
- Identifying unusual depreciation rates.
- Analysing items into age categories since last physically inspected.
- Identifying properties with no title deed reference.

General ledger

10.50 The tasks in relation to general ledger systems are most frequently intended to assist in analytical reviews. Typical tasks include:

- Comparing balances to budgets or prior year balances.
- Analysing the movements in an account balance by accounting period. It may also be useful to analyse them by transaction type where this is possible.
- Computing significant ratios or other performance indicators and comparing them to similar information from prior years.

- Examining all the transactions making up the balances at the year end and reporting exceptional or unusual transactions for further tests, either by reference to their value or by comparing them to other criteria specified by the auditor.

- Totalling the transactions for each account during an accounting period and checking that the totals correspond to the movements in account balances.

Loans, mortgages and customers' bank accounts

10.51 These items have certain characteristics similar to accounts receivable. In addition to the relevant tasks mentioned under that heading, typical tasks in relation to these items include:

- Identifying accounts where repayments are in arrears.

- Identifying accounts with unusual interest or commission rates; employees' accounts can be particularly scrutinised.

- Identifying accounts with insufficient security.

- Recalculating interest paid and received.

Other applications

10.52 Computer programs can be used in a similar way for any application in any business where data is stored on computers. For example, in the case of insurance companies, a variety of tasks can be undertaken in relation to outstanding claims.

Microcomputer software

10.53 Auditors have made increasing use of microcomputers in recent years in a variety of aspects of their work. Many of these uses are administrative and do not relate to substantive test work, for example programs for preparing audit budgets and programs for non-audit purposes such as cash flow projections. Microcomputer software is, however, also being used to assist in substantive testing in a variety of ways. Much of this software is being developed using packages which are commonly available for microcomputers such as spreadsheet and data storage and retrieval packages. The program is thus a tailored version of the standard package, commonly referred to as a **template**.

10.54 A particularly effective use of such packages may be to assist in analytical review work. For example, a template might be programmed to include the normal profit and loss account and balance sheet headings and a variety of useful ratios and comparisons can be programmed into the model. Data for a particular client can then be input to the template which will analyse the information for audit purposes. It may well be possible to use such templates to compare actual to budgeted figures or to build up a history of a client covering a number of past years.

10.55 Such programs can also be used effectively where standard calculations are carried out since these can be built into the template. Examples are the calculation of a tax liability or the preparation of a statement of cashflow. Other programs require the input of the client's trial balance and then permit ratios to be calculated and substantive testing audit working papers, such as an analysis of inventories, to be prepared. Finally, microcomputers can also be used to assist in directly interrogating the client's computerised data files as discussed in Chapter 11 "The Use of File Interrogation Software".

10.56 The usage of microcomputers by the auditor and the issues to be addressed in developing software for such machines are dealt with more fully in Chapter 12 "Microcomputers in the Audit Practice".

Resident code

10.57 **Resident code**, also known as **resident program** or **embedded code**, consists of program steps written by the auditor and inserted into the company's production programs. The auditor's coding may be included within a company's existing operational program. Alternatively, it may be written as a separate program or programs and be processed, at a predetermined point, as part of the company's programs. The principal purpose of the resident code is to review "live" transactions as they are processed, to select items according to criteria specified in the resident code, and to write the selected items to an output file for examination by the auditor. The use of resident code is illustrated in Figure 73.

10.58 Items are normally selected and output on one of the following bases:

- All items passing or failing particular tests specified in the resident code. In this case, the output file is often referred to as a System Control Audit Review File (SCARF).

- A random sample of all items passing through the resident code. In this case, the output file is often referred to as a Sample Audit Review File (SARF).

Uses of resident code

10.59 The principal reason for which the auditor is likely to use the technique of resident code is to test the validity and/or accuracy of data input

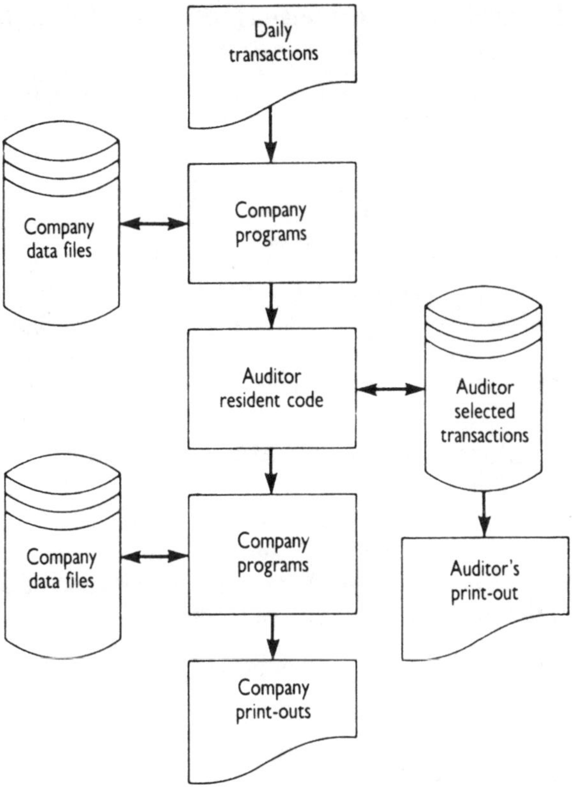

FIG. 73. Use of computer programs – resident code (para. 10.57)

to, processed, or output by the company's programs. The technique operates at a detailed level producing reports of individual transactions or items and its use by external auditors is infrequent. Internal auditors operating in only their own company's computer environment may find it more useful where they wish to review transactions in detail.

10.60 As an example of the use of this technique, the auditor may design coding to review all purchase invoices submitted to the system and carry out a range of tests thereon. Typical objectives of the resident code might be to:

(a) identify unusually high value invoices;

(b) identify invoices for particular expense accounts;

(c) match purchase invoices against a pipeline file containing details of orders placed and/or goods received;

(d) identify invoices relating to the purchase of fixed assets.

10.61 In using resident code in this way, the auditor may, provided the code is secure (see paragraph 10.63), reduce the reliance he would normally place on those user controls and programmed procedures designed to ensure the accuracy and validity of data.

10.62 The use of resident code may also be an appropriate technique for the testing of programmed procedures. For example, the auditor may include resident code to examine despatch notes input, check the calculation of sales invoices, and report high value discounts for agreement to the details on the client's exception report of high value discounts.

Procedures for the use of resident code

10.63 As with the use of file interrogation programs, it will be advisable to establish formal procedures for the use of resident code. The type of procedures that might be adopted are described in Chapter 11. In addition, because of the nature of resident code, it is necessary for the auditor to establish further procedures. These would include:

- The mechanism for turning the auditor's code "on" and "off'. A suitable method is the use of run-time parameters which indicate whether the auditor's code is to be activated or not.

- The treatment of the auditor's output. This may be put into the library to await the next audit visit or printed and despatched to the auditor.

- The security of the resident code. Unless IT controls are relied upon, the auditor needs to adopt alternative procedures to ensure the security of the resident code. A suitable means of doing this would be for the auditor to keep a copy of the relevant programs and periodically carry out a comparison between the retained copies and the operational programs.

Snapshot

10.64 **Snapshot** is a technique which can be considered as an extension of the principle of resident code. It was developed initially as an aid to program development and maintenance. Special coding is incorporated into the application programs when they are written which, when activated, will cause the application programs to record the contents of predetermined parts of main memory at predetermined stages in the processing of a transaction. By this means it is possible to check the actions taken by the program and confirm that the program is operating properly.

10.65 For example, in relation to the accumulation and analysis of the daily sales figure the following information may be reported:

- Prior to accumulation of the invoice – the value of the particular sales invoice and the value held in the accumulator set up to record the daily sales total.
- After accumulation of the invoice – the value held in the accumulator after adding in the sales invoice.
- Prior to analysis of the invoice by nominal ledger code – the values held in the accumulators for sales products.
- After analysis of the invoice – the values held in the accumulators after adding in the sales invoice.

10.66 The special coding is normally activated by an input code entered on the input documents to which it is desired to apply the monitoring procedures. This technique is not commonly used.

Interactive enquiry software

10.67 Interactive enquiry programs or languages have been developed for some on-line, real-time and database systems. Where these exist, it will be necessary for the auditor, if he wishes to use and rely on the program in preference to his own computer program, to ensure that the program functions correctly and consistently. He may, in some circumstances, gain a satisfactory degree of assurance from the manual tests on the results of the program. Alternatively or in addition, where the auditor has evaluated and tested IT controls he may be able to obtain the required assurance from these. He may also obtain assurance by carrying out direct tests on the enquiry program, usually using test data. The amount of testing required will depend on the auditor's assessment of the risk of errors in the program. The factors which he will need to take into account include whether it was supplied by an external supplier or written in-house, the extent to which it has already been tested by other users and the ease with which it could be amended.

Test data

10.68 The use of audit test data has already been discussed in Chapter 9 in relation to tests of controls, and the practical matters to be considered when using it were discussed in Appendix B to that chapter. Audit test data may also be used to test a programmed procedure which the auditor relies on as part of his substantive testing. Normally this will be done when test data is already in use for testing of controls, and additional objectives relating to substantive testing can be added reasonably easily. Test data is not otherwise usually the most efficient approach in substantive testing because of its relatively high set-up cost in relation to the objectives achieved.

Factors Affecting the Nature and Extent of Substantive Tests

10.69 The nature and extent of substantive tests is a matter for the auditor's judgement in the light of a number of different factors. Factors that are normally relevant include:

- The auditor's assessment of inherent risks relating to the account balances and classes of transactions and of the effectiveness of controls.
- The materiality of the items in relation to the accounts taken as a whole.
- The corollary assurance which the auditor obtains from substantive tests of other related accounts.
- The auditor's judgement of the most efficient and effective combination of substantive testing procedures.

10.70 These factors will have been considered on a preliminary basis when the audit strategy was decided, as discussed in Chapter 2. Before carrying out the substantive tests, it is necessary that they be reconsidered in greater detail in the light of audit work previously carried out, so that the final programme of substantive tests can be determined.

10.71 Determining levels of substantive tests requires judgement and may involve the application of some form of sampling. This is particularly so for tests of details involving confirmation, recomputation, physical inspection or examination of documentary evidence since these often require the selection of items for testing from a total population. Sampling may be defined as testing, observing or measuring part of a population in order to obtain information about the entire population. The selection of a sampling method should be made by the auditor in the light of his understanding of the characteristics of the account balance and the related audit objectives. The audit objective on which assurance is sought will also influence the population from which selection is made. For example, the primary objectives addressed by a confirmation of receivables are the existence and accuracy of the balances, and selection will normally be made from the listing of receivables balances. If the objective were to test the completeness of receivables then selection should not be made from recorded receivables, but rather from a related population such as records of despatches, with a view to ensuring that all despatches had been recorded as sales and receivables.

10.72 There are a number of different options which the auditor may adopt in designing his substantive tests, only some of which involve the use of sampling. The options may be categorised as follows:

(a) Reliance principally on internal controls supplemented by analytical reviews and procedures performed on related account balances with minimal direct substantive tests.

(b) Performing a 100 per cent examination of all items making up an account balance or of sufficient items that the amount left untested is immaterial.

(c) Performing a 100 per cent examination of selected components of an account balance with enough assurance obtained about the remainder from reliance on internal controls or other procedures such as analytical reviews.

(d) Performing a 100 per cent examination of components of an account balance, together with sampling the remainder.

(e) Sampling the whole account balance.

Only (d) and (e) involve the use of sampling. The factors affecting the nature and extent of substantive tests are considered in the following paragraphs.

Assessment of inherent risk and control effectiveness

10.73 In determining the audit strategy, the auditor will have identified inherent risks related to specific audit objectives for account balances or classes of transaction. He will also have performed an initial assessment of the control environment, accounting systems and internal controls to assess at an overall level the effectiveness of controls. Subsequently he may have performed an extended assessment of controls. In deciding upon the nature, extent and timing of substantive tests the auditor will review the inherent risks identified and consider the effectiveness of controls in preventing or detecting material misstatements which may arise from those inherent risks. Where the auditor has carried out an extended assessment of controls and concluded that they are effective, he will be able to carry out lower levels of substantive tests on related audit objectives for account balances than where no such reliance is possible, and he may also be able to carry out such tests at a date prior to the year-end.

10.74 Where the auditor cannot, or prefers not to, rely on internal controls, his audit satisfaction will be based on the performance of substantive tests. This will involve higher test levels than when reliance is placed on internal controls and the nature and timing of substantive tests may also need to be modified in these circumstances. For example, tests of the ageing of accounts receivable might include tracing individual items back to source documents instead of (as might be the case if internal controls are relied on) checking balances from the accounts receivable file, because the auditor would have no assurance that the file reflected the true position. It may also be necessary to carry out the work on the year-end figures.

10.75 Internal controls are more relevant to some account balances and audit objectives than to others. They are particularly relevant to account balances derived from a transaction processing cycle, for example, accounts receivable and sales balances. Other account balances may not be derived from an accounting system and may involve more judgement, for example, accrued receivables and payables and deferred charges and credits which are calculated at the year end. The auditor's work on internal controls will provide less assurance in relation to these balances than for those derived from transaction processing. As regards audit objectives, internal controls principally address the completeness and accuracy audit objectives and to some degree the existence and cut-off objectives. They do not generally address the objectives of valuation, rights and obligations and presentation and disclosure, although the accounting system may generate information that management uses in making valuation and disclosure judgements.

Materiality

10.76 An item or group of similar items should be judged material if knowledge of that item or its effect on the accounts could reasonably be expected to influence the decisions of users of the accounts. Size is obviously a major factor in judging whether an item is material. The nature of the item is also relevant, for example, whether it affects the determination of profit or only the balance sheet and whether it is required by law to be accounted for or disclosed in a particular manner.

Correlation with other accounts

10.77 In determining the extent of his substantive tests on a particular account, the auditor should take into account the assurance he may have gained from tests on related accounts. For example, a circularisation of accounts receivable balances will provide evidence of the existence (that is occurrence), accuracy and cut-off of sales as well as the existence of receivables. A number of profit and loss account items can be correlated with balance sheet amounts in a similar manner, for example, interest with loan balances and dividends receivable with investments. Substantive tests on the balance sheet items may well provide corollary assurance on the related profit and loss account item in such instances.

Efficiency and cost-effectiveness of substantive testing procedures

10.78 The most efficient and cost-effective substantive procedures will depend in part upon such matters as the nature and composition of the account balance or class of transactions, the way in which the accounting systems are organised, the system of controls and the quality of client personnel. The following paragraphs set out some considerations relating to the use of different techniques for particular types of account and audit objectives.

Completeness, accuracy, existence and cut-off

10.79 If account balances represent an accumulation of similar transactions, analytical review procedures commonly provide an efficient means of obtaining assurance in relation to these objectives, and they can be particularly effective in relation to the completeness objective. Tests of details are normally effective for accounts containing relatively few transactions or where a greater level of assurance is required in respect of the existence, accuracy and cut-off objectives.

Valuation, rights and obligations and presentation and disclosure

10.80 Analytical review procedures will often be efficient in providing evidence in relation to valuation, but such procedures will not usually identify consistent misapplication of accounting principles. The auditor will need to consider the appropriateness of the valuation methods applied to identify whether this has occurred. Checklists of disclosure requirements can provide assurance as to the adequacy of presentation, but the appropriateness of the accounting policies applied requires consideration of specific transactions and circumstances. Evidence in relation to rights and obligations is normally obtained during other substantive testing or by specific tests of details.

Profit and loss account

10.81 For accounts forming part of the profit and loss account, the auditor will often be able to obtain assurance in relation to completeness, accuracy, existence and, in some cases, cut-off from analytical review procedures rather than from tests of details. This is partly because profit and loss accounts are particularly susceptible to analytical review procedures, and partly because the degree of assurance required from substantive testing in this area is often low. As noted in paragraph 10.77 substantive tests on balance sheet items will often provide corollary assurance on related profit and loss account items. Furthermore, in respect of error, there is generally a low inherent risk because:

(a) profit and loss accounts are largely made up of transactions which have been settled, for example, sales where cash has been received; and

(b) these settled transactions have normally been processed by established accounting systems.

10.82 Where the auditor considers that there is a risk of material misstatement in profit and loss account items, and he has not relied on an extended assessment of controls to reduce this risk, then he may decide to carry out tests of details in respect of such items.

Order of work

10.83 It is normally most efficient to carry out analytical reviews first, followed by tests on totals or summaries of items and finally detailed tests on individual items. The reason for this is that tests at a higher level can increase the auditor's understanding of the balances involved. They may indicate areas where detailed testing can be reduced or areas of particular concern where the detailed tests should be concentrated.

Reliance on company management information and procedures

10.84 In selecting the most efficient and effective testing procedures, the auditor should consider the information available within the business and the procedures performed by management. Computer systems can produce large numbers of analyses, exception reports and summaries which the auditor can use for his analytical review work and, in some cases, for more detailed tests. Aged analyses of debtors, listings of slow moving inventories or exception reports of loan interest arrears are all examples of management reports which can be useful to the auditor. As computer systems become more sophisticated, particularly with the use of database management techniques, they are able to correlate data from many sources to provide information which would be practically unobtainable in a manual system. For example, inventory balances can be related to product component structures and sales history data to produce exception reports of component stock in excess of one year's expected usage.

10.85 The availability of such information can result in significant savings in audit time by increasing the effectiveness of analytical reviews and directing the auditor's attention more precisely at any potential problem areas. However the auditor should be aware that in using such reports he is relying on the programmed procedures within the company's systems, and he will need to satisfy himself that these are operating properly. He may gain this assurance from an extended assessment of IT controls, by reperformance of the programmed procedure or from indirect evidence from other audit tests. For example, a favourable response to a circularisation of debtors in a computerised sales system would provide some assurance that the programmed procedures which calculated sales invoices and updated them to customers' accounts were operating properly.

10.86 Management may perform its own analytical review procedures and may also carry out procedures such as inventory counts, reconciliations of suppliers' statements, and special procedures for year end accruals. In these cases the auditor may be able to improve efficiency by testing management's procedures rather than performing independent procedures of his own.

Exceptions

10.87 When exceptions (i.e. errors and deviations from established procedures) are found as a result of substantive tests, the auditor should ascertain the reasons for them and consider their effect, both in terms of its implications with respect to the functioning of the client's system of internal control and as regards the account balance under examination and any related account balances. In particular, the auditor should consider the potential for further misstatements and whether the nature, frequency or amount of the exceptions noted is such that the assessment of risk relating to the account balances, and therefore the nature, extent and timing of substantive tests, should be reconsidered. In making these judgements the auditor will take account of the following considerations:

(a) Exceptions which are the result of the incorrect application of systematic procedures for processing transactions are more likely to be repeated. An exception relating to the incorrect operation of a programmed procedure will normally be repeated every time that the program is run.

(b) Exceptions arising from infrequent procedures or unusual circumstances have a lower potential for further error.

(c) Exceptions might indicate bias and hence an increased risk of such bias in other areas. Examples might be errors in the calculation of accruals or in cut-off.

(d) Exceptions related to one account might be indicative of a failure in accounting controls and cause the auditor to reconsider the assessment of the control environment and other similar controls. An example might be the failure to reconcile a subsidiary account properly to the general ledger.

(e) Certain exceptions may be a cause of audit concern regardless of their actual or potential size. Examples are exceptions that are the result of fraud or breaches of statute or government regulations.

10.88 Where sampling is used, the purpose of performing tests on a sample is to draw conclusions about the population from which the sample is selected, and the sample result should be projected to the population to determine whether material misstatement is likely. Sometimes, the objective in performing tests is to determine whether certain procedures were properly performed so as to provide evidence in relation to the completeness, accuracy or existence of a particular transaction or account. The auditor's conclusion is either that the procedure is adequate or that the client, or in exceptional cases the auditor, will have to reperform it. In these cases it will not be appropriate to project and quantify the exceptions found. An example is the testing of a client's physical inventory counting procedures. Exceptions would normally cause the auditor to request the client to carry out further work, or to extend his own tests, until the adequacy of the count is established. A further example might be testing the additions of print-outs or ledger accounts where exceptions might indicate a serious problem and it would be impracticable to project a monetary result.

10.89 The auditor's initial response to significant exceptions noted during substantive testing should be to inform the company, with a request that known errors be adjusted and that such further work as necessary be carried out to justify the account balance. As it is the company's responsibility to produce accurate accounts, the client should be encouraged to perform the investigation. If the client is unable to do so, the auditor may need to undertake the necessary work. If, after such investigation, the auditor is unable to conclude that the account balance is not materially misstated he will need to consider a qualification in the audit report.

The Timing of Substantive Tests

Early testing

10.90 It is often desirable to perform substantive tests as at a date prior to the year end, particularly if the client wishes the audit to be completed shortly after the year end. This may be done in appropriate circumstances without impairing the effectiveness of the audit. Early testing of the profit and loss account might include, for example, analytical review on the completeness and accuracy of sales for the first nine months of the year. It is often efficient to carry out such early profit and loss account testing.

10.91 The auditor should also consider the desirability of carrying out early balance sheet testing. Such testing may well be less efficient than testing at the balance sheet date because it will need to be supplemented with other procedures to ensure that the conclusions from the early testing remain valid. In general early balance sheet testing is only likely to be cost-effective where the auditor assesses the risk of material error between the date of the early testing and the balance sheet date as low. He may gain such assurance from reviewing the operation of the accounting system and related controls during this period, or from examining evidence of the operation of special procedures established by the client for this period. If the auditor is unable to gain this assurance then early balance sheet testing will need to be supplemented by repeating some tests of details at the balance sheet date or by testing transactions in the period between the date of early testing and the balance sheet date, and this approach may not be efficient.

10.92 Where physical custody controls to safeguard assets are ineffective, early substantive testing in relation to the existence of assets will not normally be cost-effective, because the auditor will be unable to rely on controls over the custody of assets to provide assurance about the existence of assets at the balance sheet date. It is usually efficient to perform substantive tests on related accounts as at the same date. When considering early substantive testing of a specific account, the auditor should consider the relationship of that account to others and the extent to which a single substantive test will provide corollary evidence on other accounts.

Summary

10.93 Substantive tests have as their objective the substantiation of account balances and other information in the financial statements. They comprise:

(a) Analytical review which involves the comparison of recorded amounts with expectations of what such amounts should be and the investigation of significant variations.

(b) Tests of details which include direct tests of items making up the financial statements and more general procedures such as a review of minutes and letters of enquiry to lawyers. Direct tests may involve observation and enquiry, reperformance and recomputation, confirmation, physical inspection and the examination of documentary evidence.

10.94 The auditor can gain considerable improvements in both the effectiveness and efficiency of his substantive testing by using the computer to assist in the work. The computer-assisted techniques available to the auditor include file interrogation software, microcomputer software, resident code and test data. The most common of these is the use of file interrogation programs, which can examine large volumes of data much faster and more accurately than is possible manually. Such software can be used to reperform the company's programmed procedures, to select samples for audit work, or to produce additional analyses and exception reports not produced by the company's system. The use of computer programs can result in the auditor's attention being directed more precisely to areas of potential concern. However it should not be overlooked that manual audit work, often of high quality, will be needed to interpret and act on the results produced by computer programs.

10.95 The nature and extent of substantive testing will depend on a number of factors, including:

(a) Inherent risks and the effectiveness of controls. The design of substantive tests will take account of the inherent risks of misstatement in the financial statements and the effectiveness of controls in preventing or detecting such misstatements. If the auditor is able to rely on internal controls the extent of substantive testing can usually be lower, and its nature different, than if he cannot.

(b) The materiality of the item in relation to the accounts taken as a whole.

(c) Correlation with other accounts. The auditor should take into account the corollary assurance he may have gained from tests of other accounts related to the account he is testing.

(d) The efficiency and cost-effectiveness of testing procedures. Analytical review procedures can be very cost-effective and are commonly the principal test applied to the profit and loss account. Analytical reviews will normally be carried out before tests of details to increase the efficiency of the audit. Tests of details are more time consuming but can provide greater assurance in some cases. The auditor may find it efficient to rely on management's analytical review procedures, or to use the wide variety of management information available in modern computer systems in his substantive testing.

(e) Exceptions revealed by substantive tests can lead the auditor to perform additional work to determine their effect on the financial statements.

10.96 It is often desirable to perform substantive tests as at a date prior to the year end, particularly if the client wishes the audit to be completed shortly after the year end. Whether this approach is efficient will depend in part on whether the auditor is able to rely on the operation of internal controls in the period between the date of early testing and the year end.

10: Appendix A

Example of a Programme of Substantive Tests

Introduction

1 In this appendix is set out part of an audit programme relating to the testing of trade accounts receivable. This section of the programme was designed for use in either computer or non-computer systems. The design allows for the use of computer programs when trade accounts receivable are processed by computer. As a guide to the identification of those tests for which computer programs could be used to assist in testing, possible uses of computer programs have been described to the right hand side of each test.

2 Although this appendix deals only with trade accounts receivable, the same principles would apply to substantive tests for other assets and liabilities.

3 In practice the scope of the substantive tests would be greater than the examples used in this book. Additional tests would cover such things as presentation and disclosure of items in the financial statements, translation of debts in foreign currencies and tests that might be carried out before the year end, in the intervening period and at the year end where early substantive testing is performed. Since the principles of early testing are not affected by computer processing, the section of the programme that follows draws no distinction between early and year end work.

Substantive Tests

Analytical review

1 When analytical review is carried out for any audit objectives:

(a) Develop an expectation of the recorded amounts.

(b) Investigate variations in excess of acceptable amounts.

(c) Corroborate the client's explanations for the variations.

(d) Consider whether further investigation is required or, if satisfactory explanations cannot be obtained, record the amount of the exception and consider the effect on the financial statements and the audit.

Cut-off

2 (a) Note on a working paper the client's procedures for ensuring that sales around the year end date are accounted for and matched with cost of sales in the correct period.

(b) Set out below the nature and levels of substantive tests to be applied.

Notes

(1) In most cases the cut-off steps can be carried out in the inventories section of the programme.

(2) Cut-off tests will often include an examination of:

(i) records of goods despatched and services performed and related sales invoices for periods before and after the year end;

(ii) records of returns and claims from customers and related credit notes for periods before and after the year end;

(iii) records of unmatched documents referred to in (i) and (ii) as at the year end;

(iv) files of documents referred to in (i) and (ii) unmatched at the date of the visit;

(v) sales invoices and credit notes for the period subsequent to the year end to determine whether any significant invoices or credit notes that are applicable to the period under review have been appropriately reflected in the accounts.

Use of computer programs
1 Production of additional analyses, e.g.: (a) Balances compared to sales. (b) Balances compared to credit limits. (c) Balances stratified by value. (d) Balances stratified by age.
2 Identification and reporting of transactions dated after cut-off date.

Substantive tests
3 Determine from the above procedures: (a) whether receivables for goods despatched and services performed before the year end are properly recorded and that sales are not recorded in the period under review for goods despatched and services performed subsequent to the year end; (b) whether adjustments to receivables for returns and claims from customers arising before the year end are properly recorded as at the year end.
Total balance of trade accounts receivable 4 (a) Obtain an aged listing of trade accounts receivable by individual customer and compare the total with the balance reflected in the control account(s) in the general ledger. (b) Reperform (on a test basis where appropriate) the additions of the reconciliation and the amounts on the listing.
5 Test any significant adjustments made by the client in reconciling detailed accounts receivable records with the control account(s) in the general ledger.
Individual balances 6 Examine, on a test basis where appropriate, the detailed accounts receivable records making up the balances shown in the listing (step 4). During this examination: (a) verify that the balances comprise specific transactions and that the total of the transactions within each account agrees with the account balance on the listing (step 4); (b) determine whether balances have been correctly analysed on the aged listing; (c) enquire into any unusual items (e.g. transfers between accounts).

Use of computer programs
4 Reperform accumulation and ageing of all amounts including any analysis.
6 (a) Reperform the totalling of transactions comprising each balance and report disagreements. (b) Reperform the analysis of each balance by age. (c) Identification and reporting of defined items for manual investigation.

Substantive tests
Significant credit balances 7 Enquire into credit balances of significant amount identified on the listing and consider whether they indicate the possible existence of unrecorded sales.
Confirmation 8 (a) Select customers' accounts for confirmation and determine the method of confirmation (positive, negative or combination thereof); obtain statements and check with the detailed accounts receivable records or the list of balances supporting the selected accounts; and send confirmation requests. (b) Where replies to positive requests are not received within a reasonable period of time, send second requests.
9 (a) Summarise confirmation coverage and investigate any discrepancies or queries reported by customers. (b) Determine that any adjustments required are properly made. (c) Consider whether discrepancies or queries indicate weaknesses or irregularities which would cause other audit procedures to be revised.
Alternative to confirmation 10 Where confirmation is not carried out, or where it is not possible to confirm a selected account: (a) compare any subsequent remittances credited to these accounts to cash receipts records (and remittance advices if available); (b) for items not paid since the year end, examine documentation, such as despatch documents, copies of sales invoices and relevant correspondence, supporting account balances or unpaid items.

Use of computer programs
7 Identification and reporting of credit balances for manual investigation.
8 (a) Stratification and selection of accounts for confirmation and printing of requests. (b) Matching of replies, production of details regarding outstandings and printing of second requests.
9 Matching of replies and reporting of mismatches.
10 Matching of amounts outstanding at the year end with later cash receipts. Analysis of total year end balance by amount not subsequently paid.

Substantive tests

Doubtful accounts

11 Determine the adequacy of the provision for doubtful accounts at the year end, giving consideration in particular to:

(a) all large balances and particularly old balances (refer to the aged listing – step 6(b));

(b) cash collections subsequent to the year end as shown by the cash receipts records, paying particular attention to partial or round sum receipts;

(c) accounts that appear to be disputed (step 9);

(d) unusual variations in balances (step 1);

(e) any evidence of customers' inability to comply with credit terms, having regard to relevant economic conditions;

(e) security.

Other provisions

12 Consider whether other provisions should be made (e.g. for trade allowances, rebates and claims).

Debts written off

13 Select significant trade accounts receivable that have been written off during the year and review the propriety of and the authority for write-off; examine documentation supporting and authorising the write-off.

Use of computer programs

11 Production of additional analyses as an aid to manual review. Examples are:

(a) balances compared with total value of annual sales;

(b) balances on accounts marked as closed;

(c) balances for accounts where cash is required when orders are placed;

(d) balances on accounts on which dishonoured cheques have been received.

13 Investigation and reporting of items indicated as written off.

10: Appendix B

Examples of the Use of Computer Audit Programs

Introduction

1 In this appendix are given two examples of the use of computer audit programs. The first example concerns an accounts receivable ledger and illustrates the wide variety of information that can be obtained from a file holding relatively little data. The second example relates to an inventories ledger and illustrates the substantial number of objectives that can be included where a wide variety of data is held on the files.

Example I – ACCOUNTS RECEIVABLE LEDGER

Description

2 The items held on the accounts receivable file consist of outstanding invoices, credit notes, unmatched cash and adjustments. Details of cash received, credit notes and credit adjustments are matched against the appropriate invoices and debit adjustments. Cash receipts which have been matched are not written to the file but instead an indicator is set to identify items which have been fully paid and these are then deleted from the file at the end of the month. Cash which cannot be matched and payments on account are written to the file. Credit notes and adjustments are input and held separately on the file until they are deleted as part of the matching of cash receipts. There are approximately 3,000 accounts on the file with a total value of about £5 million.

3 There are two files used in the accounts receivable application, the customer master file and the customer transaction file. The customer master file holds the names and addresses of customers, together with the current outstanding balance and credit limit. The customer transaction file holds details of individual transactions.

File layouts

4 The details of the fields on the files are set out below:

(a) *Customer transaction file*

FIELD	CHARACTERS	COMMENTS
Account number	5	
Date: Year	2	
Month	2	
Day	2	
Record type indicator	1	Indicators are: 1 = invoice 2 = cash (unmatched) 3 = cash (payment on account) 4 = credit note 5 = adjustment.
Transaction value	8	In the case of invoices this field contains the invoice value net of returnable packaging and VAT thereon.
Transaction reference number	7	
Paid code	1	1 = unpaid 2 = fully paid 3 = partly paid If the transaction is not an invoice or a debit adjustment this field will not be required and accordingly is set to zero.
Status code	1	The field contains a space if the transaction still forms part of the balance outstanding. If the field contains "D" this indicates that the transaction has been matched as part of the cash matching process and that it will be deleted from the file at the end of the month.
	29	

(b) *Customer master file*

FIELD	CHARACTERS	COMMENTS
Account number	5	
Customer name	30	
Address line 1	30	
Address line 2	30	
Address line 3	30	
Postcode	8	
Balance outstanding	9	££££££ pp
Credit limit	7	££££££
Information not used by the audit program	11	
	160	

Objectives of running the program

5 The objectives included in the program are as follows:

File totals

(a) Check the additions of outstanding balances and establish totals of both debit and credit balances.

(b) Check that the outstanding balance for each customer agrees with the total of the individual outstanding transactions for that customer. Establish a total of any differences.

General information

(c) By reference to the balance outstanding field identify and print the forty largest accounts on the file.

(d) By reference to the balance outstanding field categorise each account by value and produce a histogram.

Cut-off

(e) Establish totals and provide samples of any transactions dated after the year end date to assist in cut-off audit tests.

Provision for bad and doubtful debts

(f) By reference to the record type indicator field, age by record type each of the outstanding transactions into the following categories as an aid in assessing the provision for bad and doubtful debts:

(i) current;
(ii) 1 month old;
(iii) 2 months old;
(iv) 3 months old;

(v) 4–6 months old;
(vi) 7–12 months old;
(vii) over 12 months old.

(NOTE: The company program analyses all items over 3 months old into one category.)

(g) As a further aid in assessing the bad and doubtful debts provision, and in addition to the analysis of transactions in (f) above, establish a total and print samples of accounts where twenty-five per cent of the total outstanding balance is more than three months old.

(h) Provide totals of the balances of accounts which exceed their credit limits and of the amounts by which they exceed their credit limits. Provide a separate listing and total balance of accounts for which credit limits have not been set.

Producing letters for debtors circularisation

(i) Select accounts to be used in the debtors circularisation. The selection is to be made on the following basis:

(i) By reference to the balance outstanding field select all accounts where the total value exceeds £20,000 debit or is more than £1,000 in credit.

(ii) By reference to the date and transaction value fields select all accounts where the value of transactions over three months old exceeds £500.

(iii) A random sample of the remainder.

Produce an overall control schedule suitable for monitoring replies, and for each account print a confirmation letter and detailed statement.

Achievement of objectives

6 No particular problems should be encountered in achieving the objectives set out in paragraph 5. Depending on the particular package used it may be necessary to use special routines to accumulate and store the transaction values for each account for comparison with the balance outstanding field in the customer master file (objective 5 (b)).

Example II – INVENTORIES LEDGER

Description

7 The inventory master file contains the finished goods inventory records. Inventory lines are divided into two types defined as "special lines" and "standard lines". "Special lines" are fast-moving lines which are prone to quick obsolescence, predominantly due to deterioration of the items concerned. "Special lines" held for more than twelve weeks are provided against by the company. "Standard lines" do not deteriorate so quickly. "Standard lines" are provided against by the company on a sliding scale.

8 The file is updated by receipts from suppliers, issues in respect of sales to customers, and adjustments which arise mainly through inventory being scrapped or through the correction of differences discovered during physical stock counts. Inventory is issued on a FIFO basis. There are approximately 6,000 different inventory lines on the file with a value of about £55 million.

9 Inventory is subject to a system of perpetual inventory counting which is designed to ensure that all "standard lines" are counted at least twice a year and "special lines" four times a year. All lines should be counted during the last three months of the financial year.

10 The company's system for pricing is complex. A separate file holds details of cost and selling price histories, and is used by the company to calculate average costs for each stock line monthly. The inventory master file, which is accessed by the program described in this illustration, holds the latest average cost price and the average cost price at the beginning of the financial year. It also holds the latest and opening selling prices. The price histories file is not accessed in this illustration.

11 The company maintains its future sales forecasts on the file in the form of estimated sales for the next twenty-four weeks. These are computed by another application and updated quarterly. Experience has shown the forecasts to be fairly reliable, the average error being only ±3.7%. New lines introduced during the quarter will not have a forecast and in these cases the forecast fields are blank.

12 Each inventory line is sold in up to nine variations. Separate forecasts and a separate record of inventory are maintained for each variation.

File layout

13 The details of the fields on the file records are set out below:

(a) *Forecast record*

FIELD	CHARACTERS	COMMENTS
Record type	2	Always 01
Line prefix	4	1001–1999 "special lines" 2000–8000 "standard lines"
Sub-record counter	2	Value may be 0–9 and indicates: (i) number of forecast sub-records following (ii) number of inventory records
Forecast sub-record (can occur up to 9 times indicated by the value of the sub-record counter)		
Line suffix – 3 characters		
24 week forecast – 3 characters (maximum)	54	Future quantity sales forecast in thousands
(maximum)	62	

(b) *Inventory record*

FIELD	CHARACTERS	COMMENTS
(NOTE: Certain fields not used by the program have been omitted)		There may be 0–9 inventory records. There will be 1 inventory record for each forecast sub-record (see above)
Record type	2	Always 02
Line number	7	Line prefix + suffix
Line description	15	
Stock location	6	
Supplier code	6	For generating purchase orders from suppliers' master file

FIELD	CHARACTERS	COMMENTS
Cost price	6	££££ pp-current average unit cost
Opening cost price	6	££££ pp-average unit cost at commencement of financial year
Selling price	6	££££ pp-current unit price
Opening selling price	6	££££ pp-unit price at commencement of financial year
Inventory quantity	6	Current balance
Opening inventory quantity	6	At commencement of financial year
Maximum stock level	6	
Re-order quantity	6	
Re-order level	6	
Purchases	78	13 fields of 6 characters each recording purchases of stock for each period in the financial year – blank until used
Sales	78	13 fields of 6 characters each recording sales of stock for each period in the financial year – blank until used
Weeks since last issue	2	Number of weeks since a sale was last made
Date of last stock count	6	Format DDMMYY. Blank until first count made
Last stock count difference	4	Blank until first count made
Date of next stock count	6	Format DDMMYY
Date of first receipt	6	Format DDMMYY. Date line first stocked – blank until first receipt accepted
Date of last purchase	6	Format DDMMYY
	276	

(c) *File control record*

FIELD	CHARACTERS	COMMENTS
Record type	2	Always 99
Number of inventory records ("special lines")	6	
Number of inventory records ("standard lines")	6	
File total of inventory	10	££££££££ pp-at latest cost value
	24	

Objectives of running the program

14 The objectives included in the program are as follows:

File totals

(a) Check the evaluation of inventory and establish totals of both debit and credit balances.

(b) By reference to the line prefix, analyse total inventory between "special lines" and "standard lines", providing debit and credit totals for each category.

(c) Check the totals established in (a) and (b) above with the file totals on the file control record.

(d) Produce a report of all negative stock balances for investigation, and the total value of negative stock should be reported.

Stock pricing

(e) As an aid to the assessment of the reasonableness of current average cost prices, carry out the following comparisons of fields on the file:

cost price: opening cost price;
cost price: selling price;
opening cost price: opening selling price.

Provide totals and print samples of items meeting the following conditions:

(i) current margins significantly more or less than the company's normal margins;

(ii) current margins significantly different to opening margins;

(iii) cost prices in excess of selling prices;

(iv) cost prices showing an abnormally large or small rise during the year;

(v) cost prices which have decreased or not changed during the year.

The comparisons in (i), (ii) and (iv) above will be controlled by parameters, the auditor having previously determined what might be regarded as significant or abnormal percentage changes.

Obsolete and slow moving stock

(f) In respect of "special lines", compare the inventory quantity field with the purchases for the thirteen financial periods. Evaluate and analyse inventory over the following categories:

(i) 0–4 weeks old;
(ii) 5–8 weeks old;
(iii) 9–12 weeks old;
(iv) 13–16 weeks old;
(v) over 16 weeks old.
} The company makes a 100% provision against these amounts.

Print samples from categories (iii)–(v).

(g) In respect of "special lines", divide the 24 week forecast field by two to obtain the estimated usage for the next twelve weeks. In respect of items in categories (f)(i)–(iii) above, compare the inventory quantities with the twelve weeks' estimated usage and accumulate an evaluated total and print a sample of inventory which it is forecast will not be used within the twelve-week period.

(h) In respect of "special lines" introduced in the last quarter and therefore without a valid forecast on file (objective (g) cannot therefore be achieved), compute an average four weeks' usage by reference to the date of first receipt field and the issues fields for the three most recent periods. Compare the computed average with the inventory quantity and accumulate an evaluated total of inventory which it is forecast will not be used within twelve weeks. Print a sample of items accumulated.

(i) In respect of "standard lines" other than those introduced in the last quarter, by reference to the weeks since last issued field, analyse the evaluated inventory into the following categories:

(i) no issues 0–8 weeks;
(ii) no issues 9–16 weeks;
(iii) no issues 17–24 weeks;

(iv) no issues 25–40 weeks;
(v) no issues 41–56 weeks; } The company makes a 100%
(vi) no issues over 56 weeks. } provision against these items.

(j) In respect of "standard lines", included in (i)(i)–(iv) above, compare the inventory quantity with the 24-week forecast and analyse inventory into the following categories of estimated future usage of inventory quantities:

(i) 0–12 weeks;
(ii) 13–24 weeks;
(iii) 25–48 weeks;
(iv) 49–72 weeks; } The company makes the 25%
(v) 73–96 weeks; } following provisions 50%
(vi) over 96 weeks. } against these items. 100%

Print samples from categories (iii)–(vi).

(k) In respect of "standard lines" covered in (j)(i)–(v) and new "standard lines" (introduced in the last quarter; these have been omitted from (i) and (j)), compute an average four weeks' usage by reference to the issues fields for the thirteen accounting periods and, for stock lines held for less than one year, the date of first receipt field. Compare the computed average with the inventory quantity and analyse evaluated inventory into the following categories of estimated future usage of inventory quantities:

(i) 0–12 weeks;
(ii) 13–24 weeks;
(iii) 25–48 weeks;
(iv) 49–72 weeks;
(v) 73–96 weeks;
(vi) over 96 weeks.

Print samples from categories (iii)–(vi).

(l) Accumulate a total and print a sample of "standard lines" in categories (i)(i)–(iii) and (j)(i)–(iii) where the inventory quantity is in excess of the maximum stock level. Evaluate and accumulate the excess.

Perpetual inventory

(m) By reference to the date of last stock count field establish the total number and value of stock lines which have not been subjected to a physical count in the last quarter. Analyse the totals into the following categories (include items in more than one category if appropriate):

(i) new stock lines in the last quarter (identified by reference to the date of first receipt field);

(ii) high value inventory (identified by reference to a parameter specifying the value);

(iii) high value unit cost (identified by reference to a parameter specifying the unit cost value);

(iv) "special lines" (identified by line prefix);

(v) "standard lines".

In each category the samples printed will be in descending value of inventory held. This will enable the more significant items to be identified for counting.

(n) By reference to the last stock count difference field, establish a total of high value stock count differences. A sample will be printed of high value differences for manual verification that the year end balance was correct.

Management information

15 As well as achieving objectives of direct relevance to the audit it is also possible to achieve certain objectives which are largely operational in nature. Operational objectives enable useful points to be brought to the attention of management. Objectives may be termed operational for two reasons. First, the auditor is unlikely ever to be interested in the information for the purposes of the audit. Secondly, although the information may sometimes be relevant, the auditor is not directly interested in it because other objectives in the program stand in place of those objectives.

16 The operational objectives included in the program were to:

(a) check that all "dead" stock lines were properly cleared from the file by accumulating a total of lines with nil inventory quantity and a date of last purchase more than one year ago;

(b) check that the relationship between maximum stock level, re-order quantity, and re-order level is reasonable by ensuring that re-order quantity plus re-order level does not exceed the maximum stock level;

(c) check the validity of maximum stock levels by comparing the maximum stock level field with the 24-week forecast field. Accumulate a total of items where the maximum stock level is more than twice the 24-week forecast (maximum stock levels are calculated and input manually; they should not exceed twice the 24-week forecast);

(d) provide totals and print samples of items showing an abnormally large or small selling price rise in the year.

Achievement of objectives

17 Unlike the previous sample it is likely that the achievement of the objectives set out above will require a substantial number of additional routines to be incorporated into the basic package. Routines may be required, *inter alia*, for the following purposes:

(a) to identify the number of forecast sub-records for each forecast record, based on the value of the sub-record counter;

(b) to match each forecast sub-record with its related inventory record and extract the relevant information from each;

(c) to expand the 24-week forecast field to a six character field;

(d) to manipulate date fields into the format YYMMDD.

11

The Use of File Interrogation Software

Sources of Software

Introduction

11.01 There are a number of methods which the auditor can adopt in using file interrogation software within the audit. One method is for the auditor to write a program himself, another is for him to specify the requirements of a program to be written for him by the company or some other suitable source, such as a software house. Both of these methods result in a "one-off" program which can normally only be used on a particular file at one installation. In addition, they tend to be time consuming and therefore expensive methods of developing audit software and, particularly in the case of writing programs, a high degree of technical skill is required. The external auditor, who usually wishes to run programs on a variety of applications and installations, is more likely to use one or other of the many available package programs.

Package programs

11.02 The logic required in most computer programs used by auditors is relatively simple. It is also usually similar from application to application. The auditor wants much the same from an inventories file as an accounts receivable file – accumulate field A; compare field B with field C. Field A may be the stock balance in one case and the customer's balance in another. Comparing field B with field C may be identifying slow moving inventory items in one case and overdue accounts receivable in the other. Although the difference is clear to the auditor, within the program the logic is similar.

11.03 It is from two factors – the problems of using the "one-off" program, and the broad similarity of logic required as between one program and another – that the idea of the **computer audit package** developed. These packages, which have been developed by the major accounting firms, by software houses, by computer manufacturers and by companies' internal audit or systems departments, are general purpose computer programs which can carry out similar tasks on a variety of files. It is necessary for the auditor to define the configuration on which the program is to be run and the files to be used. In addition the auditor is left to choose in each case the use he will make of the logic in the program. The auditor's definitions and requirements are input and convert the computer audit package into a specific program to do what the auditor wants in relation to the files concerned.

11.04 An effective computer audit package helps overcome most of the practical problems faced by the auditor in using computer programs. Thus the use of a package enables the auditor to avoid much of the work entailed in writing and testing a program; it also simplifies the work of specification required. The cost to the auditor of using a package is substantially less than that of developing and using a "one-off" program. As a result there has been an increasing interest in, and use of, computer audit packages.

11.05 The objectives which the auditor wishes to achieve through the use of software in a particular application will tend to be very similar from client to client, and typical tasks for common applications were included in Chapter 10 "Substantive Tests". Using a general purpose computer audit package for a particular application requires the auditor to code the logic into the program for each new client on which the package is used even though the objectives are the same as used for a previous client. In order to avoid this repetition of coding the **application specific package** was developed. The application specific package is a program into which the audit objectives for a particular application, for example accounts receivable, are pre-coded so that the auditor has only to define the configuration on which the program is to be run and to format the client's data files into the form required by the package.

Types of computer audit software

11.06 The auditor may be able to use computer software in many areas of his audit. The more common types of software which may be used have been mentioned elsewhere in this book; they may be briefly summarised as follows:

- File interrogation software which accesses the company's data files such as master files or transaction files.

- Comparison programs to compare versions of a program in either source or executable form.
- Interactive enquiry software to interrogate files in on-line systems.
- Software to analyse files in use by system software.
- Resident code to examine live transactions as they are processed.
- Microcomputer software to assist the auditor in areas such as analytical review, the preparation of audit schedules and in audit administration.

11.07 This chapter concentrates on file interrogation software, since, of the programs that access company data, this type of program is the most commonly used. However the principles outlined in the rest of this chapter can to a large extent be applied to all types of computer software used by the auditor. A wide variety of package file interrogation programs have been developed over the years. The different approaches to the use of file interrogation packages and the more important facilities, based on practical experience, that should be available in them are described in the following paragraphs.

Facilities of the File Interrogation Package

11.08 It is not a purpose of this book to review and evaluate the various computer audit file interrogation packages available. However, to aid selection the important areas to be considered are set out in paragraphs 11.09 to 11.21. Briefly, the areas that should be considered are whether the package will run on the relevant machine(s), whether it can read the data file, and whether it is capable of fulfilling the required audit objectives. The relative importance of each of these factors will vary according to each auditor's requirements. For instance an external auditor may require a package that can run on the various machines used by his clients whereas an internal auditor will often simply need to ensure that a package runs on his company's particular computer.

Ability to be used on different machine types

11.09 Each type of computer operates in a different way; thus a package which works on one type of computer will not necessarily work on any other type of computer. One solution to this problem is to produce separate versions of the package for different machines. For instance, major accounting firms and software houses often produce packages which by use of different versions are able to work on a variety of machine types. Packages sold by computer manufacturers will often work only on that manufacturer's machines. Where the package does not work on the required machine it may be possible to convert it to operate on that machine. As a minimum this will require that a version of the language in which the package is written (e.g. COBOL) is available on the machine. The ease of conversion will depend to a large extent on the language in which the package is written and the complexity of the code used. It is always easier to convert packages written in a source language such as COBOL than to convert a package using a language nearer machine code such as ASSEMBLER.

Ability to access data files

11.10 The types of data files that can be read by a package will usually depend on the nature of the package. For instance a package designed to operate on many computers will often handle simple file structures on all the machines covered, but will not be able to access databases directly. Packages developed by computer manufacturers will often access only that manufacturer's file structures. Nowadays, increasingly powerful interrogation packages are available which run on microcomputers and these can provide a cost effective method of undertaking file interrogation in an environment familiar to the auditor. Such packages commonly include facilities to assist in reformatting data to enable files from a variety of machines to be converted and read by the package.

11.11 As well as considering the ability of the package to access the data file, it is also important to consider its ability to process the different characteristics of fields that could be present. This is particularly important if it is planned to use the package against data files from other machine types since the field characteristics (such as binary) on the file may then not be standard. Remedies in use include reformatting the files using the company's or the auditor's software, writing linkage programs to access the information on the database or running against a back-up copy of the file, where data is held in conventional form. It is also important that the program is capable of accessing data held on more than one file, such as, for example, when stock prices are held on one file and quantities on another file.

Tasks

11.12 It is helpful to assess the logical power of a package in terms of the audit tasks that the auditor may wish to carry out. Examples are detailed for the various accounts items in Chapter 10 but may be considered here in general terms. The variety is, in fact, quite limited. The auditor requires totals and samples of data held on the file, or derived from the data held on the file. He also requires them to be printed out in a convenient manner in order to interpret them. These matters are discussed in the following paragraphs.

Totals

11.13 The totals required may be:

(a) an *overall* total of all items on the file, for example all accounts receivable balances;

(b) an *analysis of* all items on the file, for example accounts receivable transactions aged into different categories;

(c) totals of *specified* items on the file, for example accounts receivable whose balances are in excess of their credit limits.

The totals required will usually be of the main value field, for example fixed asset net book value. It may, however, also be of a subsidiary field, for example depreciation for the year, or of a calculated field, for example the notional depreciation charge for the year in respect of fully depreciated assets.

11.14 The requirement for a single total of all items on the file can be satisfied by a simple accumulation facility in the program. The number of simple accumulations will be conditioned by the number of totals of this nature that are required, which is usually relatively few. Typically totals of positive, negative and zero items for each category are required. It will also be necessary to be able to obtain sub-totals based on a reference number of each record, for example departmental totals.

11.15 In order to obtain analyses of all items and totals of specified items, there will need to be a facility to compare. A facility to carry out both single and multiple comparisons is normally required. Single comparisons are required to compare:

(a) any two fields on a record, for example accounts receivable balances in excess of credit limits, or inventory balances where maximum stock level exceeds usage for the year;

(b) any field on the record with a constant specified by the auditor, for example inventory balances where the stock count date is more than one year old or deposit account balances where the interest rate exceeds a specified percentage;

(c) any field on the record, with a field calculated by the program, for example fixed assets depreciation charge on file with a calculated depreciation charge;

(d) a field calculated by the program, with a constant, for example inventory valued greater than £10,000 where the value has to be calculated from quantity and price.

Multiple comparisons are required to compare any field with more than one other field or constant, for example accounts receivable balances of a certain category *and* size *and* over the credit limit.

11.16 When one field is compared with another field, it may be desirable to weight one or both fields. This is useful where only large differences are required, for example accounts receivable balances in excess of 150% of their credit limit, or to locate differences between items of data which should have a direct relationship, for example inventory items where the selling price is not equal to 150% of cost price. It will be necessary to be able to compare fields on separate files, for example accounts receivable balances on one file and credit limits on another file.

11.17 From the above it can be seen that the ability to carry out comparisons and accumulate the results into totals is the auditor's principal requirement. To this may be added the need to calculate, both before and after the comparison. Thus, in relation to accounts receivable, it might be necessary for the program to calculate the balance outstanding from the transactions on the record before comparing the calculated balance with the credit limit. Likewise, having carried out the comparison, it might be desirable to calculate the amount, if any, by which the balance exceeded the credit limit. The number of comparisons required will depend on the variety of data on the file and the ingenuity and requirements of the auditor. The number may extend from one to a hundred or more.

Samples

11.18 Several packages contain statistical sampling routines. This is advantageous when selecting items for subsequent audit tests, for example inventory balances for physical count, or accounts receivable balances for confirmation routines. In other cases, however, the auditor merely requires a sample as evidence of the items making up a total. In these cases it is useful to have the facility to:

(a) stratify the population on the file;

(b) start sampling from a random point on the file;

(c) stratify the sample into any number of levels by value, for example sample debit balances over £2,000 and credit balances over £100;

(d) specify an interval between each item selected, for example every 100th record;

(e) control the maximum number of items to be printed out, for example the first ten in the category.

It is also useful if the whole sample can be written to an output file for sorting and printing or further processing if required. In this way all items in defined categories can be produced if necessary for investigation by the company.

Print-out

11.19 The form of print-out and the presentation of information is of particular significance since the print-out will be used by the auditor and may form an important part of the audit working papers. The print-outs should be easy to understand and should be clear as to dates and contents. It is helpful if totals are printed for both value and number of records. The percentages that the totals of analyses and specified items represent of the total population can be useful but this facility is less usually provided. It is important that the total value of samples printed out and the percentage that the sample represents of the total in the category are calculated and printed out.

11.20 Relevant details of individual items should be printed, together with a reasonably full reason for their selection. Cryptic messages that need decoding are not easily dealt with by the auditor. Individual items may be sorted before printing so that all in the same category are printed together. An example of a suitable print-out of individual items is illustrated in Appendix B.

11.21 It is helpful if the auditor can select the order in which totals are printed and specify descriptive details. In this way totals can be grouped under meaningful audit objective headings. An example of part of a print-out provided in this manner is also illustrated in Appendix B.

Types of File Interrogation Package

11.22 The auditor will often need to run software against files from a large number of different applications and, for external auditors, clients. These applications will run in a variety of ways on many different machines. Since at present there is no single type of software capable of dealing with all situations, the auditor may need to use a variety of techniques to interrogate data files including the following:

- Generalised data file interrogation software.
- Fourth generation languages, report generators and query facilities supplied by computer manufacturers and software houses.

- Application specific programs.
- Skeleton source programs.
- One-off programs written in a high level language, where none of the above approaches is suitable.

These techniques are discussed in detail below.

Generalised data file interrogation software

11.23 This type of package provides the auditor with a flexible enquiry facility which may be used to produce a variety of different reports from any data file which can be read by the package. Typically they have been designed with the auditor in mind, and provide facilities needed by the auditor such as sampling. The auditor is normally required to specify the nature and layout of the data files to be read by the package and to define the reports he needs in overall terms, for example by specifying the method to be used to select items for reporting and the data fields to be reported. Based on this specification, the package will read the data file, select the items specified and produce a report, usually in a standard format.

11.24 To use this type of package effectively it is necessary to understand the way in which it will interpret the specifications used by the auditor. For example, in a task which has selection of records both for detailed reporting and totalling, it is important to know whether the totals include records which have not been selected for detailed reporting.

11.25 The package will normally work in one of the following ways:

(a) it may produce a source program in a high level language such as COBOL, which must then be compiled before it can be executed against the data file;

(b) it may produce an executable program which can be run against the data file; or

(c) it may interpret the instructions and read the data file, with no intermediate stages.

11.26 Packages which produce a source program are generally more flexible because the auditor's own source language statements can often be added to the source program. Thus the auditor can add coding to carry out tasks which the package itself is not capable of. Packages which interpret and then execute instructions are generally slower in execution than the other two types of package which permit an executable program to be created and stored.

11.27 The stages in implementing a generalised interrogation program, which generates a source program, are outlined in Figure 74. A completed example of the type of questionnaire used in such a generalised interrogation package is set out in Appendix A.

11.28 Most generalised interrogation packages only work on a limited range of machines and a problem arises when the auditor wishes to develop

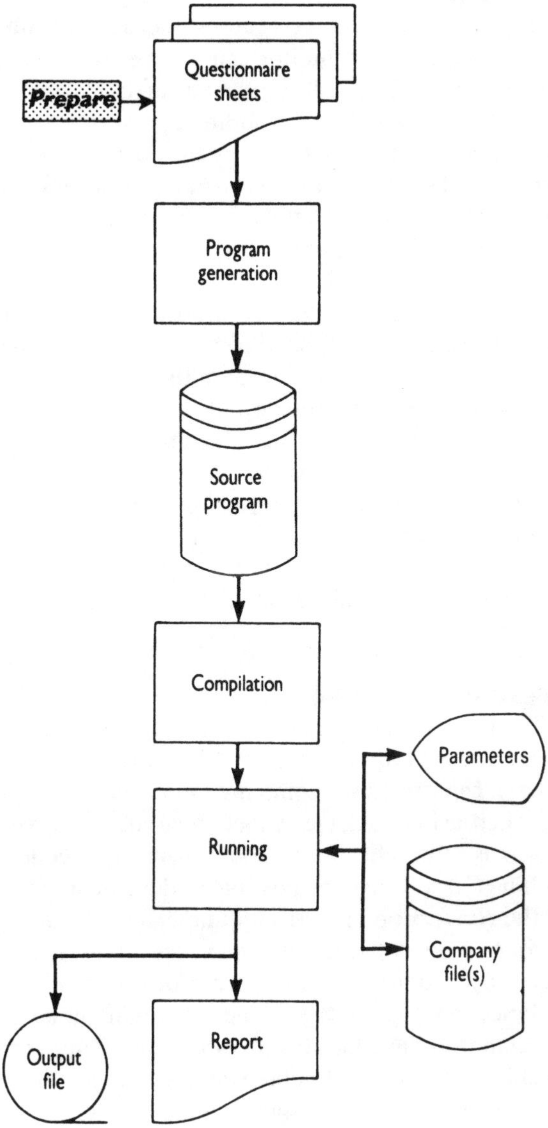

FIG. 74. Implementation of a generalised interrogation computer audit package (para. 11.27)

software for applications running on other machine types. One approach may be to use one of the other types of file interrogation software described in paragraphs 11.31 to 11.41. If, however, the auditor wishes to use generalised interrogation software there are two alternative approaches that can be adopted. These are data file conversion and program conversion. They are discussed below.

Data file conversion

11.29 When the auditor's interrogation package will not run on the company's computer the auditor can arrange for the data file to be taken to a computer which will run the package. Normally this computer will be either one owned by the auditor, possibly a microcomputer, or one at a computer bureau selected by the auditor. This approach offers the advantage that the auditor is working in a familiar environment and can thus save time. Offsetting this are the costs of running the auditor's computer or, if a bureau is used, the extra costs incurred in purchasing machine time, although this cost is not of significance where a microcomputer interrogation package can be used on the auditor's microcomputer. The auditor will need to ensure that the interrogation package can read the data file produced on the company's computer. It may be that the company can provide a file in a suitable format, or alternatively the auditor may need to use facilities within the package, a utility program or a special program to convert the file. It will be necessary to obtain the company's permission to remove the data files from the company's premises, and where the files contain confidential information the company may be reluctant to grant such permission, or the auditor may be required to take specific precautions to prevent its disclosure.

Program conversion

11.30 Under this approach the auditor runs the package on a suitable machine to generate the required source code, and then converts the code created so that it can run on the company's machine. This approach is only feasible when using packages which generate a source language program since it is impracticable to convert machine code programs between machine types. It may be possible to develop a special program to carry out the conversion process automatically. The main advantages of this approach over data file conversion are that it minimises bureau costs, where the auditor is unable to perform the interrogation on his own machine, and it solves the problem of confidentiality when the company is reluctant to have files taken away from their premises. However it is difficult to use this technique when the client's files are subject to frequent changes in format, since it is expensive to reconvert the program in order to amend the program logic. Generally, program conversion is more difficult and expensive than file conversion.

Fourth generation languages and report generators

11.31 Companies will often have purchased a report generator (sometimes known as a query language) or a fourth generation language in order to improve programmer efficiency or to enable users to develop their own reports. Sometimes such software is provided as part of the standard system software. Such languages use small numbers of very powerful commands to achieve results which would require lengthy programs if programmed in languages such as COBOL. An example of the coding used by such languages was provided in Chapter 9, Appendix D.

11.32 When a company has its own report generator or fourth generation language the auditor may be able to use it for audit purposes. An advantage of this is that the report generator or fourth generation language will often maintain within itself a dictionary of the company's files, thus overcoming one of the common practical problems in the use of interrogation software, namely misunderstanding file layout and field usage. However, report generators are often less well adapted to the needs of the auditor than a package defined specifically for audit purposes, since facilities are frequently limited. For example, although calculations and comparisons can be performed, it is often not possible to perform further calculations and selections on a previously calculated result field. Thus for example, it might not be possible to compare the debtor balances to their credit limits, as set out in paragraph 11.17. This is normally less of a problem with fourth generation languages since they usually provide a wide variety of facilities. When the auditor is not familiar with the report generator or fourth generation language he will incur additional learning costs before he can use it. This can be a significant problem when the auditor has clients using a wide variety of different packages.

11.33 The auditor will also need to satisfy himself that the package itself is working correctly. Where IT controls are tested and relied on these will normally provide a considerable degree of assurance. In addition, a great deal of assurance can be gained by agreeing file totals to the company's reports and by the tests carried out on samples produced. In extreme cases, if the auditor does not rely on IT controls, cannot obtain sufficient assurance from the manual tests, and is concerned that unauthorised amendments could have been made to the package itself, or to the directory of data files, he should either not use the facility or take further steps to ensure its accurate operation, such as creating test data and executing his program against it.

Application specific packages

11.34 For each of the common business systems the auditor will normally wish to achieve similar objectives with interrogation software irrespective of the company for which software is being developed. For example, in respect of accounts receivable applications the auditor will normally wish to cover most or all of the objectives stated in the first example in Chapter 10, Appendix B. Since it is inefficient constantly to recreate the coding to carry out identical tasks, and since most accounts receivable systems contain the same basic data, a standard package can be used which produces all the commonly required reports. Such a package is referred to in this book as an application specific package.

11.35 For a particular type of application different systems will normally hold the same basic data, but it will be held in a variety of different formats. Therefore the first program in an application specific package is normally a special reformatting program to reformat the data and produce standard files for use by the remaining programs in the package. Each time the package is used this reformatting program will need to be adapted by the auditor to read the particular file formats used by the company. The amount of work involved in adapting the reformatting program will depend on the differences in format between the client's files and those required for input to the package. For example, if an accounts receivable package requires two separate files, one containing outstanding customer transactions and the other the customer balance, name, and address, and the company's system has two files which are similar in overall format, then work required will be restricted to re-ordering individual fields from the company's files to create two files suitable for the package. A diagram depicting the structure of such an application specific package is shown in Figure 75.

11.36 The auditor will need to input parameters each time the package is run. These are necessary to provide information that varies from run to run, such as:

- The company name for report headings.
- Which tasks are to be carried out assuming the auditor can choose which parts of the package are to be run each time it is used.
- Values and other criteria which will be used in calculations and comparisons, for example, the value against which balances are to

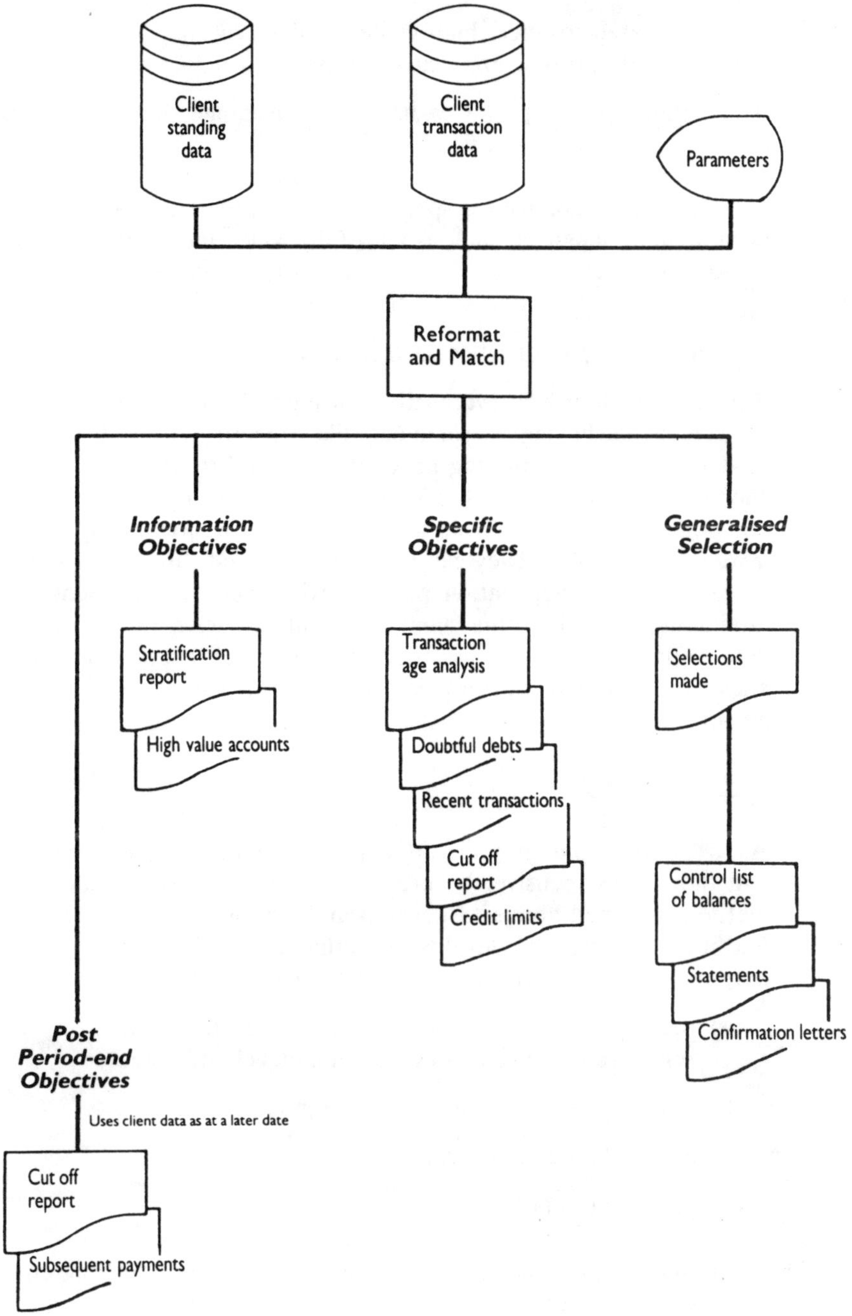

FIG. 75. Accounts receivable application specific package (para. 11.35)

be compared to select high value accounts receivable, or the date to be used in producing a cut-off report.

Application specific packages have the advantage that most of the processing logic and specification of reports is built into the package, and therefore they are cheaper to use than generalised interrogation packages. Many application specific packages are written in a standard programming language such as COBOL, which means that they can be converted relatively easily to run on different types of computer.

Application program specific packages

11.37 Where the auditor has several clients using the same accounting package, and hence having the same data file structures, it may be efficient to develop the reformatting program once and to use it on all such clients. The programs are then very specific to that application package and for the common accounting areas within it, for example sales, inventory, payables. They can thus be set up and run for each of the clients using the application package with maximum efficiency and minimum cost. Where the client's accounting package holds types of data over and above that assumed for the normal application specific package it may prove cost-effective to program extra objectives to take advantage of this data.

Use of skeleton programs

11.38 As discussed in paragraph 11.01 writing programs is time consuming, and therefore expensive. Where it is not possible to use one of the methods outlined above to develop audit software, the auditor may find it cost-effective to develop an outline program to carry out tasks that are common to virtually all developments such as:

(a) reading the parameters to obtain information that varies from run to run, such as dates, sampling level and values;

(b) selecting samples from the file population;

(c) accumulating file totals;

(d) producing reports.

11.39 Each time the program is used the auditor completes the program by writing the code to:

(a) define and read the input file;

(b) exclude from the remainder of processing unwanted record types such as file header records;

(c) carry out any necessary calculations;

(d) trigger the sampling and totalling routines;

(e) define the detailed information needed for audit use.

As with generalised audit software and application specific packages the auditor will also need to determine parameters such as sampling levels.

11.40 Since the tasks to be carried out are common to all developments, this approach is more cost-effective than writing a completely new program for each development. It may also enable the auditor to use software on a machine which has available the source language in which the skeleton program is written, but where none of the other methods for developing software outlined above is available. It is not normally as cost-effective an approach as the other methods outlined above since it requires more programming to be performed by the auditor. It also requires knowledge and skill in the particular programming language used, for example, COBOL.

One-off programs

11.41 Where no other method is available to develop software the auditor will need to write the entire program himself using a source language such as COBOL. The most common use of this technique is when databases or complicated file structures have to be accessed and a small one-off program is written to create an output file in a format suitable for further interrogation. However because this process is time consuming it will rarely be cost efficient to develop programs fulfilling a full range of audit objectives using this method.

Procedures for Using Computer Audit Software

Introduction

11.42 It is advisable to establish formal procedures for the use of computer programs. This will help ensure that programs are used only where the costs can be justified, that the right objectives are included and that the costs are budgeted and approved and then controlled against the budget. Examples of suitable procedures are outlined in the following paragraphs. The procedures are set out separately for the first year of use and for second and subsequent years.

11.43 The development of computer programs for audit use has many similarities to the development of new computer systems by clients. Procedures are needed to control both types of development to ensure that:

(a) the development is cost effective;

(b) the users' requirements are accurately interpreted;

(c) costs are budgeted and approved;

(d) the programs are documented both for audit evidence and so that they can be used in subsequent years.

11.44 Procedures for the development of computer audit programs will need to be flexible to cater for the different requirements of the various types of file interrogation software. For example, there will need to be discussions regarding the proposed report layout when using a generalised interrogation program, but not in the case of an application specific package since report layouts are fixed. Procedures that could be used to control the development of a large computer program, where a generalised interrogation program is in use, are set out in paragraphs 11.45 to 11.61. The major areas where different procedures are needed for other types of file interrogation software are identified in Figure 76.

First year

Identification

11.45 The need for, or desirability of, using file interrogation software should be identified during the audit planning process when the audit strategy is determined. It is helpful to make this identification as early as possible in order that the program can be prepared in sufficient time to assist fully in subsequent audit work.

Specification

11.46 When the need for, or the desirability of, using file interrogation software has been identified, a specification should be prepared. This specification sets out the objectives of the program, the logic by which they are to be achieved and a detailed budget. Discussions will normally be held with the company's data processing staff in order to obtain the detailed understanding of the client's application necessary to enable the software to be developed. The information that should be obtained includes details of the various record types on the data file and details of relevant fields. Particular attention should be paid to date, value and record status fields, since experience shows that

	Generalised interrogation software	Company's own report generator	Application specific package	Skeleton and one-off programs
Initial feasibility study	✓	✓	✓	✓
Detailed specification of programs	✓	✓	X	✓
Loading of package	✓	X	✓	✓*
Development and testing of reformatting program	X	X	✓	X
Detailed programming	✓	✓	X	✓
Testing of detailed programming	✓	✓	X	✓
Setting parameter levels	✓	✓	✓	✓
Testing the package itself	X	✓	X	X
Controlling production running	✓	✓	✓	✓

*Skeleton programs only.

FIG. 76. Variations in procedures for different types of computer programs (para. 11.44)

misunderstandings often arise regarding these fields. It may be helpful for the auditor to write to the client setting out his understanding of these points in order to confirm that his understanding is correct. The specification, when approved, for example by the audit partner, can then be the authority to prepare and execute the program on the lines specified. Where the program is to carry out complex processing, and the cost of preparing the specification is likely to be high, it will normally be sensible first to obtain approval to prepare a specification.

Preparation, compilation, testing and execution

Preparation

11.47 The program is prepared next. The work may involve the completion of questionnaires and the preparation of parameters.

Compilation

11.48 The questionnaire must then be input to the computer. This will normally be done at a terminal. The program will then be precompiled, if relevant, and compiled. These stages will normally produce a listing detailing the original questionnaire input and a series of diagnostic messages detailing any errors detected. The output should be reviewed to ensure that the program appears complete. Any diagnostic messages should be checked, and the original program should be corrected where appropriate, prior to the next recompile.

Testing

11.49 In the year in which the program is written, or in any year in which the program is amended, it will be necessary to carry out test runs prior to the production run to ensure that the input file definition and program logic are correct. Testing is most conveniently carried out on copies of the relevant company's files. The program may include a test facility to stop processing after reading a certain number of records when a test is made. If this facility is used, the auditor will often be unable to agree the totals produced in the test run with those produced by the company. In these cases, a print-out should be obtained of all items processed, and expected results should be calculated for comparison with the actual results of the run. Where the program is being used to identify items of an exceptional nature, such as accounts receivable balances greater than the credit limit, it is particularly important that adequate testing is carried out since incorrect logic may not be immediately apparent. For example, if no items are reported this may disguise the fact that items should have been printed out, but were not. Where all possible combinations of data do not appear to exist on the test file it may be necessary to develop specific test data to ensure that the program will cope with all possible data.

Execution

11.50 At execution time the auditor will need to ensure that the correct unamended version of his program is run against the correct data file without unauthorised intervention.

Ensuring the correct program is used

11.51 In order to ensure that the correct unamended version of the program is used the auditor will need to be able to differentiate between different versions of the same program. Procedures to ensure that the correct program version is used may include printing out the date (and time) the program was compiled each time the program is run. Reference can then be made to the compile listing to determine the version number. In addition it is likely that many versions of the program will be created during the development phase and the auditor should avoid retention of many different versions as this may cause confusion. It is, however, necessary to ensure that adequate back-up to the operational program is retained.

11.52 It is also necessary to ensure that no unauthorised amendments occur to the program after creation. Possible steps include:

(a) ensuring that the library in which the program resides is adequately protected against unauthorised access;

(b) ensuring that the period of time between creation and execution of the program is minimal;

(c) use of time and date stamps to ensure that the creation date can be checked;

(d) carrying out the procedures set out in paragraph 11.54 to ensure that the program is not subject to unauthorised amendment during execution.

Controls over operation

11.53 During execution of his program the auditor needs to ensure that:

(a) the JCL that governed the operation of the program was correct; and

(b) there has been no unauthorised intervention by the operator or other client staff.

11.54 The auditor will often write his own JCL. Should client staff be responsible for this function, the auditor should carefully scrutinise the JCL, ensuring in particular that the correct version of the program and data file are used. The auditor will need to ensure that the program was not subject to unauthorised operator intervention during the run. In the case of mainframes this can often be carried out by reviewing the extract of the console log produced as part of the output of his program which will list all instances of operator intervention. All instances of intervention should be reviewed to ensure they are acceptable, for example, fulfilling a request to mount a tape. The auditor may wish to attend the run to monitor operator intervention. In the case of micro- and minicomputers the auditor will often run his program interactively from a terminal and he is thus in a position to monitor the run. If the auditor cannot satisfy himself in any other way that the program will be run without unauthorised intervention, he should consider copying the data file and running the program at another installation.

Ensuring the correct data file is used

11.55 The auditor can normally ensure that the correct file is used by checking the control totals produced by his programs to the totals produced by the company's program when executed against the same file. He should ensure when checking file totals with the company that the totals have been taken from the correct version of the file, for example, the year end version. In addition the auditor should check the label of the data file used by his program. This check can normally be carried out in the JCL used to run the program. Where it is impossible to ensure by any other means that the correct file is being used, the auditor should consider attending the run at which the file is created and obtaining a copy for subsequent use.

Use of the auditor's computer

11.56 Where the auditor is using his own computer or a computer bureau, procedures relating to unauthorised amendments to the program and operator intervention can in practice be reduced. However it is still necessary to operate those procedures designed to prevent accidental error. Furthermore, additional procedures are likely to be required to protect confidentiality of client data.

Audit programme

11.57 The audit programme should contain a list of the objectives to be achieved, the information that will be produced and the work to be carried out on the print-outs. It is also necessary to prepare written instructions for the administrative procedures to be followed in running the software in future years. These will include the obtaining of the relevant files, the input of the parameters, the action to be taken on halts and the obtaining of the print-outs.

Completion report

11.58 After the program has been used for the first time, a formal completion report should be prepared. The report should contain a summary of the results obtained by the program, any points of general interest arising from running the program and a comparison between the actual and the budgeted costs.

Storage

11.59 Suitable storage arrangements will be required to hold the program, parameters and JCL until the next time they are used. It would not normally be appropriate for this material to be left in the client's program library.

Work plan

11.60 The work in paragraphs 11.46 to 11.59 should be carried out in accordance with a work plan which is similar to an audit programme and is signed off and filed with the program documentation. An example of a work plan is set out in Figure 77 (overleaf).

Second and subsequent years

11.61 Once the program has been written, it will often be possible to run it in the second and subsequent years without change. However, amendments may be required if there have been any changes in the relevant computer system, master file layouts, JCL or operator instructions. The auditor may also need to amend constants, such as dates and amounts, which will usually involve changes to parameters. Where changes are required to the program, audit staff who have been fully trained in the use of the program will probably be required, but otherwise it may be possible to use, in the second and subsequent years, staff who have been trained to run the program but not to prepare it.

Summary

11.62 The form of program most commonly used by the aúditor is the file interrogation package. These can be general purpose programs which can carry out similar tasks on a variety of files at different installations or packages tailored for a particular application. Although developed to cope with similar problems, the computer audit packages are all different to a greater or lesser extent.

11.63 The more important facilities, based on practical experience, that should be available in a computer audit package have been indicated including the ability to access different machine types and data files, the tasks to be undertaken and the format in which the resulting information will be provided.

11.64 It is advisable to establish formal procedures for the use of computer programs. This will help ensure that programs are used only where the costs can be justified, that the right objectives are included, and that the costs are properly controlled. Examples are given of suitable procedures to be followed, and documentation to be prepared.

WORK PLAN

Client... Application..	*Initials*	*Date*
1 Where a bureau is used, ensure that there is a formal letter setting out arrangements with the bureau. 2 Client notified in writing of: (a) intention to write/run audit software; (b) requirement for copies of file(s) to be made; (c) other requirements, e.g. terminal to be made available. 3 Written confirmation of file layout and meaning of relevant fields obtained from client. 4 Specification and budget prepared and approved. 5 Program(s) written and tested. 6 Following documents updated/prepared: (a) record of program logic (e.g. annotated program listing, flowcharts) and file layout/ explanation of data fields; (b) run diagrams; (c) run instructions; (d) explanation of parameters; (e) explanation of print-outs; (f) evidence of testing. 7 Software run and file total agreed to client total. 8 Secure copy of program(s), JCL and parameters retained. 9 Completion memorandum prepared. 10 Points of technical interest arising during the work brought to the attention of the technical manager.		
Manager Review 11 Working papers and permanent file reviewed. 12 Completion memorandom issued. 13 All important matters reported to audit manager.		

FIG. 77. A file interrogation program work plan (para. 11.60)

11: Appendix A

Examples of the Use of Questionnaires

The Package

1 In the package concerned, the user completes the questionnaires which are input to the computer using a terminal and read by an ASSEMBLER program. The questionnaires are interpreted and analysed by the program and a COBOL program is generated.

The Questionnaires

2 Two types of questionnaire have to be completed:

- *Environment specifications* – to describe the computer, peripheral equipment, and input and output files used.
- *Processing specifications* – to describe the comparisons, selections, calculations and accumulations to be carried out.

The Examples

3 Three completed examples of the questionnaires are included on the following pages. The purpose of each questionnaire is as follows:

- *Input file specifications* (AG11/12) – to specify the input files being used. In the example shown two input files are defined. The layout of each file is described on another questionnaire.
- *Selection criteria* (AG30) – to specify the items to be selected by the program. In the example shown the program will select items where all of the following conditions are satisfied:

  (a) Record type not equal to 0 or 9.

  (b) Stock number not equal to 100, 200 or 300.

  (c) Stock class between 1 and 9.

  (d) Indicator equal to 1.

- *Selection criteria – pre-selection calculations* (AG40) – to specify the calculations to be carried out on the items selected by the AG30 and how the result is to be treated. In the example shown, the stock items selected by the AG30 are valued and the resultant field will be printed out on the report under the heading "Inventory Value". A total of all items selected will be produced.

INPUT FILE SPECIFICATIONS

PRIMARY *(REQUIRED)* SECONDARY *(OPTIONAL)*

A G 1 1			A G 1 2	
1	4		1	4

***DEVICE TYPE**

R – Card reader (2540) D – Disk 2314 F – Disk 3330
S – Card reader (2501) E – Disk 2311 G – Disk 3340
(T) – Tape

D		T	
5		5	

RECORD LENGTH

Fixed length records – length of logical record
All other records – length of largest logical record

3 5		3 5	
6	9	6	9

BLOCK SIZE

Fixed length records – length of physical block
All other records – length of largest physical block

1 7 5 ∅		1 7 5 ∅	
10	13	10	13

FILE LABELS

(S) – Standard labels U – Unlabeled N – Non-standard labels

S		N	
14		14	

FORMAT

(F) – Fixed length records V – Variable length records U – Undefined record length
S – Spanned records

F		F	
15		15	

DUPLICATES ALLOWED?
(Applies only to a file matching application)

Y – Duplicates exist (N) – Duplicates do not exist

Y		Y	
16		16	

Remainder of file specifications applies only to disk files.
ACCESS – SECONDARY FILE ONLY
(Primary file is always accessed sequentially)

(S) – Sequential R – Random

S			
17		17	

ORGANIZATION

(S) – Sequential D – Direct I – Indexed Sequential

I			
18		18	

RECORD KEY (Indexed Sequential Only)
Enter input data name

S T O C K N U M			
19	28	19	28

NOMINAL OR ACTUAL KEY (Random Access Only)
Enter primary input data name or result data name of field containing
the access key

29	38		

*For non IBM codes see Appendix. O Indicates default, if omitted.

SELECTION CRITERIA

A G 3 Ø (1–4) Job # 3 (5)

PRE-SELECTIONS FOR CALCULATIONS

TEST # (6–7)	IF: DATA NAME (8–17)	IS: Relationship (18–19)	CONSTANT (20)	DATA NAME, VALUE, OR STRING OF VALUES: LOWER LIMIT (21–35) / UPPER LIMIT (36–50)	Conjunction A O (51)	ACTION IF CONDITION IS: TRUE Code (52)	TRUE # (53–54)	FALSE Code (55)	FALSE # (56–57)
Ø1	RECTYP	EQ	S	Ø,9		E		T	Ø2
Ø2	STOCKNUM	EQ	S	1ØØ,2ØØ,3ØØ		E		T	Ø3
Ø3	STKCLASS	NE	S	1,2,3,4,5,6,7,8,9		E		T	Ø4
Ø4	INDICATOR	EQ	X	1		C	Ø1	E	

Test # – Assign a number 01–99 to each test comprised of single or single or multiple statements.

Data Name – Input file data name being tested.

Relationship – EQ – Equal to; NE – Not Equal to; LT – Less than; LE – Less than or equal to; GT – Greater than; GE – Greater than or equal to; BT – Between range limits

Constant – Enter "X" if value is a constant. Enter "S" if value is constant string.

Value – Alpha or numeric constant, string of constants separated by commas (EQ or NE only), or lower and upper limits (BT).

Conjunction – Links condition test in an and/or relation (A=and, O=or). If blank, end of test is assumed.

Actions – Enter actions for true or false result of condition test. If omitted:
True action code: perform all calculations.
False action code: go to next pre-selection test. If last test, exclude record.

Code	Meaning
T	Go to pre-selection test number
C	Perform calculation number
E	Exclude this record

SELECTION CRITERIA

PRE-SELECTION CALCULATIONS

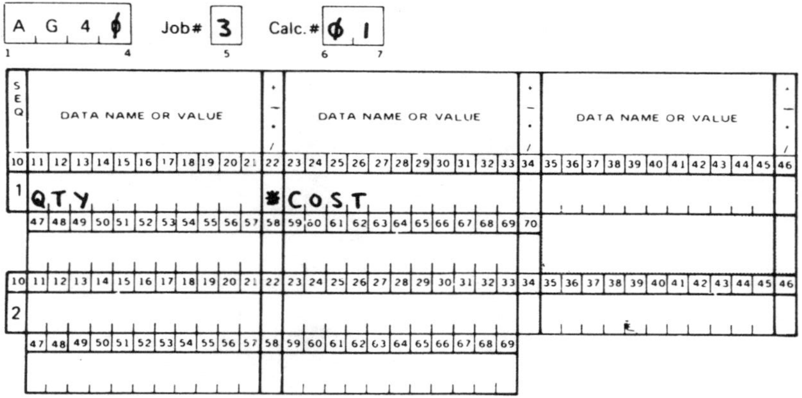

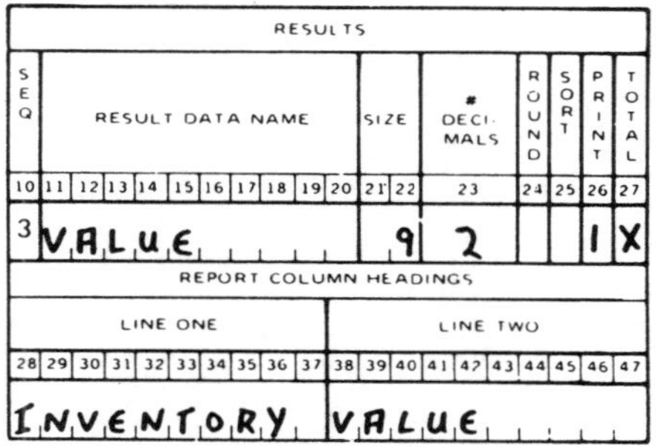

CALCULATIONS

Enter the calculation in algebraic format. Operations enclosed in parentheses ( ) will be performed first. The calculation statement consists of data names and/or numeric values (i.e., "2.5") and operations (+ add, – subtract, * multiply, / divide). A single calculation may contain up to 9 operations on up to 10 data names or numeric constants.

Calc. # – A unique two digit number identifying each calculation.

RESULTS

Result Data Name – Name assigned to the result of calculation.

Size – Size of result field in number of digits.

 # Decimals – Number of decimal positions in the result.

Round – Enter "X" if result should be rounded. If blank, result will be truncated.

Sort – If the result of the calculation is not to be used for sequencing the output report, this parameter should be blank. Indicate sort sequence priority using digits, 1, 2, 3, . . . 9 from major to minor. DO NOT use a priority number previously assigned to an input field for this job. For a descending sort, enter "D". If this is the least significant control field and level totals are not desired, enter "Z".

Print – If the result of the calculation is not printed, no entry is required. If the result is to be printed enter the relative horizontal position using digits 1, 2, . . . 9. Result fields will appear to the right of any printed input fields.

Total – If the result is to be totalled, enter "X" for level totals. If the result column is to be averaged, enter "A".

Column Headings – If the calculation result is to be printed, enter the headings to appear on the report above the result column.

11: Appendix B

Example of a Print-out

Contents of the Print-out

1 Extracts from a typical print-out produced by an AUDITPAK II program are reproduced overleaf. The print-out relates to the selection of items from a stock file. The print-out consists of individual items selected and totals of items.

Description of Job

2 Page 1 of the print-out consists of a description of the objectives to be achieved.

Individual Items Selected

3 Page 2 of the print-out shows the individual items printed. Items have been sorted so that all items printed for the same reason are grouped together. It has been possible to sort the individual items further, by printing items in descending value of transaction.

Totals of Items

4 Page 3 of the print-out shows the totals accumulated by the program. The totals are:

- the total value of transactions;
- an analysis of the total value printed-out according to the category of each transaction;
- the number of records read by the program.

Appropriate descriptions are given to each total.

REPORT NO. AUDITPAK-1
REPORT DATE 13/03/–

COOPERS & LYBRAND – AUDITPAK II
SAMPLE PRINTOUT
SELECTED TRANSACTIONS

PAGE NO. 0
PERIOD ENDED 30/06/–

```
***************************************************
*                                                 *
*    JOB 1 - OBJECTIVES                           *
*    ==================                           *
*                                                 *
*    TO VERIFY THAT THE FILE TOTAL IS MADE UP     *
*    OF INDIVIDUAL STOCK ITEMS.                   *
*                                                 *
*   THIS IS ACHIEVED BY CALCULATING THE COST OF   *
*  EACH STOCK ITEM ( UNIT COST TIMES QUANTITY     *
*  ON HAND ) AND ACCUMULATING IT FOR ALL ITEMS,   *
*  PRIOR TO PRINTING IT IN THE END OF JOB         *
*  STATISTICS.                                    *
*                                                 *
*   INDIVIDUAL ITEMS ARE SELECTED FOR PRINTING    *
*  ACCORDING TO THE EVALUATED COST OF THE ITEM;   *
*  THE CRITERIA USED IS AS FOLLOWS:-              *
*                                                 *
*   (A)  PRINT ALL ITEMS OVER £ 150,000 GIVING    *
*        A DESCRIPTION OF <HIGH VALUE>            *
*   (B)  PRINT ALL ITEMS BELOW £ - 200 GIVING     *
*        A DESCRIPTION OF <LOW VALUE>             *
*   (C)  PRINT A SAMPLE OF 1 IN 4 OF REMAINING    *
*        ITEMS GIVING A DESCRIPTION OF <SAMPLE>   *
*                                                 *
*  TOTALS FOR ITEMS PRINTED OUT ARE ALSO GIVEN    *
* IN THE END OF JOB STATISTICS                    *
*                                                 *
***************************************************
```

REPORT NO. AUDITPAK-1 | COOPERS & LYBRAND - AUDITPAK II | PAGE NO. 1
REPORT DATE 18/03/– | SAMPLE PRINTOUT | PERIOD ENDED 30/06/–
SELECTED TRANSACTIONS

STOCK REFERENCE	COST PER UNIT	SELL PRICE PER UNIT	MARGIN %	QUANTITY ON HAND	EVALUATED COST	ID DESCRIPTION
30103	16	21	31.20	23,463	375,408	HIGH VALUE ITEM
30010	217	250	15.20	1,702	369,334	HIGH VALUE ITEM
30274	6	5	16.70-	58,279	349,674	HIGH VALUE ITEM
30681	16	25	56.20	19,812	316,992	HIGH VALUE ITEM
30060	10	12	20.00	26,781	267,810	HIGH VALUE ITEM
30243	10	12	20.00	25,411	254,110	HIGH VALUE ITEM
30175	8	9	12.50	20,783	166,264	HIGH VALUE ITEM
					2,099,592	
30398	102	115	12.70	2-	204-	LOW VALUE ITEM
					204-	
30609	27	35	29.60	2,056	55,512	SAMPLED ITEM
30869	40	48	20.00	1,153	46,120	SAMPLED ITEM
11226	6	8	33.30	5,113	30,678	SAMPLED ITEM
30768	18	20	11.10	1,247	22,446	SAMPLED ITEM
10222	5	7	40.00	3,861	19,305	SAMPLED ITEM
30501	21	22	4.70	918	19,278	SAMPLED ITEM
10176	10	15	50.00	1,716	17,160	SAMPLED ITEM
21311	365	425	16.40	32	11,680	SAMPLED ITEM
30343	86	95	10.40	119	10,234	SAMPLED ITEM
20264	2,500	2,750	10.00	1	2,500	SAMPLED ITEM
30674	2	5	150.00	1,200	2,400	SAMPLED ITEM
					237,313	
					[illegible]	

REPORT NO. AUDITPAK-Z
REPORT DATE 18/03/-

END OF JOB STATISTICS
JOB NO. 1

PAGE NO. 1
PERIOD ENDED 30/06/-

STATISTIC TYPE	SELECTED ITEM COUNT	SELECTED ITEM PERCENT	SELECTED VALUE AMOUNT	SELECTED VALUE PERCENT	POPULATION ITEM COUNT	POPULATION VALUE AMOUNT
DATA NAME - VALUE		DESCRIPTION - HIGH VALUE STOCK ITEMS				
ITEM ID - HI		DESCRIPTION - HIGH VALUE ITEM				
POSITIVE	7		2,099,592			
NEGATIVE	0		0			
ZERO	0					
NET TOTAL	7		2,099,592			
DATA NAME - VALUE		DESCRIPTION - LOW VALUE STOCK ITEMS				
ITEM ID - LO		DESCRIPTION - LOW VALUE ITEM				
POSITIVE	0		0			
NEGATIVE	1		204-			
ZERO	0					
NET TOTAL	1		204-			
DATA NAME - VALUE		DESCRIPTION - STOCK ITEMS NOT INCLUDE ABOVE				
ITEM ID - RE		DESCRIPTION - SAMPLED ITEM				
POSITIVE	11		237,313			
NEGATIVE	0		0			
ZERO	0					
NET TOTAL	11		237,313			
DATA NAME - VALUE		DESCRIPTION - TOTAL VALUE OF STOCK				
POSITIVE	18	0.2	2,336,905	27.4	7,446	8,513,613
NEGATIVE	1	25.0	204-	53.1	4	384-
ZERO	0	0.0			0	
NET TOTAL	19	0.3	2,336,701	27.4	7,450	8,513,229

FILE STATISTICS

FILE	RECORDS
PRIMARY	9,238

3017-I NORMAL END OF JOB

12

Microcomputers in the Audit Practice

Introduction

12.01 In this chapter the ways in which microcomputers can be of use to the auditor will be considered. This chapter is not concerned with how to audit microcomputer-based accounting systems, since this is covered in Chapter 13 "Small Computer Systems", nor with non-audit uses of microcomputers, for example for tax computations or maintaining accounting records for clients. The auditor seeking to make use of a microcomputer will generally find it most efficient to begin by automating audit administration. The most obvious example is the automation of audit budgets and actual costs. Such administrative uses are dealt with in the first section of the chapter. Word-processing and electronic mail, although fundamental aspects of office automation which can be usefully taken advantage of within the audit process, are not within the scope of this book.

12.02 It is also possible to extend the uses of microcomputer software to tasks that are a more integral part of the audit process. For instance, audit working papers may be produced using software. Such uses are dealt with in the second section of the chapter. It is not necessary to consider microcomputer hardware until the software needs have been specified, since the availability of suitable software packages will often determine the selection of the machine. Software can be purchased, adapted or developed from scratch. Adapting or developing custom-made software demands sound control procedures and these are discussed. The final sections of this chapter then deal with a practical methodology for installing microcomputers within an audit practice and ensuring that they are being used in a cost-effective manner.

Microcomputer Software for Audit Administration

12.03 In this section the following administrative uses of microcomputers are considered:

- Audit budgets and actual costs.
- Contacts and other databases.
- Statistics.

Software for audit budgets and actual costs

12.04 Audit assignments typically require a detailed budget expressed in units of time and analysed by grade of staff and by task. Totals and sub-totals then need to be multiplied by the charge-out rates for each grade of staff so that the budget costs can be evaluated and a fee can be set. Actual costs will be accumulated from timesheets, again analysed at least by grade of staff, and ideally also by task, for example, testing controls and substantive testing. Such two-dimensional arrays of numerical data are exactly suited to the type of software known as a **spreadsheet package**.

12.05 Spreadsheet packages normally allow some degree of protection for the embedded formulae and a limited amount of programming (known as macro routines, for example), making it possible for simple systems to be prepared and data files to be maintained. Taking audit budgets as an example, a spreadsheet system could be designed:

(a) to handle any number of files of budget and of actual data, for as many years as required;

(b) to produce standard reports comparing any pair of files, for example, actual costs for this year compared to actual costs on the same client for last year;

(c) to produce summarised reports or variance reports;

(d) to accumulate and evaluate the timesheet data for each period and then to add it to the accumulating file of current year actual costs.

12.06 Other forms of budget and actual analysis are possible, designed to suit different circumstances. For instance, it will often be useful to design a simple general purpose budgeting model to handle smaller audit assignments or to deal separately with the constituent tasks in an audit, such as implementing file interrogation programs or carrying out a review of IT controls within the data processing department. Another approach might be to move away from the detail and to concentrate instead on the total time, time cost, expenses and related fees for a group of audit assignments, to monitor overall performance and margins.

12.07 Setting up any computation using a spreadsheet package is unlikely to take any less time than carrying out the computation by hand. In fact, if it takes less time then the job is probably not being done sufficiently thoroughly. Where savings arise is when the computation needs to be repeated, after adjustments or for a new set of input figures. This makes spreadsheet software very well suited for audit budget systems.

12.08 There are practical problems and some pitfalls to be avoided in using spreadsheets. These points are taken up later in this chapter in the section on software development.

Contacts and other databases

12.09 Having dealt with automating budgets, the next most common use of microcomputers by the auditor is automating various lists of names and addresses. At the simplest this will be nothing more than a mailing list, varying up through degrees of complexity to a full contacts or client database. While the potential time savings and ease of accessing data are attractive, in practice such data handling systems can often turn out to be a disappointing waste of time if they are not planned very carefully in advance. The data to be handled is text, not numbers, and therefore tends to be voluminous. It usually needs to be coded rigorously in order to:

(a) save storage space;

(b) reduce data input time; and

(c) make subsequent interrogation of the data as efficient and unambiguous as possible.

12.10 **Coding** is used here to mean the rendering of data used frequently into a shortened and unique form. For example, if a database of names and addresses is to be set up and the user wants to be able to sort and analyse the data by region, then a suitable code list might be:

Code	*Region*
1	South-East
2	South-West
3	Midlands
4	North-East
5	North-West
6	East Anglia
7	Wales
8	Scotland

Codes like this can save a lot of input typing time and file storage, helping to make the system work faster.

12.11 There are many mailing list packages that may be suitable for a simple names and addresses database, and some spreadsheet packages also offer an integral database form of processing, but any increase in the complexity of the system demands a similar increase in the complexity of the software package to be used. For example, if one client can have several different contact names and several different addresses, then there could be several names at each address. This gives a three-tiered data structure as illustrated in Figure 78.

12.12 It follows that the software package to be used must be capable of handling such a complex data file structure in a way that will provide whatever degree of flexibility is needed, for example, the maximum permitted number of addresses for each client or names at each address must be sufficient. The package must also allow whatever types of interrogation will be needed, for example:

- Can it produce a report of all Chief Accountants, showing both address and client details?

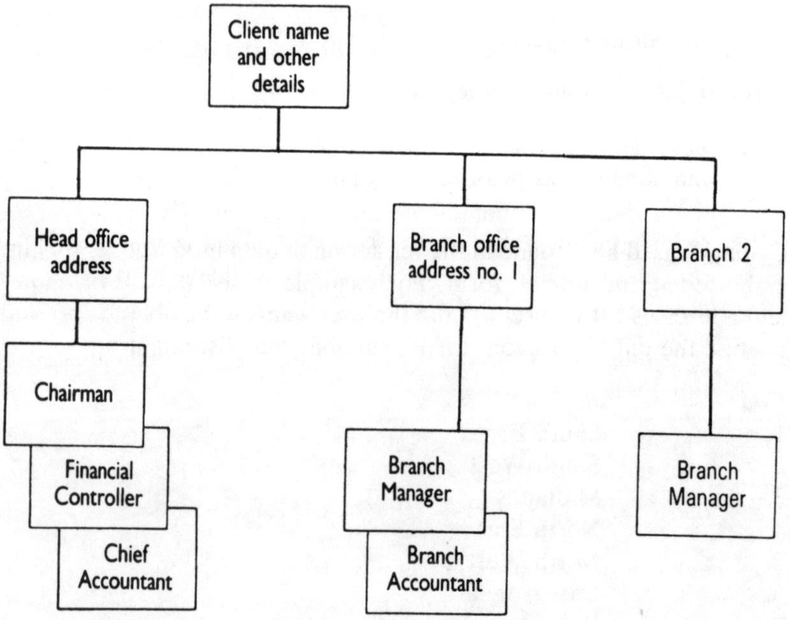

FIG. 78. Client contacts data structure (para. 12.11)

- Can it give an exception report of all clients with an office in Cheshire, without double-counting those with more than one office in Cheshire?

12.13 Data management packages can prove to be rather slow in operation, particularly where the data file structure is a complex one with many separate data files and the links between them having to be managed by the programs. The system may begin to work more slowly as more data is stored and as the data volumes begin to build up. Finally, good data input and validation routines will be needed, in order to make it as easy as possible for the user to input new data and amend existing data. Many purchased packages offer little assistance with data input and validation, aspects of the system that are of crucial importance to the establishment of a reliable up-to-date database.

12.14 Consequently, when planning a data handling system likely to be more complex than a list of names with one related address or equivalent, the auditor will be well advised to follow these steps:

(a) plan the required data to be input and reports to be output carefully, in detail and in advance;

(b) consider the likely data file structure to see how complex it will need to be;

(c) decide how many data items will need to be coded, as explained above, and will need to be validated by the data input routines;

(d) compute the likely data file sizes, with a sensible margin for expansion;

(e) then review the packages available on the market, bearing in mind that any input data validation or custom made reports (with good headings and a range of totals, for instance) will probably have to be written specially, adding to the costs of development;

(f) remember to budget for the likely true cost of initial data collection and capture;

(g) look for evidence from the supplier that the final system will not turn out to be unacceptably slow in live operation once the data files begin to build up in size.

12.15 Another form of database can be built up from the auditor's own diary of jobs that need to be done on each client assignment and the dates on which they fall due. Figure 79 illustrates a specimen report from one such system designed for a microcomputer and written using a

Ref. : ASM001
Time : 12:46:57
User : BROWN

Page : 1
Date : 02/07/9X

Client : ABC Company plc
Period End : 30/06/9X

Audit Timetable

Audit Step	Due Date	Completed Date	W/P Ref.	User Id
Understand the business/industry	31/05/9X	31/05/9X	A10	BROWN
Internal audit checklist	04/06/9X		o/s	
Perform preliminary analytical review	10/06/9X	12/06/9X	G2	BROWN
Review accounting policies	10/06/9X	13/06/9X	G4	BROWN
Account bals, instlns and applictns	20/06/9X	22/06/9X	A22	SMITH
Determine materiality	25/06/9X	01/07/9X	A30	JONES
Preliminary visits to branch locations	28/06/9X		o/s	
Meeting with Finance Director	03/07/9X	02/07/9X	B4	SMITH
Review of budgeting procedures	03/07/9X	02/07/9X	D20	BROWN
Brief audit team	04/07/9X		o/s	

*** END OF REPORT ***

FIG. 79. Specimen report (para. 12.15)

purchased database package. In addition to reports on an individual audit, the system allows exception reports to be produced for groups of clients. Such reports could be used to monitor progress on the audits of a holding company and its subsidiaries or on all of the jobs controlled by a particular audit partner or manager. Reports can also be produced by date to assist in planning work, for example, all tasks scheduled to be completed in the month ahead.

Statistics

12.16 Audit administration systems based on budgets, timesheets, client facts and figures, and audit planning have been discussed. Perhaps the most complex administration system that the auditor would be tempted to set up on a microcomputer would be one designed to produce statistics to help monitor and control aspects of his own business, for example:

- Personal data, recording staff qualifications, work experience, courses attended, and so on, to help with managing staff.
- Billing information, showing dates due and dates paid, to help with cash flow management.
- Client information, for example, data processing installation and application details, to help analyse the extent of likely future computer-assisted audit techniques needed on current audit clients.
- Information on businesses in an area, extracted from a public database, to help promote practice development.

Such systems are likely to exhibit all the problems discussed in the previous section and therefore should be approached with caution and careful planning. In the smaller office or practice where requirements may be simpler and volumes of data smaller, database and statistics systems may be easier to implement and keep up to date than in a larger office. This does not remove the requirement for careful planning in such cases. Where such systems are carefully planned and implemented, they are likely to prove invaluable.

Microcomputer Software in the Audit Process

12.17 The next step after dealing with audit administration will normally be to look for ways of using a microcomputer to play a useful labour-saving part in the audit process. In this section the following uses of microcomputer software in the audit process are discussed:

- Producing audit working papers.
- Audit test decision support systems.

- Expert systems.
- Data file interrogation for audit purposes.

12.18 Microcomputer software can provide a sound basis for automating the audit. The small to medium sized practice may find that audit automation software on a microcomputer can continue to fulfil its needs in the longer term, while medium to large practices may prefer to use microcomputer-based software as a pilot for integrated systems designed for larger machines or for use on a network.

Producing audit working papers

12.19 The working paper is an integral part of the audit. Most lead schedules and their supporting analyses vary very little from year to year. They will normally hold prior year figures as well as current year, and the percentage fluctuation will usually be computed. A word-processing or a spreadsheet package can be used to automate standard audit working papers. Efficiencies can be gained by preparing standard layouts or *templates* in the word-processing or spreadsheet package and issuing them to auditors in a *read only* form. The auditor can then copy over the required standard layout and amend it to suit the assignment, saving the amended version with a suitable *filename* so that this working paper will form part of the current audit file for the assignment, usually in both printed and computer form. For this procedure to be successful in bringing about savings in time and improvements in the standardisation of work done it is necessary for the auditors to be familiar with the word-processing or spreadsheet package and to have a reasonable level of microcomputer literacy.

12.20 Some "trial balance processing" packages for auditors are available. These packages capture the client's trial balance on the microcomputer, together with a suitable description of the way in which the trial balance items should be processed to produce the client's financial accounts, and then are used by the auditor to produce:

(a) lead schedules;

(b) supporting analyses;

(c) financial statements;

(d) adjustments;

(e) scoresheet entries;

(f) reports and ratios designed for analytical review work.

12.21 Such software may offer little cost saving in the year of implementation, as is typical of automation projects, but efficiencies and improvements in audit working practices in subsequent years can be worthwhile. Appendix A shows sample reports from an audit working paper system based on the client's trial balance.

12.22 Useful extensions to such a system can be the production of:

(a) corporation tax computations;

(b) statements of cash flow or source and application of funds;

(c) final accounts, including notes, the directors' report and even the auditor's report.

Software capable of doing all this is necessarily complex. It must be sufficiently flexible to handle a wide variety of charts of accounts without being cumbersome or slow in operation.

Audit test decision support systems

12.23 In addition to using software to produce working papers upon which to record the audit work that was done, it is also possible to use microcomputer software to assist in tasks that require the exercise of audit judgement. There are many instances where computations need to be made to help the auditor reach a decision on an audit test, and it often happens that those computations need to be made many times using different values for the most significant variables. In these cases a microcomputer can be programmed to carry out the computation in such a way that the important variables can be changed easily and the results produced as many times as may be needed to show how sensitive they are to fluctuations in the underlying assumptions. Some examples are:

(a) producing funds flow and profit forecasts;

(b) estimating future margins on long term contract work in progress;

(c) selecting possible audit sample sizes, or levels of test, using statistical or judgemental methods;

(d) making projections based on past claims experience in insurance;

(e) calculating lease balances.

12.24 A spreadsheet package could be used as the means of setting up these and many other such models. Care must be taken in the design, security and maintenance of the software since, by definition, it is to be used many times, probably by many different auditors, and some of the results it produces are likely to be relied upon for audit purposes. The best general rule to follow is to keep it as simple as possible. Good user guidance notes are essential to reduce time for the user and, more importantly, to avoid errors arising from a misunderstanding of how the software works. User guidance documentation is discussed in paragraph 12.36.

Analytical review software

12.25 Analytical review software is a particular type of audit test decision support system. Analytical review is the examination of financial information to discover any trends or particular fluctuations that cannot be readily explained by the auditor's knowledge of the business, so that further information and explanation is required. The basic financial data can be reviewed as it stands or in the form of ratios, a method that compensates to some degree for overall changes in volume. In either case, it is always important to have corresponding information for as many periods as possible. Similar information on other businesses operating in the same field will also be useful. Here, again, the microcomputer can be used to store, rearrange and report whatever growing volume of data the auditor may consider worthy of analytical review. The microcomputer can help manipulate the data, for example, making room on the analysis when new lines of business arise or deleting from the earlier periods any segments of the business that are no longer pursued. The computation of ratios and presentation of the results in the form of a graph are tasks that can usually be done with ease on most microcomputers and printers, provided the appropriate software is obtained.

Expert systems

12.26 The auditor must make many selections, decisions and judgements in the course of reaching the audit opinion. There is no doubt that microcomputer software can be used to support the auditor's decision-making, but whether it can ever go so far as to make decisions for the auditor is a different matter. Software capable of exercising judgement is generally known as an **expert system**. Such systems were referred to briefly in paragraphs 3.19 to 3.20 and it is not our purpose here to go into this complex matter in any depth. Suffice it to say that an expert system attempts to codify the knowledge and experience of one or more expert persons, in a way that incorporates the lack of precision in human opinions. Some expert systems have been developed to support aspects of audit judgement, although developers often find their systems either require more processing power than is available in the typical audit microcomputer or are too restricted to satisfy the auditors' needs. Examples of successful expert systems in auditing include the tailoring of programmes of substantive test, and the review of investment decisions. Interpretation of statutory and other regulations is an area where expert systems support has been fruitful. But expert systems remain a specialist area. They can be expensive to set up and to maintain.

File interrogation for audit purposes

12.27 File interrogation software is dealt with in detail in Chapter 11 "The Use of File Interrogation Software". Data file interrogation software on a microcomputer will be relevant in cases where the client's data file can be accessed using the audit microcomputer as a terminal or where the client's data file can be transferred to the audit microcomputer and interrogated there. Given these conditions, it is quite practical to run powerful audit interrogations on a microcomputer.

12.28 Technical assistance will generally be needed to transfer data files to a microcomputer and to reformat the file into a form that can be read by whatever interrogation software package is to be used on the microcomputer. Some proprietary packages are available to help with this process and with the subsequent interrogation routines. This technique is dealt with briefly in Chapter 11. Care must be taken to ensure that the correct file is being examined and that the interrogation is wholly under the auditor's independent control.

Hardware Selection

12.29 **Hardware** covers the microcomputer processing unit, screen, disk or diskette drives, keyboard, cables and printer. In some cases the screen, disk drives and main processing unit are combined. The processing unit usually contains a powerpack, a fan, and a variable number of circuit boards. Microchips, either providing memory or computational power, are plugged into these circuit boards. Unlike mainframe or minicomputers, microcomputers are made and supplied on the assumption that the user will probably often need to open up the main processing unit, perhaps to install more memory or a circuit board relating to some other new peripheral piece of equipment. A novice wishing to buy a microcomputer must either take advice or invest what can amount to a lot of time in studying the market and deciphering unfamiliar technical terms. There are many problems arising from incompatibility between different types of machine, for example, a microcomputer designed for five and a quarter inch diskettes cannot read data on a three and a half inch diskette even if it was produced on a machine made by the same manufacturer. There can be many unexpected extra expenses.

12.30 The best general advice is first to decide what software will be needed, both in the short and in the longer term. Selecting the hardware will generally then be a much easier task. For example, an auditor interested in automating budgets and costs in the first instance, who then intends to progress towards using audit working paper software would probably look for a machine that:

(a) supports a good spreadsheet package for use in audit budget and actual time–cost comparisons;

(b) supports whatever audit working paper software has been selected;

(c) is sufficiently transportable, together with a printer, to be moved to the client's premises for cases where using working paper software on the client's premises is likely to be cost-effective;

(d) can be linked easily to a higher quality printer back in the office, or to the office network, where applicable.

12.31 An auditor interested in complex business modelling, for cash and profits forecasts, with a view to progressing towards building a client contacts database, is going to be less interested in transportability and much more concerned with hard disks for storing large volumes of data, fast back-up devices for security and enough power to produce the required performance speed.

Software Development

12.32 There are few, if any, packages on the market specifically aimed at helping to support the audit process with automation. Proprietary spreadsheet, database or other products generally have to be tailored to suit and occasionally the tailoring will be extensive. In these cases, and whenever programs are written specifically from scratch, it will be wise to follow a systematic approach to what is, in effect, software development. The principles described in Chapter 6 for in-house systems development also apply to microcomputer developments.

12.33 The key elements of successful microcomputer software development are:

- ensuring that the system to be developed will match the users' needs and will fit in properly with their existing working practices, while leaving scope for improving and streamlining those working practices through the use of automation;
- appointing a separate person or persons to deal with development, so that they can operate independently of the users and work as productively as possible, ideally on a full-time basis;
- making sure the developers take direction from the users, or suitable representatives of the users. This could be one person appointed to this task, with the right breadth of expertise, or a team, meeting as needed;
- appointing a project manager who can ensure neither users nor developers are exercising an undue influence, since they will have needs and views likely to be in conflict and needing to be reconciled in such a way as to make the eventual product a success;
- designing the system carefully and agreeing the design widely before programming begins;
- proper documentation and very thorough user testing;
- action from the earliest stage possible to devise, agree and document the procedures by which the users will be expected to operate the system. This often reveals practical problems so the earlier it can be done the greater the chance of finding and eliminating problems before the final system goes out for live use.

These procedures may seem too much for what is often perceived as minor development work, but experience shows clearly that the cost of issuing software that people do not like or cannot use, for whatever reason, can be very expensive in more than the cost of the lost time and frustration. Users expect new software to work perfectly and when it does not they tend to lose interest in using a microcomputer altogether, which means the loss of much more than the software development time.

User representatives

12.34 It is vital to secure active participation from the people destined to use and rely on the proposed software system. If users perceive that they will have every opportunity to understand what is going on and to express their views, and will be given enough time to do the job properly, then the resulting system will be much more likely to meet their needs and suit their working practices.

The minimum size of the team

12.35 Microcomputer developments tend to be too small to need a team of programmers and analysts. It may be sufficient to use only one person to tailor the package, design the "macros" or write the programs. The minimum number of people participating in a microcomputer development should be three as follows:

- The user representative.
- The analyst/programmer.
- The manager/director who runs the project and is able to reconcile any conflicts between the user and analyst/programmer promptly and effectively.

User guidance documentation

12.36 The operating documentation, or user guide, provides the prospective users of the software with all the information they will need to use the software under controlled conditions and to ensure that it performs properly. It should be written in language the user will understand and should contain the following:

(a) A statement of what the system is for, and the benefits it can deliver when used to its full potential.

(b) How to understand and to prepare the data to be input to the system.

(c) How to put the data into the system, how to check that it is correct, and how to obtain results, whether on the screen or in a printed report.

(d) Processing instructions, showing key menus or main screens in the system.

(e) How to respond to every warning message or rejection message that may appear on the screen.

(f) Advice on diskette handling, where appropriate, and a reminder to take back-up copies of data.

The user guide should be as simple and succinct as possible. It should be capable of being used as a ready reference manual.

Technical documentation

12.37 The technical documentation provides a permanent record of what the software does, how it does it and what steps were taken to ensure that it was properly tested before it was released. It will be invaluable when changes are needed. The minimum documentation will generally include:

- *System narrative.* A concise narrative explanation of the purpose of the system. The objective is to describe what the system and programs will do, in a manner that is clear and unambiguous. The system narrative should also include any hardware or other software required to execute the system.
- *System overview flowchart.* A diagram showing the data files, the programs and their relationships.
- *Input and output.* A detailed description of each input element. This should include the origin of each element, how the element is entered into the system, what the system does with this information and what evidence is provided for the user to ensure that the input was processed. Similarly, there must be a detailed description of the output provided by the system.

12.38 Program documentation must be kept for each program module in a software application. The minimum program documentation should include:

- *Program code.* Full program listing in the appropriate program language or as a series of commands (for spreadsheet systems).
- *Program narrative.* Concise accompanying explanatory information, such as decision tables, charts and record layouts, to the extent required to explain both the purpose and the operation of the program.
- *Calculations.* An explanation of all calculations or formulae used should be provided. This explanation should also include any totalling or balancing procedures for reconciling results. Control totals must be present and, where possible, should include value totals as well as totals of the number of records processed.
- *Data file layouts.* File layouts and data element definition forms for each file in the system. Microcomputer systems often have several data files.

Microcomputers in the Audit – Practical Considerations

12.39 Introducing microcomputers to a professional practice means dealing with many practical points, as follows:

- Acquisition procedures.

- Ownership and custody of the machine.
- Maintenance.
- In-house support.
- Security.
- Confidentiality.

Acquisition procedures

12.40 There are many sources of advice, handbooks and magazines providing general guidance on the acquisition of microcomputers, and this topic is not included within the scope of this book. It is assumed that the professional practice has already purchased microcomputers or other computer equipment and is interested in acquiring microcomputers for use by auditors. Key considerations will be:

- **Consistency.** The new machine(s) should be compatible with other equipment in use in the practice, with each other, and possibly compatible with equipment commonly in use at clients in case the exchange of information on diskette can bring efficiency savings. Care is needed in exchanging diskettes, as explained later in this chapter under *Security*.
- **Portability.** Auditors work on site at clients' premises. They will normally benefit from access to portable machines with suitable portable printers, backed up by desk top machines with higher quality printers back in their own offices.
- **Ease of use.** Ease of use depends largely on the software, and is a critical success factor when use is likely to be relatively infrequent, a common condition for audit use of microcomputers. Before investing in new hardware and software for audit support it is necessary to consider the planned software *user interface* with a view to deciding whether it will be as intuitive as possible, so that the infrequent user suffers the least possible re-learning overhead.

Ownership and custody of the machine

12.41 It must be decided whether the microcomputers are to be assigned permanently to one individual or to be shared in some way among the members of one or more teams. A key factor in this decision is whether the prime purpose for the microcomputers is to improve efficiency for auditors as individuals or for an audit team as a whole. Single ownership is probably more expensive but solves many of the ongoing problems of care of the machine, security and maintenance. Ownership on a shared or pool basis can lead to staff deciding not to use machines since they are not confident of being able to get access to one when needed, and to machines being neglected or lost. Workable day-to-day procedures must be devised to ensure a system of sharing will work well in practice. The most typical use of a business microcomputer is on a personal basis, but auditing is one of the relatively few instances where a case can be made for sharing, provided the inherent disadvantages of sharing are acknowledged and dealt with.

Maintenance

12.42 Although they can be surprisingly robust and long-lived, most microcomputers will break down from time to time. Swift efficient arrangements with a dealer or other agent capable of carrying out repairs are essential, for sustaining the productivity advantage of using the microcomputer in the practice. Many repair agents effect a quick response by means of replacing the damaged machine. If using this type of service then it is necessary to be aware of the confidentiality risk associated with the removal and redeployment of the damaged machine. The repair contract should include the thorough removal of data from the hard disk of any machine taken away on this basis.

In-house support

12.43 The size of the practice and of the investment in microcomputer hardware and software will dictate whether in-house support services are cost effective. Two distinct types of support will be needed in practice:

- Technical support, concerned with the continued and proper operation of the hardware and of proprietary software packages. This support should be provided by staff with the necessary specialist technical expertise. Professional staff are generally best used on their mainstream professional work and should normally not be deployed as microcomputer support technicians. If resources do not permit employing a technician full-time then some external or part-time arrangements should be considered, possibly as part of the maintenance arrangements.
- Advice on how best to use the software systems for audit-related purposes. This form of support can be provided by members of the professional staff, and this can often be done successfully on a part-time basis.

Security

12.44 Reasonable steps must be taken to secure the investment in hardware and software. As noted above, microcomputers owned by individuals tend to be looked after rather better than microcomputers shared among members of one or more teams. If sharing is unavoidable then special attention needs to be paid to the associated arrangements for physical custody, and for protection against accidental damage or loss. For example, portable machines should be booked in and out and someone should be made responsible for seeing that the booking system is observed and works well in practice. New users need to be made aware of the risk of loss if they fail to back up their work regularly or if their library and labelling procedures for diskettes are inadequate over time.

12.45 Viruses constitute a particular risk for microcomputer users. A machine which has suffered attack by a virus program is unusable until the virus has been cleared, and diskettes used on that machine can spread the virus to other machines unless they too are cleared. The subject of viruses is dealt with in Chapter 15. Key points for the microcomputer user to consider are:

- **Protection.** Microcomputer viruses are normally spread on diskettes. All users should be instructed never to accept a diskette from any outside source, including clients, until it has been checked and declared clear of viruses. A separate microcomputer, perhaps an old machine, should be kept apart for this purpose, with virus checking software installed on it.

- **Coping with a virus attack.** All users should be instructed on how to proceed should they suspect a virus attack has taken place. This will normally mean switching off the suspect machine, gathering up all diskettes likely to have been used on it and putting them aside in quarantine until they have been checked. It is also necessary to find out as a matter of urgency whether any of the suspect diskettes have been used on other microcomputers, thus possibly spreading the virus within the organisation. Specialist software can then be used to check and clear the damaged machines.

Confidentiality

12.46 It is important to ensure that confidential data is kept under appropriately secure control, and can only be acquired or used by authorised personnel. Normal audit standards for confidentiality of clients' data should be applied. The same standards should also be applied to software. Diskettes containing programs or data should only be available to authorised staff and all diskettes should be cleared away and locked up out of normal working hours. The requirements of the Data

Protection Act apply to personal data processed on microcomputers and are dealt with in Chapter 16 "Computer Security".

Summary

12.47 This chapter considered how microcomputers can be useful in an audit practice, first by automating administrative tasks and second by automating aspects of the audit work, particularly the audit working papers.

12.48 The selection of computer hardware should generally follow the selection of software, and where the auditor writes his own software for microcomputers, controls are needed over the development process. Successful acquisition and use of microcomputers within an audit practice requires attention to practical aspects of the care and use of the systems.

12: Appendix A

Example of an Audit Working Paper System for Microcomputers

Introduction

1 In this appendix a microcomputer working paper system called Pre-audit is described and specimen reports are shown. Pre-audit is an interactive menu-driven system written in COBOL. The "Print/Display Reports" menu, illustrated below, gives an outline of the main features of the system.

Input of Trial Balance

2 Pre-audit is based on the client's trial balance, which must be typed into the microcomputer or read in automatically. Automatic input may be by direct connection to the client's nominal ledger system or by extraction of data and conversion to the appropriate format on a diskette suitable for input to the microcomputer.

C&L | PRE-AUDIT

MEGA LIMITED

Print/Display Reports

Input Forms
Definition of Financial Structure
Account Balance Information
Journal Entries
Lead Schedules
Common Size Analysis
Ratio Analysis
Statement of Cash Flows
Worksheets for Consolidation
Financial Statements

3 It is not necessary to wait until the final trial balance is available before input. A preliminary trial balance can be captured and then kept in step with the client's records by processing the same or equivalent journal vouchers using Pre-audit.

Working with the Trial Balance

4 The trial balance is input and amended, after having first set up the "financial statement structure". The first specimen report in this appendix is a page of a full trial balance print-out.

Lead Schedules

5 This option has its own detailed sub-menu (not illustrated) which includes, among other things, the ability to print a wide range of summary or "lead" schedules covering particular areas of the accounts, for example, debtors and prepayments. The second specimen report is a typical standard lead schedule, showing the full accounts structure with detailed descriptions for cash and bank balances. In this example cash has been defined as "financial line" 70, which is made up of detailed trial balance accounts. Note from this example that Pre-audit conforms to good practice in producing audit working papers, and in particular includes:

(a) full descriptive headings for each report, including period end and report date;

(b) comparative figures for last year and the fluctuation from last year calculated as a percentage.

6 Specialised lead schedules can also be produced (not illustrated) to deal with the extra information which may be required, for example, for fixed assets.

Ratios

7 Pre-audit can also be used to calculate ratios. The third specimen report shows one possible summary ratio report.

Journal Entries and Potential Adjustments

8 Journal entries may be entered and adjusted in the trial balance. Scoresheet entries are items which the auditor has discovered that may require to be adjusted but which have not necessarily been accepted by the client and so cannot be entered as journals. The final specimen report in this appendix shows how Pre-audit can record the current scoresheet entries while still holding the scoresheet entries in suspense.

* FS040S-3 * PRE-AUDIT PAGE 1
REPORT DATE 26/07/XX MEGA LIMITED PERIOD ENDED 30/12/XX
(JOURNAL ENTRIES INCL) * * * TRIAL BALANCE * * *

ACCOUNT NUMBER	USER REF.	FIN. NO.	ACCOUNT DESCRIPTION	CURRENT PERIOD	PRIOR PERIOD	DIFFERENCE	FLUCT.
0000000160		010	LAND AND BUILDINGS COST.......	152,294.12	145,675.06	6,619.06	4.54
0000000165		020	BUILDINGS DEPN................	41,769.00-	35,952.00-	5,817.00-	16.18
0000000170		013	PLANT & MACHINERY COST........	424,388.00	352,804.00	71,584.00	20.29
0000000175		023	PLANT & MACHINERY DEP'N.......	209,494.00-	172,875.00-	36,619.00-	21.18
0000000180		014	FIXTURES COST.................	75,085.00	77,045.00	1,960.00-	2.54-
0000000185		024	FIXTURES DEP'N................	47,238.00-	39,921.00-	7,317.00-	18.33
0000001110		104	STERLING BK A\C...............	0.00	178,742.65-	178,742.65	100.00-
0000001117		070	BK DEP A\C....................	4,800.00	0.00	4,800.00	100.00
0000001120		070	DOLLAR BK A/C.................	1,327.62	3,146.08	1,818.46-	57.80-
0000001150		070	PETTY CASH....................	200.00	320.00	120.00-	37.50-
0000001160		070	DLR CASH BOOK EXCH PROV'N.....	0.00	1,673.73	1,673.73-	100.00-
0000001401		050	SALES LEDGER..................	0.00-	1,009,198.02	1,009,198.02-	100.00-
0000001421		055	EMPLOYEE DEBTORS..............	0.00	945.00	945.00-	100.00-
0000001488		050	PROVISION FOR BAD DEBTS.......	0.00	76,400.00-	76,400.00	100.00-
0000001490		050	EXPORT SALES LEDGER EX PRVN...	0.00	7,598.09	7,598.09-	100.00-
0000001502		040	CLUBS RAW MATERIALS...........	0.00	28,968.00	28,968.00-	100.00-
0000001503		040	CARTS RAW MATERIALS...........	103,768.00	95,068.00	8,700.00	9.15
0000001523		042	CAR WORK IN PROGRESS..........	33,593.00	31,691.00	1,902.00	6.00
0000001531		044	BALLS FINISHED GOODS..........	331,581.00	276,825.00	54,756.00	19.78
0000001532		044	CLUBS FINISHED GOODS..........	221,188.00	290,911.00	69,723.00-	23.97-
0000001533		044	CARTS FINISHED GOODS..........	85,510.00	50,868.00	34,642.00	68.10
0000001535		044	OTHER FINISHED GOODS..........	118,214.00	61,766.00	56,448.00	91.39
0000001541		044	F.GDS OBSOLETE STOCK PROVISION	43,579.00-	62,814.00-	19,235.00	30.62-
0000001542		040	R.M. PROVISION OBSOLETE STOCK	5,322.00-	10,400.00-	5,078.00	48.83-
0000001543		042	W.I.P.PROVISION OBSOLETE STOCK	431.00-	1,145.00-	714.00	62.36-
0000001571		044	RETURNABLE PALLETS............	250.00	250.00	0.00	0.00
0000001581		044	BALLS GOODS IN TRANSIT........	186,064.58	110,097.04	75,967.54	69.00
0000001582		044	CLUBS GOODS IN TRANSIT........	40,850.20	58,987.40	18,137.20-	30.75-
0000001585		044	OTHER GOODS IN TRANSIT........	2,831.80	18,369.42	15,537.62-	84.58-
0000001601		059	PREPAID INSURANCE.............	0.00	1,605.59	1,605.59-	100.00-
0000001625		059	PREPAID OTHER.................	0.00	13,331.71	13,331.71-	100.00-
0000002201		010	LAND..........................	15,209.10	15,209.10	0.00	0.00
0000002927		005	GOODWILL......................	193,681.33	193,681.33	0.00	0.00
0000002928		005	AMORTIZATION OF GOODWILL......	45,999.30-	41,157.30-	4,842.00-	11.76
0000003201		106	ACCOUNTS PAYABLE TRADE........	271,217.16-	174,346.57-	96,870.59-	55.56
0000003212		110	CREDITORS A.C.USERS SALES.....	724,444.96-	254,863.74-	469,581.22-	184.25
0000003213		110	CREDITORS A.C.USERS SALES CO..	24,967.00	965.80	24,001.20	999.99
0000003218		110	INTER CO EXCH PROVISION.......	9,008.22-	4,201.69-	4,806.53-	114.40
0000003304		114	STAT SICK PAY.................	405.60	724.50	318.90-	44.02-
0000003305		114	EMPLOYEES WITH G. PAYE/NHI....	23,727.75-	21,452.61-	2,275.14-	10.61
0000003306		114	EMPLOYEES WITHOLDING TSBS.....	125.00-	25.00-	100.00-	400.00
0000003401		114	ACCRUED WAGES CONTROL.........	33,175.34-	27,797.81-	5,377.53-	19.35

FS050R-4 PRE-AUDIT PAGE 1
REPORT DATE 26/07/XX MEGA LIMITED PERIOD ENDED 30/12/XX
NO. 12 ****** Cash and Bank (inc overdrafts) ******

ACCT. NO.	ACCOUNT DESCRIPTION	CURRENT PERIOD	PRIOR PERIOD	FLUCT. %
FINANCIAL LINE: 070 Cash at bank & in hand				
0000001117	BK DEP A\C...............	4,800.00	0.00	100.00
0000001120	DOLLAR BK A/C............	1,327.62	3,146.08	57.80-
0000001150	PETTY CASH...............	200.00	320.00	37.50-
0000001160	DLR CASH BOOK EXCH PROV'N	0.00	1,673.73	100.00-
TOTAL FINANCIAL LINE 070		6,327.62	5,139.81	23.11
TOTAL Cash and Bank (inc overdrafts)		6,327.62	5,139.81	23.11

FS071R-3 PRE-AUDIT PAGE 1
REPORT DATE 26/07/XX MEGA LIMITED PERIOD ENDED 30/12/XX
* * * SUMMARY RATIO REPORT * * *

RATIO NO.	RATIO DESCRIPTION	4 YEARS BACK	3 YEARS BACK	2 YEARS BACK	PRIOR	CURRENT
01	CURRENT	0.00	0.00	0.00	1.65	0.56
02	QUICK	0.00	0.00	0.00	0.83	0.00
03	SALES TO RECEIVABLES	0.00	0.00	0.00	5.84	0.00
04	DAYS RECEIVABLES	0.00	0.00	0.00	62.49	0.00
05	COST OF SALES TO PAYABLES	0.00	0.00	0.00	9.96	5.45
06	INVENTORY TURNOVER	0.00	0.00	0.00	4.83	4.97
07	DAYS INVENTORY	0.00	0.00	0.00	75.55	73.43
08	WORKING CAPITAL TURNOVER	0.00	0.00	0.00	7.39	8.33-
09	EBIT TO INTEREST	0.00	0.00	0.00	11.45	999.99
10	CASH FLOW TO CUR. DEBT	0.00	0.00	0.00	0.00	0.00
11	FIXED ASSETS TO WORTH	0.00	0.00	0.00	0.49	0.89-
12	DEBT TO WORTH	0.00	0.00	0.00	1.23	3.48-
13	INCOME TO WORTH	0.00	0.00	0.00	46.18	191.25-
14	INCOME TO TOTAL ASSETS	0.00	0.00	0.00	19.43	70.08
15	SALES TO FIXED ASSETS	0.00	0.00	0.00	11.29	13.71
16	SALES TO TOTAL ASSETS	0.00	0.00	0.00	2.32	4.45
17	DEPRECIATION TO SALES	0.00	0.00	0.00	0.00	0.00
18	LEASE EXP. TO SALES	0.00	0.00	0.00	0.00	0.00
19	OFFICERS COMP. TO SALES	0.00	0.00	0.00	0.00	0.00
20	FINISHED GOODS TURNOVER	0.00	0.00	0.00	5.70	5.66
21	EQUITY TO TOTAL ASSETS	0.00	0.00	0.00	0.48	1.04
22	RETURN ON COMMON STOCK	0.00	0.00	0.00	0.69	1.61
23	SALES TO EQUITY	0.00	0.00	0.00	4.80	4.30
24	RETURN ON ASSETS	0.00	0.00	0.00	0.21	0.70
25	LIABILITIES TO TOTAL ASSETS	0.00	0.00	0.00	0.52	1.27

REPORT NO. FS100R-2 PRE-AUDIT PAGE 1
REPORT DATE 26/07/XX MEGA LIMITED PERIOD ENDED 30/12/XX
* * * SCORESHEET ENTRY LISTING * * *

S.E. NO.	TRANS NO.	FIN. NO.	FINANCIAL LINE DESCRIPTION	SUBGRP NO.	GROUP	AMOUNT
01			STOCK PROVISION	POSSIBLE OMISSIONS		
	01	044	Finished goods	15	A	50,000.00-
	02	210	Cost of sales	50	I	50,000.00
			TOTAL SCORESHEET ENTRY NO. 01			0.00
02			OMISSIONS FROM ACCRUALS			
	01	222	Administrative expenses	55	C	15,954.36
	02	118	Accruals & deferred inc	25	L	15,954.36-
			TOTAL SCORESHEET ENTRY NO. 02			0.00

13

Small Computer Systems

Introduction

13.01 In recent years there has been something of a revolution in the accounting world. This has been brought about by the increasing availability of small, cheap computer systems and the use of these by businesses of all sizes for accounting purposes. It is now practicable for any business, from multinational down to family shop, to own and run a computerised accounting system. The cost/performance ratio of computers has fallen consistently and this trend shows no sign of halting. Today's microcomputers, purchased over the counter in high street stores, are as powerful as the mainframe computers of a few years ago.

13.02 The subject of how best to audit small business computer systems has received much attention, not least because there are perceived to be very significant difficulties in applying an audit approach other than substantive testing. This chapter will discuss the characteristics of small computer systems and the controls over them, covering user controls, programmed procedures and IT controls. It will then show how the audit approach outlined in this book can be applied effectively to small computer systems, including a discussion of the use of audit software.

General Characteristics of Small Computer Systems

13.03 It is helpful to give a general description of the characteristics of small computer systems. The term "small computer system" is difficult to define. Traditionally computers have been divided into three categories – "mainframe", "mini" and "micro" computers – and it has been possible to define the differences between them in terms of cost, size and computing power. However the dividing line between microcomputers and minicomputers has largely disappeared with the availability of large, multi-user microcomputers or networks of smaller microcomputers with the capabilities of traditional minicomputers. Even the distinction between mini and mainframe computers has become less clear with the advent of "super minis" which bridge the gaps in power and cost between the two categories.

13.04 However there remains a useful distinction between the large, traditional computer system and those systems which, in accordance with common usage, we will term "small business computers". The first category approximately corresponds to mainframe and large minicomputers whilst the second is roughly equivalent to the smaller minicomputers and microcomputers. A more useful distinction between the two can be drawn in terms of the size and type of the organisation using the system and the manner of its use, since these are likely to determine the nature of the controls over the system.

13.05 Small business computer systems can also be characterised as follows:

- They will typically be found situated in a normal office environment, rather than in a separate data processing department.
- They will frequently be operated and controlled by user departments rather than by specialist computer operators, although occasionally a minimal team of one or two specialist operators will be employed.
- The application programs in use will normally be purchased as packages rather than written in-house since there will be few, if any, in-house programmers. The people responsible for selecting and implementing the system may have no computer expertise or experience.
- They will generally be on-line or real-time systems controlled almost entirely from menus displayed on terminals.
- The various ledgers or other records maintained by the systems are likely to be "integrated". That is, transactions will be input only once and automatically posted to all the appropriate ledgers, rather than having to be input separately to different ledgers. For example, sales invoices will automatically be posted to the debtors, stock and general ledgers.
- The volumes of data processed by the systems will generally, though not invariably, be lower than in a larger organisation.

13.06 This chapter is intended to cover small computer systems used by relatively small organisations, usually running on mini- or microcomputers and exhibiting the characteristics described above. It is not intended to cover systems running on small computers which form part of distributed processing systems in large organisations, for example where sales order processing and stock control are processed on a small computer at a branch and accounting transactions transmitted to a central computer for updating to the debtors and general ledgers. Similarly it is not intended to cover small computers used for the automatic collection of data to be transmitted to a larger computer system, for example metering the usage of telephones or collecting accounting data from automated manufacturing assembly lines. The reason for this is that the audit risks, the volumes of transactions and the controls in such systems will be those applicable to the large organisation. Thus those computers can usually be treated as components in a larger computer system.

Controls Over Small Computer Systems

The need for controls

13.07 The effect on a company of implementing a computerised accounting system is considerable. There are significant benefits to be obtained in terms of faster and more efficient customer service, better management information and reduced administrative costs. There can often be considerable improvements in the working lives of the company's staff. Furthermore computers have the potential to improve the controls over the processing of data both because they can carry out control procedures which would be too time-consuming if done manually and because the processes carried out by computer programs will, under normal circumstances, be consistent from one day to the next.

13.08 On the other hand, when a computer system is implemented, the administrative processes and the data needed to run the business tend to become concentrated within it. For example, a sales order processing system may process sales from order entry through invoicing up to their posting to the debtors and stock ledgers automatically, to the extent that it would be very difficult to revert to manual processing if this was ever necessary. The company may thus become completely dependent upon its computer, often without realising this, and any problems regarding the performance of the system, its continued availability or the accuracy and completeness of the business records it maintains are likely to have a serious effect on the company.

13.09 Furthermore in manual systems, particularly in smaller organisations, management often place considerable reliance on the common sense of the people processing transactions and their knowledge of the business in order to detect and correct any apparent errors. The advent of a computer system reduces the amount of manual scrutiny to which transactions are subjected in the course of being processed. Any errors, arising either from incorrect input or from errors in the computer programs, are thus less likely to be detected unless positive action is taken to implement controls for this purpose.

13.10 For example, the production of despatch notes and invoices, and the posting of the debtors, stock and general ledgers may be entirely automatic following the input of a sales order. If the order had been incorrectly priced, either manually when it was input or because the wrong price was recorded in a price file in the system, this would probably not be detected unless a specific control existed to check prices. A suitable control might be a programmed comparison between sales prices and cost prices with a report of abnormal margins. In the corresponding manual system incorrect prices on sales orders might be picked up by a sales invoicing clerk or sales ledger clerk who knew the correct value of the item concerned.

13.11 For these reasons it is more necessary to implement controls over small computer systems than over the equivalent manual systems. These controls are as important to management, in order to ensure that the system continues to be available and to produce reliable results, as they are to the auditor. Unfortunately one of the characteristics of small computer systems is that they are often implemented, operated and controlled by people with little or no training in how to do so. Thus controls which would be taken for granted in specialised data processing departments may be absent.

13.12 This chapter will cover the user controls and programmed procedures needed to control the processing of accounting data, as well as the IT controls which ensure the continued reliability of the computer system itself. One of its principal themes will be that an adequate level of control is practicable, as well as being necessary, in small computer systems. This will be demonstrated by means of individual controls which are practicable in small systems, but it is useful to recognise that it must be true as a general statement since a large number of small businesses are able to run successful small computer systems producing reliable results.

User controls and programmed procedures

13.13 In small, manual accounting systems it is frequently not practicable to institute strong controls over the processing of accounting data because of the high cost of such controls. We have already seen that stronger controls are needed in a computer system since transactions are generally subject to less manual scrutiny as they are processed.

13.14 Fortunately it is also possible to control computer systems more cheaply and efficiently than corresponding manual systems by using the computer to check and correlate information. For example:

- Checking input data such as stock reference codes against a stock file or values against pre-set upper and lower limits (an accuracy control).
- Exception reporting, for example, comparing sales price against standard costs and reporting unusually high or low gross profit margins (a validity or accuracy control).
- Sequence checking or matching of input transactions (completeness controls).
- Periodically reconciling the movements in stock with totals of purchases and sales (an updating and file continuity control).

13.15 Furthermore computer systems often result in better management summaries and analyses being available – indeed the ability to produce better management information is often a major reason for the purchase of a computer system. This results in close examination of results of the business by management, and this can act as a control leading to the detection of any major processing errors. For example, an error in a sales price file might be picked up during an examination of an analysis of gross profit by product. In small organisations top management are generally more closely involved in the detailed, day-to-day transactions and can thus control the accuracy of the accounting records by scrutinising the output from the system.

13.16 It is thus possible for reasonable controls to exist over small business computer systems. These controls will depend heavily on editing, exception reporting, reconciliations and other control procedures within computer programs. There is therefore likely to be considerable reliance on programmed procedures in any efficient audit strategy which involves reliance on controls for small business computers.

13.17 In order to implement controls of this type, it is necessary that the computer programs incorporate the relevant control features such as edit checks and exception reports. Since many such systems are purchased packages rather than programs written in-house, the company will need to assess when selecting a system the suitability of the control features within it.

13.18 Ideally the package chosen should have more than the basic and commonly available facilities to input and check batch totals and to print out a log of all transactions input. Many packages also incorporate password protection systems and limited editing of input data. Some packages also include report generators which allow a limited range of user defined reports to be produced. However, if the controls over the system are to be efficient in operation, it will normally be necessary for the selected package to provide reconciliations between accepted transactions and movements in file totals, and exception reports of transactions requiring authorisation or balances requiring investigation or action.

13.19 Where a package is in use which lacks important control features, it may be possible to substitute manual controls. For example, a manual reconciliation between transaction totals and the movement in a file total can often be prepared easily from totals reported at different points in the system in order to provide an adequate updating and file continuity control. Alternatively it may be possible to add control features to the system. This is usually only practicable where no change is required to existing programs or files, for example the creation of a new program to produce an exception report. This may be done with the aid of a report generator or one of the very high level programming languages discussed in Chapter 6, paragraph 30. Alternatively the supplier of the package may be asked to write a suitable program: the cost of this would not normally be high where no change is required to the existing programs and files.

13.20 Where weaknesses exist in the update or file continuity controls, or in the user controls over a programmed procedure such as producing an invoice, the degree of risk arising must be assessed. Frequently in a small system the risk is considerably lower and thus the weaknesses less important than in a larger computer system. For example, the programs will often be purchased as packages, there may be no utility programs which can amend programs or data files, and the system may have been designed so that there is very little scope for computer operator error in setting up the system and running programs. These areas are considered in the section on IT controls later in this chapter.

Supervision and division of duties

13.21 It is generally recognised that smaller organisations cannot devote as much time to formal supervision as large organisations, neither do they have sufficient staff to permit a high degree of division of duties. However the auditor should not conclude that control is necessarily inadequate in such cases.

13.22 In large organisations senior management are more remote from the day-to-day transactions of the business and the work of the staff processing them. They therefore exercise control by means of supervisory hierarchies and by arranging that staff check each others' work. In smaller organisations, the close contact between management and staff, and the detailed scrutiny of transactions by management, may compensate for less supervision and division of duties.

IT controls in small computer installations

13.23 We have already seen that programmed procedures are likely to be an important part of any small business computer system. It is therefore necessary to consider whether the IT controls in such an installation are sufficient to ensure the continued and proper operation of such procedures. Common sense suggests that they should be, at least from a management, if not necessarily from an audit, point of view, since many small businesses demonstrably and successfully place considerable reliance on their systems.

13.24 Many of the IT controls procedures already discussed in respect of large installations involve considerable work; for example the review and approval of system specifications, or detailed program and system testing. Furthermore in a large installation reliance is placed on extensive disciplines such as supervision of computer operators and the segregation of the system development, operations and user functions. In small business computer installations the same effort cannot be applied to controls and their supervision, and the division of duties between computer operations and users often does not exist because small business computers are typically operated by user departments.

13.25 However the areas of IT controls risk for small computer systems are less than for larger systems for two reasons:

(a) Small systems are normally purchased as packages, and are therefore usually tried and tested.

(b) Small systems are commonly designed to be operated by user departments rather than by specialist computer staff, and hence to minimise the scope for operator error.

These points will be expanded upon in subsequent paragraphs. Frequently their effect is to make it possible to implement some effective IT controls over small computer installations despite the impracticality of many of the formal controls which are found in larger installations.

13.26 In this section the differences between the small and the large computer installation, and the way in which these affect the control requirements and the types of control which are practicable are considered.

Implementation controls, computer operations controls and security controls are discussed separately.

Implementation controls

13.27 Small business computer systems are generally purchased packages. Where packages are modified to meet the requirements of the company, these modifications will normally be carried out by the supplier because of the lack of system development capability within the company. Thus the controls over the in-house development of systems do not apply. Implementation controls in small business computer installations therefore consist of controls over the specification, selection, implementation and subsequent maintenance of packages.

Specification and selection

13.28 The specification and selection of a small computer system is frequently undertaken by user departments since they are the only people available to do this. The problem experienced in larger organisations, of inadequate user involvement in specifying and selecting the system, is therefore not usually present. However, as a result of their lack of computer expertise, the users may not realise the problems and risks involved. It is not uncommon for the auditor to be asked to advise his client on the selection of a system.

13.29 The risks relating to the selection of a small computer package are no less than those relating to the selection of a large package. If anything the smaller business is often more vulnerable since it will usually be less able to absorb the extra administrative costs caused by any system problems. The considerations discussed in Chapter 6 relating to package selection therefore apply equally to smaller systems.

13.30 In most cases, even in small organisations, it will be necessary to produce a statement of requirements listing the features of the required system which are essential or highly desirable to the company. This will necessarily be produced by user departments, who may need guidance on what to include. It is important to include any control-related requirements such as exception reports or reconciliations, since in a small organisation it may be difficult to compensate by manual controls for control facilities not included in the computer programs.

13.31 When selecting a small computer package, it is usually particularly important to assess the quality and reliability of the support available since the company will often have no in-house expertise to call upon if this is deficient. Areas to be considered will include maintenance of the hardware and software, training and documentation. The reputation and financial stability of the suppliers is important since they will often be smaller companies than would be found supplying packages for large computers. It may be an advantage if a turnkey supplier can be found to take responsibility for both the hardware and the software.

Testing

13.32 The testing of a small business computer system is likely to be less detailed than that of a package bought for larger installations. The reason for this is that a larger number of existing users of the package are normally found, and hence a greater degree of reliance can be placed on these users to have detected any errors in the package. It is, however, still important to assess their experience of the package and to carry out some user testing as described in Chapter 6.

Implementation

13.33 The amount of work involved in implementing a computer system is frequently under-estimated, and can pose serious problems in a small organisation. The suppliers of a system will often provide help in implementing it as part of their support service. For example, installing such a system frequently involves setting parameters and selecting options so as to make the system operate in accordance with users' requirements. This requires some knowledge of the system, and is usually done by the suppliers. The suppliers may also provide a data input service to convert the previous manual records into the computer files required by the new system. Most suppliers provide training in the operation of their systems, though the design of clerical procedures is likely to be the responsibility of the purchaser. The availability of such assistance will be assessed when selecting the package since it will contribute to the selection decision.

13.34 It is important to assess the controls exercised by the supplier over the set-up of programs and data files, since these will take the place of the equivalent in-house controls in larger computer installations. It is also desirable to carry out some independent checks on the accuracy of installation and file conversion. For example control totals and spot checks on individual data items could be used to ensure that accounting data had been transferred accurately to the new computer files.

Modifications to packages

13.35 Modifications to packages should generally be kept to the minimum possible, since modifications will increase the risk of system errors and will make it difficult to obtain maintenance support for the package. This is particularly true in respect of small computer systems where in-house maintenance support is generally not available and the cost of external maintenance support is less easily absorbed by the purchaser.

Where modifications are essential it is good practice to restrict these to the addition of new programs, which will not affect the existing programs within the package, for example programs to produce additional reports.

13.36 Where modifications are carried out by the suppliers of a package, the users will need to agree their specifications, cost and delivery timetable in writing with the suppliers. It is commercial prudence to do this before agreeing to buy the package. They will also need to ensure that the suppliers have sufficient technical expertise to carry out the modifications, that adequate warranties are given in respect of the modifications, and that adequate maintenance for the modified package will be available. The users will not normally be involved in the technical aspects of modifying the package, but they should carry out adequate, independent testing to ensure that the modifications have been completed satisfactorily and have not adversely affected other aspects of the package. The need to do this is another reason why modifications should be kept to the minimum in small organisations, since testing of major new programs is likely to be time consuming.

13.37 Where, in rare cases, a small organisation elects to modify a package in-house it will often not be practicable to exercise the development controls which would apply in a large organisation. Considerable responsibility will inevitably be given to the programmers and systems analysts to design, test and document the modifications with little or no supervision. In some cases user departments may be involved in modifying systems. It is fair to say that in many organisations where unskilled users have attempted to learn programming and write or modify programs, the results have been at best amateur and at worst abortive. Consequently the recruitment of staff with suitable experience and expertise will be important. Extensive user testing will be important, since this will often be the only independent control possible over the design of the modifications. The company will normally need to provide internally for the maintenance of the package in future and this will be easier if the modifications are kept to the minimum and do not affect the existing programs in the package.

Computer operations controls

13.38 The main difference between the computer operations controls for small business computer systems and those for large computer systems is that small business computer systems are operated primarily by users rather than by specialist computer operators. This changes the nature of the controls that are possible, so systems need to be designed to minimise the need for operator intervention and to provide automatic checks on or prompts for operator actions wherever possible. However, this does not eliminate the need for controls. For example, it is still important to ensure that the correct files are used, and that back-up copies are taken regularly of all files.

Scheduling and set-up

13.39 Most small business computer systems are now designed to minimise the risks of operator error in the scheduling and set-up of programs, on the assumption that they will be operated largely by users. This is typically achieved in three ways: by the use of menus, by internal checks carried out within the system and by user controls over parameters input by the operators.

13.40 Menus are used to help the user to run the right programs by allowing him to select the programs to be run from a menu, and often by combining into one menu option a number of related programs. For example the operators of a large system might, at the month end, schedule and run several different programs which respectively reorganise the sales database, update all sales ledger transactions to the general ledger, print debtors' statements and reports, create back-up copies of sales ledger files and finally purge all matched transactions. Computer operation controls would be required to ensure that they run the correct programs in the right sequence. Typically in a small business system the user would select an option on the main menu described as "month end procedures", and a master program in the system would automatically call in the appropriate programs in the correct sequence.

13.41 Internal checks are carried out within many systems to ensure that the actions of users are consistent with the current status of the system, a record of which is maintained automatically in a computer file. For example, it would be common for a system to keep a record of the date when the latest back-up file was created, and to ensure that the operators create new back-up copies before closing down the system at the end of the day. Another common control is the prevention of any input in respect of the next accounting period until the month end procedure for the current one has been satisfactorily completed.

13.42 The number of parameters which are required to be input by the operators of a small business computer system is usually small. Such systems are normally designed to maintain their own internal records of parameters such as the date (for example by maintaining a real-time system clock) and accounting period (for example held in a file and increased by one at each period end). Any other necessary parameters such as exchange rates would need to be controlled in the same way as transaction or standing data. Detailed manual checking is often an appropriate technique because such parameters are both infrequent and often highly important.

Use of correct data files

13.43 In small installations, the operators normally have much less direct involvement in the selection and use of data files. Typically the operator loads a disc containing all the data files onto the system at the start of each day, and each program selects the appropriate data files automatically. The scope for operator error is thus limited to the loading of the wrong disc at the start of each day. Control over this is often achieved by software label checking. For example, the system might check the dates stored as part of the file label with the system date when a file is first loaded each day to ensure that it is the one created during the previous working day.

Back-up and recovery procedures

13.44 Control over the integrity of the system following a system failure or abnormal situation is equally necessary in small and large installations. The controls necessary in small installations, as in larger ones, will usually consist of:

- Regular creation of back-up copies of files and programs. In a small installation the programs will often ensure by means of internal checking that back-up copies of files are taken regularly. The need to take back-up copies of programs will depend upon how frequently the programs are amended and whether the suppliers can be relied upon to supply new copies of the programs promptly.
- Clear recovery procedures to be followed in the event of a failure. In a small installation, these will normally be provided as part of the system documentation by the supplier. However additional clerical procedures may need to be devised covering the reinput of transactions where necessary.
- The reporting and subsequent review of operator actions. A well designed system should produce a log showing all failures and the action taken to correct them. It is important, even in a small installation, that this is reviewed by a responsible official since system failures are one of the most common causes of errors in data files.

13.45 Fortunately in a small installation system failures are generally less frequent than in a large installation. The reason for this is that many of the causes of system failures in large installations are absent in the typical small installation. For example, operator errors will be less frequent because of the use of menus and internal checks within the system. Similarly small installations normally use tried and tested packages, and thus program failures will be less frequent.

Security controls

13.46 The greatest problem in the control of small business computer systems is usually the security of programs and data files. It is often difficult to achieve as high a degree of security as would be considered necessary in a larger installation. For example, there is frequently no suitable access control software for small computers.

13.47 As a result of this, security has often been given little emphasis in small installations. Traditionally it has been argued that the user of a small business computer could afford to some extent to ignore security, because management was more closely in touch with the day-to-day transactions processed through it and because the systems themselves were often simple systems which could only be accessed from one department. However this is unlikely to continue to be the case for several reasons:

- First, small computers are becoming more powerful and disc storage capacities are increasing dramatically so that small computers are being used for ever larger and more complex systems where management involvement cannot necessarily be relied upon to detect errors.
- Second, as small business computer systems become more powerful and process more operational information, the users are likely to find that they keep more confidential information on computer files which they need to protect from unauthorised access.
- Third, legislation on data protection gives users of small business computers a duty to protect and control data files containing personal information, such as payroll and personnel files.
- Finally small business computers nowadays are often either multi-user systems or connected together in networks, making access to them from a variety of departments easier and control over security correspondingly more important.

Software access controls

13.48 Historically the access control software available for small computers has been less sophisticated than that for larger computers. One reason for this is that it has been more difficult to implement sophisticated security techniques because of the limitations in the power and memory capacities of small computers. Another is that less attention has so far been given to security systems for small computers.

13.49 These problems can be expected to diminish as the price/performance ratio of small computers continues to fall and as the small computer market matures. Password systems are now incorporated into many of the better application program packages, and where security is important to the users the password facilities will need to be assessed when they are selecting a system. As security features are seen to be beneficial in marketing hardware and software, so it is likely that system designers will pay more attention to them.

13.50 The same considerations regarding the security of passwords and the reporting of unauthorised attempts to gain access apply as in larger systems. Some systems incorporate a facility to restrict programs so that they can only be run from certain physical terminals as well as requiring the input of a password. For example, it may be possible to specify that the payroll program can only be run from the terminal in the payroll department, as well as requiring the payroll supervisor password to be input in order to run it.

Physical security

13.51 Physical security over files and terminals may become important when password facilities are inadequate. For example, sensitive files and programs may be physically removed from the system when not in use and stored in a safe under the control of a senior official of the company.

Utility programs

13.52 Large installations often need utility programs which can amend programs and data files, by-passing the normal application programs and any security controls within them. These are frequently used to maintain the system software, or to create test files and to make emergency alterations to data files following a software failure, often in a new system.

13.53 In small installations there will normally be no need to use such utility programs because the systems in use will be tried and tested packages and thus there should be no need to make emergency corrections to data files or programs. In addition, there is no need to make amendments to programs in-house, since all amendments are provided by the supplier of the programs. Thus it is often practicable to remove from the system any utility programs with the ability to amend directly programs and data files.

The Audit of Small Computer Systems

13.54 The auditor of a small business computer system is faced with several problems arising both from the nature of the system itself and, often more importantly, from the nature of the organisation using it. In general the main problems can be classified as follows:

(a) There are likely to be less formal controls than in a larger organisation, particularly in the areas of supervision and division of duties.

(b) The computer department is generally small or non-existent, and consequently IT controls where they exist are less formalised than in a larger organisation.

(c) It is often relatively more expensive to implement file interrogation software on small computers than on larger ones.

These problems have to be overcome in the face of the tight constraints which are invariably imposed on audit costs in relation to small organisations. They are discussed in turn in the following paragraphs.

User controls and programmed procedures

13.55 In any organisation, the auditor should find that the user controls and programmed procedures are adequate to enable management to ensure the accuracy and reliability of the accounting records. If this is not the case then the audit reaction would be the same in a large or a small organisation; namely to report weaknesses to management and adopt a substantive testing audit strategy. However, in judging the adequacy of controls the auditor must take into account the nature of the organisation.

13.56 As has already been discussed in paragraph 13.15, control in a smaller company may be exercised to a considerable extent by means of direct review by management of the company who are familiar with the detailed transactions of the company, and by direct management contact with all the staff working for them. Thus the absence of formal controls in some areas, and of formal supervision procedures and division of duties, need not necessarily constitute a weakness. The auditor must evaluate and test both the formal and the less formal controls which exist in smaller organisations.

13.57 The auditor can normally evaluate the effectiveness of management review by discussing with management the way in which information is reviewed and the extent to which any errors would be detected. He will need to review for himself the management information to ensure that it is adequate for the purpose.

13.58 Management reviews can be tested in the same way as any other control. Evidence of management review can often be obtained from annotations on the documents reviewed and documentary evidence of action taken as a result. Alternatively, some assurance can be obtained by discussing accounting balances with management and noting the degree to which management appear to be aware of the detailed transactions making them up. The auditor may also decide to reperform the review and subsequent investigation of unusual items, particularly where management do not adequately evidence their review.

13.59 Informal supervision of the type often found in small organisations is less easy to evaluate and test for audit purposes. Some assurance can be obtained by observation and by discussion with management and staff. However, this is usually less conclusive than a test of formal, evidenced supervision in a larger organisation since it is more liable to fluctuate according to the individuals involved. Consequently the auditor may decide to perform more extensive tests on the underlying control procedures to compensate for his inability to place as much reliance on the supervision over them.

13.60 Where the volume of transactions processed by the system is low, the savings in substantive tests to be made from placing reliance on controls will be lower. Thus in some cases the auditor may adopt a substantive testing audit approach even where controls are adequate.

13.61 As has already been discussed, the most efficient controls are those which are automated. Thus in a small organisation, where alternative controls are unlikely to be practical, it will be important to ensure when selecting a system that the relevant programmed procedures are included as requirements in the selection or design of the computer system. It is beneficial for the auditor to review the proposed system specifications before they are finalised to ensure that the necessary control-related programmed procedures are included.

13.62 As set out in paragraphs 2.67 to 2.68 the auditor may gain assurance for audit purposes about the continued and proper operation of programmed procedures by:

(a) reliance on IT controls;

(b) reliance on user controls where these ensure that the programmed procedures operate properly; or

(c) performing direct tests of the programmed procedures.

13.63 These approaches may be combined in different ways and the discussion in paragraphs 2.63 to 2.71 on determining the extent of reliance on controls at the audit strategy stage is relevant here. As noted in these paragraphs it is becoming increasingly rare for user controls to ensure the continued and proper operation of programmed procedures. The auditor is therefore likely to place emphasis on tests of IT controls and possibly on direct tests of programmed procedures where he wishes to perform an extended assessment of controls as part of his audit.

13.64 The techniques for direct tests of programmed procedures are set out in paragraph 2.68 and include manual reperformance, simulation, the use of test data or software and program code analysis. These techniques are discussed in detail in Chapter 9 "Testing Controls and the Response to Weaknesses". With the smaller client the auditor may wish to place reliance on such direct tests, and particularly manual reperformance and simulation, possibly in combination with a degree of reliance on IT controls as discussed in paragraph 13.65 to 13.70 below. It may even be that management themselves use some form of periodic direct testing of programmed procedures in order to gain increased assurance on the operation of such procedures.

IT controls

13.65 Certain basic IT controls are necessary in all organisations in order that the systems function satisfactorily. These controls can usually be achieved even in small computer installations where there is no formal data processing department. Provided these basic controls exist there is no reason why the auditor should not be able to place some degree of reliance on IT controls in small computer installations.

13.66 The nature of small computer systems is likely to reduce the risk of error and the cost of evaluating and testing IT controls. A number of factors are relevant:

(a) Usually the systems are purchased as packages, and have a large number of other users. Where this is so, an initial presumption can be made that they are reliable.

(b) Modifications are not normally undertaken in-house by the user companies, and for commercial reasons the suppliers are likely to test modifications thoroughly before releasing them to all their customers.

(c) The systems are designed to be user-operated, and therefore their operation is made deliberately easy.

(d) All system software will be supplied by the vendor of the machine and the user will make no changes to it.

13.67 These factors reduce the risk of errors in the programs, operational errors or corruption of programs and data files. Thus the auditor may find that it takes less time to evaluate IT controls, and he may decide that he needs a lower level of testing of specific IT controls in a small installation than in a larger one in order to provide assurance against the risk of error in the operation of programmed procedures and the erroneous amendment of data files.

13.68 In addition, it is likely that the IT controls in a small installation are less complex than in a larger one. For example, there will be a review of the experience of other users of a package instead of detailed program testing, system testing and live testing of a new system. The evaluation and testing of those IT controls which are at present in small installations is likely to be simpler, requiring less technical knowledge, and therefore cheaper than in a large one.

13.69 The principal weakness which the auditor may find is that security controls to protect against fraudulent amendment of programs and data files are weak due to the absence of formal supervision and division of duties in respect of those controls which exist. Frequently there will be one person with overall responsibility for operating the machine and this person will have full access to all programs and data files. This should not prevent the auditor relying on IT controls in respect of the risk of error. The risk of material misstatement through fraud may be responded to by other procedures, such as substantive tests including analytical review of results.

13.70 In general the cost of evaluating and testing IT controls in a small installation is likely to be considerably lower than in a large installation. Thus where the auditor wishes to perform an extended assessment of controls he may well find it efficient to place some reliance on IT controls.

File interrogation software

13.71 File interrogation software is dealt with in Chapter 11 "The Use of File Interrogation Software". In auditing large computer systems there are two principal reasons for using file interrogation software as follows:

(a) to improve audit efficiency where the volume of data to be examined is large enough to be difficult to manage manually; or

(b) less frequently to overcome a loss of visible evidence where there is inadequate printed evidence to enable tests to be carried out manually.

13.72 The auditor of a small computer system is likely to find in most cases that the volume of transactions is relatively small. Therefore the case for using computer file interrogation software will not usually be as strong as it is in larger installations. Furthermore, the audit budget for clients using small computer systems may well be low. Since the cost of developing interrogation software does not decrease in proportion to the size of the machine, it can be relatively more expensive to develop software for small machines than for large ones. Nevertheless the auditor will sometimes find that he needs to use interrogation software when he faces a loss of visible evidence or, increasingly, when a small computer system processes a relatively large volume of data and poor controls lead him to adopt a substantive testing audit approach.

Techniques available

13.73 The techniques available to the auditor to enable him to interrogate small business computer files include the following:

- Data file conversion.
- Generalised interrogation facilities built into the client's system.
- The purchase of independent copies of accounting packages which the auditor encounters frequently.
- Standard programs written by the auditor for accounting packages which he encounters frequently.

13.74 There have been substantial improvements in recent years in the availability of generalised interrogation packages which run on microcomputers, and which can be used to read data files converted from a client's system. Such packages commonly include facilities to assist in reformatting data to enable it to be read by the package. Clients may be able to provide files readable on a microcomputer which can then be reformatted, and such packages may also include facilities to enable other types of file such as tape files to be converted and read on the microcomputer. The efficiency of such packages reduces the cost of their use and this assists in overcoming the high relative cost of software for smaller machines. Costs may be further reduced by the fact that the auditor is carrying out the interrogation in a familiar environment using his own microcomputer. In some cases the auditor may use such a package to reformat a data file and then use other software, such as his own application specific package, to interrogate the data on the microcomputer.

13.75 Generalised interrogation facilities are increasingly found as part of small business computer systems. Frequently they take the form of report generators built into individual ledger packages, and their flexibility and power varies greatly. However they are often capable of producing a range of summary and exception reports of use to the auditor. When using such facilities the auditor should consider how much reliance he can place on the interrogation software itself and whether it is susceptible to manipulation by the client's staff. Where the software is a package with a large number of other users, and supplied only in object form, the auditor may be able to place considerable reliance on it.

13.76 Where the auditor has several clients using the same accounting package he may wish to purchase a copy of the package or parts of it himself. This can be particularly useful when the package includes a generalised interrogation facility, since the use of his own, independent copy enables the auditor to place much greater reliance on it. The auditor will need either to ensure that the licensing agreement with the supplier of the package allows him to use it at several different clients' sites, or to obtain his clients' permission to remove copies of their accounting files to his own office.

13.77 Alternatively, where several clients use the same accounting package, the auditor can develop standard programs to use at each client. Whilst the development cost may still be high, the ability to spread it across several clients may make this cost-effective.

13.78 One practical difficulty facing the auditor may be a shortage of computer time available to him in small systems. In a large installation, the computer power used by the auditor is generally too little to affect other users, whereas in a small installation it may represent a significant fraction of the power of the machine. This is particularly true where he uses interrogation facilities which have been designed for occasional use only, and are therefore often relatively inefficient in operation. Furthermore, where there is only a small number of computer terminals, the use of one terminal by the auditor when typing in and running his programs may delay other users. In some very small systems, it may not be possible for other users to access the system while the auditor runs his interrogation programs. This problem does not arise when the auditor converts the client's data files for interrogation on his own machine, and is a further advantage of such an approach.

Training

13.79 The audit of small computer systems poses a particular problem in the training of audit staff. The smaller audit budgets, as compared to those for large systems, may make it inappropriate to involve specialist computer audit staff to a significant extent. Nevertheless it is important for the staff on the audit to be able to apply computer audit techniques such as the use of generalised interrogation facilities, and to be able to identify the extent to which reliance can be placed on programmed procedures.

13.80 Furthermore, this type of client is much more likely to need the auditor's advice on the selection, implementation and control of computer systems, as discussed in paragraphs 13.82 and 13.83. While specialists can be brought in to give detailed advice, the audit staff are the only people in day-to-day contact with the client. It is desirable for them to have some familiarity with the issues in order to know when and how to involve the specialists.

13.81 Thus auditors will need to plan for their audit staff to be sufficiently trained in small computer systems. Such training needs to be a mixture of general familiarisation, training in the use of computer audit techniques and training in the issues raised by small business computer systems.

Services Outside the Audit

13.82 In many cases companies buying small computer systems lack the skills and experience which a larger company can bring to bear. The auditor is likely to find that his advice is sought on a number of issues, including:

(a) The accounting and audit requirements for computer systems.

(b) The controls required to select and implement a system properly.

(c) The programmed procedures which need to be built into a system to enable it to be controlled adequately.

(d) Other regulatory or fiscal requirements such as those relating to VAT records or to the statutory requirements on the protection and control of personal data incorporated in the United Kingdom in the Data Protection Act.

In such cases the auditor's knowledge will enable him to be of considerable assistance to clients. Furthermore the work he carries out for this purpose may also assist him in the audit. By combining the audit work with other services to his client he may be able to achieve efficiency savings.

13.83 The auditor should be aware, however, that the requirements of audit and control are only a small part of his client's overall requirements in selecting a system. For example, the needs of management information must be taken into account in deciding on the requirements for a computer system in addition to the basic accounting records and accounting controls. The auditor may wish to ensure that his is able to give advice in all aspects of selecting, implementing and subsequently managing a computer system for the benefit of clients with no such knowledge within their own organisations.

Summary

13.84 Controls are both necessary and practical in a small business computer system if it is to operate effectively. These are of two types:

(a) User controls and programmed procedures, making use of the power of the computer to minimise the manual overhead of controls.

(b) IT controls to ensure the reliability of the system and the integrity of the accounting records in the event of any system failures.

13.85 The adoption of appropriate procedures for the selection and implementation of a system is crucial, in order to ensure that it will be both suitable and reliable, and that sufficient controls are built into it. It is important that the auditor is involved at this stage to ensure that appropriate controls exist.

13.86 The auditor will frequently be able to place reliance on controls. The degree of assurance he can obtain will generally be lower than in a larger installation because the arrangements for supervision will be less formal and the division of duties will be less. However he will often be able to place some additional reliance on the closer management scrutiny of the accounts as compared to a larger organisation. Where the volume of transactions is low, the savings in substantive tests will be lower, and the auditor may decide to adopt a substantive testing approach on efficiency grounds.

13.87 The auditor will also be able to use computer audit interrogation programs, and there have been significant improvements in the availability of interrogation software for microcomputers in recent years.

13.88 The auditor will find that small businesses need advice on the selection, implementation and control of computer systems. He will need to be able to provide such advice, and this poses staff training problems.

14

Electronic Data Interchange (EDI) and Electronic Funds Transfer (EFT)

Introduction

14.01 Recent years have seen rapid growth in the use of computers to communicate directly between organisations for the processing of business transactions, thus removing the necessity for the exchange of paper documents. Electronic data interchange (EDI) is the computer to computer exchange of business documents in a standard format between two or more trading partners. Electronic funds transfer (EFT) is the initiation, approval and execution of payments and other transfers of funds using a computer network rather than paper. EDI and EFT may be used in conjunction, for example purchase orders and invoices may be communicated between a supplier and a customer by EDI with EFT used by the customer to pay outstanding invoices.

14.02 The use of EDI and EFT has significant implications for users including increased dependence on computer systems and networks, the need to consider the legal and tax implications of electronic trading and the need to ensure that effective controls are implemented including both direct controls over transactions and controls over the operation and security of the system and network. EDI and EFT are relevant to the auditor because they may change the risks to which the organisation is subject, they will necessitate changes in the nature of controls and they are likely to result in the loss of documentary and visible evidence of transactions.

14.03 In the first part of this chapter, the technology used for EDI and EFT is considered together with the risks to which an organisation may be subject when using it. In the second part of the chapter the effect of EDI and EFT on application and IT controls is discussed.

The Technology and Its Uses

EDI

14.04 EDI was first used in the late 1960s by the transport industry to help alleviate delivery delays that resulted from a large volume of paper documentation. Today, most major industries worldwide use EDI including the transport, automotive, manufacturing, pharmaceutical, insurance, financial services and retail industries. EDI involves the sender and receiver using EDI software to process electronic transactions and pass them to existing application systems. Packaged software is available to handle these processes which can run on a mainframe, minicomputer or microcomputer.

14.05 Although early EDI transmissions were made directly from trading partner to trading partner, most users today use a value added network (VAN) to provide a store and forward service for EDI transactions. This is often the most cost-effective method of exchanging documents between multiple trading partners and the use of a value added network for EDI processing is illustrated in Figure 80. Value added networks available within the United Kingdom include 'Tradanet' operated by INS, 'Infotrac' operated by AT&T Istel and the IBM Information Network.

14.06 The majority of EDI transactions, referred to as messages, are formatted using established document standards to allow different systems to communicate with each other. Various countries and industries have developed different standards, although initiatives are

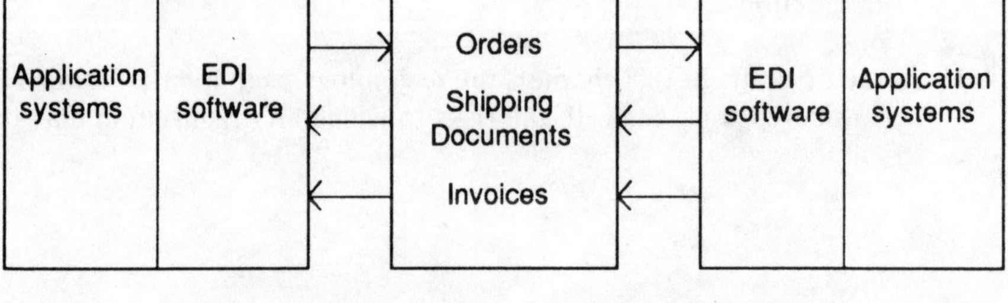

FIG. 80. Use of value added networks (para. 14.05)

underway to bring these together into a common international standard. The major standards in use include the international standard EDIFACT developed under the auspices of the United Nations and ANSI X 12 developed in the USA.

14.07 Support for using EDI is provided by a number of associations and user groups within the UK and Europe, including:

- Trade EDI Systems (TEDIS) – an initiative by the Commission of the European Communities designed to increase the awareness of and co-ordinate EDI developments.
- International Chamber of Commerce (ICC) – this organisation developed the uniform rules of conduct for the interchange of trade data by teletransmission, or UNCID rules, which outline agreed rules of conduct between trading partners.
- Comité Européen de Normalisation (CEN) – a European committee concerned with establishing standards for use across Europe.
- Consultative Committee for International Telegraph and Telephone (CCITT) – this committee is a part of the International Telecommunications Union which advises the public telephone and telegraphy companies (PTTs).
- Simplification of International Trade Procedures Board (SITPRO) – this is a UK government agency set up to provide guidance materials on using EDI and to promote common standards.
- EDI Association (EDIA) – this is a members' funded UK organisation focusing on international trade and transport.

14.08 Examples of the way in which EDI is used in various industries include:

- **Manufacturing** EDI is used to send a variety of transactions including purchase orders, invoices, shipping notes and production schedules. It is used to improve inventory and cash management and, in more advanced situations, to integrate with 'just in time' inventory procedures.
- **Insurance** EDI allows a faster response to customers through the exchange of quotations and proposals and the processing of claims settlements electronically. EDI processing in the UK and Europe is supported by networks such as LIMNET for the London insurance market and RINET for cross-border reinsurance business.
- **International trade and transport** EDI is used to improve transport management through speedier communication of documents with trading partners and customs authorities. The UK initiative, 'Data

Interchange for Shipping' (DISH) and the electronic communication capabilities of HM Customs and Excise are facilitating EDI usage.

14.09 The benefits of using EDI effectively can include:

(a) cost savings on transaction processing by reducing manual preparation, paper and mailing costs;

(b) improved speed of processing and communication with trading partners;

(c) reduced errors and greater accuracy of processing;

(d) improved inventory and cash management; and

(e) enhanced relations with customers and suppliers.

14.10 Benefits will be greater if the majority of similar transactions can be processed using EDI, thus eliminating the need to process many transactions on parallel systems. The willingness of major trading partners to move to EDI is therefore of great importance in achieving the potential benefits.

EFT

14.11 Most major banks in the United Kingdom now offer EFT services by providing computer terminals on their customers' premises to be used for issuing EFT instructions. These services are commonly used for applications such as payment of suppliers. There has also been substantial growth in the use of EFT within the retail industry with payment for goods and services being made using EFT at the point of sale (EFTPOS). In some cases EFT systems can also be used to provide information from banks relating to the movement of funds. For example, when a customer pays an invoice by EFT an electronic remittance advice might be provided by the bank and used to update the sales ledger.

14.12 In the United Kingdom EFT frequently makes use of the bank clearing system. There are four major clearing companies involved in this system as follows:

- Clearing House Automated Payments System (CHAPS) and Town Clearing Company. This organisation deals with same day clearing of high value items. CHAPS provides electronic clearing while Town Clearing deals with cheques in the City of London.

- Bankers' Automated Clearing Services (BACS). BACS handles electronic bulk clearing of direct debits and automated credit transfers.

- Electronic Funds Transfer at Point of Sale (EFTPOS) UK. EFTPOS deals with point of sale transaction clearing.

- Cheque and Credit Clearing Company. This company handles bulk paper clearing, for example cheques.

14.13 These companies process EFT data and cheques and pass information to the Bank of England where daily settlement between the banks is made. The Society for Worldwide Interbank Financial Telecommunication (SWIFT) deals with international fund transfers.

14.14 An organisation wishing to make use of EFT payments or credit facilities has two options, as follows:

(a) It can install a dedicated terminal or extension of its existing computer system which is connected to the system operated by its bank. The organisation then issues instructions from its terminal to its bank.

(b) It can produce information in a format which can be processed directly by one of the clearing companies, for example, a file of payments to be processed by BACS.

The format of payment messages will be determined by the requirements of the bank or clearing company processing the transaction.

14.15 Examples of the way in which EFT is used in various industries include:

- **Manufacturing** EFT is used to make payments to suppliers and employees and also to receive electronic payments from customers, with a resulting improvement in cash management.

- **Retail** EFT allows faster processing of customer payments using a plastic card, thus avoiding the time required for writing cheques or handling cash. This may benefit sales as customers may be lost if there are excessive queues at cash tills. In addition the security of cash is a less significant problem.

- **Local government** EFT is used to make benefit payments, such as housing benefits, to recipients. Substantial savings in the manual preparation and reconciliation of payments can be achieved and, since many payments are recurring, payments can be scheduled for a number of periods ahead resulting in further savings.

- **Insurance** As well as making and receiving payments, EFT is used to deal with investment of funds. It enables funds to be moved rapidly and with accuracy so as to maximise investment potential.

14.16 The benefits of using EFT can include:

(a) improved cash and treasury management by more exact control over funds;

(b) cost savings by reducing cheque preparation and paper and by reduction in bank charges;

(c) reduced errors and greater accuracy of processing;

(d) improved security and control with less cash handling and enhanced confidentiality over sensitive payments such as salaries.

Risks Arising from EDI and EFT

14.17 The use of EDI and EFT changes the environment in which transactions are processed and consequently can change or introduce new risks to which the user of these technologies is subject. These risks are discussed in the following paragraphs. Overall an organisation will become increasingly dependent on its trading partners for the efficient continued operation and control of its business. Specific measures to limit the risks are set out below, but the development of good informal relationships with trading partners is also vital.

Lack of human intervention and written evidence

14.18 When EDI and EFT are used, headed paper, cheques, voice and signature are replaced by streams of electronic signals. There is significantly less human intervention in the processing of transactions and consequently less opportunity for the exercise of judgement and intuition in reviewing written evidence. More of the control processes become automated with an increased reliance on programmed procedures and IT controls over the operation of the computer systems and network.

Legal and taxation implications

14.19 Legal and taxation issues are likely to arise from the use of EDI and EFT and these need to be addressed in establishing relationships with the other parties to the transactions. A legally binding contract should exist between parties using EDI and EFT dealing with, *inter alia*, the following matters:

(a) the definition of what constitutes a transaction;

(b) the form of any acknowledgement of receipt or acceptance of a transaction;

(c) the legal position if a transaction fails to get delivered or acted upon;

(d) the legal position if an unauthorised transaction is submitted;

(e) which country's legal system applies for international transactions.

14.20 Consideration should be given as to whether the system would be able to provide legally admissible evidence if required. It is also important to ensure that, if appropriate, the system is adequate to support invoicing for VAT purposes and customs requirements for international trading. The EDI Association has drawn up a standard interchange agreement which may be used as the basis for an agreement with a trading partner. Suitable legal agreements should also be established with network service providers specifying agreed service levels.

Risk of errors in processing

14.21 The use of EDI and EFT gives rise to additional risks of error in the processing of transactions. These errors may include:

(a) duplication of transactions;

(b) corruption of messages whilst in transit;

(c) misrouting of transactions; and

(d) delay or failure to process transactions.

14.22 Effective controls must be established both as part of the operation of the EDI or EFT software and processing environment, and within the total framework of controls performed by users over the application of which the EDI or EFT processing forms a part. For example, the EDI or EFT software may include acknowledgement of receipt of transactions, sound controls over the development or maintenance of the software will assist in limiting errors and users may exercise controls such as reconciliation of payments totals with bank balances which would identify missing or duplicate items.

Increased risk of fraud

14.23 There may be an increased risk of fraud arising from the use of EDI or EFT either from an unauthorised individual gaining access to processing facilities or from outsiders penetrating the system. This risk is more pronounced in EFT systems, since these are involved in the transfer of funds, and in part arises from the reduced level of human intervention in such systems. There is a particular risk of one-off large frauds being perpetrated using EFT systems with the culprit absconding before the fraud is detected. This possibility is increased due to the fact that funds can be transferred instantly using such systems.

14.24 Effective controls over the authorisation of transactions and over access to processing facilities are necessary to minimise the risk. Controls over access to EFT systems frequently include passwords combined with physical devices such as keys and magnetic tokens such as diskettes. In some cases two or more individuals may be required to input separate passwords in order to authorise processing. The software sending the message may encrypt the message and incorporate data to authenticate the sender of the message. The more general IT controls over physical and software access discussed in Chapter 7 are also of importance.

Breach of confidentiality

14.25 EDI and EFT involve the use of computer networks and require an organisation to link its computer systems to those of its trading partners and banks. This may give rise to an increased risk of a breach of confidentiality whereby confidential information on an EDI or EFT network might be inadvertently or deliberately disclosed. The controls over authorisation of transactions and access to the network referred to in paragraph 14.24 above are again of importance in protecting against such breaches of confidentiality. It is important to agree security standards with trading partners and network service providers to ensure that they are also operating an adequate level of security.

Business dependence on EDI and EFT systems

14.26 The growing use of EDI and EFT has made businesses increasingly dependent on these systems in order to be able to carry on their trading operations. Consequently a loss or disruption of EDI or EFT systems, including the non-availability of VAN services, can cause significant business disruption. For example, a retailer that suffers failure of its EFTPOS system may immediately start to lose business from customers intending to pay by this method. A manufacturer who is unable to place orders to replenish a 'just-in-time' inventory system may face significant disruption to production in a very short timescale.

14.27 To protect against such risks a business should ensure that its EDI and EFT systems are designed so as to be robust and resilient. It will also be necessary to prepare a contingency plan for recovery in the event of a loss of EDI or EFT facilities. Achievement of the first of these objectives may involve the use of fault-tolerant equipment so that failure of one component does not prevent the system from operating. Achievement of the second may require alternative processing capability at a second site to be used if the main EDI or EFT facilities are damaged or destroyed. The subjects of availability of computer processing facilities, software and hardware integrity and contingency planning are considered in more detail in Chapter 16 'Computer Security'.

Application and IT Controls Over EDI and EFT

14.28 Exchanging data electronically using EDI or EFT changes the nature of transaction processing within an organisation, and new or amended manual or automated control techniques will be required at each major stage of processing. The auditor will need to consider the effects of these changes on the application and IT controls, and to take them into account in any work he performs on the controls.

14.29 In the case of EDI the major stages of processing are illustrated in Figure 81 and comprise:

- **The application interface** which passes transactions from the application systems.

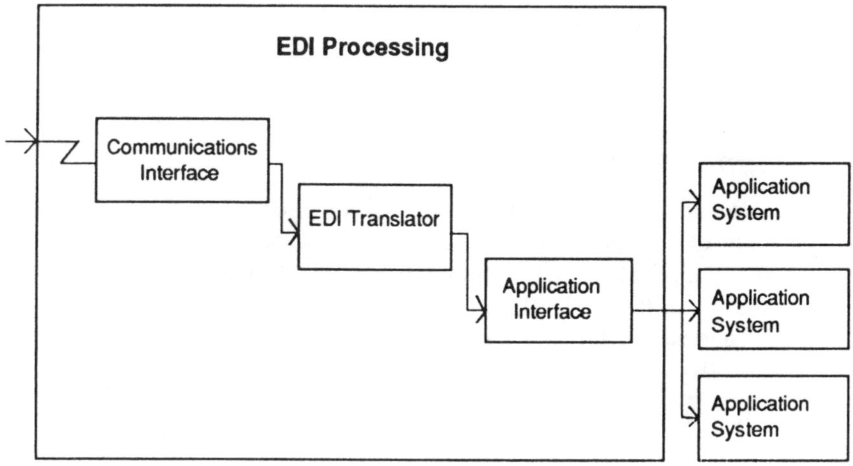

FIG. 81. EDI processing (para. 14.29)

- **The EDI translator** which translates transactions to the standard format used for EDI transmission from the format used by the organisation's applications.
- **The communications interface** which transmits EDI transactions to trading partners or value added networks used for such transmission.

The processing is reversed for incoming transactions.

14.30 There are similar stages in the processing of EFT transactions. There may be an automated interface with the organisation's applications or data may be manually entered to the EFT system, for example using a dedicated terminal supplied by a bank. There will normally be some processing of EFT transactions by the EFT system and this may well include the encryption of data before transmission and the inclusion of control and identification data within the message to enable the recipient to ensure its authenticity. A communications interface may transmit transactions directly to the network of a bank. In some cases a file on magnetic media, such as a tape file of computer payments, may be physically sent to an organisation such as BACS.

14.31 In the following paragraphs the general effect of EDI and EFT processing on application and IT controls is discussed. In practice the impact of EDI and EFT on controls and thus on the audit will vary with the nature of the system. For example, the application controls over a retail outlet using EFTPOS will differ from those over a company paying its wages and salaries using BACS. As regards IT controls, where a dedicated EFT terminal and system is provided by a bank, reliance will be placed on implementation and maintenance controls operated by the bank over the software. Where software has been written in-house to interface with existing applications then controls over the implementation and maintenance of such software will be relevant.

Application controls

14.32 EDI and EFT deal with the processing of transactions as part of the input or output of application systems. Once transactions are passed to the application system they will be subject to the normal application controls relating to the processing, update and continuity of data. As a result, EDI and EFT processing principally affect the control objectives of:

(a) completeness of input;

(b) accuracy of input; and

(c) authorisation of transactions.

Completeness of input

14.33 For incoming transmissions, controls over completeness of input are designed to ensure that all transactions sent are received, processed by the EDI or EFT system and input once and once only to the appropriate application. Control techniques used may include transmitting acknowledgement of transactions received back to the sender, the use of sequence numbers, the use of control or hash totals and the batching of transactions for processing by application systems. Controls over outward transactions are similar.

Accuracy of input

14.34 For incoming transmissions, controls over accuracy of input are designed to ensure that transactions are accurately received, processed by the EDI or EFT system and input to the appropriate application. Control techniques used include checking within the communications software for transmission errors or failures, the use of control, hash or batch totals, and the editing of transactions within the EDI or EFT system or within the application system.

Authorisation of transactions

14.35 It is important that transactions received or sent via EDI or EFT systems are suitably authorised. Authorisation is of particular importance in outward transactions within EFT systems. For incoming EDI transactions controls might include the checking of transmissions against a trading partner masterfile to verify that the trading partner is authorised to send the type of transaction being received. For outward transactions controls may include manual authorisation, for example of physical files transferred on magnetic media, on-line authorisation using passwords as described in paragraphs 5.71 to 5.77, the use of physical keys or magnetic tokens to limit access to authorised individuals, encryption of data and authentication of messages by inclusion of control and identification data within them to enable recipients to ensure that they are from an authorised source. Controls over the security of programs and data are likely to be an important part of controls over authorisation.

IT controls

14.36 Since EDI and EFT are automated processes all aspects of IT controls will be relevant to the control of EDI and EFT. Many of the IT controls already discussed in Chapters 6, 7 and 8 will apply to EDI and EFT systems. Particular features of control for EDI and EFT are set out below for each area of IT controls.

Implementation

14.37 Implementation controls are relevant when a new EDI or EFT system is implemented. Where a system, for example an EFT system, is provided by a third party, such as a bank, the implementation will be more similar to the acquisition of a vendor supplied package than to an in-house systems development. As with other systems it is necessary to ensure that there is adequate user involvement in the development of the new system if the business benefits are to be achieved.

14.38 EDI and EFT involve closer integration with the computer systems of third parties with which an organisation deals, and may also involve the use of separate networks provided by independent service providers. New system developments must be integrated with these third parties. There may well be industry sector user groups for a technology such as EDI and these can be useful sources of expertise and advice. As well as providing information on such things as industry standard message structures, such groups will have a longer term influence on the development of EDI within an industry. Similarly, an established network service provider may well have a network user group. Joining such a group will provide greater opportunities to influence the quality of service and security of the network.

14.39 Since many application controls will be dependent upon the operation of programmed procedures, the initial system specification should include procedures necessary to ensure completeness, accuracy and authorisation of transactions. Clerical user controls to complement the programmed procedures should be designed as part of the implementation process. As with all significant system developments, it is important to ensure that adequate training is given to all personnel who will be involved with the new system, whether as a user or in a more technical role. Appropriate documentation should be prepared of the system and operational and user procedures.

System maintenance

14.40 Controls over system maintenance will be of relevance when EDI or EFT systems are subject to change. Examples of such changes include adding a new EFT transaction, adding a new EDI trading partner, changing message format standards and changing the value added network (VAN) used for communication.

Computer operations

14.41 The existing controls over computer operations will normally be of relevance in controlling EDI and EFT. New procedures will be required to deal with the communications interface, the acknowledgement of transmission and receipt of messages and error correction and re-transmission when messages fail. Also of importance are restart and recovery procedures when the system fails and back-up procedures for programs and data files.

Program and data file security

14.42 Program and data file security controls are of increased importance in EDI and EFT systems because the linkage of the organisation's computer systems with computer systems of trading partners and banks creates new risks of security breaches. In addition EFT systems are used to transfer funds and this activity presents a particular fraud risk. To some extent security will become dependent on the quality of control exercised by network service providers and third parties with which the organisation deals. It is important to agree with these other parties the level of security to be enforced over the system and responsibility therefor. This can be done directly as part of the trading agreement with the other party or through joint agreement in user groups.

14.43 All aspects of program and data file security controls, as discussed in Chapter 7, are of importance in dealing with EDI and EFT. Software and physical access controls are discussed in paragraphs 7.14 to 7.39 and are of particular importance. Techniques such as passwords, physical devices to control access, encryption and authentication of messages may well be used, particularly in EFT systems.

System software

14.44 The existing system software controls will be of relevance to EDI and EFT systems in the same way as for other computer systems. For example, controls over the implementation and maintenance of a security package may well be of importance to an EDI or EFT application in the same way as for other applications. The use of EDI or EFT may involve the use of new communications software and system software controls will need to be effected over this software.

Summary

14.45 EDI and EFT involve the use of computer systems and networks to transmit transactions and funds transfers between independent trading partners, in place of the exchange of paper documents. Such systems often use third party networks for processing transactions and there has been significant progress in the development of standards for formatting and exchanging messages between trading parties. Many banks provide EFT systems and, in the United Kingdom, such systems commonly make use of the bank clearing system in processing transfers of funds.

14.46 There can be significant benefits arising from the use of EDI and EFT including cost savings, increased speed of processing, greater accuracy and improved inventory and cash management. EDI and EFT are used in most major industries worldwide and their usage is growing rapidly.

14.47 The use of EDI or EFT makes an organisation more dependent on its trading partners for the efficient continued operation and control of its business. A clear legal agreement must be established with trading partners to establish the basis of trading, and good informal relationships are also of great importance. EDI and EFT give rise to new or changed risks of error, fraud, breach of confidentiality, infringement of taxation legislation, and disruption to the business through non-availability of the system. The organisation should seek to protect itself against these risks by effective control measures. As regards application and IT controls, the general guidance on these remains applicable, but there are also some specific considerations which should be addressed in relation to EDI and EFT systems.

15

Computer Fraud and Computer Misuse

Introduction

15.01 There has been increasing publicity in recent years about the threats to computer systems from computer fraud, hacking and computer viruses. In the case of computer fraud this has to a large extent resulted from the vastly increased use of computers. Most financial systems are computerised nowadays so that most frauds will involve the use of the computer to some degree. Hacking and viruses are particular threats to computer systems which have become more serious, and which led to the introduction of the Computer Misuse Act in 1990 in the United Kingdom. This chapter considers the nature of the threats arising from computer fraud, hacking and viruses, and summarises the provisions of the Computer Misuse Act.

Computer Fraud

15.02 Before examining the nature of computer fraud, it is helpful to consider the factors which may make computer systems particularly susceptible to fraud. These may be summarised as follows:

- **Speed of processing** Computers can process transactions very quickly, and in some cases instantaneously. A fraudulent transaction such as a funds transfer may be processed very rapidly with the proceeds of the fraud available before the fraud has even been discovered.
- **Wide access to system** In order to maximise their usefulness, wide access is frequently granted to computer systems. This access may be misused for fraudulent purposes.
- **Lack of human intervention** As the functionality of computer systems increases so human intervention and the opportunity to detect fraudulent activity by manual procedures decreases.
- **Large volumes of data** Computer systems often process and store large volumes of data making the detection of a fraudulent item more difficult.

- **Complexity** Computer systems can be very complex and may include powerful facilities for review or amendment of data. Gaps in control procedures may arise as a result of the complexity, and facilities within the system may be misused for fraudulent purposes.
- **Technical personnel** Data processing specialist staff are often needed to develop, maintain and operate computer systems. Such personnel have specialised technical knowledge and may be difficult to supervise, with a resulting risk that their skills may be used to commit fraud.

15.03 Published surveys quote widely differing figures regarding the extent of computer fraud. In part the different estimates result from the difficulty of defining computer fraud since many frauds involve both manual and computer procedures, and in particular the manipulation of data before it is processed by the computer. In some cases the fraud may be very similar to the sort of fraud which might be committed in a manual system, with the computer merely used as the method of processing transactions. In other cases the computer may be used to facilitate a fraud which would otherwise have been difficult to perpetrate. An example of the first might be the processing of an unauthorised purchase invoice for payment by the computer which is similar to the submission of a fraudulently authorised invoice for manual payment in a non-computer system. An example of the second might be the use of a utility program to transfer funds directly between accounts in a bank.

15.04 In general, computer frauds fall into one of the following three categories:

- **Defalcation** whereby computer processing is used to assist in the unauthorised obtaining of assets belonging to the company.
- **Misrepresentation** whereby computer processing is used to assist in the production of financial information which is not derived from authorised transactions.
- **Misuse of resources** where, as a result of a breach of security, data or programs are accessed in an unauthorised manner, computer equipment is attacked, or computer facilities are used in an unauthorised manner, including access or use by people outside the organisation.

15.05 It is important for the auditor to distinguish between these types of computer fraud because different factors affect the risk of each type of fraud occurring. For example, the factors which lead to risk of a fraudulent computer payment are very different from the factors which lead to a risk of management manipulation of the accounts. Poor authorisation controls and password security may lead to the first while management remuneration dependent on profits combined with an adverse business climate may increase the risk of the second. An understanding of the risk factors will assist the auditor in evaluating controls, and each of the major types of fraud together with the related risk factors is discussed in the following paragraphs.

Defalcation

15.06 The main factors giving rise to a risk of defalcation include:

(a) Poor physical controls over the custody of assets.

(b) Poor user controls over the initial recording and subsequent processing of transactions. Controls over standing data are often weak due to the infrequency of changes to it, and effective control over computer output may also be overlooked. The opportunity to process fraudulent items is increased where wide access is given to the system through terminals, which may be located remotely from the computer.

(c) Weak division of duties and supervision, for example inadequate authorisation of payments. It should also be recognised that collusion to commit fraud is not uncommon.

(d) Weak IT controls over the security of programs and data so that access to these is inadequately controlled. Such weaknesses may extend to the access granted to computer operators and to controls over utility programs which may be used to change programs or data.

(e) IT controls that are ineffective in preventing fraudulent changes to programs or data during the implementation of a new system or maintenance of existing systems. These periods of change in systems represent a particular risk.

(f) Inadequate personnel procedures for recruiting and controlling staff, including the taking up of references, staff counselling to identify potential problems and procedures for dismissal. Frauds are committed by people and employing the wrong people creates a risk of fraud. It should also be recognised that many frauds are committed by people in supervisory positions.

15.07 There are two main methods by which computer processing can be used to assist in the unauthorised obtaining of assets belonging to the company – fraudulent steps in the program and the processing of unauthorised data.

Fraudulent program steps

15.08 The most common methods of program manipulation are:

(a) including unauthorised amendments as part of normal authorised changes to programs;

(b) making temporary changes, perhaps when emergency corrections are made after program failure, or permitted by inadequate access controls;

(c) making unauthorised runs of authorised programs;

(d) the use of utilities, as described in Chapter 7, which can amend programs directly often leaving little audit trail.

15.09 All of the published surveys on computer fraud show that there are relatively few cases of program manipulation reported. The reasons for this may include:

(a) the fear of leaving fraudulent steps in a program over a period of time;

(b) the difficulty in obtaining sufficient knowledge of the system as a whole and of the data processed and user control procedures to enable the fraudulent steps to be safely included;

(c) the fact that it is a complex fraud and only certain systems such as payroll or cash recording in banks are really susceptible to such frauds, since in many other systems it may be difficult to gain access to the assets.

15.10 The risk of program manipulation therefore appears to be less serious than the risk of some other types of fraud and particularly of input manipulation. This does not mean that it can be ignored. With the growth in computerised payment and funds transfer systems there is an increasing risk of one-off very large frauds where the culprit then absconds and such frauds may involve the amendment of programs or direct changes to data using utilities. In such systems it may be considered that stringent controls are needed in spite of their cost since the potential loss is very high.

15.11 The most effective controls to guard against fraudulent program steps are a suitable division of duties (whereby programmers have no detailed knowledge of the surrounding manual parts of the system and the user controls), adequate testing of new systems and program changes and control over access to programs. Protection can be enhanced by using modular programming techniques whereby no single programmer has knowledge of the full computer system. In addition, personnel policies such as taking up references for programmers and staff counselling to identify disgruntled employees are important.

Processing unauthorised data

15.12 Defalcation by processing unauthorised data is the most common method of computer fraud. This is not surprising since often only limited skill is needed to amend input data and many staff involved in processing transactions have the opportunity to amend input to the computer. Most recent surveys have shown that the majority of frauds by both number and value involve processing unauthorised data with purchases and claims systems being particularly susceptible. Processing unauthorised data can arise through the input of unauthorised data, manipulation of files, improper use of the printer or suppression of print-outs.

15.13 In batch systems the input is usually made with batches of valid data being processed in a particular application, for example, payroll. In real-time and on-line systems the fraudulent data can be input separately from valid data through a terminal. This usually involves an additional stage, namely the breaching of the physical or software protection of the terminal. These breaches are potentially serious since they may expose programs and data for a variety of applications to abuse.

15.14 The most effective measures to guard against processing unauthorised data are good application and IT controls. In particular, it is important that there should be good physical controls over assets and computer output, an appropriate level and timing of authorisation of important transactions, standing data amendments and adjustments, strong controls over access to data files in on-line systems, regular controls over the continuity of data on files, and strong division of duties. Personnel procedures are also relevant. The linkage between application and IT controls is important. For example, it is ineffective to implement very tight controls over the original manual authorisation of transactions prior to processing if password security over the system is weak so that many people could make changes to authorised data after it has been processed.

15.15 The computer should be used to assist in exercising control. Extensive validation of input can be carried out by the computer, using information stored on files or databases. Records of transactions input and processed and of data communications can be logged to provide a record of activity. The logical consistency of files and databases can be periodically checked by program. Well designed output including exception reports of discrepancies, errors or unusual items can often provide evidence of fraudulent activity where it has occurred. It is very important that such output and even minor discrepancies reported by other parties such as customers, suppliers or employees, are subject to proper follow-up since evidence from detected fraud frequently shows that such discrepancies were reported but not pursued for some time before the discovery of the fraud. Overall, the published surveys show that where input frauds occur there are often blatant weaknesses in control procedures.

Misrepresentation

15.16 Misrepresentation, whereby computer processing is used to assist in the production of financial information which is not derived from authorised transactions, usually involves a significant degree of collusion. Almost certainly material error will arise and therefore the auditor should identify the fraud through audit procedures. However, frauds of this nature are probably easier to perpetrate in computer systems because of the computer's ability to process large volumes of data without the need to involve numerous staff.

15.17 There are a considerable number of risk factors giving rise to a possibility of misrepresentation. The auditor should determine the risk of misrepresentation by considering all of the relevant factors in the light of the circumstances of each particular case. It is quite possible that the auditor will conclude that there is little risk of misrepresentation in a particular case even though one or more of the risk factors is present. Among the more important risk factors are the existence of the following circumstances:

(a) a small autocratic management team;

(b) an ineffective board of directors or audit committee;

(c) management remuneration dependent on profits;

(d) significant ownership of shares by management and incentive to keep share price high, for example, when a flotation is planned;

(e) individuals within management under personal financial pressure;

(f) declining position within the industry or declining industry;

(g) borrowing up to credit limits.

Misuse of resources

15.18 Misuse of computer resources can cover a wide range of activities including unauthorised use of computer resources, breaches in security whereby programs and data are accessed in an unauthorised manner including access by external hackers, the propagation of computer viruses, physical attacks and industrial action. The information contained in programs and data is likely to be a valuable asset to the organisation, and in some cases such information may be stolen after unauthorised access to it has been obtained. Such theft may occur by copying or printing the information, by reading it at a recognised terminal, by reading it from outside the organisation, commonly known as hacking, or by listening in to messages passed through telecommunications networks.

15.19 In reviewing the risk factors which may give rise to misuse of resources, it is helpful to consider all types of misuse together, although it may be argued that, since some of them do not involve deception, they are not strictly computer frauds. The risk factors include:

(a) poor physical control over access to the computer installation or hardware in user areas;

(b) poor software control over access to on-line systems for data processing staff, users and possibly outsiders;

(c) poor physical and software controls over networks using telecommunications, for example allowing dial-up to sensitive applications without dial-back;

(d) weak staff policies including such things as not ensuring that staff dismissed leave the premises immediately and have passwords deleted;

(e) poor procedures for controlling distribution and disposal of printed output;

(f) weak control over the operation and usage of computer resources so that there is no check that resources are used only for valid purposes;

(g) the location of the installation, for example, in a country subject to a high level of terrorist acts.

15.20 The growth in on-line systems and networks has resulted in an increase in this type of activity and the published surveys generally show it to be the most common occurrence after input frauds. Cases include use of computer resources for personal gain such as a programmer running a personal bureau, acts of sabotage by staff or outsiders and cases of external hackers breaking into systems and causing disruption. Some of the risks related to misuse of resources are beyond the scope of normal audit work. However, the auditor may be well placed to carry out security reviews and further guidance on these and on some aspects of misuse of resources is included in Chapter 16 "Computer Security". Legislation has been introduced in the United Kingdom to deal with unauthorised access to computers or unauthorised modification of computer material. This legislation will assist in combating the threats from hacking and computer viruses. These threats and the Computer Misuse Act 1990 are considered in more detail in the second part of this chapter.

Other risk factors

15.21 The risks will also vary with the type of organisation, application and computer installation. As regards organisation, in a banking environment a key risk area may be the system for electronic funds transfers whereas in a pension fund the custody of investments and risk that pensions will still be claimed for deceased pensioners may be more important. Similarly the risks vary for different applications. For example, in a stock system the risk may comprise poor physical control over stock coupled with poor control over processing stock adjustments whereas in a payroll system it may consist of weak controls over processing standing data such as starters and leavers.

15.22 The type of computer installation will also affect the risks. In a minicomputer system where the organisation uses packaged programs and does not have access to source code or a programming capability there may be relatively little risk of fraud through amendment of programs. However, there will probably be a limited number of staff involved in accounting and computer processing and thus division of duties will be restricted and this will increase risk. A large mainframe installation may well write and maintain its own programs and will have skilled staff who could amend programs fraudulently giving a greater risk of fraudulent amendment to programs. On the other hand, division of duties and supervision of work should be better so that staff will work in a controlled environment and might also find it difficult to access assets.

Future trends

15.23 The evidence of computer frauds in published surveys relates to frauds which have occurred in the past. It is therefore helpful to consider how current and future trends in the use of computers are likely to affect the risk of fraud. One of the most significant trends will be the growth in networks and communications which will provide wider access to data and systems. This access will extend to customers and users outside of the organisation which operates the computer system. An example is the growth in electronic data interchange (EDI) discussed in Chapter 14. Within an organisation there will be greater use of on-line communications with less paper and human intervention making it more difficult to check items manually. These trends can be expected to increase the opportunity for computer fraud.

15.24 The expected growth of electronic funds transfer (EFT) systems arising from the same trends represents a particular risk. The data used in these systems constitutes an asset since fraud can be committed by manipulating the data without any need to access physical assets or negotiable instruments. As the use of these systems spreads beyond the banking sector opportunities for fraud can be expected to increase. To counteract these increased risks more emphasis will be placed on programmed checking of transactions and data and improved access control techniques. These techniques are likely to include improved security software, tamperproof hardware, encryption and authentication devices and software, and improved personal identification systems such as smart cards, signature, voice or biometric recognition.

15.25 The progressive improvement in price/performance ratios of computer equipment is likely to mean that powerful and sophisticated computer facilities become increasingly available in smaller businesses and departments or branches of large businesses. Whilst there is likely to be substantial business benefit from such systems, the concentration of functionality and limited staff numbers is likely to increase the opportunities for fraud. For example, in a small business a sophisticated software package might be able to handle all financial processing, including funds transfers, with little division of duties.

15.26 There is an increasing trend for users to take more responsibility for systems development using powerful computer based tools. In some cases this may be by downloading data from a central system for manipulation and subsequent uploading back to the central system. The division of duties between those writing programs and those using them is likely to disappear in such cases, and unless users are properly educated in the need for effective controls to be built into the development process, there is a risk of fraud within such development activity. Finally, as the sophistication of computer systems grows so that they maintain significant corporate expertise, there is an increased risk of theft or misuse of the systems themselves.

15.27 A number of the above trends will increase the risk of computer fraud. However, there are likely to be substantial business benefits to such developments and they should not be held back solely because of increased fraud risks. The techniques for control can also be expected to improve, and there is no reason why effective controls cannot be developed to match the changes in fraud risks provided enough resource and priority is given to them.

Computer Misuse

15.28 The wide range of activities which may be described as computer misuse, and the risk factors which may give rise to them, were described in paragraphs 15.18 to 15.20. Further consideration of all of the threats to computer security, including computer misuse, is included in Chapter 16 "Computer Security". Concern about computer misuse has grown significantly in recent years and, in the United Kingdom, the Computer Misuse Act was passed in 1990. This Act creates new criminal offences to deal with unauthorised access to computers and the unauthorised modification of computer material. In particular, it will combat the threats of hacking into computer systems by insiders or outsiders and of the spreading of computer viruses. These threats and the provisions of the Act are discussed in the following paragraphs.

Hacking

15.29 Hacking is a term applied to the process of accessing computer systems by persons who have no legitimate access to the system, or at least not to that part of the system. It may be carried out by people outside the organisation or by insiders who are users of the system but who attempt to gain access to parts of the system they are not authorised to access. Access may be gained by a number of means including:

(a) Exploiting facilities provided by the system.

(b) Exploiting flaws in the security mechanisms of the system.

(c) Guessing or obtaining the log-on names and passwords of legitimate users.

15.30 There are many reasons why people hack into computer systems. Sometimes it is done to obtain confidential information or commit fraud, sometimes to cause disruption to the target organisation, but often there is no malicious intent, merely a desire for intellectual amusement. Whatever the hacker's objective, he can cause disruption and adverse publicity to the organisation he attacks.

15.31 There have been several well-publicised examples of hacking as follows:

(a) In 1988 two individuals were accused of hacking into British Telecom's Prestel system, after discovering a system administrator's user name and password. Prosecutions were ultimately unsuccessful.

(b) US police alleged that a 14-year old boy in California used his home computer in August 1989 to hack into New York's Citibank computer and obtain more than $11,000 of mail order goods and a Visa gold credit card with a limit of $10,000.

(c) A large international system was entered by a hacker who appeared to have acquired a sufficiently high level of privilege to be able to read and collect passwords. The entire system was closed down, and the software rebuilt to exclude any possibility of the hacker's having rendered it insecure. The work had to be completed within 72 hours in order for the system to remain functional, and occupied upwards of 10,000 man-hours of highly skilled staff.

15.32 Many cases of hacking involve people inside the organisation and often the objective in such cases is to obtain access to confidential files such as the payroll master file. Where networks are used and dial-up facilities are provided the risk of remote hacking by outsiders is increased. The effects of hacking can include direct financial loss, loss of confidential information and significant business disruption caused by the corruption of programs or data and the substantial time which can be required to investigate and resolve the problem. Adverse publicity can also result.

Viruses

15.33 Viruses, trojan horses, logic bombs and worms are different forms of 'hostile' computer programs. The terms are often used somewhat loosely, but the commonly accepted definitions are set out below.

- **Viruses** are programs which reproduce themselves to 'infect' systems, although they do require the unknowing co-operation of the user. They usually make copies of themselves onto any diskette which is placed into an infected machine, and if this diskette is placed into another machine it too can become infected. Thus, the virus propagates itself. Once a single copy of a virus is introduced into an office environment, frequently attached to 'pirated' software, it can rapidly spread to other machines. Viruses may also propagate through networks, either by the originator's design or by the machine's owner making use of networked programs.

- **A trojan horse** is the name given to any program which performs some action of which the user is unaware at the time it is executed.
- **A logic bomb** is a part of a program which, whenever it is executed, tests some condition known as the trigger, and performs some (usually destructive) action if the condition is found to be true. The trigger may be a simple count, a date check, or a more complex specialised test. Viruses and trojan horses usually have logic bombs attached to them – the virus or trojan horse acts as a delivery system for the logic bomb 'warhead'.
- **A worm** is an example of a type of self-reproducing program that is often confused with a virus. The difference between the two is that a worm reproduces without attaching itself to other programs, whereas a virus always attaches itself to some other program. In general, worms tend to be large, complex programs, whereas viruses tend to be small and simple.

15.34 There have been several recent examples of viruses, as follows:

(a) The AIDS information program which was mailed to 10,000 computer users in the UK in December 1989 is an example of a trojan horse. This program claimed to (and did) give information on the disease AIDS. It also, however, installed a hidden program on the disk of the computer which would damage files if a fee was not paid by the user.

(b) On Friday 13 October 1989, two separate viruses were triggered – the Jerusalem Friday the 13th virus and the Datacrime virus. The Jerusalem virus is activated to delete any programs which a user attempts to run on a Friday the 13th of any month. The Datacrime virus deletes directory and other information on any date after the 12 October. Neither of these viruses was widespread in the UK, but many systems were affected in the USA and elsewhere.

(c) The Internet worm was a large, complex program which was released into the US Advanced Projects Research Agency (APRA) network in 1988. The program used several independent techniques to break into computer systems, and contained several mechanisms which aimed at avoiding detection. Fortunately for users, one of these mechanisms did not function as intended and the worm was discovered. Had it not been discovered, it could easily have infected all the 13,000 machines on the network. Although methods are now known which would prevent the same worm from successfully infecting systems, many systems in the UK are known to be still at risk.

15.35 In principle, any type of machine could be infected by a virus. In practice microcomputers are the most popular target, because of their widespread use, the free availability of programming tools and the use of diskettes which are transferred between machines. Since viruses are spread with computer programs, inadequate controls over obtaining and loading software onto microcomputers represents the major threat. The main effect of viruses is disruption of business, as a result of lost or corrupted data and programs and the time required to investigate and attempt to repair the damage. Adverse publicity can also result.

The Computer Misuse Act 1990

Background to the Act

15.36 In September 1988 the Law Commission issued a working paper reviewing the current status of the law against computer misuse and considering possible changes. Comment was requested from all interested parties and a substantial majority of those responding urged that unauthorised access to a computer should be made a criminal offence.

15.37 Following further consultation by the Law Commission to obtain more specific evidence of the problems which have arisen, the Commission published its report 'Computer Misuse' in October 1989. The report recommended legislation because of the cost and disruption caused by such activity, the risk of it being a preliminary to other criminal offences and the disincentive it provides to greater investment in computer systems.

15.38 A Private Member's Bill was introduced by Michael Colvin MP in December 1989 and received Royal Assent on 29 June 1990. The Act creates three new criminal offences which are described in the following paragraphs. A major effect of change in the law will be to deter those who may have regarded hacking or the writing of a virus as a game.

The 'basic unauthorised access' offence

15.39 Under the new Act it is an offence to cause a computer to perform any function with intent to secure access to any program or data held in a computer, in the knowledge that this access is unauthorised.

15.40 This offence is designed to deal with cases of browsing of computer systems. The wording clearly covers attempted access or 'probing' of a computer system which, it may be argued, does not constitute accessing data directly, since the act of entering a user's password causes the system to perform a function with intent to secure access. Purely physical access to the system is excluded.

15.41 The actions of employees authorised to use a computer, but who intentionally exceed the bounds of their authority, would be covered. However, it is understood that the Act is not intended to cover the use of a computer by employees for unauthorised purposes, for example typing a personal letter. The recommended maximum penalty for this offence is six months' imprisonment or a fine.

The 'ulterior intent' offence

15.42 The second provision is that it is an offence to commit the basic unauthorised access offence with intent to commit or to facilitate the commission of a further crime (in general one for which the maximum penalty is imprisonment for five years or more).

15.43 This more serious offence is intended to deal with cases where unauthorised access is obtained with intent to commit a further crime, but where a charge of attempting to commit the crime under the Criminal Attempts Act 1981 would not be sustainable. For example, someone who hacks into a computer to obtain personal information to be used to blackmail someone else could not be guilty of attempted blackmail until the attempt is made, but would be guilty of the offence of unauthorised access with intent to blackmail. The maximum penalty for this offence is five years' imprisonment.

15.44 It is immaterial for the purposes of this offence whether the further crime is to be committed by another person or whether it is to be committed on the same occasion as the unauthorised access offence or on any future occasion. A person can be guilty under this section even if the facts are such that the commission of the further offence is impossible.

The 'unauthorised modification of computer material' offence

15.45 The third provision is that it is an offence knowingly to cause an unauthorised modification of the contents of any computer with intent thereby to impair the operation of any computer, to prevent or hinder access to any program or data held in any computer or to impair the operation of any such program or the reliability of any such data. It is immaterial for the purposes of this offence whether the unauthorised modification or any intended effect of it is, or is intended to be, permanent or merely temporary.

15.46 This offence is intended to cover several forms of conduct, the most important of which are the following:

- Simple unauthorised modification where a person intentionally and without authorisation (electronically) alters or erases programs or data contained in a computer's memory or on a storage medium. Physical damage is not intended to be covered.
- The putting into circulation of diskettes which are 'infected' with a virus, intending that the diskette will cause some person somewhere to suffer a modification that will impair the operation of his computer.
- The unauthorised addition of a virus or 'worm' to a computer's library of programs, intending thereby to impair the operation of the computer simply by using up its capacity.
- The unauthorised addition of a password to a data file, thereby rendering that data inaccessible to anyone who does not know the password.

The maximum penalty for this offence is five years' imprisonment.

15.47 The Act applies to England and Wales, Scotland and Northern Ireland. There is a wide jurisdiction for the new offences and, in general, domestic courts have jurisdiction over computer misuse that either originates from, or is directed against computers located in the home countries. It should be noted that in the majority of cases computer viruses have originated outside the UK, although they have had effect in the UK. In practice it may be difficult to prosecute offenders successfully in such cases.

Reliance on the Act

15.48 The Law Commission report stressed that no legislation can take the place, in protecting the legitimate interests of computer users, of proper investment in security systems, and the stringent administration of such systems once they are installed. Furthermore, the onus is on the prosecution to prove that access was unauthorised. For employees this means that the status of the person controlling access must be clearly established, the limits of authorisation of each employee must be clearly defined and it must be proved that the employee has knowingly and intentionally exceeded that level of authority. The law may not protect employers who have not implemented clear security procedures. Guidance on such procedures is included in Chapters 7 and 16.

Summary

15.49 There has been a significant increase in computer fraud and computer misuse in recent years and these activities have attracted greater public attention. Computer fraud may involve defalcation, misrepresentation or misuse of resources and different risk factors may be likely to lead to each of these. Defalcation by processing unauthorised data is the most common method of computer fraud. Future changes in technology are likely to create greater opportunities for fraud, and resources will need to be devoted to ensuring that control techniques keep pace with these risks.

15.50 The increase in the incidence of computer misuse has to a significant extent resulted from an increase in unauthorised access or hacking into computers and the spread of computer viruses. In the United Kingdom, the Computer Misuse Act 1990 has been introduced to deal with unauthorised access to computers and the unauthorised modification of computer material.

16

Computer Security

Introduction

Relevance to the auditor

16.01 In recent years the rapid improvements in computer facilities have led to an unprecedented increase in the use of automated systems to communicate, process and store information. Today data processing and information systems have become critical components in ensuring the continued operation of an organisation's business activities as well as being used for the processing and storage of financial data. Businesses are more and more dependent on the availability of their computer resources for their daily operations, and in many cases could not continue to operate if deprived of them. Typically networks of terminals are used in making business decisions such as quoting premium rates for insurance or checking a customer's credit rating and accepting an order. Information is thus a key asset to the business and in these circumstances it is more than ever essential that the processing capability, as well as the data itself, is safeguarded and protected. Computer security is usually defined as meaning that data is processed completely and accurately, that access is restricted to appropriate people and that the computer facilities, and the information they hold, are available at all required times. These three elements of security are generally referred to as integrity, confidentiality and availability.

16.02 This chapter considers all three elements of computer security. Some of the concerns relating to security have been considered in previous chapters and reference will be made to these where appropriate. In particular, the complete and accurate processing of authorised financial data and access to data, insofar as it relates to authorised data not being altered, has always been a major concern to the auditor, and this has been dealt with in earlier chapters. In this chapter the importance of the correctness of non-financial data will also be considered. The subjects of computer fraud and computer misuse, including in particular the threats from hacking and computer viruses were considered in Chapter 15 "Computer Fraud and Computer Misuse" together with the provisions of the Computer Misuse Act 1990. This chapter deals with the other risks of misappropriation of information or computer facilities and protection against disruption of processing, which are of major concern to management.

16.03 Data security has become of greater importance to the external auditor because the growth in on-line systems and networks has made traditional controls over input, authorisation and update of data increasingly dependent on controls over data security. The Institute of Chartered Accountants in England and Wales published an Information Technology Statement in June 1985 entitled *Security and Confidentiality of Data* dealing with the concerns in this area. Security reviews can form an important part of the work of internal audit departments, and may also be performed by external auditors as a special service to clients.

16.04 The issue of confidentiality and privacy of data held on computer systems and relating to individuals has also become of far greater concern in recent years and, in the United Kingdom, the Data Protection Act was passed in 1984 to deal with this subject. One of the requirements of the Act is that data relating to individuals should be kept adequately secure, and the effects of this legislation are dealt with in this chapter.

The need for security

16.05 In all systems, computer or otherwise, there is always a risk, no matter how remote, of inaccurate information, physical disruption and misappropriation of data and facilities. In a computerised environment the magnitude of these risks is greater as a result of the following factors:

(a) *The physical concentration of data processing* and storage in one or a small number of locations. As a result the disruption of a relatively small physical unit can have a disproportionate effect on the general data processing of the organisation. Partly in order to overcome this some organisations have distributed their data processing functions. This arrangement is designed to provide resilience since processing may be carried on using computers in other locations while one site is inoperable. However, at a local level, failure of a system may still have an adverse effect on the operations carried out within that area, and this may have a subsequent effect on the proper and efficient operation of the organisation as a whole. The security over communications between computer installations will also need to be considered in such circumstances.

(b) *The complexity of computer processing.* This leads to a concentration, in the hands of a relatively small number of people, of the knowledge of a company's computer systems, and thus of the ability to create and modify them. This increases the opportunity for one or more members of this group, intentionally or otherwise, to be able to influence the procedures carried out by the computer systems, and thereby in some way affect the company adversely.

(c) *The development of networks* to provide real-time and on-line systems where remote users communicate directly with the centralised, distributed and local data processing facilities. The proper processing of data input through remote terminals follows the same principles as outlined in earlier sections of this book. However, in respect of security, special regard must be paid to:

(i) terminals and their capabilities both locally and as regards the network as a whole;

(ii) hardware not under central control to which unauthorised peripherals could be attached;

(iii) communication lines where unauthorised equipment could be used to intercept, read or amend transferred data; and

(iv) responsibilities for hardware and software at remote locations.

These factors make it more difficult to identify and control the usage of processing and storage facilities.

(d) *The use of computers to carry out processes which could not easily be performed by manual systems.* This increases the dependence on the computer and leads to the danger that, should processing be interrupted, it would be difficult to introduce alternative manual procedures.

(e) *The scale of operation of many computer systems.* While providing greater reliability, speed and accuracy, the large scale and inter-connected nature of modern systems introduces the risk that a processing failure will have a greater and more widespread effect than a failure in a corresponding manual system.

(f) *The move towards the 'paperless office'.* Increasingly businesses are relying on computers, rather than paper documents, to initiate and record transactions. There has been a substantial growth in electronic funds transfer (EFT) and electronic data interchange (EDI). Electronic records are often the prime, and in some cases the sole, record of a particular transaction.

Components of Computer Security

Definition of computer security

16.06 Computer security, or information systems security, is a term used to cover the security of all the information processed by an organisation's computer systems, and of the equipment and facilities used to process the information. The three components of security – integrity, confidentiality and availability – are dealt with in turn in the following paragraphs.

Integrity

16.07 Integrity is about ensuring that information is complete, not duplicated, accurate, authorised and kept secure. Integrity is considered first because it is perhaps the most familiar to the auditor; the earlier chapters on application and IT controls were particularly concerned with controls directed at preserving the integrity of data, in other words protecting it from error and fraud. However whereas the focus of an auditor has traditionally been the integrity of financial systems, in practice it may well be that errors in non-financial systems would be more serious. Consider for example the following functions carried out by computers:

(a) air traffic control;

(b) control of a nuclear power generator;

(c) pharmaceutical batch records;

(d) computer-aided design.

Although these systems are non-financial, errors in any of them could have very serious consequences.

Confidentiality

16.08 There are different reasons why an organisation may wish to keep information confidential. The example that springs most readily to mind is personal information, such as salary, health records or information about criminal convictions. In many countries, including the United Kingdom, this type of information is protected by legislation. There are however many other types of confidential information; some examples are given below:

(a) *'Top secret' information* which could prejudice national security. Such information may be held by commercial organisations in the defence industry.

(b) *Trade secrets* such as product formulations and designs and market research data.

(c) *Information which could attract adverse publicity,* such as details of animal experiments or trade with an unpopular foreign regime.

(d) *Information which is confidential in the period before its release,* such as a company's financial results or information relating to a takeover.

Confidential information must be protected no matter what form it is in. It will be necessary to consider data input, output, stored, transmitted along communication links or displayed on a screen.

16.09 One of the interesting facts about confidential information is that it is often held in computer systems which are outside the control of the main data centre. In most businesses a snooper or troublemaker would find it more rewarding to penetrate word processing systems used by senior executives' secretaries than to attempt to hack into the mainframe. Research information of considerable value to a competitor may be held on a minicomputer in the research department in an informal processing environment. It is therefore of concern that many office systems and research computers are set up and run with scant regard for security.

16.10 Sometimes it will be the computer systems themselves, rather than the data, that are confidential. Examples would be a new operating system developed by a computer vendor which has yet to reach the marketplace, or an expert system used for providing tax advice developed by an accounting practice.

Availability

16.11 Information should be accessible when it is wanted. The major aspects of availability are described below:

(a) *Response time.* The response time is the delay between pressing the 'enter' or 'return' key on a terminal and obtaining a response back from the computer (an error message or confirmation that the transaction has been accepted).

(b) *Back-up procedures.* All parts of a system require regular back-up in case they are lost or damaged. Potentially this includes data, application software and system software, although in practice package software and system software may be standard and a replacement therefore easily obtainable from the original suppliers.

(c) *Fallback arrangements.* Fallback arrangements are needed to offer an alternative means of operation if the normal computer system is not useable for some reason such as a fire. Fallback arrangements can range in sophistication from a paper-based manual operation to a complete duplicate data centre which can be 'switched in' at a moment's notice.

(d) *Redundancy/resilience.* It is desirable wherever possible to design the hardware configuration such that the loss of one component is tolerable. For example if three computers are linked together in a ring rather than a line, loss of any one link will not prevent them from communicating with one another. If several disk drives are used, then two disk controllers rather than one will allow at least some of the disk drives to be useable if one controller fails.

16.12 Availability requirements will vary considerably according to the type of system. They may also vary with time in any particular system. For example, response or turnaround time may become quite critical for a general ledger or consolidation system at the financial year end, whereas process control systems are likely to have very high availability requirements at all times. Availability requirements need to be considered from the users' perspective. If response time exceeds a certain level, for example, the user may consider the system to be unavailable since it is of no practical use. The assumptions made in setting up fallback arrangements such as the order of priorities in application system reinstatement, or the length of time before systems are working again must be understood and agreed by users.

A model for computer security

16.13 As part of a study of network security commissioned by the European Commission, Coopers & Lybrand devised the 'House Model' to provide a conceptual framework for understanding security. In this model there are four complementary layers of computer security which work together to provide a secure environment in a cost-effective manner, as follows:

- **The foundation** The basis for good security is the attitude of an organisation's senior management. This can be demonstrated in practice by:

  (a) a statement of **policy** on security;

  (b) the allocation of **responsibilities** for security;

  (c) high levels of **awareness** of security issues.

- **Baseline controls** These are control procedures generally accepted as standard good practice, which will be implemented in any well-run organisation without the need for elaborate analysis and cost-justification. They are the computer equivalent of a bank reconciliation; no accountant debates about whether regular bank reconciliations are worthwhile.

- **System-specific controls** There will usually be some systems which require stronger controls in particular areas. Examples are the need for strong access control over electronic funds transfer and good fallback arrangements for process control systems. These system-specific controls are defined by considering the particular functions of each system, ideally at the design stage.

- **Management processes** These are required to ensure that security remains effective even though people, systems and technology change. Effective processes are required for implementation, administration, monitoring, auditing, reviewing and change management for security procedures.

Following this study, the European Security Forum, a group of leading organisations across Europe which are advanced users of IT, was founded by Coopers & Lybrand. The Forum provides various services for members including research into advanced security techniques and advice on the cost-effective application of security in commercial and public sector enterprises.

Threats to Security

16.14 There are many factors, internal and external to an organisation, which may threaten its security. The threats may be accidental, such as air conditioning failure, or deliberate, such as computer-assisted fraud. In some cases, the same event can be caused either accidentally or deliberately; a fire which destroys the whole data centre may be the result of a chance electrical short-circuit or the deliberate act of a disaffected security guard. It will often be the case that deliberate acts are the more serious, as they will have been planned to avoid detection and cause the maximum damage. A computer operator who deliberately destroys important data files may also be in a position to destroy the back-up files as well. The main threats to the security of a typical computer installation are set out below.

Hardware damage or breakdown

16.15 Hardware damage or breakdown can have many causes:

(a) *Natural calamities.* Both the computer hardware and its environment may be damaged by external forces. The most likely of these is fire. However, the less frequent hazard of flooding, and even a catastrophe such as an earthquake or the crash of an aircraft should not be ignored.

(b) *Power supply failure.* This can affect one or more of the computer itself, data storage devices, printers or terminals. Frequently the impact of failure may be different for each piece of equipment. For example, the central system may be unaffected by the lack of power to remote terminals, although where the organisation relies on those terminals for the input of data or providing users with essential up-to-date information, such an interruption may be unacceptable.

(c) *Hardware malfunction.* It is to be expected that, from time to time, one or more of the components in the computer hardware will malfunction. When this occurs, it may degrade the performance of the system or cause it to fail completely.

(d) *Air conditioning failure.* Many larger computer systems require air conditioning. They may be able to run for some time when deprived of their normal requirements for air conditioning, but this is likely to increase the probability of hardware malfunction.

(e) *Deliberate interference with hardware.* Certain employees, such as computer operators, security guards and cleaners, may have unsupervised access to computer equipment and be in a position to damage it.

Fraud

16.16 Fraud is a subject of particular concern to the auditor, and is discussed in Chapter 15 "Computer Fraud and Computer Misuse".

Theft

16.17 Hardware, software and computer time are all vulnerable to theft, as follows:

(a) *Hardware.* Some items of computer hardware are both portable and re-saleable. Terminals, personal computers and communications equipment may be easily concealed in normal-sized bags.

(b) *Software.* Software may also be subject to theft. The threat is usually confined to widely used proprietary microcomputer software such as spreadsheets, database systems and word processing systems, which can be taken away on an easily concealed diskette. Other software, both production programs and system software, developed by a company or obtained from a supplier, may also be stolen if they could be valuable to a competitor. The software may be misappropriated by copying files, obtaining print-outs or accessing systems through terminals. The system and programming documentation is as important in this respect as the software itself. This threat is of particular relevance when staff leave a company's computer department to join competitors or software companies.

(c) *Computer time.* Computer staff have been known to sell computer time to outsiders or to use computer time to develop their own programs, either for financial gain or purely from technical interest. This is most relevant in a time-sharing environment where many users have access to the system, in small organisations where little formal control is exercised over the use of the computer facility or where microcomputers are used extensively.

Misuse of information

16.18 There are many opportunities for information to be obtained from a computer system as follows:

(a) *Copying of magnetic media.*

(b) *Extra copies of print-outs* can be obtained.

(c) *Misuse of terminals* and other communications equipment. These are frequently less physically secure than the central installation and may be accessible to large numbers of people. Terminals may be left connected to the computer but unattended; logging-on routines showing passwords may be left visible on unattended terminals or in waste bins; unauthorised equipment may be connected to teleprocessing systems to intercept, disrupt or amend data being transferred.

(d) *Availability of waste output.* User output may become obsolete once an updated output is received but may still have considerable value. A mistake by a computer operator, for example the incorrect set-up of the printer, may necessitate the re-running of work, and the output, although described as waste, may contain valuable information. Waste paper disposed of as a result of test running new production programs or utilities may also contain valuable information.

(e) *Printed output can be examined in an unauthorised manner* during handling in the computer department or after it has been passed to users.

16.19 The scale and importance of the misappropriation can range from a situation where a sales clerk who has access to customer credit information gives this information orally to others who can make use of it, to one where complete copies of important files, such as price lists or customer details, are taken in magnetic or paper form and sold to competitors or a ransom demanded for their return.

16.20 Sometimes there is no intention to use the information in a way which could be described as fraud or theft. Members of staff who have access to information for certain purposes may use it in other ways, or those who should not have access to the information may obtain it. Examples of this misuse could be computer operators learning of the salaries being paid to other employees and discussing them, or casual visitors to an organisation being allowed sight of, and time to examine, sensitive output on print-outs or screens such as bad debt lists or company profit figures. To the extent that information is obtained by causing a computer to perform a function in the knowledge that access is unauthorised, it is likely that a criminal offence will have been committed under the Computer Misuse Act. This Act is discussed in Chapter 15 "Computer Fraud and Computer Misuse".

Sabotage

16.21 Malicious destruction of hardware can be carried out by an employee or an intruder. For many businesses, deliberate destruction or amendment of programs or data can be even more disruptive, especially as the perpetrator may be in a position to destroy back-up copies as well, making recovery very difficult. Again the Computer Misuse Act dealt with in Chapter 15 may make such acts a criminal offence if they involve unauthorised access to a computer or modification of computer material.

Pervasive or significant data or programming errors

16.22 The writing of software, both for operating systems and application systems, involves many thousands of instructions. No matter how well these systems are tested, they will fail from time to time. The effects of such a failure can vary from minimal to catastrophic.

Operating errors

16.23 While simple operator errors normally have only a minimal impact on the running of the system, it is possible that such errors may, on occasion, have a significant impact, where for example a direct debit tape is processed twice. It might take a considerable time to restore the situation, should an operator accidentally disrupt a complex communications system. As computer operations become more automated there is less scope for operator error. However in emergency situations, for example a disk failure in a time-critical system, it is often necessary for operators to override automated procedures in a hurry, and this is when mistakes are likely to occur.

Personnel problems

16.24 Increasing automation reduces the number of people needed to run a computer system, but often has the effect of concentrating the technical skills and experience in a few individuals. If these people are sick, leave or go on strike, this can have a major impact on the business. The withdrawal of a few key individuals from the computer department during an industrial dispute can be a very effective bargaining tool, and senior management, particularly in state-run or paternalistic organisations, may consider it too provocative to employee relations to develop a contingency plan for this eventuality.

Hacking and computer viruses

16.25 The threats from hacking and computer viruses are dealt with in Chapter 15 "Computer Fraud and Computer Misuse".

Computer Security Controls

16.26 The adverse effects of breaches in security on a business can be minimised by procedures or steps designed to:

(a) Prevent the security breach.

(b) Detect the security breach.

(c) Recover from the security breach.

In practice an organisation will employ a combination of these types of control. The following sections describe features of good practice and procedures often employed to achieve effective security. The procedures described are reasonably comprehensive and would be most likely to be applied in a large computer installation. Similar principles apply to smaller installations but the less complex computer environment means that the procedures necessary are more straightforward.

Software access controls

16.27 It will usually be necessary to restrict access to production data, programs and system software, to protect them from hazards such as theft, malicious or accidental destruction, unauthorised alteration and unauthorised examination. The main method of achieving this is software or logical access control. Software access control techniques have already been described in Chapter 7 on program and data file security. It must be remembered however that the major concern there was to prevent unauthorised amendments. In the wider context of security, controls over the ability to read (confidentiality) and delete (availability) both data and programs are also of concern. It is also necessary to consider non-financial systems, for example office automation, manufacturing control and research and design systems, which may be run on separate computers under separate control.

Software and hardware integrity

16.28 To ensure the correct functioning of both the software and hardware components of application systems, security must be considered at all phases of the project life-cycle.

Statement of requirements

16.29 It is normal practice to prepare a statement of requirements for an application, to provide a basis against which an in-house development, or a tender, can be evaluated. Security requirements should be clearly specified in this document, for example:

(a) The need to restrict certain functions/data elements/data values to certain terminals and/or user IDs.

(b) Control over accuracy of data input and processing.

(c) The separation of enquiry functions from update functions.

(d) Confidentiality requirements, for example, where data contains personal information or information of value to a competitor.

(e) Requirements as regards availability, such as the maximum acceptable length of time that the application could be unavailable, or the required response time.

These requirements should be specified in as much detail as possible from the outset. It is not adequate merely to include such statements as 'Fall-back : revert to manual procedures' or 'Information held within this system should be regarded as confidential'. The requirements should be refined as the development proceeds and the development measured against these requirements; software selection procedures should include an evaluation of the proposed solution against the stated security requirements. The advantages of a comprehensive systems development and testing methodology have already been described in Chapter 6. It is important that the systems development checkpoints and sign-offs cover the security requirements set out in the system specification.

Contractual arrangements

16.30 Contracts for the supply or maintenance of hardware and software should specify security requirements, where relevant, and should deal with the following matters relating particularly to software:

(a) Ownership of software.

(b) Confidentiality of software and data, including test data extracted from live information, and data left on magnetic media which have been taken off the premises for maintenance.

(c) Arrangements for ensuring the continued use of the software by the purchaser, in the event that the supplier ceases to trade, for example, escrow arrangements for systems documentation and source code.

16.31 Arrangements (preferably contractual) should be made for the routine and emergency maintenance of hardware and software. These should specify the response time and the action to be taken when a repair cannot be effected within the specified time, for example, the supply of a replacement item.

Project management

16.32 The relevance of good project management to security is that it should help to ensure a disciplined development process with adequate time for testing, and adherence to the chosen methodology. Project management is as important for projects to upgrade or change hardware and system software as it is for software developments.

Development, testing and cataloguing

16.33 It is vital that systems development and testing takes place in a processing environment which is separate from the normal production ('live') environment. This has already been discussed in Chapter 6. Change management and cataloguing procedures should control the transfer of tested and approved programs into the production environment. They should also cover the hardware and system software environment. Linked to the change management system there should be an up-to-date record of all hardware and software, together with model/version numbers and dates of installation. This is particularly useful in a distributed environment where problems may arise through the use of different versions at different locations, and considerable system down-time may occur while the problem is investigated. The change management system may also be linked to a problem management system, where problems and their clearance are logged.

Computer operations

16.34 Many aspects of computer operations controls have already been covered insofar as they relate to integrity. Areas which are particularly relevant to confidentiality and availability are as follows:

- **Media management** Arrangements should be made for the orderly and secure storage of diskettes, disks, tapes and input documents (see also the sections on Physical Security and Office Systems). Magnetic media should be examined periodically to ensure that it is still usable. If output is printed centrally, appropriate arrangements should be made to ensure that it is stored and distributed securely, and that its confidentiality is preserved.

- **Back-up** Periodically the adequacy of back-up arrangements should be tested by reloading the back-up and attempting to resume processing with it. Where tape back-ups are to be kept for several years, they should be recopied periodically, say every two years. At least one set of back-ups should be kept offsite in a secure location, and arrangements made to ensure that they are transported safely to and from the storage location.

- **Performance** System performance standards should be set, and actual performance monitored and compared with the standards. Faults and problems should be formally recorded in problem log, and the steps taken to resolve the problems should also be recorded.

Communications security

16.35 There should be written standards for network design, implementation, operation and maintenance. Special security requirements, such as encryption of very confidential transmitted information, should be included. An up-to-date inventory of the different components of the network should be maintained, which shows the model/version numbers of all hardware and software.There should be clearly defined responsibilities for the operation, maintenance and safe custody of all hardware and software components, wherever situated. If at all possible, resilience should be built into the network by duplicating critical components or links and by physically separating duplicated components, to reduce the likelihood that both items would be damaged by the same incident.

16.36 Changes to hardware or software, even apparently minor changes such as the installation of new versions of software, should be subject to formal change control procedures.

16.37 Network performance standards should be set, and actual performance monitored and compared with these standards. Faults and problems should be formally recorded in a problem log, and the steps taken to resolve the problems should also be recorded.

16.38 It should be borne in mind that unauthorised intrusion into a network can impair confidentiality and availability, as well as integrity. Controls over network access, including dial-up, are covered in Chapter 7.

Contingency planning

16.39 A formal contingency plan should be prepared. This should take into account all systems and all locations. Full user department participation is needed to ensure that the plan reflects the importance to the business of each computer system, and to establish an order of priorities for reinstatement of the systems, where this is to be done in a phased manner. The contingency plan should cover both interim processing arrangements and the steps necessary for full normal processing to be resumed, including actions required by users. There has been a tendency for contingency planning to concentrate solely on restoration of the computer facilities. In fact what is required is a plan which will enable the business to resume normal operation, and nowadays the process is sometimes referred to as business contingency planning or business resumption planning.

16.40 Different fallback options are available commercially for the computers themselves, but of course the more convenient and comprehensive an arrangement is, the more it is likely to cost. The main options are:

(a) *Warm/hot standby* comprising a machine room containing a computer on which the systems software and the application software is already installed.

(b) *Cold standby* comprising a machine room containing a computer on which standard system software is installed.

(c) *A portable machine room* in which a computer obtained from the manufacturer can be installed.

16.41 A business impact assessment can be used to balance cost with risk and assist in selecting the appropriate option. A common area of difficulty is that of communications links which are unlikely to be in place at the fallback site unless it is a dedicated site belonging to the organisation itself.

16.42 The contingency plan should also cover user department procedures for continuing to operate in the interim. It is important that these procedures are thought through in detail, so that any possible problems can be tackled. For example, where the intention is to fall back to a recent hard copy of the contents of a file, it will be necessary to ensure that the whole file is printed out, or is available to be printed out perhaps at a bureau, at regular intervals. This is more likely to be a problem with database files which may be difficult to reload and print at a bureau, particularly where unusual or bespoke database management software is used.

16.43 The plan should be kept up-to-date for changes to applications, system software and hardware. This is particularly important where the intention is to use similar facilities, which are not under the direct control of the organisation, at a bureau or another company. The use of one of the proprietary contingency planning software packages with integral cross-referencing facilities, makes updating more convenient. Disaster recovery considerations should also be incorporated into change management arrangements to ensure that the plan is routinely updated for hardware and software changes as they occur.

16.44 The drafting of a contingency plan needs meticulous attention to detail. Testing plays a vital role in checking that nothing has been forgotten; in fact it would be more accurate to say that it will highlight what has been forgotten. It is particularly necessary when the plan is for partial reinstatement of systems, since it will bring to light any unsuspected system dependencies. Regular testing is necessary for two main reasons, firstly to ensure that the plan has been updated for all changes to hardware and software, and secondly to familiarise people with the fallback procedures. A typical test frequency would be once a year, and most suppliers of fallback arrangements offer annual testing facilities as part of the contract.

16.45 A copy of the plan should be stored securely off-site. Where the plan relies on the hardware or software suppliers or other third parties providing replacement hardware, software or services, this arrangement should if possible be contractual. Failing this, correspondence expressing intentions should be retained.

Security management and administration

16.46 Good security will only be achieved if all employees understand their responsibilities. This needs an unambiguous statement of policy and regular training and communications designed to foster awareness of security issues, and a working atmosphere in which good security is desired and routinely achieved. A regular 'security audit' can check that the required procedures are in place and are being followed. Many organisations are expressing an intention to apply for BS5750 (British Standard in Quality Service) and this may be an effective mechanism for demonstrating management commitment to quality in general and security in particular.

16.47 A good security policy includes the following features:

(a) the endorsement of senior management;

(b) a statement of objectives of computer security;

(c) responsibilities for security;

(d) general principles of security.

A security policy should be a statement of general principles and will not need frequent updating. To supplement this general statement, security procedures manuals are needed which provide detailed, specific guidance. The procedures manuals will need regular updating to reflect technical and procedural changes.

16.48 The overall responsibility for IT security should be clearly defined. A specific individual should be allocated responsibility for computer security. If possible he should be independent of individual user departments and the data processing department, report to a senior official of the company and have adequate status, authority and resources. It may be helpful to set up a security committee with representatives from user departments, the data processing department, the finance function, personnel and security management.

16.49 Insurance cover should be regularly checked to ensure that it remains adequate. If practicable and cost effective it should cover all risks, including employee fidelity, sabotage, and accidental error, and all losses including business interruption, consequential losses, restoration of records, third party liability and replacement value of equipment. Where third parties or subcontractors are used it will be necessary to check that they themselves are covered for losses caused by security breaches, including negligence, errors and omissions.

16.50 Some security controls may need careful administration, for example:

(a) authorisation and implementation of rights of access to systems;

(b) removal of access rights when employees leave or change departments;

(c) control over remote access, for example by a third party responsible for maintenance of application software or systems software;

(d) arranging for the reporting and investigation of security violations.

These tasks are fundamental to the secure operation of the computer systems, and therefore must be carried out regularly by a suitably trained employee, if possible independent of user department and data processing department responsibilities, and supervised.

Physical security

Physical access control

16.51 The nature of physical access controls required will depend on the location of the equipment, the type of business and the other uses of the building in which the computer equipment is located. For example, extra precautions may be needed in the cases listed below:

(a) A neighbourhood where vandalism is common.

(b) The organisation is a possible target for political attack, for example, a laboratory performing animal experiments, a business with links with an unpopular foreign regime.

(c) The public, or a large number of employees, has access to parts of the building (local government office, retail outlet, canteen).

(d) The building contains valuable items which could be the target of theft.

(e) The computer systems/data could be the target of criminal activity such as fraud or theft of confidential information.

16.52 A knowledge of the likelihood of physical attack, and the value of assets being protected, will allow an assessment of the cost-effectiveness of various security measures which might include:

(a) Site security including guards and cameras.

(b) Buildings security, operational during office hours and at other times, and covering employees, visitors, engineers, contract staff and cleaners.

(c) Sound building construction, for example, avoiding flimsy partitions or large windows.

(d) Computer equipment not obvious to the casual observer, for example, avoiding external windows, external or internal direction indicators.

(e) Control of access to rooms containing computer equipment.

(f) Control of access to areas next to rooms housing computer equipment, including communications equipment.

(g) Logging of access to sensitive areas.

(h) 'Zoned' physical access control with the most sensitive area, to which access is strictly limited, sited inside a somewhat less secure area to which access is also controlled, although less tightly.

(i) Intrusion detection equipment and cameras out-of-hours or in unmanned locations.

(j) Secure storage for important documents and magnetic media.

Fire protection

16.53 Fire protection measures which will always be appropriate are listed below:

(a) Hand-held fire extinguishers appropriate to the type of fire/material being protected.

(b) Regular fire practices including evacuation and use of fire-fighting equipment.

(c) Regular inspection by a Fire Prevention Officer.

(d) Clear emergency signs, for example to exits and fire-fighting equipment.

(e) Storage of bulk paper and inflammable materials, such as printing fluids, as far away from computer equipment as possible.

(f) Metallic waste bins.

(g) 'No smoking' regulations.

(h) Fireproof cabinets for storage of important documents and magnetic media.

Circumstances may warrant additional precautions such as smoke/heat detection equipment and automatic fire suppression systems.

Environmental conditions

16.54 In general, the larger an item of computer hardware the more heat it generates, and the more demanding its requirements in terms of controlled temperature, humidity and sensitivity to air-borne dust. The trend is for computers to become less demanding, with sealed units, less self-generated heat and greater tolerance to fluctuations. Where equipment needs a controlled environment, this will be specified by the manufacturer. If there are no stated requirements, then it can be assumed that the equipment will function in normal office conditions. However, unless the manufacturer gives a specific assurance to the contrary it should still be protected from extreme conditions such as excessive dust or vibrations caused by heavy machinery. Where environmental control equipment is needed, it should be regularly maintained and monitored (particularly at times when the computer room is unmanned) and fallback arrangements made.

Power supply

16.55 Computer equipment should be fed by a 'clean' power supply, that is one protected from spikes and surges. An uninterruptable power supply (UPS) will, in the event of a power cut, as a minimum allow the equipment to be powered down in an orderly manner, or allow processing to be continued until a standby generator is activated. The UPS (and standby generator) should be regularly tested. The power requirements of other ancillary equipment such as air conditioning units, computer peripherals, terminals and emergency heating and lighting, should also be taken into account.

Water hazards

16.56 Unnecessary risks should be avoided by keeping computers and water as far apart as possible. If possible, the following precautions should be taken:

(a) No tanks or pipes should be sited in the ceiling or higher floors above the computer.

(b) Where a computer is under a flat roof, the roof should be checked regularly.

(c) Care should be taken with the siting of water-cooled air conditioning equipment, and water detectors should be installed to warn of leaks before major damage occurs.

First aid

16.57 Other matters which should be considered under the general heading of physical security are training in first aid for selected employees and the provision of first aid cabinets and sick rooms.

Office systems

16.58 The proliferation of microcomputers in office environments over the last few years has brought considerable security problems. Their users are often self-taught, and liable to focus on the quick achievement of results rather than compliance with sound practice. Also their managers may not be sufficiently familiar with computers to provide them with adequate guidance and supervision. It is no easy task to educate users to understand the need for security, but they must be made aware that office systems often hold very confidential data (board minutes, spreadsheets containing confidential financial information) and appropriate measures should be taken to protect it as follows:

(a) Data should not be left on the hard disk of a microcomputer, unless security software is in use. If microcomputers are networked, data is usually safer stored on the file server where logical access control facilities are likely to be more effective.

(b) Diskettes should be locked up.

(c) Special precautions should be taken to remove confidential data when a machine is removed for repair.

16.59 It is not uncommon to find microcomputer-based applications developed in spreadsheet or database products which have taken weeks of development effort. Clearly these represent a corporate asset and need to be effectively backed up.

16.60 Where work-stations are networked, back-up is most conveniently performed as a separate regular function on the file server or central minicomputer. For stand-alone machines, guidelines should be issued on the preferred back-up method and frequency. The common practice of keeping diskette back-ups immediately next to the microcomputer is not a good idea. Guidance on standard file naming conventions is also helpful to enable colleagues to locate a file in someone's absence.

16.61 Employees also need to be made aware of the dangers of viruses. Diskettes from machines outside the organisation (including employees' home computers) should be checked for viruses before being used. It is also possible to instal virus-checking software on microcomputers which will warn if viruses are introduced.

16.62 Physical security is needed to protect the equipment itself, which is often portable and easily sold, and also the data which it holds. Normal office security should prevent equipment being taken off the premises without written authorisation. Where further precautions are deemed advisable, it may be considered necessary to secure the equipment to furniture using clamps or chains.

16.63 Procurement of office systems software and hardware should be handled centrally:

(a) to obtain the best terms;

(b) to ensure that inventories are up-to-date and that maintenance contracts are in force for all items; and

(c) to encourage users to select items from a short-list of recommended products (which will simplify maintenance, upgrades and support).

Further guidance on the acquisition, use and security of microcomputers, with particular relevance to usage within an audit practice, is contained in Chapter 12 "Microcomputers in the Audit Practice".

Personnel procedures

16.64 Personnel procedures for computer department staff are important because considerable reliance is often placed on their conscientiousness and integrity. There may well be no-one within the organisation who is technically competent to supervise their work in detail, and they often work outside normal office hours when few people are around. It is not uncommon to find that they have the knowledge and the opportunity to make fraudulent changes to data or to disrupt processing dramatically. When recruiting computer staff references should always be obtained and should be followed up. Contracts of employment should be appropriate to a computer environment, dealing for example with confidentiality requirements and with the private use of computer resources. Accurate job descriptions should be prepared. Employees should receive regular training in emergency procedures and computer security. Regular counselling sessions should be held to ensure as far as possible that employees' work-related and other problems do not go unnoticed.

16.65 When an employee is dismissed, or leaves in unhappy circumstances, it will usually be best to remove him immediately from any tasks which would allow him scope for malicious activity. Indeed, it may be appropriate to escort him off the premises immediately. Any access privileges which he has (cards, badges, ID) should also be cancelled straight away.

16.66 Particularly in smaller organisations, considerable reliance may be placed on a few key individuals. While this is often unavoidable, the problem should be minimised as far as possible by training back-up staff for key tasks, and by insisting that adequate systems and operational documentation is maintained and kept secure.

16.67 Support service staff such as cleaners should be adequately supervised to prevent unauthorised access to sensitive locations or information. Contracts for the supply of support services should include security provisions, and where appropriate, contractors and consultants should be asked to sign non-disclosure agreements.

Risk Assessment

16.68 Breaches in security are only important insofar as they have an adverse effect on the business. Business impact analysis endeavours to quantify, in business terms, the effects on the business of various possible incident scenarios. The control environment can then be reviewed in the light of this, to ensure that effort in security improvement is directed at those areas where weak security leaves the business most exposed. It can also help to ensure that the amount spent on security is not out of proportion with the risk. This is particularly useful where major expenditure is required to improve security, for example in the area of contingency planning. Business impact analysis usually focuses on the total cost of a possible breakdown in security. As a refinement to this process, it is possible to consider also the probability that a breakdown in security will occur. This technique is known as risk assessment.

16.69 A 'top down', management-driven, approach to risk assessment is desirable because:

(a) Senior management determine the shape and direction of an organisation.

(b) Senior management will have overall knowledge of risks and their likely impacts; they know how the organisation stands in the market place.

The risk assessment process must reflect these factors in order to make the security improvement programme business-based i.e., practical, cost-effective, acceptable and supported by senior management.

16.70 Methods of risk assessment may be broadly categorised into two types:

(a) a quantitative or statistical approach giving an expected monetary loss;

(b) a qualitative or subjective approach which ranks the significance of the threat and its impact to the business.

These are described further below.

Statistical approach

16.71 The most widely encountered statistical approach makes use of the concept of annual loss expectancy (ALE). The two components of the calculation are the probability, sometimes referred to as expectancy, that an incident will occur in any one year, and the cost (impact) of that incident if it does occur. The annual loss expectancy, that is the average 'cost' per year, is obtained by multiplying these two numbers. Examples are as follows:

Risk A:	*Major flood*	
	Probability	: 1 every 50 years
	Total cost	: £5m
	ALE	: £5m × 1/50 = £100,000
Risk B:	*Major fire*	
	Probability	: 1 every 20 years
	Total cost	: £500,000
	ALE	: £500,000 × 1/20 = £25,000
Risk C:	*Data entry error*	
	Probability	: 1000 per year
	Total cost	: £25 per error (average)
	ALE	: £25 × 1000 = £25,000

16.72 This method is attractive because it allows each risk to be quantified in a way which takes into account both cost and probability. However it has the following drawbacks:

(a) The risks of a major fire and data entry errors have impacts which are vastly different, yet in the above example they produce the same ALE.

(b) The figures will never be the actual loss for a 'real' year. A major flood costing £5m might actually destroy the business.

(c) Although probability figures for certain incidents such as fires are readily available from insurance industry statistics, there are no reliable probabilities for some other types of incident such as fraud.

(d) The probability figures may not reflect the exact circumstances of the organisation under consideration, which may have security measures in place which are very much better, or very much worse, than the average.

Qualitative approach

16.73 An alternative approach to risk assessment is to keep the two components, that is impact and expectancy, separate. They may also be ranked, say on a scale of 0 to 10, rather than assigned an absolute value. These rankings can then be plotted on a risk matrix, in one of four quadrants as illustrated in Figure 82.

16.74 The quadrant into which a particular problem falls will depend on the business and the controls in place. Thus data entry errors have been categorised in the illustration as low impact/ high expectancy because

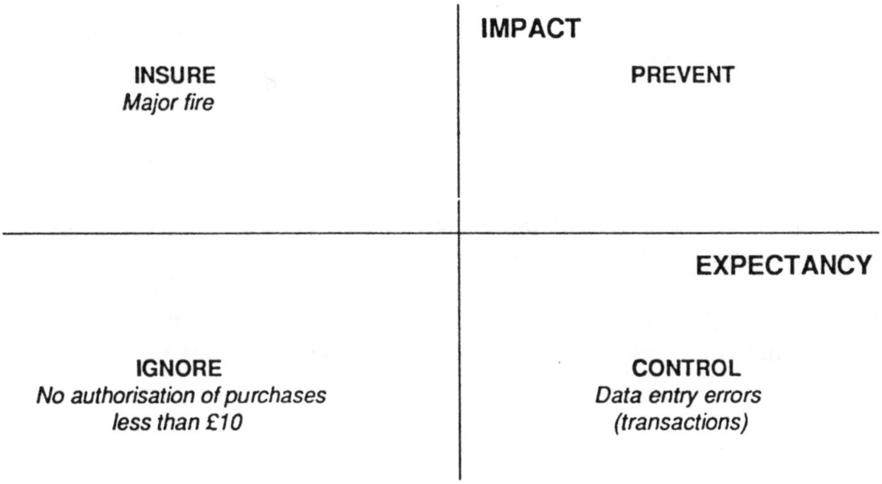

FIG. 82. Risk matrix (para. 16.73)

it has been assumed that errors in transactions either will not be sufficiently large to cause a major impact, or will be easily identified and corrected before any real damage is done. The matrix includes a suggested response to each type of risk, for example, the implementation of controls to protect against data errors. In practice the response will be determined by the precise circumstances of each risk.

16.75 There are no items in the high impact/high expectancy quadrant because it is to be expected that an organisation will have controls in place to prevent such occurrences. However, as an example of such a risk, if a computer room full of inflammable materials was sited next to a canteen, then the risk would fall into this quadrant, and immediate action would be needed.

16.76 There are many different ways in which a breach of security can have an impact on the business including:

(a) *Fraud:* fraudulent diversion of assets or funds.

(b) *Immediate loss of business/profits:* loss of business or reduction in profits as a direct result of the problem.

(c) *Loss of public confidence:* damage to public, customer and supplier confidence, resulting in long term loss of business, effect on share price or damage to public image.

(d) *Additional costs:* for example interest penalties.

(e) *Legal liability:* breaches in legal, regulatory or contract requirements.

16.77 Impact is assessed by considering, for each incident scenario, the adverse effects on the business in the areas indicated above. This is mainly a 'top down' process using senior management for the policy and corporate strategy issues, and middle management, both IT and user, for the detailed, day-to-day impacts.

16.78 As regards expectancy, statistics may be available for some risks; these should be discussed with management to determine their applicability and then ranked on an appropriate scale.

16.79 The benefits of the matrix approach are that it is:

(a) *Easy to understand.* It uses rankings of risks rather than exact probabilities which may not be reliable.

(b) *Visual.* The quadrants give some indication of the action required.

(c) *Realistic.* Expectancy and impact are assessed specifically for the organisation's circumstances enabling a cost-effective and practical solution to be identified.

Risk management

16.80 Whatever method is adopted for assessing risk, management will use the results of the assessment to identify the relative importance of different threats to the business. In the light of this assessment the cost of implementing control procedures can be measured against the risk to the business and cost effective security procedures can be implemented. This process is sometimes referred to as risk management.

Confidentiality and Privacy

Data protection legislation

16.81 There has been much concern in recent years about the keeping of computerised records relating to individuals, the accuracy of the information held in such records and its use. Legislation has been passed in a number of countries, and in the United Kingdom the Data Protection Act was passed in 1984. One objective of the Act was to ratify the European Convention for the Protection of Individuals with regard to the Automatic Processing of Personal Data.

16.82 The Data Protection Act also attempts to deal with the threat to privacy posed by the rapid growth in the use of computers, and it applies to information relating to living individuals which is processed automatically, irrespective of the size of the computer. In this context personal data relates only to living individuals and data relating to companies is excluded. Detailed interpretation of the Act and its applicability are outside the scope of this book, but a brief summary of the major provisions is included below.

The general principles

16.83 All affected users must register and the Act sets out eight principles concerning data protection with which they must comply:

(a) The information to be held should be obtained and processed fairly and lawfully.

(b) Personal data should be held only for one or more specified (i.e. registered) and lawful purposes.

(c) Personal data held for any purpose should not be used or disclosed in any manner incompatible with that purpose.

(d) Personal data held for any purpose should be 'adequate, relevant and not excessive' in relation to that purpose.

(e) Personal data should be accurate and, where necessary, kept up to date.

(f) Personal data held for any purpose should not be kept for longer than is necessary for that purpose.

(g) A data subject is entitled:

(i) at reasonable intervals and without undue delay or expense:
- to be informed by any data user whether he holds personal data concerning that individual;
- to have access to any such data;

(ii) where appropriate, to have such data corrected or erased.

(h) Appropriate security measures must be taken against unauthorised access to, or alteration, disclosure or destruction of, personal data, and against accidental loss or destruction of personal data. Computer bureaux need to comply only with this principle.

Registration

16.84 The Act established a Data Protection Registrar, who maintains a register of users of personal data and computer bureaux which process personal data within the United Kingdom. The Registrar has the power to ensure that personal data is used in accordance with the generic principles set out in 16.83. Users must register the following particulars:

(a) The name and address of the data user or computer bureau.

(b) A description of the personal data and the purpose or purposes for which the data is held.

(c) A description of the sources from which the data user intends or may wish to obtain the data.

(d) A description of persons to whom the data user intends or may wish to disclose the data.

(e) The names or a description of any countries or territories outside the United Kingdom to which the data user intends to transfer the data.

(f) One or more addresses where data subjects may send requests for access to the data.

16.85 It has been suggested by a number of bodies that the registration requirement is unduly burdensome and unnecessary except where particularly sensitive processing is carried out. The Data Protection Registrar has taken a number of steps to simplify the registration process for small businesses performing only standard commercial data processing.

Rights of the individual

16.86 Individuals have rights concerning data held relating to them, and in particular, the right to be informed by any data user whether the data held by him includes that subject's personal data and the right to be supplied by any data user with a copy, in intelligible form, of any such personal data held. The data user may make a reasonable charge for this request but must comply within forty days. Data subjects may sue in the courts on the grounds of failure to receive copies of data or damage suffered by inaccuracy of data, by loss or destruction of data without permission of the data user, or by unauthorised disclosure except in accordance with planned disclosure noted in the register.

Exemptions

16.87 The definitions within the Act are drawn very widely and exemptions are therefore limited. The exemption of interest to most businesses is that relating to computerised accounting systems. The Act exempts data used only for the following purposes:

(a) calculating amounts payable by way of remuneration or pensions in respect of service in any employment or office or making payments of, or of sums deducted from, such remuneration or pensions; or

(b) keeping accounts relating to any business or other activity carried out by the data user or keeping records of purchases, sales or other transactions for the purpose of ensuring that the requisite payments are made by or to him in respect of those transactions or for the purpose of making financial or management forecasts to assist him in the conduct of any such business or activity.

It should be noted, however, that where accounting systems include additional personal data not required for the above purposes, for example details of qualifications and age on a payroll system, then the system is apparently not exempt. In practice, therefore, many accounting systems are not exempt.

Relevance to the auditor

16.88 The requirements of the Act are not of primary concern in forming an audit opinion but the auditor should be aware of them in order to make appropriate comments to management. The internal auditor may well be more closely involved in monitoring compliance with the Act. The following considerations should be borne in mind:

(a) Personal data should be accurately recorded, kept up to date and held no longer than is necessary. To ensure that information is correctly processed within and held on a computer system appropriate controls will need to exist as discussed in Chapter 5. In reviewing and evaluating the effectiveness of the controls to ensure that financial and management information is accurate and up to date the auditor may wish to pay special attention to data which will be subject to registration under the Act. Previously there may have been only informal controls operating over the processing and maintenance of personal data which was of secondary importance to maintaining financial records, for example, character assessments, social background or educational detail in a personnel system.

(b) Appropriate security measures must be taken against unauthorised access to, or alteration, disclosure or destruction of personal data and against accidental loss or destruction of personal data. In this respect it may be helpful for the auditor to assess the adequacy of IT controls to ensure that personal data is not subject to unauthorised access or amendment and also the relevant security controls discussed earlier in this chapter.

Proposed directive on data protection

16.89 The Commission of the European Communities has issued a draft of a proposed future directive on data protection. In its draft form the directive would:

(a) extend the right of individuals to be given access to information held about them on computer files and to have it corrected or erased if it is incorrect;

(b) extend the right of an individual to have greater control over data processing of which he or she is the subject, particularly through the right to oppose, and to refuse to allow, the computerised processing of data defining personality or personal profile;

(c) extend the requirements for those who process personal data to exercise effective control over their data processing operations.

16.90 The directive, as presently drafted, would appear to extend data protection to manual as well as computer records and there are concerns about whether this would be workable in practice. It also contains no exemptions and includes registration requirements which would impose a significant administrative burden. Comments on these matters and on the directive in general have been made by many bodies during the comment period for the draft.

Summary

16.91 Computer security is usually defined as meaning that data is processed completely and accurately, that access to the data in computer systems is restricted to appropriate people, and that the computer facilities, and the information they hold, are available at all required times. These three elements of security are generally referred to as integrity, confidentiality and availability. Some aspects of computer security are of particular concern to the auditor in carrying out a financial audit, while others may have less effect on the audit but are of concern to management.

16.92 There are many factors, internal and external to an organisation which may threaten its security. These include hardware damage or breakdown, fraud, theft, misuse of information, sabotage, data or programming errors, operating errors, personnel problems, hacking or computer viruses. A variety of control techniques exist to protect against the threats. The control techniques may address logical access, software and hardware integrity, computer operations, communications, contingency planning, security management and administration, physical security, office systems, support services and personnel procedures.

16.93 The threats to security should be carefully considered and suitable protective measures determined. This process is the responsibility of management and is often called risk management. Management commitment is essential to establish adequate security techniques, the objective of which is to provide and maintain a stable and secure installation. Most security techniques involve some cost and it is thus important that they are directed towards those threats which create a significant risk. It is also important that the benefits and cost of security precautions are carefully considered in each case, as the requirements and remedies may differ.

16.94 The Data Protection Act has imposed new requirements on management concerning information relating to living individuals and processed by automatic means. These requirements have been considered briefly in this chapter.

17

Organisation and Training

Introduction

17.01 In this chapter are outlined some considerations regarding, first, the organisation of computer auditing within a practising firm or internal audit department and, secondly, the training requirements and how these can best be satisfied. The discussion in this chapter is principally concerned with organisation and training to provide specialist computer audit support to the audit process. It is recognised that in practice staff who provide this support may spend a large proportion of their time on special assignments carried out for management such as security reviews or reviews of controls in new systems.

17.02 Different organisational structures are used in different firms, varying from use of consultants to total integration of 'specialists' within audit groups. The comments in this chapter are based on our practical experience and procedures in a large practice office applying the approach and techniques set out in this book. However, the organisation is similar in our firm's smaller offices in the United Kingdom and in offices of varying sizes overseas. It is therefore hoped that the suggestions made will be of relevance and practical assistance to organisations of all sizes.

The Organisation of Computer Auditing

Policy

17.03 Specific responsibility will need to be assigned for developing the organisation and techniques for carrying out computer audit work and the related training. In a larger firm this responsibility can be assigned to a specialist committee. In a smaller firm the responsibility is probably more conveniently assigned to an individual.

17.04 Where there is a specialist committee, it will normally comprise those partners responsible for computer auditing possibly together with the audit technical partner and one or more general practice partners who can comment on proposals from the general audit viewpoint. Where the firm has a consulting division with computer expertise, it may be useful for a member of that division to be a member of the committee.

17.05 The committee or individual will be particularly concerned in developing the firm's techniques and training and in monitoring performance.

Client work

17.06 The extent of the skill required to carry out computer audit work successfully will depend primarily on the complexity of the system and the audit techniques used. For example, more skill will be required to evaluate the controls in a complex integrated system, and where computer audit programs are used, than in a simple system, where the controls are largely manually based and where conventional audit techniques are appropriate. Likewise, different levels of skill will be required for the various parts of the audit. For example, the preparation of computer audit programs will require more technical skill than the carrying out of manual audit tests.

Computer audit specialists and general audit staff

17.07 In order to carry out computer audit work in the most efficient manner, it is necessary in the training and use of audit staff to recognise the different levels of skill required. It seems best to recognise and train two distinct levels of technical ability although, where computer audit work is extensive, further levels may be advantageously developed. A high level of skill is taught to certain staff to enable them to undertake the more complex computer audit work that may be encountered. These staff are hereafter referred to as **computer audit specialists**. A lower level of skill is taught to the majority of the audit staff, referred to as **general audit staff**, so that they can undertake those aspects of the work which can be effectively taught to large numbers in a short time, and so that their training reflects the balance of their practice work.

Organisation of computer audit specialists

17.08 Where practicable, it is beneficial for the computer audit specialists to be organised into a separate group or department, referred to in this chapter as a **computer audit group**. In larger firms there may need to be several groups in different offices. In smaller firms there may be a single group serving several offices. It seems preferable, where practicable, to restrict the work of such a group to computer auditing and related special work for clients. Where there are a number of small offices, it appears better to create a central group of suitable computer audit specialists from the various offices rather than to rely on individuals in each office, who may often only need to spend part of their time on computer auditing.

17.09 The group will normally be headed by a manager who has himself worked as a computer audit specialist (the **computer audit manager**). He is responsible for planning and reviewing the work of the computer audit specialists on the group. The computer audit manager will report to the partner responsible for the group (the **computer audit partner**). It is advantageous if the partner has also worked as a computer audit specialist.

17.10 In small firms it will not be practicable, or necessary, to have this formal group structure. Where, for example, only one computer audit specialist is needed, it is usually best to train either a manager or a member of staff who is likely to become a manager in the near future. More reliance can be placed on the work of someone in this category who can supervise the work of general audit staff. This individual can also form the nucleus of the group that may subsequently be needed if further computer audit work arises.

Selection of staff

17.11 Computer audit specialists may be recruited directly, either as students training to be chartered accountants or externally whether they are chartered accountants or computer specialists, or they may be selected from among the general audit staff and given the necessary technical training. However, with the growth in complex systems and the use of techniques such as computer audit programs, there is an increasing opportunity for using technical computer staff as computer audit specialists.

17.12 Selection of computer audit specialists from the general audit staff is not normally restricted to any particular grade or age of staff, although the majority are newly-qualified accountants. Suitability may be based on aptitude tests and/or on proficiency and interest in auditing and computers generally.

17.13 The length of time that staff will normally remain on the computer audit group depends on the policy of the firm. Some firms regard the computer audit group as providing the basis for a career and, in that case, the computer audit specialists serve on the group permanently. This has the advantage of building up a high level of skill on the computer audit group but, on the other hand, may emphasise the separateness of computer auditing and care is necessary to ensure that the development of the skill of general audit staff is not thereby overlooked. Other firms second staff to the computer audit group for, say, two years. At the conclusion of their secondment they return to the general audit staff. If staff are carefully selected for this work, the firm can gradually build up a significant number of senior staff with computer audit training and experience. However, in these situations, it is less easy to maintain a high level of technical knowledge in the computer audit group.

17.14 One solution may be a combination of the two approaches, whereby there is a permanent group of specialists, with both audit and computer background, on the computer audit group, and a number of selected audit staff on secondment at any time.

17.15 In large firms, where the general audit staff are organised on a group basis with specific clients allocated to each group, it may be possible to train computer audit specialists who are then resident in the groups. This is particularly useful where an audit group serves one or major clients with numerous computer-based accounting systems. The computer audit specialist's work would continue to be reviewed by the computer audit manager, unless the general audit group manager possessed the necessary skill and experience, perhaps as a result of having previously worked on the computer audit group.

Division of work

17.16 Under the arrangements in our firm, the overall responsibility for computer audit work rests with the general audit staff, and it is for them to call in the computer audit specialist when needed to carry out specific work. Detailed suggestions, based on our practice, for the division of work between computer audit specialists and general audit staff that they may be found suitable are outlined in the following paragraphs under the headings of the main stages of computer audit work.

Determination of the audit strategy

17.17 As discussed in Chapter 2, in order to determine the most efficient audit strategy, the auditor will need to obtain a preliminary understanding of the accounting system and related internal controls. A decision will need to be made as to whether general audit staff or computer audit specialists will perform this work. In general, it can be beneficial for computer audit specialists to gain the understanding in respect of complex computerised systems or where major changes have been made to computerised systems. This is because the auditor will need to gain an understanding of the significant features and controls within complex computerised systems in a very short timescale, and this requires a high level of technical skill and understanding of the manner in which complex systems work. For less complex systems or routine updating of the review in subsequent years, general audit staff will generally carry out the work.

17.18 Where computer audit specialists perform the initial review of computer systems they may prepare overview documentation of the system and controls as described in Chapters 3 and 4, together with a brief report outlining the main features of the system and making recommendations as regards the audit strategy. This report will include the potential for the use of computer audit programs, and, where an extended assessment of controls is to be performed a proposal as to whether the work should be carried out by computer audit specialists or general audit staff and the budgeted costs of the work.

17.19 The general audit group manager should inform the computer audit manager as soon as he is aware that a company is planning to install a computer, change its current machine or make substantial amendments to an existing system. It is important that the computer audit manager is informed in good time so that the implications of the change for the audit are considered and, if required by the client, advice can be given on controls to be implemented in the system in good time before the system goes live.

Recording the system and evaluating the controls

17.20 The recording and evaluating of accounting systems may be carried out by either computer audit specialists or general audit staff, depending on the complexity of the system. In general, since it is to be expected that the majority of accounting systems will be computerised, general audit staff should carry out the work of recording and evaluating accounting systems in most cases. A particular exception to this is the evaluation of IT controls, where the degree of technical skill required means that computer audit specialists should carry out such work. In addition, it may be desirable for computer audit specialists to record and evaluate particularly complex accounting applications in the first instance.

17.21 With the exception of IT controls, once the initial recording and evaluation have been carried out, general audit staff will normally carry out the annual updating for all systems. Another factor influencing the division of work is the number of computer audit specialist staff available and the volume of computer audit work. In particular, where the volume is low, it will usually be more efficient to maximise the evaluation work carried out by the computer audit specialist in order to keep him fully employed on computer audit work.

17.22 An indication of complexity is the nature of the data processing environment in which processing takes place. It is possible to purchase a packaged order entry sales or purchases system as described in Chapter 3 to operate on a microcomputer, and in practice the manner in which such a system is operated and controlled may be relatively straightforward. Alternatively, such a system may be operated in a highly complex distributed network with transactions input at a large number of terminals in a variety of locations resulting in a complex structure of controls over such aspects as access to the system and the ability to update transactions.

Tests of controls

17.23 Where it is decided to use computer programs, or other computer assisted techniques, the design and implementation work should be carried out by computer audit specialists with assistance from the general audit staff in the setting of objectives, the inclusion in the audit programme of the appropriate instructions regarding the running of the program or other techniques and the audit work to be carried out on the results.

17.24 The responsibility for carrying out tests of controls will normally be conditioned by the degree of technical skill required. Computer audit staff will usually carry out the tests on the IT controls. In those cases where it is deemed necessary to use program code analysis, computer programs or audit test data this work will also normally be carried out by computer audit specialists, although general audit staff may be able to perform some of the work in the second and subsequent years. General audit staff will normally be responsible for carrying out all other tests of controls.

Substantive tests

17.25 The standard programme of substantive tests will need to be amended to take account of the precise nature of computer processing and the testing techniques used. The responsibility for making the alterations will depend on the degree of technical skill required. In general, where the alterations relate to substantive tests that are manually based, the changes will be made by general audit staff. It may be desirable for the revised audit programme to be reviewed by the computer audit manager. Where it is decided to use computer programs, the design and implementation work will be carried out by computer audit specialists with assistance from the general audit staff, particularly with regard to the setting of objectives, and the inclusion in the audit programme of appropriate instructions regarding the running of the program and the audit work to be carried out on the results.

17.26 The responsibility for carrying out substantive tests will normally rest with the general audit staff, subject to the need for computer audit specialists, as already indicated, to run computer programs.

Functions of computer audit specialists

17.27 The principal functions of computer audit specialists as regards client work may thus be summarised as follows:

- The gaining of the preliminary understanding to determine audit strategy for complex computer-based accounting systems or where major changes have been made to computerised systems. This will include making recommendations as regards the audit strategy including the potential for use of computer audit programs and, where an extended assessment of controls is to be performed, whether the work should be carried out by computer audit specialists or general audit staff.
- The evaluation of IT controls. This work is seldom carried out by general audit staff because of its technical nature. For the same reason, computer audit specialists will carry out the tests of IT controls.
- The recording of the system and evaluation of the controls over complex computer-based accounting systems.
- The setting up of computer programs, and running them in the first year of use. In many cases, for reasons of technical difficulty, computer audit specialists will continue to run them on behalf of general audit staff in subsequent years. Other computer-assisted audit techniques such as test data and program code analysis will usually be carried out by computer audit specialists.

In addition, computer audit specialists would be available to give any other assistance, such as commenting on the content of management letters, or carrying out a security review as requested by general audit staff or the client. Work carried out by computer audit specialists should be reviewed and approved by computer audit managers and partners.

Functions of general audit staff

17.28 The main functions of general audit staff in this area may be summarised as follows:

- The recording of the preliminary understanding to determine audit strategy for the less complex computer-based accounting systems, and the updating of the understanding for all systems after the first year.

- The recording of the system and evaluation of the controls in respect of most computer-based accounting systems, where appropriate.
- The carrying out of the tests of controls and substantive tests on the annual audit, other than for IT controls and where computer audit specialists make use of computer-assisted audit techniques.

In addition, it is the responsibility of the general audit staff to ensure that the computer audit specialists are called in at the appropriate time to carry out audit strategy and subsequent work, or where there is doubt whether the most current and effective computer audit techniques are in use.

The role of the manager and partner

17.29 It is an important feature of the audit approach described in this book that managers and partners are involved at each important stage in the audit. In addition to reviewing the results of tests of controls and substantive tests managers and partners are required to participate in planning the work to be done and deciding on the audit response to strengths and weaknesses disclosed by each part of the work.

17.30 The most important decisions requiring manager and partner consideration and approval are:

- Determination of the audit strategy and, in particular, whether an extended assessment of controls is to be performed.
- Which systems and controls are both relevant and material in relation to the audit, and the extent to which controls will be tested.
- The level of tests to be carried out.
- The proposed audit response to weaknesses and exceptions.

The involvement of managers and partners in these decisions helps ensure that, on the one hand, important audit work is not omitted and, on the other hand, time is not wasted on unnecessary procedures.

17.31 The need to involve audit managers and partners at each important stage is of particular importance where the accounting is computer-based. Although such managers and partners will retain full responsibility for the audit as a whole, certain work will often be delegated to computer audit specialists and will be planned and reviewed by the computer audit manager and partner. Procedures are needed to ensure that the audit manager and partner are involved in decisions arising from work undertaken by computer audit specialists.

17.32 For complex computer systems or where major changes have been made to computer systems, the report prepared after the preliminary review has been carried out, as described in paragraph 17.18, provides a convenient basis for the audit manager and partner to plan with the computer audit manager and partner the work required in relation to computer systems. At this stage the following matters should be agreed:

- The extent of evaluation and testing of controls to be performed.
- Whether this work is to be carried out by computer audit specialists or general audit staff.
- Whether reliance should be placed on IT controls or user controls to ensure the continued and proper operation of programmed procedures or whether direct tests of the programmed procedures should be performed.
- Whether it is likely that proposals will subsequently be made to use computer assisted audit techniques, for example, computer programs.
- The budgeted costs of the work to be carried out by computer audit specialists.

17.33 The audit work carried out will be planned, controlled and reviewed either by the audit manager and partner or the computer audit manager and partner, depending on whether the work is done by general audit staff or computer audit specialists. Where work is carried out by computer audit specialists, the detailed budgets should be approved by both the computer audit manager and partner and the audit manager and partner. Where computer programs, audit test data or program code analysis are to be used, proposals will be prepared on the lines indicated earlier in this book. Audit managers and partners should give their approval to these proposals before work commences. Reports of all work carried out by computer audit specialists should be prepared and submitted to the audit manager and partner after approval by the computer audit manager and partner.

Training and development work

Training

17.34 Where the firm undertakes its own training, the computer audit group may bear a significant portion of the responsibility for developing the computer audit course material for training both computer audit specialists and general audit staff. In doing so they will work with both the firm's training department and with general audit staff. Computer audit specialists may also present the courses, either alone or in conjunction with training department staff. This approach has the advantage that those teaching have practical experience of the subject. In addition, the development of training material is improved if those responsible have experience of teaching.

Development work

17.35 If a computer audit group is established, it should normally be responsible for developing the firm's computer audit techniques and approach under the direction of the relevant committee or partner. The amount of this work will depend mainly on the extent to which it is decided to develop documentation specific to the firm as opposed to using published material. Larger firms may wish to design their own documentation so as to integrate this with their existing audit approach and methods. This is likely to apply in particular to the detailed methods of recording the system and evaluating the controls. Specimen tests will also need to be designed. Greater technical skill is necessary to design questions for evaluating IT controls and more use is likely to be made of published material. Considerable technical support is required to develop computer audit software packages to interrogate clients' data files and only the larger firms are likely to find it worthwhile to allocate resources to projects of this nature. Most firms are, however, likely to find that effective use can be made of standard interrogation, spreadsheet, database or other software packages on microcomputers for such purposes as file interrogation, audit planning or corporation tax computations. Particular applications of such software may be developed by computer audit specialists for use by general audit staff.

Control of time

17.36 Experience shows that training and development work can, unless carefully controlled, absorb a disproportionate amount of computer audit specialists' time. It is, therefore, appropriate for the computer audit committee to set budgets for the percentage of time to be allocated to training and development work and for the actual use of time to be monitored against these budgets.

Training

Scope of training

17.37 In all firms involved in computer auditing, there is likely to be a need to train, or provide training for, both general audit staff and computer audit specialists. In this part of the chapter, suggestions as to the training requirements, and how these requirements may be met and from what source, are outlined for both types of staff.

General audit staff

Training requirements

17.38 The training requirements for general audit staff in this area will depend on their role in the computer audit. If their functions are similar to those outlined in paragraph 17.28, the requirement will be a mixture of learning certain techniques and gaining an appreciation of others.

17.39 The techniques that must be learnt are how to record the preliminary understanding of less complex systems to determine audit strategy, how to record and evaluate systems, and how to select and carry out manual tests of controls and substantive tests.

17.40 In order to carry out these functions satisfactorily, particularly the determination of the audit strategy and the recording and evaluating of systems, general audit staff require a good appreciation of how computers process data and familiarity with examples of typical computer-based accounting systems. Such an understanding will also assist in selecting and performing tests of controls and substantive tests. They also need to ensure that their audits are being conducted using the most current and effective methods. This means that they require an appreciation of the audit techniques that may be used by computer audit specialists such as computer programs, and less commonly audit test data and program code analysis. This appreciation should include guidance as to the circumstances in which the use of these techniques, and particularly file interrogation software, is likely to be appropriate.

Training courses

17.41 The training required to satisfy the requirements outlined above can be provided either as part of an overall training programme where manual and computer audit training are integrated, or by separate computer audit courses. In general the first approach is to be preferred. Since general audit staff can expect to find computerised systems at the majority of their clients, it is desirable that all auditing courses which they attend should take account of this fact by dealing with the techniques and methods applied in auditing computerised systems.

17.42 General audit partners and managers will benefit from regular refresher courses in order to keep up to date with the new techniques that become available to assist in the audit of computer systems. Courses of this nature can be quite short; they provide a useful means of communication and discussion between computer audit specialists and general audit staff.

Sources of training

17.43 Larger firms can provide their own training but smaller firms may depend on outside sources. There is no shortage of courses on computer auditing organised by various bodies. Care is needed to ensure that any particular course is relevant and of practical use. The Institute of Chartered Accountants in England and Wales provides suitable training for general audit staff, managers and partners, and details can be obtained from the courses department. In addition, the IT Faculty of the Institute runs a conference on auditing in a computer environment every year where the latest techniques and issues are discussed.

Computer audit specialists

17.44 The training requirements for computer audit specialists will depend on their role in computer audit work and on the complexity of the systems which they have to audit. Because there will be fewer computer audit specialists than general audit staff, it is possible to be more flexible in their training. Computer audit specialists will need:

(a) sufficient computer technical knowledge to evaluate the more complex computer-based accounting systems; and

(b) the ability to apply the more advanced computer audit techniques used by their firm.

These requirements and possible sources of training are discussed in the following paragraphs.

Technical knowledge

17.45 Computer audit specialists are likely to require a knowledge of the control requirements and techniques appropriate to all types of computer systems discussed in Chapter 3. They will find it necessary to acquire a general knowledge of input devices, the software which handles communications and processing of data, the structure of databases, the role of database management systems and their relationship with the application programs and the system software including security packages used in many sophisticated systems. This general knowledge can then be supplemented by studying any specific features which the auditor will meet at his clients.

17.46 The larger firms may be able to provide training in these matters but it is more likely that the computer audit specialist will attend courses run by the relevant manufacturers. Care will need to be taken to ensure that the courses selected are appropriate to the level of knowledge and the skill required.

More advanced audit techniques

17.47 The computer audit specialist will also require to be trained, as appropriate, in the use of computer-assisted audit techniques including computer programs, and possibly audit test data and program code analysis. The computer programs in use may include both those for examining data on files and those to assist in the testing of IT controls discussed in Chapter 9.

17.48 The training required in respect of computer audit programs will depend on the nature of the skill being taught. In larger firms, it may be the firm's own computer audit packages that will be taught and, depending on the complexity of the programs and the amount of technical involvement required of the user, this may take up to several days. In both larger and smaller firms, it may be decided to train staff in externally available computer audit packages, in which case the scope and length of training will be governed by whoever owns each package. If it is desired to provide computer audit specialists with the ability to do their own coding of programs, they will, if unskilled in programming, also need to attend a suitable programming course.

17.49 It will also be necessary for computer audit specialists, who wish to carry out program code analysis, to attend courses and obtain practical programming experience, unless they are already competent in programming.

Keeping up to date

17.50 The training outlined earlier for computer audit specialists can only be considered as a basic course; in such a fast-developing area, it is important that they receive such additional specialised knowledge as is necessary to keep up to date. In larger firms it will probably be helpful to hold regular meetings of computer audit specialists, at which technical and audit developments can be discussed, dealing with such matters as operating systems, security software for various machine types and newer technologies such as EDI and EFT. In smaller firms, computer audit specialists can attend some of the various seminars that are held by computer and accountancy bodies.

17.51 It is helpful to keep in one place reports on the use of techniques such as computer audit programs, and copies of letters commenting on weaknesses in IT controls. In this way computer audit specialists can read of recent experience. The periodicals issued by manufacturers and other relevant bodies can also be helpful as background reading.

Summary

17.52 It is desirable to allocate specific responsibility for the development, organisation and training in respect of computer auditing within a firm. In carrying out the work, at least two levels of skill are necessary. Thus, computer audit specialists might undertake preliminary reviews of complex systems to determine audit strategy, evaluate IT controls, and use computer programs, audit test data and program code analysis, while general audit staff might be responsible for the preliminary review of less complex systems, the evaluation of systems and for carrying out manual tests of controls and substantive tests. Managers and partners should be involved at each important stage in the audit.

17.53 In larger firms, the computer audit specialists may be responsible for development work and the training of computer audit specialists and to some extent of general audit staff. In smaller firms much of the training may have to be obtained from suitable outside sources. There is no shortage of appropriate courses organised by various bodies.

Conclusion

1 The approach outlined in this book, with its documentation, techniques, division of work between computer audit specialists and general audit staff and training, is being practised on a widespread basis. It has been designed so as to be applicable successfully to real-time, on-line and batch systems and to systems using databases and communications networks.

2 It is certain that the advancement of systems will lead to further audit developments. There will need to be a greater awareness by auditors of new techniques and a recognition that the balance of audit effort may change. For example, it is likely that there will be a greater degree of reliance placed by auditors on IT controls, and in particular upon security software features, and a development of new techniques to carry out tests thereon. The computer audit specialist will need a greater measure of technical knowledge.

3 However, it is important that these developments should take place within an overall audit framework that seeks to integrate the manual and computer elements of the audit and thus relate the increasingly

technical computer elements to a specific audit purpose. Only in this way can the potential benefits of advances in computer technology, and the related audit techniques, be properly realised for the auditor.

4 It is hoped that the suggestions in this book will make a contribution to these developments.

Index